THE GREAT EARTHQUAKE AND FIRESTORMS OF 1906

UNIVERSITY OF CALIFORNIA PRESS   BERKELEY   LOS ANGELES   LONDON

THE GREAT EARTHQUAKE
AND FIRESTORMS OF 1906

HOW SAN FRANCISCO
NEARLY DESTROYED ITSELF

WITH A NEW PREFACE

PHILIP L. FRADKIN

University of California Press
Berkeley and Los Angeles, California

University of California Press, Ltd.
London, England

First paperback printing 2006

Library of Congress Cataloging-in-Publication Data

Fradkin, Philip L.
    The great earthquake and firestorms of 1906 : how San
Francisco nearly destroyed itself / Philip L. Fradkin.
        p.   cm.
    Includes bibliographical references and index.
    ISBN 0-520-24820-1 (pbk : alk. paper)
    1. Earthquakes—California—San Francisco—
History—20th century.   2. Fires—California—San
Francisco—History—20th century.   3. San Francisco
(Calif.)—History—20th century.   I. Title.
F869.S357F735 2005
979.4'6103—dc22   2004018506

Manufactured in the United States of America
14   13   12   11   10   09   08   07   06
10   9   8   7   6   5   4   3   2   1

The paper used in this publication meets the minimum
requirements of ANSI/NISO Z39.48-1992 (R 1997)
(*Permanence of Paper*).

For Kevin Starr

Towards the close of the nineteenth century the city of San Francisco was totally engulfed by an earthquake. Although the whole coast-line must have been much shaken, the accident seems to have been purely local, and even the city of Oakland escaped.

BRET HARTE, "THE RUINS OF SAN FRANCISCO," a satirical sketch, 1872

Earthquake and Fire—can you conceive engines of war more devastating! And yet we knew of the imminent danger from both. Knowing, we did nothing to protect ourselves from disaster.

RAPHAEL WEIL, the first "Sunday Sermon" to be written by "well known merchants of San Francisco on the upbuilding of the city," *San Francisco Call,* August 5, 1906

What lessons are to be learned for the benefit of the future if nearly everything which has happened is to be misrepresented?

KATHERINE HOOKER, a 1906 fire victim

Nobody has pointed out that the destruction of Berlin established the fact that it is now possible to destroy a city and that every city, but for the hairline distinction between the potential and the actual, is afire, its landmarks gone and its population homeless.

"TALK OF THE TOWN," *The New Yorker,* December 11, 1943

My argument is not simply that natural disasters bear a strong human component, but that those in power (politicians; federal, state, and city policymakers; and corporate leaders) have tended to view these events as purely natural in an effort to justify a set of responses that has proved both environmentally unsound, and socially, if not morally, bankrupt.

TED STEINBERG, *Acts of God: The Unnatural History of Natural Disaster in America,* 2000

CONTENTS

Illustrations follow pages 40, 191, and 344.

PREFACE TO THE PAPERBACK EDITION

As I skimmed the hardcover edition of this book five months after its initial publication in April 2005, I realized how close I had come to the goal of writing an accurate disaster manual for the future. What I hadn't realized at the time was that it would be a disaster manual for the *very* near future. In the waning months of the summer of 2005, the deeply tragic events of Hurricane Katrina and its devastating aftermath began to unfold in a manner I was well acquainted with.

Listening to radio reports of the hurricane while driving home to California from Montana, I was gripped by the same slightly elevated feeling of anxiety that prevailed during the time I researched and wrote this book. For I was not only describing events that had taken place one hundred years ago but also attempting to locate myself in the present by drawing on all the nerve-jangling catastrophes and the civil unrest I had witnessed as a journalist and had experienced firsthand as a resident of California for nearly fifty years.

We Californians are self-proclaimed experts in natural disasters, but we are not alone in experiencing them. As I wrote in my original preface, "It may seem at times that Californians are different; but all peoples are the same. Earthquakes, fires, tornadoes, typhoons, hurricanes, floods, droughts, wars, and acts of terrorism shape our species."

Parallels between San Francisco in 1906 and New Orleans in 2005 flitted across my mind as I drove westward through the silent, empty nighttime spaces of the interior West. That there were similarities, and that others were seeking them, was confirmed when I arrived home in the late afternoon of the next day to find numerous messages from journalists across the United States. Can you tell us, they asked, what happened then that illuminates the now?

There are marked similarities and differences.

First, the similarities: San Francisco and New Orleans were portrayed as fun-loving, extravagant, and sinful places, although both were actually quite gritty cities surrounded by water. In both cities huge discrepancies in wealth and political power existed between races and ethnic groupings.

Both cities had been forewarned of disaster: San Francisco by previous earthquakes and fires and New Orleans by earlier floods and hurricanes. Both cities and their populations ignored the warnings and were, as a result, woefully unprepared. They were, in other words, ripe for major catastrophes.

Both disasters struck in two linked pulses, the second being far more deadly than the first. The earthquake was immediately followed by the disastrous firestorms in San Francisco, and the hurricane preceded the far more catastrophic flooding caused by the failure of the dikes in New Orleans. Silence descended on both flattened cities. They became war zones. Guns bristled. The middle class and the rich had a better chance than the poor of finding adequate shelter elsewhere. Outlying areas received far less attention than the two major urban centers.

The differences are less numerous. There was no advance warning for the earthquake, whereas days of inadequate planning predated the hurricane in the Gulf. Army troops were already stationed in San Francisco; none were present in New Orleans. Refugees from San Francisco, regardless of their wealth, could board free ferries for Oakland or walk ahead of the flames to the west or south, where they could either continue on their way or camp. Most poor residents of New Orleans were trapped.

History, not current events, is my principal guide. The former serves to enlighten the latter. History has made me skeptical of what I have read, heard, and watched in the last two weeks. No, I am not talking about any vast media conspiracy, although it seemed that once again people of privilege, like myself, were describing the travails of people of far fewer advantages and that a tremendous gap existed between the two.

What I am referring to is the inability—which I experienced as a journalist in the 1960s and 1970s—to comprehend the totality of such large-scale, horrific events. I am experiencing this very same difficulty as I write these words. I cannot sufficiently grasp what is occurring now nor write about the hurricane with any great authority unless I view it through the perspective of history. Then I feel more secure.

This is what history tells me.

Natural disasters, whether in California, the Gulf states, or New York (as a child I recall being evacuated from the Long Island shore before the 1938 and subsequent hurricanes), are part of the human condition. It is a characteristic of our species, lodged in the hubris gene, to believe we can deflect or escape them entirely. But we can't. In fact, we are responsible for them.

Such disasters are caused not by nature but by building flimsy structures and living in dangerous places.

That is not about to change. Based on what occurred in northern California one hundred years ago, New Orleans and all the smaller parishes, cities, and towns, will eventually emerge bigger, brighter, and more vulnerable to such catastrophes in the future. The dark horror of the moment will be erased from our collective memories and will be replaced with glittering facades unveiled at staged events marking the return of the coastline of the Gulf states to a condition beyond normality.

Such disasters also spawn wartime conditions for civilian populations—fear, trauma, chaos, hunger, thirst, exposure to the elements, misinformation, and the inability to communicate with anyone except nearby fellow sufferers. We haven't experienced the punishing effects of warfare on United States soil since the Civil War, although we have inflicted death and destruction on countless others. We are a pampered nation. We demand order, but order is not a historical constant or a given in any society.

Regardless of one's overall opinion of President George W. Bush and his leadership—or lack of it—in this crisis, there was little that he or the government of the richest nation in the world could have done in the immediate aftermath, when the forces of nature and chaos, rather than humans, were in control. Even an activist president such as Theodore Roosevelt could do little to effectively aid the inhabitants of San Francisco in the first few weeks following the 1906 disaster. Only the coincidental presence of troops and an ambitious general acting without orders allowed a quick military response.

But the military's first priority was to protect private property while neglecting other, more immediate and basic human needs. In urban disasters an inordinate amount of attention is paid to what is called looting, whether for survival or personal gain. The intense emphasis on looting and a massive military response to it, both in 1906 and 2005, represents more than a simple police action: it discloses an underlying fear that the dominant class will be overthrown during a period of chaos.

That fear is also expressed in other ways. Urban legends dormant since the Middle Ages, such as stories about "ghouls" chewing off earrings and rings from the ears and fingers of supine white women, reemerge during great disasters. Germans in the Chicago fire of 1871, African Americans in the Galveston hurricane of 1900, and the Chinese in San Francisco were depicted as the evil threats of their times. Although I am not aware of any public reports of the "ghoul" legend surfacing in New Orleans, I have no doubt that it is circulating privately.

Other wild, unsubstantiated rumors—including the nonexistent mass murders of the injured in a large San Francisco auditorium and mental patients in a San Jose state hospital in 1906 (read the New Orleans Superdome and convention center in 2005)—circulated to reinforce the fear of class revolt. Such stories have been given credence in New Orleans by attributing them to what "police believe" or citing anonymous "reports of" prowling gangs (think African Americans), gun battles, rapes of women and children, beatings, robberies, burglaries, and multiple murders.

Why am I so skeptical? Because of reason and history.

Earlier, tens of thousands were supposedly dead in the South. As of this writing, the figure is in the low one hundreds and is likely to rise somewhat. The New Orleans police chief, who first pushed the concept of a massive crime wave, more recently declared: "This is the safest city in America." I wonder who spoke to him, just as I wonder who kept the death toll low in San Francisco; laid the blame on fire; suppressed news of the post-quake plague, smallpox, and typhoid epidemics; and denied there were any earthquake faults in California.

The instinctive threat of revolution hangs over such catastrophes. The Chinese, with three thousand years of recorded earthquakes causing some thirteen million deaths, regard such upheavals as harbingers of regime change. Emperors and Communist leaders alike acted with great care—or force, if necessary—to preserve the status quo. In San Francisco an oligarchy of the wealthy and powerful took over the civil government within hours after the earthquake and held onto power afterwards. The group issued an infamous order, through the pliant mayor, to "KILL" anyone suspected of committing a crime. As a result, an undetermined number of people were dispatched by troops and vigilantes. The governor of Louisiana used similar language. "Those troops know how to shoot and kill," she said to signal the beginning of a period of curtailed civil rights that followed the precedent of other urban disasters.

In the aftermath of the San Francisco conflagration, reform was the political battle cry. Graft was the specific target then; corruption is now. Reform, however, was in the eye of the beholder. Reform did not extend to those of different ethnic and racial backgrounds. But the real goal of maintaining social and political stability was achieved.

The process of rebuilding after a great disaster follows a historical pattern as well. Money and goods from across the country and around the world poured into San Francisco, just as they have in New Orleans. The federal contributions were massive in 1906 and 2005. Who qualified for insurance was a matter of contention in San Francisco, just as it is now in New Orleans: then, a thin line separated insurable fire from uninsurable earthquake damage; now, it separates wind from flood losses. In San Francisco hasty and massive rebuilding repeated the mistakes of the past on a larger scale, the local economy was given a tremendous boost in the process, and the city was soon humming again. I suspect that will also be the case along the Gulf coast.

There is no way to accurately determine the number of dead or the dollar amount of damages for such massive catastrophes. The death toll in 1906 was between three and five thousand. A dollar amount for damages in 1906 that is equivalent to 2005 monetary values cannot be accurately calculated. (See the Author's Note on pages 345–346 for a list of imponderables.) In any case, numbers are manipulated for political, economic, and journalistic purposes.

No standard—whether deaths, amount of damage, economic fallout, or a combination of the three (which I used in this book)—exists to rank disasters. Hurricane Katrina may yet emerge as this country's greatest urban disaster and supplant the 1906 earthquake and firestorms. Then again, it may not. What is certain is that some disaster will eventually win the dubious honor of being "the worst" or "the greatest."

In terms of story, I hope the historical records of the hurricane will not be lost, as was the case in 1906. I also hope there will be a suitable memorial. I doubt there will be one, as 1906 has never been properly commemorated in any permanent manner, the impulse being to substitute myth for reality and to forget. Some thoughtful author with the perspective and careful research that only time permits will eventually publish the full story of the Gulf disaster, although quickie books—just as in 1906—are doubtless already in the works.

And what might the future be in the event of a large earthquake in the San Francisco Bay region? Such a disaster was one of three distinct possibilities that the Federal Emergency Management Agency (FEMA) studied, the other two being a terrorist attack on New York City and a hurricane in New Orleans. Using studies current in the mid-1990s, I wrote a scenario for a magnitude 8 earthquake in the book *Magnitude 8: Earthquakes and Life Along the San Andreas Fault,* first published in 1998.

Such an event would, once again, be truly overwhelming. Twenty-eight thousand deaths would be a conservative estimate. There would be ninety thousand serious injuries, along with damages ranging from $170 billion to

$225 billion. I ended that documented scenario thusly: "I realize this account is difficult to accept, but history demonstrates that it will occur in a similar form and place in the near future. No one can know with any degree of certainty when or where such a catastrophe will strike."

That conclusion also pertains to what will inevitably follow Hurricane Katrina.

P.L.F.
September 11, 2005

PREFACE

The principal theme of this book is that San Franciscans, not the inanimate forces of nature, were primarily responsible for the extensive chaos, damage, injuries, and deaths in the great earthquake and firestorms of 1906. Despite earlier devastating earthquakes and fires that should have served as warnings, they were dismissive of the past and failed to prepare for the future. During the earthquake and fire, military and civilian officials reacted foolishly under great duress. The rich and powerful then usurped the functions of government. When it was over—and this is the most telling period of all—the city was not only physically ruined but also morally bankrupt.

Fear, like a radioactive element, has a half-life much longer than the original exposure to catastrophe. It was fear that caused the cancer within the society that lasted for years after the events of 1906. Few cities had fallen so quickly from the height of such great prosperity to the nadir of despair.

The manipulation and abuse of power is the primary theme I have chosen to trace during and after the disaster. While the three days and nights of earthquake and fire have been the climax of previous accounts, I view the aftermath as the less obvious but more fascinating surface manifestation of the fractures that occurred within the earth. The trail of power is the best proof I can offer that nature, in the guise of an earthquake and fire, can significantly alter history and human destinies.

The implication for the future is that change brought about by similar forces will occur again. I have no doubt it will. I can also say with absolute certainty that no one knows when or on what scale the next major disaster will occur. So this book, although its title contains the date 1906, is very much about the next one hundred years. In other words, I have told a story about the past, and simultaneously I have written a disaster manual for the future.

What follows is not a conventional retelling of the earthquake and fire story. Besides incorporating many documents not previously published, probing beyond established boundaries, and seeking the core reality of events, I have joined the natural and human components of the before, during, and after phases of the catastrophe in one continuous narrative and placed them within an appropriate historical context. I have written this book not as a disinterested observer from afar but rather as a Californian who has lived adjacent to the San Andreas Fault for the past thirty years.

This volume is the decade-long culmination of a series of books of mine that have dealt with earthquakes. *The Seven States of California* (1995) was the progenitor of an earthquake trilogy. In *Seven States* I picked emblematic landscape features and showed how they affected the human histories that swirled around them. The San Andreas Fault along the central coast defined "The Fractured Province" chapter.

The first two books in the trilogy were *Magnitude 8* (1998) and *Wildest Alaska* (2001). *Magnitude 8* was an overall and a California-oriented history of earthquakes and their cultural impacts. It included a tour of the San Andreas Fault. I also took a look at the science of earthquakes and found it lacking. A remote bay in *Wildest Alaska* was the setting for a study of seismic-generated activity and historic parallels in a wilderness setting. Finally, this book—the last in the trilogy—locates the natural phenomenon and the resulting human responses in an urban setting.

I am personally acquainted with large-scale disasters. I have experienced earthquakes in southern and northern California over the past forty-five years. As a newspaper reporter and correspondent, I witnessed the chaos of catastrophic wildfires and other natural disasters, urban riots and conflagrations, and foreign wars. I have lost a home to fire, the twin of earthquakes.

It may seem, at times, that Californians are different; but all peoples are the same. Earthquakes, fires, tornadoes, typhoons, hurricanes, floods, droughts, wars, and acts of terrorism shape our species.

P.L.F.

The seeds of trauma are scattered within individuals, and collectively within societies. All that is needed for them to sprout is a shake of our established worlds, and then, like black bulbs, they bloom again and again.

A woman whose remarkable handwritten account does not reveal her identity was driven from her home on Chestnut Street.

> With such a sense of relief, such a weight of anxiety removed we re-entered our homes, but it was a short-lived reprieve; a terrific tidal wave of fire had started somewhere down in the Valley and rushing outside I saw in the heavens what seemed a funnel shaped cloud enlarging until the size of a turn table, into this yawning black chasm, the flames seemed to leap a hundred feet into the air, one glance showed our section was doomed. A shout from a soldier that they were dynamiting our home, caused me to rush to the street and start for my pre-arranged place of safety. . . . All this time this terrific whirlwind was catching up big pieces of timber roofing, everything whirling through the air, & with difficulty one could walk, reaching the seawall I was hurried on I knew not where.

The woman took refuge behind some freight cars. They burst into flames.

"Nearly blinded with dust and the air thick with flying debris" she ducked into a shed, only to watch the roof catch fire.

A "liquid mass of flame" rolled toward her from the west.

The cyclone carried tin roofs and ridge poles through the air as if they were merely soaring kites.

She ran and ducked and dodged. Her hair and heavy woolen clothing caught fire twice. She had eaten once in the last three days and had "an awful thirst from the hot sun and the furnace of the fire."

On board a navy tug, Midshipman John E. Pond witnessed the same wild scene from the bay.

As we steamed north along the waterfront we watched a long thin twister arising from the center of the burning city like a giant waterspout. It whipped about over the city for a long time, changing color alternatively from black through gray to yellow as the setting sun shone on different parts of its writhing column. The wind was blowing off shore in strong gusts, carrying showers of large cinders, sometimes burning shingles, or large pieces of roofing material.

The district north of Jackson Street was now becoming a veritable purgatory. Some sulfur was burning and the fumes from it made breathing very difficult. The wind was blowing a gale. . . . I think the continued heat, rising for several days from this great fire, accompanied by some change in the local atmospheric conditions, had at last created a miniature cyclone, and that the cinders now falling in such great quantities had been carried up by the twister previously described.[1]

The woman labored up the steps to the top of Telegraph Hill, seeking safety. "Here were huddled hundreds of miserable people seemingly mostly the poorer classes. Pictures of despair and terror."

She rested for a moment. She was surrounded by human misery and blackened ruins "as far as the eye could search."

The fire blocked escape toward the Western Addition. She walked southeast on Broadway, keeping to the middle of the hot pavement in order to avoid the flames on either side and dodging the dangling electric wires. She reached the ferry and made it to the relative safety of Berkeley.

The woman concluded her tale. "While traversing the City those three days and nights I saw no tears, heard not one loud word, the utter calmness of man, woman, and child was marvelous, whether the apathy of despair or a dazed condition from terror or the undaunted spirit that cannot give up, it was something never to be forgotten."[2]

Others also remarked on the numbing silence.

Thirteen years after the San Francisco earthquake and fire, George Stratton, a professor of psychology at the University of California at Berkeley, located just across San Francisco Bay from the reconstructed city, gave more than two hundred students in his classes an assignment to write about their experiences during that stressful time.

The young adults had been impressionable children on April 18, 1906. Some lapsed into the voices of the youngsters they had been. Others employed the psychological jargon they thought the professor wanted. Still others wrote with the dignity and clarity of adults.

Stratton's purpose in assigning the short exercise was to collect material for a journal article or a book that was never completed. When he eventually got around to writing the draft, he entitled it "When Children Are in Mortal Danger." He began, "I have long had some unopened papers which perplex me, now that I have read them." In his "plan" for the article or book, Stratton commented that it was "a strange scientific work."

Had it been published, the study could have been a clear demonstration of the long-lasting psychological effects of a disaster of great magnitude. Fear is palpably imbedded in the dusty responses of the students' papers that have lain forgotten in the archives of the Bancroft Library at the university where Stratton taught. For many of the children it was their first encounter with the possibility of violent death.

These were Stratton's instructions to the students:

> Write as detailed and precise an account as you can of your own recollections of the earthquake and fire of 1906. Tell if you remember them, the events of the day and evening before the earthquake, the doings and thoughts of yourself during and after the earthquake, the doings of your family and neighbors,—all these for the days and weeks following until the earthquake no longer figures in the events. Tell nothing <u>that you do not personally remember</u>. If you remember little tell that carefully.

These were their responses.

Barbara, age four at the time, cried. Her brother laughed as he was flung from his bed in their Oakland home. From their damaged house they went to their uncle's home on the other side of Lake Merritt. Twenty-four people took refuge there. Others were camped along the shore of the lake. Both children contracted typhoid fever. Afterward, Barbara had "a terrible fear" of insects.

An older student, who was eleven years old at the time and living in Ukiah to the north, recalled the great excitement. He was playing outside on the afternoon of April 18. The weather was unusually sultry, and the sky was filled with smoke from Santa Rosa, whose downtown district was burning. Play turned to terror. The boy was "paralyzed with an indescribable fear."

In the San Joaquin Valley, 150 miles east of the burning city, a female student recalled: "We children all thought that the fire was going to sweep all thru California. We were so frightened that we couldn't even play our childish games. . . . One of the neighbors, who was a good Presbyterian, said that San Francisco was so wicked and bad that God had to strike it down, so as to punish it."

In San Francisco, the shock was more immediate. A father, on going to the window on the morning of April 18, exclaimed: "My God, the city's on fire." His daughter recalled, "For years and years that came back to me. I knew at the time it signified something terrible." With mattresses piled high on top of a cart, the family fled to Palo Alto. "I can still feel the heat of those flames as we rode through the burning district," the student wrote in 1919.

A girl was asleep with her mother. The bedroom was decorated with oriental fixtures, including two scimitars. When the quake struck, the hanging swords landed about a foot from her head. The family camped in the Panhandle of Golden Gate Park and cooked on a stove. A soldier told them to put the fire out because of the danger of it spreading. They bribed the soldier with a sandwich.

A shot shattered the glass in the lighted window of a San Francisco home. A soldier said no lights were permitted because of the fire danger. The young girl's father, a doctor, explained that he was "attending an urgent case."

It was "a lark" for another girl. Her aunts and uncles came to stay with her family. They cooked and ate outside. She was teased by small boys who said she was afraid to sleep in the house because she did not want to get trapped by the tidal wave, rumored to be on its way ever since a large water tank collapsed nearby.

People fled the city. Gregory, age eight, lived in the Mission District, part of which remained unburned. The refugees were quiet as they filed past his home. They spoke in whispers. Later, at a friend's house on San Bruno Road, he gave the refugees water as they streamed south. He could still picture clearly "groups of Chinamen, lone Chinamen, old women, young women, and children, old men and young men and even cattle, as surging masses trudging along San Bruno Road." Gregory, the college student, said, "Nothing can efface the memory of the earthquake and fire of San Francisco from my mind."

Other students were themselves refugees. "I remember the long walk we took to the ferry. The street cars had stopped and we had to walk. There were throngs like ourselves, who were struggling to get to the ferry. Men stood at the side of the road with little cans willing to give us a drink." The family made it safely to the other side of the bay. Guilt was the young woman's predominant legacy. She didn't recall the horror, just the slight discomforts. She worried at the age of eighteen that she had been "a selfish and narrow-minded girl."

A number of students viewed the conflagration safely from a distance. "The flames were fierce as those of a forest fire and frightened me," said one. She traveled to San Francisco after the fire and found a gleaming white marble in "the cold gray ashes" of the ruins. Another student remembered visiting San Francisco, as did many sightseers after the fire, and picking up bright pieces of molten glass.

A dark specter had followed them through their young lives. One student had a fear of being swallowed by the earth. For another it was a fear of the instability of the entire earth. A third feared a heart attack. "The shock was too much for me," she said, "and my heart is not quite normal yet."

What stuck in one young woman's mind was being awakened by "some unknown and unseen thing." That memory remained with her. "In looking back over the experience," she wrote, "I am almost certain that my fear started with the earthquake. Afterwards, I was always frightened to be left alone. I was afraid of the dark, but mostly I was afraid of thunder (for we moved back to Montana in May). Its rumbling and shaking reminded me too clearly of the earthquake. And in truth, it has been in recent years that I have transferred my fear of thunder to lightning."

When Stratton, a pioneer in the field of social psychology, looked over the raw research materials some years later, he wrote: "Earthquakes show human nature?—human culture also!—in this, like War."[3]

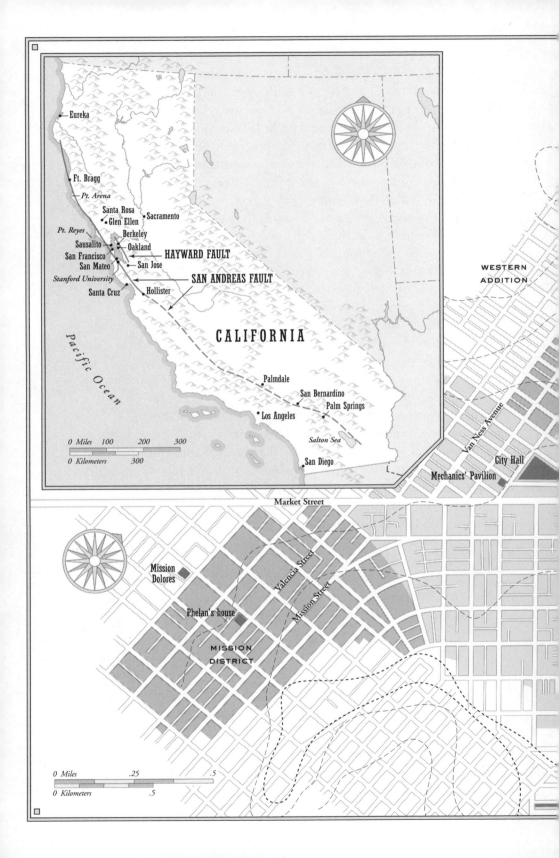

Eureka

Ft. Bragg

Pt. Arena

Santa Rosa
• Glen Ellen   • Sacramento
Pt. Reyes
Berkeley
Sausalito
Oakland
San Francisco
San Mateo   • San Jose
Stanford University
Santa Cruz   • Hollister

HAYWARD FAULT

SAN ANDREAS FAULT

Pacific Ocean

CALIFORNIA

Palmdale

San Bernardino
• Palm Springs
• Los Angeles

Salton Sea

0 Miles   100   200   300

0 Kilometers   300

San Diego

WESTERN
ADDITION

Van Ness Avenue

City Hall
Mechanics' Pavilion

Market Street

Mission
Dolores

Valencia Street

Mission Street

Phelan's house

MISSION
DISTRICT

0 Miles   .25   .5

0 Kilometers   .5

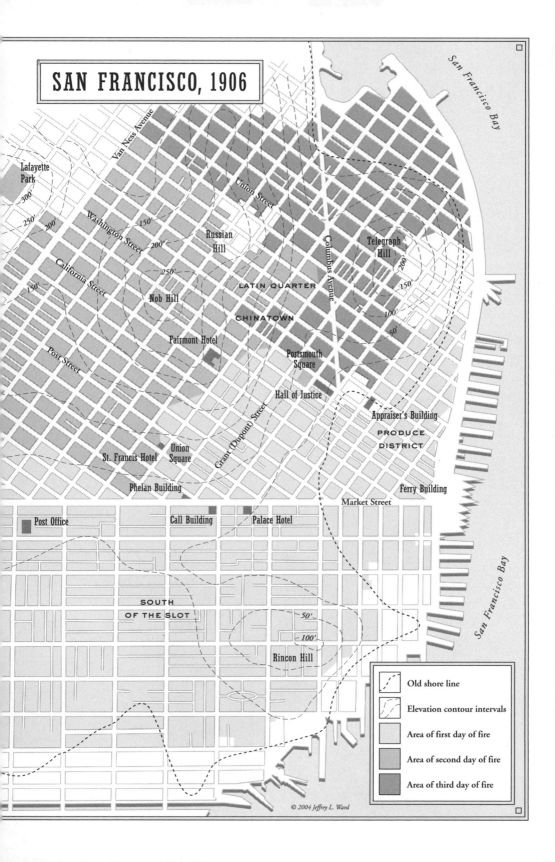

I

BEFORE

BEGINNINGS

SAN FRANCISCO AND NEW YORK CITY

Northern California has never been an easy place to live, although it might seem otherwise to the casual visitor. Eventually, earthquakes, fires, floods, and droughts—not to mention less frequent threats, such as tornadoes, volcanoes, and serial killers—overtake long-term inhabitants and unlucky transients alike. Such was the case at 5:12 A.M. on Wednesday, April 18, 1906. What followed that fateful moment was this country's greatest urban catastrophe.

Writing about megacity disasters, one historian said that "the San Francisco earthquake and fire of 1906 are widely considered America's worst urban disaster and one of the world's greatest urban conflagrations." Another described the 1906 earthquake as "the very epitome of bigness," an event "canonized as the natural disaster to end all disasters" in the public consciousness. "The 1906 San Francisco earthquake is arguably the event that defines calamity in the popular imagination," he added. "It is the Big One that lurks in the back of the American mind."[1]

The story of the 1906 earthquake and fire reveals in bold outline how people react to extreme events. The same could be said for such great disasters as the London fire of 1666, the Chicago fire of 1871, the Galveston hurricane of 1900, or the destruction of the World Trade Center in 2001.

There are, in fact, striking parallels to the terrorist attack on New York. The mightier force that rose unexpectedly from the earth's interior was no less fearsome than the airplanes that descended apocalyptically from the sky. Both San Francisco and New York City were ill prepared. Both had been forewarned: one by numerous smaller earthquakes and six fires that destroyed large portions of the city, the other by the previous bombing of the

World Trade Center. Civil liberties were thought to be a luxury after both disasters. The respective populations were traumatized. Offers of help and donations poured into both cities. Their tarnished mayors rose to the occasion. The cities' elites determined the form of reconstruction. And, like gleaming phoenixes from the ashes, the structures of both cities rose—or, in the case of New York, are due to rise—more glorious and vulnerable than before.[2]

There was one major difference, however. The attack on New York's World Trade Center did not come close to obliterating an entire American city.

A UNIQUE DISASTER

Because of the chaotic nature of large-scale catastrophes, accurate quantifications are, at best, educated guesses. Numbers can be—and have been—manipulated for political, economic, and journalistic purposes. Some general comparisons, however, are possible.

In terms of other war-related tragedies, the British sack of Washington, D.C., during the War of 1812 and General William Tecumseh Sherman's burning of Atlanta during the Civil War resulted in far fewer deaths and less property damage than the 1906 earthquake and fire. In peacetime, the flames that followed the earthquake destroyed an area six times greater than London's "Great Fire" and twice as large as the Chicago fire.[3]

The only comparable civil disaster in terms of the death toll was the Galveston hurricane of 1900. Perhaps six thousand people died in Galveston and outlying areas, although the number has never been verified. But the extent of property damage, the economic loss, local political repercussions, national political ramifications, and foreign policy considerations were minimal in the small Texas city when compared to what took place in California.

In 1906, not only did San Francisco suffer but also the entire West. The largest city west of the Mississippi River, San Francisco was the commercial hub of the region beyond the Rocky Mountains. Commerce was stalled or greatly altered in Seattle, Portland, Los Angeles, Salt Lake City, Phoenix, and elsewhere. San Francisco's urban satellites and outlying suburban and rural areas were either lightly damaged, badly shaken, or rocked and then consumed by fire—as were San Jose, Santa Rosa, and Fort Bragg—along a 270-mile swath of the San Andreas Fault. It was truly a northern California disaster.

The ruins of San Francisco and Santa Rosa to the north—dramatically documented in photographs—matched similar scenes of destruction caused by mass bombings and incendiary fires in London, Hamburg, Dresden, Tokyo, and Hiroshima nearly forty years later. The 1906 earthquake and firestorms were the closest this country has come to experiencing the widespread ravages of modern warfare.

After examining more than six thousand photographs, some taken after the earthquake but before the fire, and reading numerous first-person accounts, I came to the conclusion that the damage from the earthquake alone was considerable but not all-consuming, given the final scale of the catastrophe. But by itself the earthquake would still have been a major disaster. Most deaths were caused by the instantaneous shaking. People could walk away from the fire if they were not trapped by the debris. Most of the damage was caused during the three days of fire.

It could have been much worse. California has been extremely fortunate. No major earthquakes centered near urban areas have struck during those hours between Monday and Friday when most people are either working or in school. That was certainly the case on April 18. Had the earthquake struck three or four hours later—when the city would have been crowded with students, workers, and shoppers—the number of casualties would have been in the tens of thousands instead of the thousands.

There were national and international repercussions in addition to the regional devastation. The failure of the city's private water system when it was needed most gave impetus to the drive for a municipal water supply that would draw from Yosemite's Hetch Hetchy Valley. The first major conservation battle of the twentieth century ended with the damming of the valley in Yosemite National Park, compounding the vulnerability of San Francisco's water system, which now crosses two major faults instead of one.

The nascent Progressive movement was given impetus by the events unleashed in San Francisco. Progressive business leaders, lawyers, and politicians rode the emotionally charged events to prominence. President Theodore Roosevelt took an active interest in San Francisco's internal affairs. He encouraged the urban reformers but sought to dampen the anti-Japanese fervor of the Progressives that led to a war scare. "Nothing during my Presidency has given me more concern than these troubles," said Roosevelt, referring to "the infernal fools" in San Francisco.

The postquake city became the nexus for Roosevelt's foreign policy with Asia. Given the emergence of Japan as a major power following the Russo-Japanese War and anti-Asian racism in California, the United States, with its largest western port destroyed, suddenly seemed quite vulnerable to a Japanese attack. When rioting erupted in San Francisco following a school board vote to segregate Asian students, the president, who was concerned about the reaction of the Japanese, stationed U.S. troops on the streets of San Francisco.

Following these racial incidents, both the United States and Japan undertook the construction of more battleships, and Roosevelt dispatched the Great White Fleet to San Francisco. "By intimating that San Francisco would be the fleet's farthest port of call," wrote biographer Edmund Morris, Roosevelt "encouraged California alarmists to think it was being dispatched for their 'protection.'" While under way, the fleet's cruise was extended around the globe, and in this manner the United States emerged as a military power with global aspirations.[4]

Who, or what, was to blame for the earthquake and its violent aftermath? Not nature, which merely set the events in motion. San Francisco was the city that nearly destroyed itself, and is poised to do so again for most of the same reasons.

A short history filled with natural disasters was ignored. A rabbit warren of poorly constructed, fire-prone buildings was located on the tip of a peninsula from which escape was tenuous. The water system was vulnerable to violent movements of the earth generated by the two major faults that straddle San Francisco—the Hayward to the east and the San Andreas to the west. The center of the city is equidistant from both. The fire spread because of the lack of water and the extensive and inept use of explosives.

Political power shifted from a labor-oriented movement to a wealthy elite, and it remained there for some time. An oligarchy of privileged citizens formed a provisional government. Edicts were issued—including one to "KILL" anyone suspected of committing a crime. Soldiers, police, and vigilantes were empowered to carry out the perceived needs of the moment. The results were the hasty abandonment of democracy and the legal system, and instant death for some. Innocent people were shot or dealt with summarily for minor offenses.

During most great natural disasters and wars some civil liberties—out of necessity—are curbed and civil constraints are imposed. There have been few exceptions. President James Madison avoided a state of wartime governance in 1812. But Abraham Lincoln during the Civil War, Franklin Roosevelt in World War II, and President George W. Bush in the wake of September 11 imposed restrictions on civil liberties. *Inter arma silent leges*—

in time of war, the law is silent—wrote William Rehnquist, chief justice of the U.S. Supreme Court, three years before the terrorist attacks in 2001. And so it was on the streets of San Francisco in 1906.[5]

Although martial law was created to deal with such extraordinary events, martial law was never officially declared in San Francisco, yet nearly everyone was under the impression that it had been. A twilight zone existed in which all actions by those in power—later termed a "dictatorship"—were condoned.[6] The writer Mary Austin, who was in the city at the time, later tried to explain these hasty and illegal actions: "The will of the people was toward authority, and everywhere the tread of soldiery brought a relieved sense of things orderly and secure. It was not as if the city had waited for martial law to be declared, but as if it precipitated itself into that state by instinct as its best refuge."[7]

When the turmoil was over, the deceptions began. Those in power denied that a state of martial law had existed, although the convenient ambiguity had permitted their unconstrained use of force. They also emphasized the destructiveness of the fire and exorcised the word *earthquake* from public discourse. Fire is visible, seemingly controllable, and fairly predictable; earthquakes are invisible, uncontrollable rogue events. Insurance companies and banks that might help reconstruct the city regarded fires more favorably. Besides, fire was covered by insurance; earthquakes weren't.

Although the eastern money men were not deceived, San Franciscans believed the locally generated propaganda. Lines portraying earthquake faults were struck from state maps, the number of casualties was downplayed, geologists were discouraged from probing for explanations, a history of the earthquake was never published, and the city was rebuilt as quickly as possible with scant regard for future cataclysms.

The city was purged in other ways. Civic graft prosecutions—more accurately termed persecutions—followed the natural catastrophe and became the means whereby the elite, who had illegally seized the reins of government during the disaster, held onto the bucking horse of power.

The rebuilding of San Francisco was astonishingly fast and on a heroic scale, but the price for such speed, besides another disaster-prone city, was a depletion of the West's natural resources. Time and the need to move on softened memories. A coda was supplied in the form of the gaudy 1915 Panama-Pacific International Exposition, located on the very ground that had been filled with the charred debris of the city in 1906 and that would turn to jelly in the 1989 Loma Prieta earthquake.

One hundred years later, there is good reason to believe that little, except externalities, will be different when a great catastrophe strikes again. The 1906 earthquake that sparked the conflagration and subsequent events was not a truly great seismic event. At magnitude 9.2, the Alaska earthquake of 1964 released twice the energy of the 7.7 to 7.9 San Francisco temblor. Yet the largest earthquake ever recorded on a seismograph in the Northern Hemisphere killed only slightly more than one hundred people. The differences were population density, concentration and type of structures, and fire.[8]

There will be more earthquakes—and larger and more devastating ones—because California, located on an intertwined system of active faults, is prime earthquake country where the human population and the size and concentration of structures keep on growing and growing and growing.

EARLY EARTHQUAKES

According to Native American legend, the ocean once covered the land around San Francisco. When the water retreated behind the coastal hills to become a bay, the outlets became the Santa Clara Valley and the Salinas River plain to the south and the Russian River to the north. A great earthquake split the barrier asunder, forming the Golden Gate, now the lone outlet from San Francisco Bay to the Pacific Ocean.[9]

In the mid-seventeenth century, according to scientists, a huge earthquake—termed a penultimate event—rippled across the Pacific Northwest and northern California. It could easily have destroyed what later became Seattle, Portland, and San Francisco. But structures were small and flexible, and people were scattered in small tribes along the Pacific Coast.[10]

One such tribe was the Yuroks. Anthropologist A. L. Kroeber, who recorded their tales, noted that "all the Indians of California have a name for the earthquake, and most of them personify it." The Yuroks on the northwest coast of California believed that Earthquake shook the ground when he raced against Thunder, an interesting choice for a competitor, since many earthquakes are accompanied by deep, rumbling noises. Earthquake's huge steps created coastal lagoons—perhaps a reference to the subsidence caused by the massive seventeenth-century event. The Yuroks also had an explanation for the 1906 earthquake. An informant named Dick told Kroeber in 1907: "Now Earthquake is angry because the Americans have bought up Indian treasure and formulas and taken them away to San Francisco to keep. He knew that, so he tore the ground up there."[11]

The Tolowa of northern California and southern Oregon related a story of a tsunami generated by an earthquake. The ground shook a number of times, said the Tolowa. Everything standing fell over. A flood of biblical proportions drowned all, except a brother and a sister who fled into the mountains. They had children, and The People survived.[12]

When the Spanish and then the Mexicans began displacing the Native American populations, they, too, experienced earthquakes, first in southern California and then in the northern half of the state. Churches were not immune from these random events. In fact, the relatively tall adobe and masonry structures were particularly vulnerable to this phenomenon. Earthquakes shook the rigid missions—the oldest structures of European derivation in the state—and contributed to their physical decline.

From 1800 onward the mission at San Juan Bautista near the southern end of the 1906 fracture zone was repeatedly damaged and repaired. In 1812, half the missions were damaged in southern California. Some forty Indians were killed while attending mass at the San Juan Capistrano Mission, the first recorded earthquake deaths in California. The year became known as *el año de los temblors*.[13]

A moderately large earthquake shook the area east of Monterey in 1836, and a larger one caused damage from Yerba Buena (shortly to be renamed San Francisco) to San Juan Bautista in 1838. The shaking in 1838 was equivalent to what would be experienced in 1906. Adobe walls cracked, trees splintered, and water sloshed in creek beds. In Monterey, the capital and largest settlement in Alta California, "the inhabitants were scared out of their wits," according to an American naval officer.[14]

EARLY FIRES

Six fires plagued gold rush San Francisco.

With the nascent city booming, fire destroyed the few buildings of value on Christmas Eve of 1849. Among the fifty structures destroyed was the two-story Parker House, a hotel and gambling casino.

There were three fires in 1850. On May 4 the city's merchants, who had built up extensive inventories at great cost, suffered the most when fire broke out in another drinking and gambling establishment. Water to fight the fire was scarce, structures in the path of the flames were blown up, and an undetermined number of people perished. A larger fire began in a bakery on June 14 and spread through the gold rush settlement quickly. A third conflagration on September 17 consumed mostly shanties. The losses were rated less than in previous fires, there being little left to burn.

Each time the settlement rebuilt quickly. The ashes of destroyed buildings simply served as fertilizer for the rapid growth of new structures. John S. Hittell, the historian of early San Francisco, wrote: "The ground burned over was in a few months covered with better buildings than before; and the growth and business of the city appeared to be rather stimulated than checked by the disaster."

In 1851, on the anniversary of the May 4 fire of the previous year, another "Great Fire" destroyed sixteen blocks and fifteen hundred structures during a three-day firestorm. "Many of the brick buildings supposed to be fireproof," wrote Hittell, "were unable to withstand the intense heat of half a mile of flame fanned by a high wind." Theaters, banks, hotels, and the customs house were incinerated, as were an undetermined number of inhabitants.

Samuel R. Weed, who would soon join the fire department and eventually become a New York City fire insurance underwriter, recalled: "The wind was calm and still in the beginning, but in a few minutes the wind was a roaring hurricane, and the fire was devouring buildings and contents in its onward march." Weed said the damage bore the same proportions in 1851 as in 1906—meaning that three-fourths of San Francisco was destroyed.

Employees remained inside supposedly fireproof brick buildings and risked their lives in the hope of saving structures and merchandise. Some succeeded; others failed. One unharmed survivor in a bank where three later died of burn wounds and all others were scarred for life described the 1851 firestorm thus:

> The deep thunder sound of that roar seemed to my startled ears like the voice of hell, howling at our resistance. I placed my hand upon the brick wall that separated my office by only twelve inches from the dread fire that surrounded us and felt the stove-like heat.
>
> Meeting with the impediment of the solid wall, the flames were carried by the wind along it, upward and over the roof, pouring down each chimney flue and through the fireplaces into the rooms, burning cinders and inky streams of stifling smoke like the black fumes coming through a steamboat smokestack from a bituminous coal furnace.

Arson was the suspected cause. A suspect was caught and beaten to death. Vigilante committees formed, and soon their self-appointed duties expanded beyond mere fire protection to the policing of a wide range of suspected criminal activities. The city rebuilt yet again.

One month later, in June 1851, another "great" fire destroyed both the city hall and the city hospital. Several hospital patients burned to death. Refugees fled—as they would a half-century later—on steamboats to other parts of the Bay Area. A suspected arsonist was captured and nearly lynched, but he managed to escape.

This fire, like the previous ones, was portrayed as a blessing. "The day after the fire," wrote Hittell, ever the civic booster, "another wonderful scene was presented. Instead of sorrow, idleness or despair, the city seemed to be gifted with new life." Reconstruction began immediately, but building materials and labor were quite costly. Trees from the Northwest were shipped south. Granite from China, lava from Hawaii, and bricks from Sydney, London, and New York were imported. New structures—again, more imposing than the previous ones—rose in the city whose official seal now bore the likeness of the phoenix.

Some inhabitants had rebuilt four or five times. One such landowner was William Rabe, who owned property on the south side of Clay Street, just west of Montgomery Street. When Rabe rebuilt for the last time, he had the words *Nil Desperandum* (Never despair) carved in large letters on the façade of his house. He was flattered when people called him by that name. The structure was destroyed in the 1906 fire.[15]

1865 AND 1868

San Francisco experienced a moderate shake on October 8, 1865. Centered to the south in the Santa Cruz Mountains, the quake was experienced as a slight shock followed by "a rapid shake, powerful and convulsive" and "a frightful roaring sound." Cornices, chimneys, windows, and walls fell in San Francisco.

This event was witnessed by the author Mark Twain, who was walking on Third Street shortly after noon on that Sunday when his gait was suddenly checked "just as a strong wind will do when you turn a corner and face it suddenly." The city hall was "dismembered," in the words of Twain's published sketch titled "The Great Earthquake in San Francisco." (From 1865 to 1906 each successively stronger earthquake was given the title of "great," just as the successive fires had been labeled.) Damage was also reported in Santa Cruz, New Almaden, San Jose, and Santa Clara to the south and Petaluma and Napa to the north.[16]

Three years later, on October 19, 1868, there was yet another "great" earthquake centered on the Hayward Fault on the east side of San Francisco Bay. Thirty people were killed. It could have been worse; the earthquake struck shortly before 8 A.M. The damage and deaths were greatest in such East Bay communities as Hayward and San Leandro. In Hayward a badly frightened man, lame since birth, walked eighteen feet without his cane for the first time in his life.

San Francisco was also hit hard, the damage occurring mostly on the bayside "made land" east of Montgomery Street that had been filled with dirt and debris to allow development. Such loosely compacted soil was especially susceptible to liquefaction. A half-dozen people were killed in the city, and some fifty were injured. There was sufficient water to put out the few fires. The city hall was again badly damaged. In a letter to his mother, a resident, William Henry Knight, cited the "visible and audible manifestations of power so vast as to make one feel the littleness and impotence of human might."[17]

Civic leaders moved quickly to minimize the "exaggerated accounts" dispatched eastward to New York City and other financial centers. Eastern money would be needed to rebuild the city. In one united chorus, San Francisco newspapers chanted that the damage was due to human error and could easily be corrected by building better. A chamber of commerce subcommittee report on the earthquake may—or may not—have been completed and then conveniently lost. The less publicity, the better, the thinking went.[18]

After 1868 a period of deceptive calm settled over the city and its inhabitants. Bret Harte wrote a farcical sketch in 1872 that began, "Towards the close of the nineteenth century the city of San Francisco was totally engulfed by an earthquake." "For many years" before sinking beneath the surface of the Pacific Ocean, Harte noted, "California had been subject to slight earthquakes, more or less generally felt, but not of sufficient importance to awaken anxiety or fear."[19]

The inhabitants of San Francisco dozed fitfully. "The average Californian becomes accustomed to the earthquakes which produce 'temblors' of sufficient intensity to rattle windows," an earthquake scientist wrote in 1907. "Prior to the great earthquake of April 18, 1906, these temblors were of frequent occurrence, but occasioned no alarm and, indeed, scarcely excited a passing interest."[20]

The action after 1868 shifted eastward, where the Chicago fire of 1871 and the Galveston hurricane of 1900 established precedents for large-scale disasters in this country, precedents that would be codified in 1906.

THE TALE OF TWO CITIES

CHICAGO

Termed "the Black Year" by newspapers, 1871 was exceptionally dry throughout the Midwest. Both rural forests and the crowded, poorly built wooden structures of Chicago burst into searing flames during the prolonged drought.

On the eve of the fire that began in Patrick and Catherine O'Leary's cow barn, Chicago was a thriving city that had risen quickly from swampland to become the self-proclaimed "City of the West." Then, on the night of October 8, 1871, an intense firestorm fanned by gale-force winds struck the city and raged for the next twenty-six hours. Perhaps three hundred died, thousands were injured, one-third of the city's population was made homeless, and eighteen thousand structures, making up one-fourth of Chicago, were destroyed. Chicago became the symbol of a great American city susceptible to an equally great catastrophe.

From the ashes rose not only gleaming new structures but also a benign, self-congratulatory history that failed to acknowledge the sharp conflicts that had emerged during the disaster. While Chicago missed the instantaneous terror of an earthquake preceding the fire, there were other similarities with what would transpire in San Francisco in 1906.

The supposed safeguards that cities construct, such as fire departments, were overwhelmed by the sheer immensity of the event. Firemen and their equipment were both helpless and useless. "Fireproof" buildings were consumed by leaping orange swaths of flame. Only when little remained to burn in its path did the fire fizzle out on the northern edge of the prairie.

Smaller structures were dynamited on the South Side, forming a firebreak that halted the blaze.

Wealth was a decided advantage. The wealthy tended to live in less fire-prone homes. They had servants to fetch and carry, could afford to hire transportation to carry them away from danger, and had friends in safe places to which they could flee. Their stories survived to dominate histories of the event. The poor suffered the most. Not only were they uninsured or underinsured but the fire also began in a poor area of the city. Most of those who died were poor, and the poorer survivors were the last to find new lodgings.

Class and ethnic prejudices were evident in the aftermath of the disaster. The Irish, Scandinavian, and German newcomers were unjustly suspected of looting and other crimes. An Irish family was said to have caused the fire, although the evidence indicates only that it started in the O'Learys' barn. The Germans in Chicago faced the possibility of losing their ethnic enclave after the fire, just as the Chinese would experience in San Francisco.

Disasters on the scale of Chicago present a unique opportunity to glimpse behind the lace curtains and see who actually wields power. The mercantile elite of Chicago—Anglo, Protestant, native born of New England stock—denounced the existing municipal government as weak and corrupt and quickly formed citizens' committees to take over many of the functions of local government. "In all of these instances," an insightful history of the Chicago fire pointed out, "a native-born urban elite presented their own beliefs and preferences as those that best served all of the people of the city." Karen Sawislak of Stanford University posed some key questions in her book on the Chicago fire: "How do people claim to represent the 'public interest'? How is power legitimated? And how, finally, is it won and exercised? The subject is power, and, in some ways, the classic urban studies query of 'who governs?'"

Power was appropriated not only by privileged citizens but also by the military. The Illinois governor bitterly opposed use of federal troops, believing the Illinois militia and local police were sufficient. The governor and his supporters argued that the military should not dictate policy to democratically elected public officials in a time of peace. But Chicago business leaders were willing to surrender control over policing and criminal justice functions to federal troops to preserve the existing social order. At the insistence of the business community, U.S. troops patrolled Chicago streets for two weeks.[1]

Rumors circulated and were given credence in the press. "Heartless killers, vigilante mobs, and miscellaneous looters, incendiaries, thieves, and extortionists" were on the loose. Fear of a takeover by the masses prevailed and provided the pretext for summary law enforcement. An overexcited lawyer wrote his mother in New Hampshire:

> As far as the fire reached the city is thronged with desperadoes who are plundering & trying to set new fires. The police are vigilant. Thousands of special police are on duty. Every block has its patrolmen and instructions are explicit to each officer to shoot any man who acts suspicious and will not answer when spoken [to] the second time. Several were shot & others hung to lamp posts last night under these instructions.[2]

Unfounded stories, such as accounts about the lynching of criminals or the slicing off of the fingers and ears of the dead to obtain rings and earrings, are common after large disasters. Folklorist Jan Harold Brunvand has identified the cut finger story as an urban legend, that is, "a story . . . with traditional variants that indicate its legendary character."[3]

Imagined crimes were also attributed to the underclasses. "The tales of arson and drunkenness and crime spoke mainly on a symbolic level, revealing a desire for greater control of 'dangerous' elements," wrote a Northwestern University professor. "The anxiety behind this desire was that social chaos, not fire, was the most severe threat to the future of the city."

The ultimate sanction was placed on the relatively harmless crime of looting. Allan Pinkerton ordered his private police force to kill suspected looters, even though people seeking food or personal belongings in the ruins could be, and were, easily mistaken for offenders. Whereas looting was envisioned as a class crime, little attention—and certainly not the extreme penalty of death—was paid to price gouging, perhaps an even greater crime committed against the needy in times of crisis.

To handle the crime wave that never materialized, volunteers were armed and designated "special" peace officers. The vigilantes and the more disciplined troops were ordered to shoot to kill anyone who disobeyed an order. One volunteer killed a prominent citizen who didn't know that night's password and made the mistake of turning his back and walking away from the guard.[4] Another prominent citizen would be shot under similar circumstances in San Francisco. The deaths of such persons received extensive newspaper coverage in both cities, while the killing of more ordinary people rated a few paragraphs, at most.

As would also be the case in San Francisco, most newspaper attention focused on the more easily accessible disaster in the city, while nearby events of equal or greater importance in the countryside were seriously underreported or ignored entirely. On the same day as the Chicago fire, a forest fire broke out near the small lumbering town of Peshtigo, just north of Green Bay, Wisconsin, killing approximately twelve hundred residents. The town was encircled by a bone-dry pine forest. There was no escape.[5]

The Peshtigo wildfire was the same type of megafire experienced in urban Chicago and later in San Francisco. What little is known about urban firestorms dates back to World War II, when the fire-blackened cities of Europe and Asia resembled the ruins of the West Coast city in 1906.

Called large fires, mass fires, or firestorms, these holocausts have been described by fire historian Stephen J. Pyne as "a synergistic phenomenon of extreme burning" that responds to the dynamics of its own internal energy. In other words, the fire feeds upon itself and advances inexorably in fits and starts. As small fires converge to form a large fire, much like separate streams joining to form a roaring waterfall, cool air is sucked into the vacuum left by the expelled hot air. Convective winds or updrafts of over one hundred miles per hour are generated. The cyclonic winds carry flames, fireballs, hot embers, billows of smoke, and large objects aloft into a darkening sky. Volatile gasses released by the intense heat explode in the air; embers float to the ground; flames spread in surges.

Under such conditions "traveling sheets of flame," as one witness to the Peshtigo fire described them, do not need to touch people or structures directly in order to kill, maim horribly, or destroy. Given the intensity of the toxic gasses and the radiant heat, people die from asphyxiation, burns, and the inhalation of poison gasses such as carbon monoxide. Their remains are roasted, and their bodies resemble charred lumps.

In regard to the flammability index, the application of which would be vividly demonstrated in San Francisco, wool provides more protection than cotton or linen garments, and silk is the most combustible fabric of all. Wood bursts into flames at 500 degrees Fahrenheit, iron melts at 2,000 degrees, and steel is contorted into weird shapes at 2,500 degrees.

Mass fires can release the energy equivalent of a Hiroshima-type atomic bomb every five to fifteen minutes. Pyne wrote a composite description of a mass fire that could apply equally to cities, towns, or forests: "Winds felled trees as if they were blades of grass; darkness covered the land; firewhirls danced across the blackened skies like an aurora borealis from hell; the air was electric with tension, as if the earth itself were ready to explode into flame. And everywhere people heard the roar, like a thousand trains crossing a thousand steel trestles."[6]

The ancients had known fire as a weapon. The term *firestorm* was applied to Peshtigo, Chicago, and San Francisco, and was employed during World War II to describe the firebombings of cities.

First the British and then the Americans resurrected fire as a major weapon. The urban counterpart to Pyne's description, and one that is also applicable to 1906, depicts the firestorm generated in Hamburg by incendiary bombs:

> The fire, now rising two thousand meters into the sky, snatched oxygen to itself so violently that the air currents reached hurricane force, resonating like mighty organs with all their stops pulled out at once. The fire burned like this for three hours. At its height, the storm lifted gables and roofs from buildings, flung rafters and entire advertising billboards through the air, tore trees from the ground, and drove human beings before it like living torches. Behind collapsing facades, the flames shot up as high as houses, rolled like a tidal wave through the streets at a speed of over a hundred and fifty kilometers an hour, spun across open squares in strange rhythms like rolling cylinders of fire. The water in some of the canals was ablaze. The glass in the tram car windows melted; stocks of sugar boiled in the bakery cellars. Those who had fled from their air-raid shelters sank, with grotesque contortions, in the thick bubbles thrown up by the melting asphalt. No one knows for certain how many lost their lives that night, or how many went mad before they died.

Striking parallels between San Francisco and Germany were inadvertently drawn by W. G. Sebald, a native of Germany who taught European history at the university level in England. They were the following: the unprecedented scale of destruction, the inability to grasp what it meant, the unquestioned heroism attributed indiscriminately to firefighters and survivors, the flight of refugees, the immediate necessity to clear the debris from the cities and build anew, the bleak depression, the need to "sanitize or eliminate" painful knowledge, the inability of novelists and historians to confront reality, the use of clichés by eyewitnesses to "neutralize experiences beyond our ability to comprehend . . . the depths of trauma suffered by those who came away from the epicenters of the catastrophes," "the true state of material and moral ruin," and "the well-kept secret of the corpses built into the foundation of our [city]."[7]

The Japanese also experienced similar firestorms during World War II. Sixty-five Japanese cities—including Tokyo, Osaka, and Kobe—were destroyed by conventional incendiary devices and two additional cities by atomic bombs. What was called "warfare by fire-from-the-sky" made American military planners wonder about the safety of their own cities.[8]

After the Chicago fire, eastern moneymen needed reassurance that the right people were in power before they loaned any funds to rebuild the city. The political candidates of the moneyed, commercially oriented interests, joined by a sympathetic press that vilified the existing municipal administration as plunderers, won election on a reform platform that benefited business interests.

There was much to do. Personal property losses amounted to approximately $196 million, bankrupting fifty-eight insurance companies. Even though only half the claims were paid, reconstruction was on a massive scale. New structures rose quickly with only a modicum of regard for fireproofing. The greatly romanticized reconstruction effort was virtually complete in eighteen months. The fire provided the opportunity for an urban renaissance in the form of the emergence of the Chicago school of architecture, whose designs of steel-framed skyscrapers were later exported to San Francisco.

The frenzy of the recovery effort had secondary effects. "It also induced the temporary amnesia one often needs in order to get on with life after a searing loss," wrote a Chicago historian. The emphasis was on forgetting, or not remembering accurately. Nine years later *Harper's Weekly* stated that no one had died in the fire. Like San Francisco's 1915 Panama-Pacific International Exposition, the World's Columbian Exposition in 1893 provided Chicago with the opportunity to present a reimagined self to the world. The White City of this exposition bore little relationship to the grittiness of the real Chicago. The gleaming buildings of the fair, designed by Daniel Burnham, who would also attempt to reinvent San Francisco a dozen years later, were torched by an arsonist in 1894. The pasteboard structures "melted in a parody of the 1871 catastrophe," wrote one author.[9]

Fast forward to Galveston, Texas, in 1900. The port city of 38,000 inhabitants on a low-lying, sandy island facing the Gulf of Mexico was, like Chicago and San Francisco, on the cusp of a period of great prosperity. It had hopes of catching up to San Francisco, its more urban counterpart on the West Coast.

The people of Galveston were no strangers to disaster. Since 1776, when a Spanish mission was destroyed, hurricanes had periodically raked the Gulf of Mexico coast—at least eleven times in the nineteenth century. Yet the inhabitants denied the threat to their island community. The ruinous storm of 1886 was referred to in the local newspaper as "yesterday's squall," although the town was flooded and people died. A Texas historian later wrote, "Such a lesson should have been plain for Galveston. It was not."

The intense storm of September 8, 1900, which destroyed one-third of the city and left one-fourth its population either dead or injured, was itself viewed as an abnormality. "There prevails a belief that Galveston is subject to severe storms," wrote the editor of the *Galveston Tribune* after the 1900 hurricane. "That is a mistake."[10]

Before the hurricane struck, the citizens of Galveston knew it was on its way. They just had no conception of its lethal strength. Instead of fleeing, they gawked. Among those residents who flocked to the beach was a young King Vidor, who would go on to fame as a Hollywood director. Years later he recalled: "I was only six years old then but I remember now that it seemed as if we were in a bowl looking up toward the level of the sea and as we stood there in the sandy street, my mother and I, I wanted to take my mother's hand and hurry her away. I felt as if the sea was going to break over the edge of the bowl and come pouring down upon us."[11]

It did. Thirty-foot waves battered the city and a nine-foot storm surge inundated it. The winds that tore the anemometer apart exceeded 120 miles per hour. Besides some six thousand dead and an uncounted number of injured in the small city, four thousand structures were destroyed. The monetary losses were estimated at $30 million.[12]

After the storm, rumors served as the pretext to arm citizens, who functioned as a semiofficial vigilante force, and to summon the military. Both were given carte blanche. The editor of the *Tribune* wrote that "the military regime, which was an absolute dictatorship, [was] without precedent and without restriction."[13]

Reprisals for looting, for suspected looting, or for just being of another race or ethnicity rippled across flattened Galveston with deadly results. "Rumor and apocrypha supercharged the night," wrote Eric Larson in *Isaac's Storm*. Mostly African Americans, but also "foreigners," meaning Mexicans and southern Europeans, were depicted as skulking ghouls who lopped off body parts to steal jewelry. Repeating the stories circulated by word of mouth and in printed newspaper accounts, a Galveston mother wrote her out-of-town daughters that "ears and hands have been cut off the dead, because of ear-rings and rings. Fingers have been found in the pockets of looters, mostly Negroes, one of whom had sixteen and another eleven."

Reports varied. Anywhere from a half-dozen to one hundred blacks and foreigners were shot. "White fears of blacks—fed by racial stereotypes—surfaced and shaped the post-storm recovery," stated a book published on the centennial of the disaster.

The political power had shifted, in the terms of historians, to an "urban elite" in Chicago and a "power elite" in Galveston. Additionally, post-hurricane Galveston altered its form of government from mayor-alderman to a commission, the change being hailed as the "greatest contribution to urban progressivism" at the time.[14]

Such shifts in the structure of power are not unusual in times of crisis. Large disasters breed unrest and change. The Chinese, who have a history of seismic calamities dating back 4,500 years, have traditionally regarded them as harbingers of great political upheavals. Chinese historians predicted the fall of the Zhou and Hahn dynasties, centuries before the birth of Christ, on the basis that "all political turmoils were consistent with natural calamities," earthquakes being chief among them.

Given the scale of casualties in Chinese history—half the world's 6.3 million deaths from earthquakes have occurred in China—it is understandable that empires were at risk in China while municipal governments were transformed in this country. The political lessons and science so painfully and painstakingly acquired in China, however, were lost upon the Americans.[15]

SCIENCE, POLITICS, AND SAN FRANCISCO

SCIENCE

The earth science that was being practiced at the time, who held political power and who sought it, and the physical and demographic realities of San Francisco were the montages against which the traumatic events of April 18, 1906, unfolded. Each backdrop was irrevocably altered in the aftermath.

The science that should have concerned itself with earthquakes was almost entirely applied to the extraction of valuable minerals in mid- to late-nineteenth-century California. Geologists were "slaves to Mammon." There had been fleeting interest in the phenomenon of shaking at the time of the 1865 and 1868 earthquakes, but that had quickly evaporated. California scientists, and those who passed as such, tended to be broadly and informally educated. Geologists in Britain, Italy, Germany, and particularly Japan were more specialized in seismic matters.

The San Francisco Bay Area was the center of what little scientific curiosity existed in the state. Founded in 1853, the California Academy of Science in San Francisco consisted mainly of Victorian gentlemen posing as scientists. The real scientists—meaning the great surveyors of the American West, such as Josiah Whitney, Clarence King, and William Brewer—came from the East. They rode through California with only a passing interest in earthquakes. In a brief aside folded into an article on Italian earthquakes, published one year after the "great" earthquake of 1868, Whitney wrote of the California attitude toward earthquakes:

> The prevailing tone in that region, at present, is that of assumed indifference to the dangers of earthquake calamities,—the author of

a voluminous work on California, recently published in San Francisco, even going so far as to speak of earthquakes as "harmless disturbances." But earthquakes are not to be "bluffed off." They will come, and will do a great deal of damage.[1]

The establishment of the University of California across the bay in Berkeley in 1868 attracted eastern scholars to the West Coast. Among them was Joseph LeConte, the university's first professor of geology, botany, and natural history. LeConte arrived in Berkeley when classes began in September 1869. He had studied under the famed naturalist Louis Agassiz at Harvard University. The new professor brought with him the latest thinking about earthquakes. Unfortunately, those ideas represented a theoretical viewpoint based on the European experience, which had been heavily influenced by volcanic eruptions in the Mediterranean area.[2]

Three years after his arrival in California, LeConte aired his scientific theories in a four-part series in the university's newspaper. First, he demolished the local theory that earthquakes were caused by electricity. LeConte believed there was a close relationship between earthquakes and volcanoes, which, of course, was true in Europe, Hawaii, and the Cascade Range in the Pacific Northwest. He did not mention the possibility of faulting as the cause in California.[3]

Grove Karl Gilbert of the U.S. Geological Survey (USGS) was an early advocate of the faulting theory. Gilbert traveled widely in the American West and was the author of the first Geological Survey paper on earthquakes. He was an advocate of observational geology—being there, seeing it, and describing it.[4] Gilbert studied the forces that built mountains in Utah. He cited an upthrusting movement of unspecified origin that broke the surface of the earth, causing earthquakes and the rise of mountains like the Wasatch Range. Of the perceived danger and the use of different types of building materials, Gilbert posed a question and supplied an answer relevant to this day:

> What are the citizens going to do about it? Probably nothing. They are not likely to abandon brick and stone and adobe, and build all new houses of wood. If they did, they would put themselves at the mercy of fire; and fire, in the long run, unquestionably destroys more property than earthquakes. It is the loss of life that renders earthquakes so terrible. Possibly some combination of building materials will afford security against both dangers.[5]

The haphazard study of earthquakes took a step forward in 1887 when the first two seismographs in the Western Hemisphere were installed at the Students' Observatory on the Berkeley campus and the university's Lick Observatory atop Mount Hamilton, east of San Jose. Both instruments were operated by astronomers, who were primarily interested in the effects of earth movements on their delicate telescopes. The first quiver recorded at Berkeley was an explosion in a nearby powder works on August 11. Eight days later an earthquake was detected.

One important outgrowth of the installation of the seismographs was the compilation of an extensive earthquake catalogue by Edward S. Holden, the director of the Lick Observatory. Holden's 1898 catalogue was later considered "a cornerstone of the centrally important catalogue of historical western seismicity" that was published in 1939.

At the time, however, Holden's catalogue and its accompanying text, published by the Smithsonian Institution, were virtually ignored; a visiting civil engineer could not find a copy in Bay Area libraries shortly after the 1906 earthquake. When Frederick G. Plummer returned to Washington, D.C., he located one copy in the USGS library. Its pages were uncut. The engineer wrote Gilbert: "Several teachers of geology in the West have informed me that they have never seen the catalogue although it was issued in 1898 and was reprinted for distribution by the Government."

Holden thought the origins of earthquakes were local and credited "faulting in the underground strata" rather than volcanic activity as the predominant cause. Given few truly destructive shocks and the perceived ability to build earthquake-resistant structures, the astronomer concluded: "I am firmly of the opinion that the earthquakes of California are not so much to be dreaded as is generally supposed; in fact, they are far less dangerous to life and property than are the hurricanes of the South or the summer tornadoes of the North."[6]

Holden was remarkably prescient on another matter, however. The *Mining and Scientific Press,* a respected journal published in San Francisco, noted after the 1906 earthquake:

There is room for comment here on the short memories of humankind. Here was an authority—E. S. Holden—who reported on the last serious earthquake forty years ago, and emphasized the danger of building "on the made land between Montgomery street and the Bay." Nevertheless, during the years since that report was published, people have continued to build there in disregard of the evidence that

it was dangerous to do so without taking proper precautions. . . .
The amount of dishonest construction that escapes undetected in a
big city is appalling and it is this that the earthquake, like a relentless
inspector, exposes.[7]

The University of California's greatest contribution to the knowledge of
earthquakes resulted from the hiring of Andrew C. Lawson. The Scotland-
born Lawson came to California by way of the Canadian Geological Survey.
The assistant professor of mineralogy and geology devoted his energies to
the science of geology, while LeConte dealt with the philosophical aspects.
Lawson set off, alone or with students, to explore the Coast Range that surrounded the Bay Area. In the process, he stumbled across a section of the
San Andreas Fault.

In 1893 Lawson published a description of a short part of this fault, then
unnamed, which lay south of San Francisco. The unusual narrow and
indented San Andreas and Crystal Springs valleys and the nature of the
drainage system had caught Lawson's attention. Gilbert congratulated
Lawson: "The West Coast now has a geologist who appreciates and applies
the principles of the new geology." In another publication two years later,
Lawson called his discovery "the San Andreas fault" after the valley, which
had been named Canada de San Andrés by the Franciscan missionary
Francisco Palóu on the feast day of Saint Andrew in 1774.

Others recognized small sections of the fault in northern and southern
California. But until after the 1906 earthquake no one advanced the notion
of one single fault extending 660 miles from just north of Shelter Cove in
Humboldt County to the Salton Sea in Imperial County. It would take
another sixty years before the concept of plate tectonics would be accepted
by the scientific community.

The theory of plate tectonics holds that there are seven large plates and
a number of smaller ones that pave the surface of the earth. These gigantic
slabs creep or jerk spasmodically, causing barely detectable or violent movements. The force or forces that move the plates are not known with any certainty. The western margin of California is bisected by the Pacific Plate to
the west and the North American Plate to the east. The San Andreas Fault
is the world's best-known demarcation between plates and the longest and
most active of the many faults in California. The movement along the San
Andreas is mostly horizontal, with the Pacific Plate heading toward Alaska.
The fault lies offshore of San Francisco and meets the coastline a few miles
north and south of the Golden Gate.[8]

A spate of small quakes led up to the 1906 event. Temblors peppered the San Jose area in the summer of 1903. More minor Bay Area earthquakes struck in 1904. In December Lawson wrote in the University of California's newspaper, the *Daily Californian:* "History and records show that earthquakes in this locality have never been of a very violent nature, and so far as I can judge from the nature of the recent disturbances and from accounts of past occurrences there is no occasion for alarm at the present time."

On New Year's Day of 1905, windows, loose crockery, and bric-a-brac were broken in San Francisco. A local newspaper assured the public: "College professors call them geotectonic. A geotectonic earthquake is a sort of tame variety which may chafe against its chain now and then, but never really does any harm." A second shake in August damaged many of the larger buildings in San Jose.[9]

POLITICS: THE IRISH CATHOLIC
AND THE FRENCH JEW

Human nature echoed the findings of science. The intertwined fates of two men—one an Irish Catholic and the other a French Jew—personified the fractured nature of the landscape. The stories of James D. Phelan (pronounced *feelan*), perceived in his time as the white knight, and Abraham Ruef (pronounced *roof*), cast in the role of the dark prince, illustrate the shift of political power during and after the transformative event. Each pursued power in his own way. Neither shaped events so much as he was shaped by them.

Their antagonism grew from who they were and what they represented. Phelan, a self-described capitalist, was a politician, a civic leader, and one of San Francisco's richest businessmen. Ruef, a successful attorney, was affiliated with a labor-oriented political movement and served as an informal adviser to the mayor who succeeded Phelan in that office.

Their stories, which give a human dimension to these events, are not equally well documented. Partly because their power was exercised differently—Phelan being out front and Ruef behind the scenes—the extent of their public records differ. Virtually every scrap of paper created by Phelan after 1906 has survived and is available in an archive. Ruef instructed his heirs to destroy his papers.

Both men came from privileged backgrounds, Phelan's being decidedly more so. His father, also named James, arrived in San Francisco at the height of the gold rush in 1849. He did not pursue the elusive mineral sought by so many others. Phelan senior opted for more prosaic goods, such as liquor, iron safes, and cooking supplies. He then graduated to insurance companies, banks, and real estate throughout northern California. His growing empire was directed from the imposing five-story Phelan Building, built in 1882 at the corner of Market and O'Farrell streets.

The elder Phelan constructed a modest mansion on three and one-half acres at Valencia and Seventeenth streets, an easy walk to the Mission Dolores Church in the Mission District. With his retiring wife, Phelan raised three children: Alice, James, and Mary Louise, known as Mollie. Alice would marry, but her brother and sister did not and remained housemates.

Young James had a sheltered upbringing that included a grand tour of Europe at the age of eight and a Jesuit education through graduation from St. Ignatius College. He did not complete his studies at Hastings College of the Law, preferring to embark on an extended tour of Europe, where he gained a lifelong passion for things Parisian and Mediterranean. He returned home, went to work for his father, and took over the family business when the elder Phelan died in 1892. Not a serious Catholic, although connected to the church for political and charitable purposes, Phelan's public persona was bathed in the Victorian glow of morality, respectability, and rectitude.

Phelan was a short, stiff man who viewed issues and people in black-and-white terms. He sought—continuously, assiduously, and with the degree of success that money and power can ensure—to be the master of the immediate situation, whether dealing with his mistress or financing the relief effort after the earthquake. "His life was one of organization and calculation," wrote his biographers, James P. Walsh and Timothy J. O'Keefe, who termed the young Phelan "the most prominent Californian of the upcoming generation." Phelan was considered one of the two most prominent California Democrats in the Progressive era. He was described by historian Philip J. Ethington as "the leading citizen who leads the leading citizens" in a flawed urban reform movement.[10]

The San Francisco banker-capitalist was extraordinarily well connected. Telegrams and personal notes went back and forth between Phelan and President Roosevelt. After fellow San Franciscan Franklin K. Lane, a member of the Interstate Commerce Commission, lunched with the president, he wrote Phelan: "He [Roosevelt] has, I think, very great confidence in you, such, in fact, as he has in few men on our coast." Lane wrote Phelan on commission stationery that he, the USGS, and the president supported Phelan on obtaining a water source for San Francisco from Hetch Hetchy

Valley in Yosemite National Park. (Phelan was referred to as "the father of our water supply" by future San Francisco civic leaders.) Roosevelt wrote Phelan to thank him for pushing the Progressive urban reform agenda in San Francisco.[11]

Phelan's influence extended to the military. He was close to the two top army commanders on the West Coast while they were stationed in San Francisco and after they had moved on to other posts. Major General Adolphus W. Greely asked Phelan to intercede with the president for the promotion in rank of his son as "proper recognition of my relief work in San Francisco." Greely praised Phelan for standing by San Francisco "so nobly," and later asked him for an appointment to the Hetch Hetchy Water Commission.

Phelan lobbied Brigadier General Frederick Funston to move the army's headquarters offices back into the rebuilt Phelan Building after the earthquake. Although Funston praised him as "an excellent landlord," the army remained at Fort Mason. Funston later asked Phelan to put a word in for him as army chief of staff, a position he failed to obtain.[12]

There was a public and a private Phelan. He was involved in a number of sexual liaisons, at least one with a married woman and another with a divorced woman who became his long-term mistress. Both liaisons continued as friendships into old age. The unhappily married woman, from Phelan's own upper-class social stratum, recognized Phelan's need for discretion as a public figure. The other woman, Florence Ellon, sought out the willing twenty-seven-year-old Phelan in 1888 and then threatened disclosure in 1905, stating, among other reasons: "I have had the finger of scorn pointed at me all these years in protecting you while you posed before the World as a good and lovable man." Over the years Phelan gave Ellon considerable amounts of money and property. She furnished receipts for all "claims," "services," and "demands" to the businesslike Phelan. Florence was "Dear Firenze" and James was "Dear Jimmy" in their lengthy and, at times, loving and considerate correspondence.[13]

In a glowing profile for the *Wasp,* a weekly San Francisco journal of social commentary, the writer took note of the tasteful paintings, bronze statues, thoughtful books, Turkish rugs, and suite of rooms that served as both Phelan's office and the site of his secret assignations. Unaware of the dual use of the rooms, the writer remarked: "Altogether, the offices were just what one would expect of the work-rooms of a man of ambition, education and refinement, with a superabundance of money to procure what his tastes suggest." As for the "distinguished and handsome" occupant whose one stated passion was motoring, Phelan was "a thorough American of the purest type."[14]

Phelan's public life included three two-year terms as mayor of San Francisco and one six-year term as a U.S. senator. Between holding public offices, he maintained a high profile as a promoter of civic causes, a member of city commissions, a public orator, a dispenser of earthquake relief funds, and president of the exclusive Bohemian Club.

Like Phelan's personal life, the dominant political movement of the time had two faces. Publicly, the Progressives personified disinterested reform. Privately, they sought to gain political power, and their racist attitudes and policies hurt some people. Phelan's strongest statements in his extensive private correspondence and his public utterances pertained to racial matters. He saw "non-assimilable people" as "a menace to the existence of republican institutions." The "non-assimilable" phrase occurred constantly in Phelan's correspondence.

His racial views were not unusual at the time. California was still a raw, untutored land where vigilantes and frontier justice had ruled within the last fifty years in both San Francisco and Los Angeles. In fact, Catholics like Phelan were not immune from discrimination themselves. One of Phelan's political advisers, assessing his chances in the 1914 senatorial race, believed he had a better chance in Catholic San Francisco than statewide.

Jews were one target of the Catholics and others. Phelan was a member of Ignatian Council No. 35 of the Young Men's Institute, the Irish Catholic equivalent, for men between the ages of eighteen and thirty-five, of the Protestant-dominated Young Men's Christian Association. The council was active in supporting the mayoral candidacy of "our Brother James D. Phelan" and other candidates of the Democratic Party, which "has shown itself loyal to our most holy cause." The institute's campaign literature, circulated by hand to aid Phelan's mayoral reelection, touched briefly on the Catholics losing ground in Europe. It then stated: "If we succeed the Public Schools [boldface in the original] and the City government will be ours, and there will be no place in them for Jews, Protestants, or other heretics. . . . Brother Phelan's past appointees, his present County Committee, his ticket now before us, vouch for the future."[15]

Phelan, president of the Mutual Savings Bank, refused to advertise in the *Jewish Times,* which billed itself as "The Pioneer Jewish Weekly of the Pacific Coast." The newspaper's managing editor complained to Phelan that ads for the bank appeared in all other weeklies "except the columns of *The*

Jewish Times. . . . We see no reason why *The Jewish Times* should be discriminated against." There was no reply.[16]

Phelan was particularly bellicose toward the Japanese, who had supplanted the Chinese at the turn of the century as the principal target for racism in California. He told one correspondent that "the law of self preservation is our warrant" for a war with Japan. He continued his virulent attacks against the Japanese as a U.S. senator, stating in 1920: "It is a race as well as an economic problem." This statement mirrored the Progressives' position on rural and urban racial matters in California.[17]

Others—like Phelan's close friends, those in his social set, and his fellow Progressives—were publicly more outspoken about Jews. Abraham Ruef emerged as the principal target of their anti-Semitic attacks, which at times surpassed the merely vituperative and became apoplectic.

The Bay Area author Gertrude Atherton, Phelan's close friend and frequent correspondent, undertook the writing of a book on California. Asked by her New York editors to include material on Ruef and the postquake graft trials that brought him down, she queried Phelan: "Has anybody written a paper or series of papers on the subject—from the right point of view—which I could use as a skeleton upon which to base my story—which must be correct as well as interesting?"

In the subsequent book, dedicated to Phelan, Atherton wrote: "Ruef was a little ferret-faced, black-eyed French Jew, of abilities so striking that he could have become one of the most respected and useful citizens in the history of San Francisco had he not deliberately chosen the 'crooked' role. . . . He was one of the most innately vicious men this country has spawned, and one of the most destructive incubated by poor San Francisco."[18]

Ruef was portrayed as a "crafty adventurer" in a book financed by San Francisco's two leading "reformers," Phelan and his wealthy friend, traveling companion, business partner, and fellow Progressive Rudolph Spreckels of the sugar clan. Written by the Progressive journalist Franklin Hichborn, *The System: As Uncovered by the San Francisco Graft Prosecution* was also financially subsidized, read in draft form, and advertised by its two benefactors. It is regarded as a seminal work. Writers who came later depended—many uncritically—on Hichborn's book.[19]

McClure's magazine in New York joined the Progressive chorus with an article titled "The Fight for Reform in San Francisco" by George Kennan. To explain the reelection of the labor-oriented Mayor Eugene Schmitz in 1905, Kennan lumped saloon keepers, brothel proprietors, prizefight promoters, gamblers, Catholics, and Jews together. The group as a whole, he explained, obtained "a wide-open town" from the election. "Most of the six thousand Jewish voters supported him," Kennan said, "partly because they knew that they could buy favors from him and partly because he had allied himself with a boss [Ruef] of their own race."[20]

Another New York publication, the *New York Times,* owned by German Jews, chimed in from afar: "The government of San Francisco has been turned over to a little, thin, shabby French Jew, with gray curly hair and dark, dull, fishlike eyes. Insignificance personified, Ruef looks like a peddler. He still wears the shabbiest clothes and there is absolutely nothing distinctive about him, unless it is his hands; delicate hands with long graceful fingers; the hands of the man who acquires." Overlooking some homegrown products, including Boss Tweed, the *Times* remarked that Ruef was "the most remarkable boss in the history of municipal administration."[21]

The antipathy directed toward Ruef, which would increase in tempo and virulence after the earthquake, raises the question: Who really was Abraham Ruef, besides the California equivalent of Alfred Dreyfus, the French army captain imprisoned as the result of an anti-Semitic plot and finally exonerated in 1906. (Ruef even had his Émile Zola, although his was of far lesser stature than the French novelist. The newspaper editor Fremont Older led the first attacks but later sought Ruef's release from prison through use of the written word.)

There is little doubt that Ruef, like Phelan, was both perpetrator of questionable actions and victim of his ambitions during this troubled time. The similarities between Ruef and Phelan are striking: both were proud of being born in San Francisco and were active in nativist societies; both were physically small; both were lifelong bachelors; both were fastidious dressers; both lost their homes and property in the fire that followed the 1906 earthquake; both wielded considerable political power; both speculated in real estate; and both were sophisticates within their respective cultures. Yet they became mortal enemies whose actions resembled a shadow play projected against the backdrop of a physically and morally fractured city.

Ruef's family came from the upper middle class. His parents emigrated from France and arrived in California in 1862. His father, Meyer, operated a dry goods store and later went into real estate. The elder Ruef, like the Phelans, listed himself as a "capitalist" in city directories. Abraham Ruef was the oldest child, he had three sisters, and he was devoted to his family. A niece described him as "a doting bachelor uncle."[22]

The young Ruef stood out from his fellow Californians in a number of ways. He was a brilliant student, graduating second in his class at the

University of California at the age of eighteen. One of three students to give a commencement address in 1883, Ruef received a "Special Certificate of Eminent Scholarship." He would have been named a medalist, the highest honor, had he not been a Jew.[23]

Ruef majored in the classics; was fluent in Greek, Latin, French, and German; and was intensely interested in art, music, and philosophy. He neither smoked nor drank liquor in an age when both were considered marks of manhood. While Phelan never completed his legal studies, Ruef graduated from Hastings College of Law at the age of twenty-one in 1886 and was admitted to the bar that same year. Ruef listed himself as an attorney in the city directory and shared an office with his father on California Street. He unsuccessfully courted Bella Gerstle, the daughter of a prominent Jewish family.[24]

The newly minted attorney took an interest in reform activities and local Republican politics. He became fascinated with urban politics, which was unusual for a Jew. "The dynamics of local power captivated him every bit as much as they did the eastern Irish who used political machines to crawl from teeming tenement slums," wrote James Walsh in an article titled, "Abe Ruef Was No Boss."[25]

Ruef's law practice flourished. He employed seven clerks and four attorneys. As they did for Phelan, real estate ventures provided income. He built the Sentinel Building, modeled on New York's Flatiron Building. (The movie director Francis Ford Coppola would later buy the structure, now known as the Columbus Tower.) Ruef was also the attorney for the city tax collector and public administrator offices.[26]

His appearance and behavior, as seen by his kindest biographers, were described by such words as "short," "dark," "curly-haired," "drooping mustache," "elegant," "neat," "affable," and "ingratiating." To this was added the following by less kind writers: "smirked," "little," "dull fish-like eyes," "nimble of movement," "glib," possessed of "the lust of avarice," and "a clever lawyer, a fundamental liar, and vain, emotional, unscrupulous, and daring in all his schemes, with a thrifty respect for the almighty dollar in small or large sums."[27]

The political careers of the two men collided.

Phelan, a Democrat, won the mayoral election as the reform candidate in 1896 with the help of Gavin McNab, who was termed a "good boss." After

Mayor Phelan sided with employers in the bloody teamsters' and waterfront strike in the summer of 1901, he lost his popularity and chose not to seek a fourth term. At a farewell banquet attended by many of the judges, prosecutors, and fellow Progressives who would later side with him against Ruef, Phelan spoke with prophetic words. Referring to his accomplishments, the outgoing mayor said: "It is not the constructive work that attracts attention. It is not the slow process by which cities are built, but it is the earthquake that strikes the crowd breathless. It is the conflict of battle."[28]

It was an earthquake that would propel Phelan to national prominence, and it was his battle with Ruef that would cause civic mayhem.

Ruef persuaded Eugene E. Schmitz, the handsome, charismatic leader of a theater orchestra and the musicians' union, to run for mayor. Schmitz and the labor ticket swept to victory in November 1901. Ruef then hitched his considerable talents to Schmitz's mayoral career. He was listed in a 1902 directory as the unpaid attorney for the mayor's office.[29]

Up until the newspaper attacks on Ruef began shortly before the earthquake, he was described in municipal and state directories as a promising young attorney. One stated: "He has always been a strong opponent of misrule in city government, and his efforts have ever been on the side of reform and progress in this direction." Soon thereafter he became known by the pejoratives "Boss Ruef" or "the curly-haired boss" in newspaper and magazine articles. Mayor Schmitz was unflatteringly referred to as "the protégé of thrifty Abraham."[30]

SAN FRANCISCO

San Francisco differed from other cities in terms of its physical setting and demographics; its isolation contributed to the extent of the tragedy.

Most of the City and County of San Francisco was either a wilderness or farm land on the eve of the catastrophe. The Sunset District to the west consisted of sand dunes on which a street grid had been superimposed on paper. Of the forty-eight-square-mile city, perhaps slightly less than half was occupied to some extent. The densest districts were grouped around the waterfront on the north and east edges of the tip of the peninsula.

Nights and days of cool, gray fog, the hills, and the surrounding ocean and bay isolated the jutting peninsula from the remainder of sunny California. "A city the color of dust and ashes; a summerless, winterless city," wrote a contemporary English novelist.[31]

San Franciscans bent against the strong, prevailing wind from the ocean and thought themselves different. The city, or rather "The City," as locals preferred (please, they said, then and now, never "Frisco"), was remote, insular, prideful, and self-conscious. Its cultural models resided on the East Coast and in Europe. Farther inland, other communities and their inhabitants strung along the San Andreas Fault or along the Hayward Fault on the opposite shore of the bay more closely resembled their western counterparts.

Those who could afford the better things depicted life as gay and inconsequential. A diffuse mist blunted the hard realities of the island city. Historians, journalists, artists, and the public relations arm of the Southern Pacific Railroad, along with other commercial interests, contributed to the obfuscation of the real San Francisco. A native bard, Will Irwin, called San Francisco "the bonny, merry city—the good, gray city." The photographer Arnold Genthe viewed the city through a romantic viewfinder. The fog, he said, "was not an enveloping blanket but a luminous drift, conferring a magic patina on the most common-place structures, giving them an air of age and mystery." Genthe prowled Chinatown with a hidden camera and produced misty images of the ghetto that was to become a blazing hell for its inhabitants.[32]

Then there were the sounds, described by Ansel Adams, at that time a youngster but later to become a better-known photographer than Genthe. Adams caught the grinding reality of city life.

> There was always the distant bustle of the city, a deep and throbbing space-filling rumble of ironclad wagon wheels on cobbled streets and the grind of streetcars. It was almost like the sound of the ocean or the wind in the forest, yet deep with the brutality that only a city can offer in fact and spirit, no matter how glamorous the environment or euphoric the social veneer.[33]

There was much to celebrate at the turn of the century. San Francisco ranked among the top ten American cities in population and was the largest city west of St. Louis. The West Coast center for finance, manufacturing, and shipping, it was experiencing one of the greatest booms in its short history of constant booms and busts. But the predominance of San Francisco during the first fifty years of West Coast urban history was being challenged for the first time. Seattle, Portland, and Los Angeles were cutting into the city's business and growth rate.

San Francisco was in flux. Underneath the surface, where the zone of fracture lay, ethnic, racial, and social tensions vibrated. Of the four hundred thousand estimated inhabitants in 1905, three out of four were either immigrants or the children of immigrants. Newly arrived immigrants from southern and eastern Europe were pressing the older immigrant families from northern Europe. There were substantial numbers of Irish (the largest single voting bloc), Italians, and Germans. The largest concentration of Chinese in any American city (though declining because of immigration laws) lived within the confines of Chinatown. There were twenty thousand Chinese and an equal number of Jews. Most Japanese moved inland to agricultural areas.

San Francisco was overwhelmingly a Catholic city. The literacy rate was high for an American city at the time. Of eight major cities, San Francisco had the highest ratio of males to females (55 to 45 percent), correspondingly fewer children, and a large labor force. Nearly forty thousand factory workers made relatively high wages, one of the draws of San Francisco. Unions were strong. Asians were barred from union membership.[34]

Beneath the gaiety and prosperity there was uneasiness. The melding of races was an issue of great importance to the whites at the time. When President Theodore Roosevelt visited the city in 1903, the newspaper headlines applauded the fact that white Christian schoolchildren lined the parade route. "Race Suicide Not Evident Here," proudly proclaimed one headline. The anonymous reporter wrote: "Race suicide should be a buried theme with President Roosevelt from this time on. Whatever the decadence of the race may be in the effete East, the vigorous West has surely demonstrated to him that the Pacific Slope will supply and is supplying enough healthy, happy and intelligent children to replenish the stock of mankind throughout the United States."[35]

The times were bountiful for many. The setting was gorgeous. But the city was not particularly beautiful. "Instead of taking advantage of its remarkable natural beauty," wrote Judd Kahn in *Imperial San Francisco,* "San Francisco was a homely city, dirty, cramped, with few broad avenues, public places, or handsome buildings. With life so mean, San Francisco was losing its magnetism for new residents and tourists." Something had to be done. Attention focused on Chinatown.[36]

Chinatown consisted of approximately a dozen blocks bounded by Broadway on the north and California Street on the south and Kearny and

Stockton streets on the east and west. Its population had declined by half since the Chinese Exclusion Act of 1882 created an aging bachelor society. The ghetto, colony, and ethnic and cultural island, as historian Ronald Takaki called it, was colorful, crowded, and exotic. At least it seemed that way to tourists during daylight hours. Its forbidden nighttime entertainments were added attractions, and its varied forms of commerce contributed to the local economy. Therein lay its political clout.[37]

There had been periodic attempts to remove the Chinese since the 1870s. When the bubonic plague struck the Chinese section of San Francisco in 1900, Chinatown was cordoned off by police and armed guards from the rest of the city. Travel outside the city by Chinese and Japanese could only be undertaken with a certificate of vaccination. The Japanese were included because the plague was thought to be "a rice-eaters' disease."

What plague? The precedent of public denials of catastrophes continued. Merchants, the mayor, the governor, and the state board of health said there was no plague. But their actions belied their words.

The authorities moved quickly to seize the opportunity of the moment. Filth and unsanitary conditions were thought to be the breeding ground of the dreaded disease and were used as the pretext to move the Chinese from their valuable real estate in the middle of the city. "I desire to say," Mayor Phelan declared, "that they are fortunate, with the unclean habits of their coolies and their filthy hovels, to be permitted to remain within the corporate limits of any American city." The newspapers, Phelan, and the mayor's appointees to the board of health called for the razing of Chinatown and the removal of its inhabitants to detention centers on either remote Mission Rock or Angel Island in the middle of the bay. "Clear the foul spot from San Francisco and give the debris to the flames," editorialized the remarkably prescient *San Francisco Call*.

Instead of being moved, Chinatown—the site of the first plague epidemic in North America—was fumigated, sponged, gassed, and scrubbed with highly toxic substances. More than one hundred structures were demolished along with wooden decks, platforms, and balconies, where rats, then believed to be the sole source of the disease, were thought to cluster. City and state business associations demanded the removal of the fumigated Chinese to a location south of the city. In an editorial comment that accompanied the article containing the demands, the *San Francisco Chronicle* stated: "The allied commercial interests of this city have declared themselves unequivocally in favor of wiping out Chinatown, the delight of the tourist and the unclean abode of a thousand smells, with all its bizarre effects and all its contempt of Caucasian law and civilization, and condemning its site for the purpose of a public park." But the Chinese remained in place. During the four years of plague, there were 113 deaths.[38]

The next attempt to move Chinatown piggybacked on the nationwide City Beautiful movement, an offshoot of the Progressive program initiated in San Francisco by Phelan. The former mayor had been the city's representative to the Chicago world's fair in 1893, where he had encountered architect Daniel Burnham's concept of the Great White City. Ideally, the thinking of the Progressives went, physical beauty would foster social harmony and both would ensure prosperity.

Phelan, one of the city's largest landowners, brought Burnham to San Francisco to work his city planning magic, which derived from the design of European capitals and had been imported to Washington, D.C. He also formed a group called the Association for the Improvement and Adornment of San Francisco "in response to the well-publicized demand that the city do something positive about its appearance or lose its metropolitan status to the more energetic and unified Los Angeles." This elite group served as the model for the oligarchy that ran the city during and immediately after the earthquake and fire. Of the association's composition and planning aims, the historian Kevin Starr wrote: "San Francisco was to be refashioned by men who counted for the sake of men who counted."

The monumental plan, as it evolved, encompassed the entire city. It concentrated on a radical redesign of the street system and an enormous expansion of parks and open spaces. Order would replace chaos, beauty would be substituted for ugliness, society would benefit. But there would be a huge price to pay.[39]

The Chinese would pay the most, in the words of a modern California historian, for "the deep anxieties and desire for white male supremacy in Phelan's particular—and successful—brand of urban reform." A 1905 circular explained how to get rid of the Chinese by forming a company:

> The object of this company is to get title to at least two-thirds of Chinatown, remove the whole Chinese community to a proper and well improved location on the Bay shore, clean out the tumble-down rookeries of the present quarter, and to erect thereon a new business and residence section with buildings architecturally beautiful and harmonious. The whole is to be approached by a broad and beautiful boulevard.[40]

Besides dealing with Chinatown, the plan presented to the board of supervisors in September 1905 served urban aesthetic sensibilities for parks, boulevards, and a grand civic center. The plan was designed to impart a feeling of pleasure. But certain essentials were lacking, like what to do with the industrial, commercial, and waterfront areas. When bound copies of the report were delivered to city hall a few days before the earthquake, they contained no suggestions for implementation.[41]

While civic energies and private funds were expended on this grandiose plan, a far more serious matter was being neglected. One can only guess what the results would have been had priorities been different. The National Board of Fire Underwriters, which served the fire insurance industry, formed a committee after a fire in Baltimore in 1904 to make recommendations on how to reduce the fire hazards in cities. The committee focused its attention on "congested, or heavy value districts," meaning downtown commercial areas. A staff of engineers reported to the Committee of Twenty, which issued its report for San Francisco in October 1905. In terms of firefighting capabilities, the report, which did not mention the possibility of an earthquake, concluded: "Water supply ample in quantity for present demands, but decided probability of local failure in emergency, due to faulty distribution system, which is particularly bad in outlying sections. Fire department efficient and in general adequate. Fire alarm system fairly extensive, but only moderately reliable."

Given intense congestion, lack of firebreaks, tall buildings, highly combustible materials, high winds, narrow streets, and the lack of modern protective devices such as sprinklers, the probability for a major fire was rated "alarmingly severe." Ninety percent of the structures in the city, including some that were four and five stories high, were wooden framed—a higher proportion than in any other city of comparable size in the country. There were forty-eight steel-framed—so-called fireproof—structures, mostly office buildings. The structural conditions and hazards section of the report ended:

> While two of the five sections into which the congested value district is divided involve only a mild conflagration hazard within their own limits, they are badly exposed by the others in which all elements of

the conflagration hazard are present to a marked degree. . . . *In fact, San Francisco has violated all underwriting traditions and precedent by not burning up. That it has not done so is largely due to the vigilance of the fire department, which cannot be relied upon indefinitely to stave off the inevitable* [emphasis added].[42]

No one, however, linked earthquakes to the possible lack of water and a large fire.

Despite Phelan's efforts, the Spring Valley Water Company was still privately owned in 1906. The city's low monetary valuation of the system, in anticipation of its eventual purchase, and the resulting low rates did not provide an incentive for the company to maintain the water works in optimum condition.

The three principal reservoirs outside the city and the three large cast-iron conduits that linked them to nine distributing reservoirs within the city were directly on, crossed, or, in some cases, closely paralleled the San Andreas Fault. Those lines traversed canyons and swamps on vulnerable wooden trestles, the longest being three thousand feet. From the nine distributing reservoirs within the city, 441.5 miles of asphalt-coated wrought iron pipe fanned out like a delicate spider web over numerous patches of soft ground. From the large distribution lines, tens of thousands of smaller cast-iron pipes with inflexible couplings served every imaginable type of user in San Francisco. Additionally, there were twenty-five underground cisterns remaining from earlier days with limited supplies of water.

A salt water auxiliary system that would serve at least part of the city was under consideration at the time. Fire Chief Dennis T. Sullivan urged the board of supervisors: "No effort should be spared to hasten construction of this system at as early a date as possible." Nothing was done.[43]

The city's board of fire commissioners looked into another alternative in 1904. The board asked the army if it could depend on the military for trained sappers and use of explosives in case there was a major fire. A report was ordered by Major General Arthur MacArthur, who was then commander of the Pacific division. Yes, this could be done, the military concluded. But the city would have to come up with the $1,000 cost of constructing a brick vault in which the explosives would be stored at the Presidio. No money was forthcoming.[44]

The fire department consisted of a force of 584 uniformed firemen. It was equipped with 38 steam fire engines, 39 hose wagons, 7 chemical engines, 13 buggies, 320 horses, and 4 automobiles in "good condition" and "regular" service. Few firemen lived close to the forty-four firehouses, some residing across the bay. All the fire equipment was drawn by horses: three horses for the hook and ladders and pumping steamers, two horses for the hose wagons, and one horse for the chiefs' buggies.[45]

Firefighting procedures were clear-cut. Alarm bells in towers and the station houses around the city indicated which fire alarm box had been pulled to report a fire. When an alarm rang in fire houses, the horses that pulled the engines ran beneath hanging harnesses. It took fifteen seconds to hitch a three-horse team to a hook and ladder or a pumping steamer. Each fire house had a dog, usually a Dalmatian, that acted as a four-footed siren. When the horses were ready to depart, the dog rushed into the center of the street and barked a warning. The dog then dashed to the next intersection and barked.[46]

Like the heterogeneous population, microclimates, and terrain, the neighborhoods of San Francisco were varied. All that was needed for the city to destroy itself was the initial shake and the spark that would topple and ignite the warehouses, factories, rooming houses, and small homes of the working class south of Market Street, or "South of the Slot," as it was called; the tall newspaper buildings and luxurious Palace Hotel arrayed along the diagonal slash of the 120-foot-wide Market Street dividing the flat from the hilly sections of the city, and the nearby City Hall—all imposing structures built with a certain amount of hubris in known earthquake country; the modest frame buildings in the Mission District surrounding the squat Mission Dolores, survivor of previous earthquakes and fires; the crowded wooden structures in "The Latin Quarter," meaning the Italian-dominated North Beach located between Telegraph and Russian hills; the three noisy blocks of dance halls and other entertainments servicing the floating population of the Barbary Coast; crowded Chinatown; the frame homes of the middle class that climbed Nob Hill from Chinatown to the faux-European monstrosities of the silver and railroad barons on the broad summit; the wooden homes and apartments that crept westward from Mason Street to the 125-foot-wide swath that divided the older from the newer residential sections of the city, this being north-south Van Ness Avenue, where once-fashionable mansions were being converted to boarding houses; and the comfortable homes of the nouveau riche along the quiet east-west streets stretching westward to Pacific Heights and the wilderness of Golden Gate Park, collectively known as the Western Addition.

To the north and south of San Francisco, the rolling hillsides were more open and lacked the dense vegetation that softens the suburbs today. Bare grasslands predominated, and trees clung to valley watercourses where scattered ranches, villages, and large towns like San Jose and Santa Rosa nestled, vulnerable to shaking on the loose soil of flood plains.[47] The spring of 1906 was gorgeous. Late rains meant an abundant display of wildflowers.

The ruins of the May 1851 San Francisco fire.
The Bancroft Library, University of California, Berkeley.

Damage in San Francisco from the 1868 earthquake.
The Bancroft Library, University of California, Berkeley.

President Theodore Roosevelt parades through a bedecked San Francisco in 1903.
The Bancroft Library, University of California, Berkeley.

Chinatown before the earthquake and fire.
The Bancroft Library, University of California, Berkeley.

The prequake view down Market Street toward the Ferry Building,
with the Palace Hotel in the lower right corner.
The Bancroft Library, University of California, Berkeley.

James D. Phelan.

Abraham Ruef.
The Bancroft Library, University of California, Berkeley.

Enrico Caruso.
California Historical Society, San Francisco.

THE HOTEL AND THE OPERA HOUSE

THE PALACE

The Eastertide weather in 1906 was unusually pleasant in San Francisco, where a building and a gala event symbolized the aura of well-being and extravagance that was prevalent at the time. The structure was the Palace Hotel; the event, the opening of the opera season.

It had been nearly seventy years since a grizzly bear was killed on the sand dunes that became the location for the luxury hotel. The sand from the building site was carted to the nearby water where it was dumped, thus creating valuable new bayside property. This unstable ground at the foot of Market Street was known as "made land." The hotel that rose from the sandy soil was soon acclaimed the grandest in the land.

There was nothing impermanent about the Palace Hotel, at least nothing that could be imagined at the time, for its original owner, the banker William Ralston, was mindful of the recent 1868 earthquake that had demolished brick buildings and of the fires that periodically swept the city. The hotel's outer brick walls were two feet thick and were cemented with the best mortar. Three thousand tons of iron, known as band iron, encased the huge structure in a metal corset. Thick interior walls buttressed the building, creating a veritable fortress.

The Palace, as it came to be known, had its own water supply and distribution system that were independent of city facilities. Twenty thousand feet of fire hose could be uncoiled when one of the "automatic fire detectors" in the eight hundred rooms sounded an alarm. Watchmen patrolled the subbasement, basement, and each of the seven floors at thirty-minute intervals. The hotel was "as near earthquake-proof as human skill could devise." And as for fires, well: "The protection against fire is perfect." The guests were assured that they could sleep soundly regardless of what they had heard about the dangers of life in this new city. If any of the guests had looked about carefully, however, they would have seen oak floors, thick redwood paneling, and ornate bedrooms furnished in lush Louis XV style, all of which were extremely flammable when exposed to intense heat.

Over the years, presidents, dictators, generals, the infamous, and the famous (Bernhardt, Kipling, Melba, Rockefeller, Morgan, and Carnegie) had occupied the Palace's sumptuous rooms, each with a bay window. The vertical banks of windows formed a series of undulating waves that rippled across the façade—an exterior "more monstrous than elegant," according to one European visitor.

There had been changes at the Palace over the years. Most noticeably, the glass-domed grand court, where horse-drawn carriages entered a circular drive and guests alighted within an atrium, was transformed into an enclosed lounge. An exterior entrance served the belching automobiles that were replacing the slower carriages. After thirty years, the Palace was considered "venerable" and "historic." Newer hotels, like the St. Francis, were attracting the younger smart set. The Fairmont was rising like a huge, squat mushroom atop Nob Hill. San Francisco was well on its way to becoming a city of expensive hotels.[1]

THE GRAND OPERA HOUSE

It was toward the fading elegance of the Palace Hotel that the touring Metropolitan Opera Company headed on Easter Sunday. The hotel would be home for the Met's traveling management, conductors, and singers during the two-week engagement.[2]

This was the golden age of opera. Singers were the Hollywood celebrities of their time, and the newspapers assiduously reported their comings and goings. The Italian tenor Enrico Caruso had been the sensation of the season in New York and all across the country.

The tour had begun in Baltimore, where the critic for the *Sun* wrote that Caruso "is without doubt one of the greatest living tenors, and perhaps the greatest heard in this country in many years." President Roosevelt came backstage and warmly congratulated the tenor in Washington, D.C. The president gave the singer a signed photograph of himself, a picture that would later turn out to be Caruso's passport out of a burning San Francisco.

Other triumphant performances followed—in Pittsburgh, Chicago, St.

Louis, and Kansas City—before the long haul to the end of the transcontinental railroad line. Caruso played poker for sixteen hours a day in the dining car with other members of the company, who pulled the shades down while crossing the Sierra Nevada so as not to be distracted by the mountain scenery. On their arrival, reporters were present to record Caruso's expressions of delight at being in San Francisco, and great sadness at the recent eruption of Vesuvius, near his hometown of Naples.[3]

· News of the disaster was being trumpeted on the front pages of the San Francisco newspapers. A headline screamed: "VICTIMS OF VESUVIUS MAY NUMBER 2,000/Fertile Country Converted into a Desert of Ashes and Sand." The Hearst newspapers established a relief fund for the victims. Within the week the headlines and relief efforts would be directed toward San Francisco.[4]

Hidden halfway down an inside page of Easter Sunday's *San Francisco Examiner* was a short one-column story listing a dozen natural disasters that had killed many thousands within the past year. "A remarkable record of natural calamities, perhaps the most notable in modern times," according to the newspaper. Besides the eruption of Vesuvius, there had been volcanoes in Nicaragua, Samoa, and Mexico; earthquakes in India, Albania, Italy, Columbia, the West Indies, Mexico, and two in Formosa. A great tidal wave had swept the Society Islands and smaller islands near Tahiti. The North American continent had been spared, so far.[5]

The cross-country tour had been exhausting, and the next day would be the gala opening of the San Francisco opera season. At the Palace Hotel, Caruso turned down the first suite that was offered to him, stating that it was too depressing. The second set of rooms, where President Ulysses S. Grant had once slept, was adorned with French chandeliers, an English marble fireplace, Turkish carpets, a Persian bedspread, and satin-covered walls. That was more to his liking.

At the age of thirty-three, Caruso presented a rotund figure and a pleasing, neatly mustached face to his many fans. He was known for his abundant appetites, impeccable clothes, and passionate singing. Caruso's French was much better than his English, which was fortunate because Bizet's *Carmen,* in which he would appear as Don José on the second night of the season, was sung in French. By 1906, Caruso had been singing professionally for eleven years and was just entering his prime.[6]

Caruso, *Carmen,* and San Francisco were made for one another. The rollicking, boisterous opera, with its Mediterranean setting and its emphasis on love and sensuality, was a perfect fit. San Franciscans loved a lively opera, and many could afford the exorbitant prices that the Met charged. Twice as many performances were scheduled for the city by the bay than for any of the six previous cities on the spring tour, and the prices were adjusted upward.[7]

The opening-night opera, *The Queen of Sheba,* was a heavy work and a poor choice for San Francisco. Sung by a travel-weary company, it was a great disappointment. San Franciscans adapted quickly, however, terming the second night the *real* opening and raising their expectations for Caruso accordingly. The *Examiner's* Lillian Ferguson wrote that the first night "was the predecessor of the storm that awaits Caruso and Fremstad to-night."[8]

Although hardly remembered today, Olive Fremstad was a leading soprano of her time who was better known for her Wagnerian roles than for her Carmen. Described by her contemporaries as tempestuous, intelligent, and beautiful, Fremstad fit the stereotype of a prima donna. She later served as the model for Thea Kronberg, the Wagnerian soprano in Willa Cather's novel *The Song of the Lark.* After being secretly married in Salt Lake City on the way westward, she sought privacy from her many fans so did not stay at the Palace Hotel with the rest of the company but rather chose a more discreet hotel on Van Ness Avenue.[9]

The Met was booked into the three-tiered Grand Opera House on Mission Street, a barnlike structure that was far from living up to the name. Capitalizing on opera fever, the newspapers published stories that Sunday announcing that a new opera house, "one of which any city in the world might be proud," would be completed near Union Square by that time the following year. It would be "absolutely fireproof," said the stories. There was no mention of it also being earthquake-proof.[10]

Dramatic plays, light comedies, and more pedestrian entertainments at the Grand Opera House rated programs with black-and-white covers. The stylish cover for the Metropolitan Opera program was rendered in color, perhaps by Maynard Dixon, who was then the city's leading illustrator. An elegant woman in a white gown with a shawl draped gracefully from her head was juxtaposed against a looming black silhouette of a man in opera cape and top hat. The program contained the same type of upscale ads that adorn similar publications today. The ads were for "gold medal" pianos, whalebone corsets "Frenchily embellished with lace," Southern Pacific Railroad resorts, safe-deposit boxes, Red Seal Victor Records, after-opera dining, and thirty and forty horsepower Pierce-Arrows available from the Mobile Carriage Company. Caruso's name was invoked in a poem whose purpose was to sell real estate in the Oakland Hills:

The Music of Caruso's voice
Makes every hearer's heart rejoice,
But more rejoiceful would you be
If, where the sun shines merrily
On Piedmont's hills of green and gold
Where waves anear the whispering wold,
You owned a cottage vine-embowered
Where roses bloomed and lilacs flowered.[11]

DIAMONDS, PEARLS, AND RUBIES

The evening was the apex of the excesses of the Gilded Age in San Francisco, the home of vast sums of railroad and mineral wealth and other land- and sea-based fortunes. The weather was perfect—in fact unusually warm, windless, and fogless for spring—thus allowing for a larger than usual turnout of topless automobiles on the second night of the opera season. Policemen kept the long line of horse-drawn carriages and expensive autos moving toward the main entrance.

Inside, no standing room was allowed on this night, so many of the most ardent opera lovers, those from lower-income groups, were absent. The police chief, detectives clad in mufti, and uniformed patrolmen were on the lookout for "persons of suspicious character," who "were speedily and noiselessly removed beyond the temptation afforded them by the dazzling jewel show."[12]

The jewels, if the society reporters were to be believed, were beyond mere dazzling. In fact, it was the greatest display of wealth in the city's history. Attention was focused on old Mary Leary Flood, delicately identified as Mrs. James Flood in the newspapers. Mary was an Irish immigrant who had tended bar with her husband in a saloon while on their way toward a great silver-mining fortune.

Mrs. Flood was a virtual beacon of shimmering light: "the cynosure of all eyes," according to Madame La Bavarde, the pen name of the *San Francisco Bulletin*'s society reporter. Perched somewhat askew atop her head was a diamond tiara embedded with six huge pearls followed, in descending order, by a thick dog collar studded with diamonds, pearls, and rubies; the famous Flood pearls around her "fair neck"; diamond-encrusted shoulder straps; a diamond stomacher; and innumerable small diamond and pearl corsage arrangements scattered about her white silk gown. This entire vibrant package was encased in a silver wrap.[13]

Then there were the other "glitter gowns," many having been worn two nights in succession. No longer were plunging necklines, termed "pneumonia corsages," the style, but rather there was "a high-necked rule" that season. The *Examiner* awarded first prize to Mrs. Clement Tobin of the banking family.[14]

Mrs. Flood and Mrs. Tobin were seated in opposite proscenium boxes directly above the stage. The young actor John Barrymore was also in a box. He had been appearing in a small part in Richard Harding Davis's play *The Dictator* and was scheduled to depart the next day for Australia. The performance "drew a marvelous and appreciative audience; all of San Francisco and his wife was there," commented Barrymore.[15]

During the intermission, the *Call's* James Hopper circulated in the smoky foyer and collected the witty bon mots of the men who gathered there. The previous night a handful of women had attempted to invade this bastion of "the somberly-coated, tobacco burners, but their stay was very brief. Nor did they seem to enjoy it while it lasted," wrote another reporter.[16]

Arnold Genthe, the society photographer, was engaged in an animated conversation with Judge William P. Lawlor, who would play a key role in the graft trials after the earthquake. The two men declined to pronounce their verdict on the opera, giving Hopper an opportunity to exercise his wit: "They seemed very happy and, like many Judges, may reserve their decision."

James Phelan was present. He thought the Met and the two principal singers "a brilliant company." (Three weeks later, in a letter to a friend, Phelan noted that the roof of the Grand Opera House collapsed a few hours later. "So you see," Phelan wrote, "we are very thankful that the earthquake arrived too late to do us any bodily harm.")[17]

Laurence M. Klauber, a Stanford University sophomore, sat in the gallery with a friend. He wrote, in typical sophomoric prose: "Caruso was the goods as José. . . . The toot assembly was also good." Klauber almost missed the theater train to Palo Alto. (Had he remained in the city at his sister's home, he would have been killed or badly injured by the huge stones from the chimney of a neighboring synagogue that crushed his customary third-floor bed.)[18]

From the first bravo of the season in the first act, Caruso stole the show. Fremstad's new Carmen was difficult for San Franciscans to accept. The full-page headline in the next morning's *Call*, published before the earthquake, set the tone: "CARUSO MAKES DON JOSE THE LEADING ROLE." The most discerning critic, Ashton Stevens of the *Examiner*, agreed, terming Fremstad's performance "Dutchy," meaning too Germanic.[19]

The lusty bravos and many curtain calls lasted for ten minutes. After accepting his customary adulation, Caruso escaped to the Palace's bar for a cognac with other male members of the company. With his close friend the baritone Antonio Scotti, Caruso took a hack to Zinkand's, a restaurant that specialized in the Italian food he loved. Caruso had eaten at Zinkand's the previous night. The owner tolerated Caruso's habit of dashing off quick caricatures of himself, colleagues, and friends on tablecloths, then snipping them out and giving the whimsical drawings to the assembled guests.

A young Elsa Maxwell, who went on to international fame as a hostess, finagled an invitation to the small party. Maxwell later said that she played Caruso's favorite arias on the piano. The tenor, who did not like her first name because it was too Wagnerian, nicknamed the stout young woman *mio popone,* meaning "my melon."[20]

Hopper later wrote this description of the end of the opera and the start of the next day, April 18, 1906:

> I see him stab, I hear Fremstad's scream, Caruso's wail of remorse, glutted passion and remorse commingled; I see his magnificent crawling movement to her as the curtain comes down. I see myself walking back slowly to my paper, the *Call,* a few steps away, and I am saying to myself: "Surely, what I have felt to-night is the summit of human emotion." And now when I think of that, I almost laugh.

After turning in his copy, Hopper walked the six blocks up Post Street to his room at the Neptune Hotel. The horses at the livery stable at Powell and Mason streets seemed unusually restless. Otherwise, it was a peaceful night. Hopper went to bed at 3 A.M.[21]

Within twenty-four hours much of that fairy-tale wealth and make-believe world would be reduced to bitter ashes.

II
DURING

WEDNESDAY, APRIL 18, 1906

As seen from Berkeley, twelve miles across the Bay, the burning of San Francisco presented a succession of appearances. Within half an hour after the earthquake shock, a hump of dark smoke appeared over the City, growing during the succeeding hours until it rose through the quiet air like the clouds made by a volcano. When night came, the whole front of San Francisco was ablaze, the flames shooting upward at particular centers with the glowing discharge of a blast furnace; the light of the conflagration illumined the heavy clouds of smoke with a pink glow and the occasional rumble of a dynamite explosion gave the picture a suggestion of warfare.

MINING AND SCIENTIFIC PRESS,
April 28, 1906

EARTHQUAKE WEATHER

There is a brief moment of pure magic before a large earthquake strikes and all hell breaks loose and fear runs amok across the trembling land. Animals may fidget, strange lights flash, deep noises rumble within the earth, and shallow waves roll past, leaving structures untouched.

The weather that early morning was unusually "clear and pleasant," according to the weather bureau. The usual damp early morning fog was missing. There had been no measurable rainfall for more than two weeks. A ridge of high pressure extended over eastern Washington and Idaho with a low pressure area to the south, forcing desert winds to flow from the northeast toward the central California coast—the reverse of the usual pattern of cool northwesterlies that blow from the ocean toward the land. The warm, dry conditions were known to locals as "earthquake weather."

Three years before the earthquake Alexander G. McAdie, professor of meteorology and head of the San Francisco Weather Bureau, had written that earthquake weather was "a well-defined belief among the older residents

51

of California," but that there was "no known relation between earthquakes and the weather." After the earthquake, McAdie, a highly regarded scientist whose agency kept the seismological records at the time, was unsure of his earlier opinion. "There seems to be some evidence," McAdie wrote a fellow scientist, "that certain tremors are associated with changes in [high and low] pressure distribution." The Harvard-educated meteorologist repeated his view in the *Bulletin of the California Physical Geography Club* and a catalogue of Pacific Coast earthquakes published in 1907 by the Smithsonian Institution, although stating that the evidence was "obscure and indefinite."

For the first three days after the earthquake, the city was buffeted by wildly gyrating winds generated by the changing patterns of weather and the internal workings of the firestorms. On the first day, the prevailing northwesterly wind and the unusual easterlies dueled for dominance, spreading the flames to the east and the west. The easterlies increased in tempo on the second day; the fires were then driven westward. By late Friday, a strong northwesterly wind from off the ocean had reasserted its dominance, cooling the city and forcing the fire back toward the waterfront and across fresh combustibles. On Saturday there was rain, which ended the fires but discomforted the many refugees sleeping in the open or temporary shelters.

The temperatures were ideal for a huge conflagration. On the second day the thermometer jumped a dozen degrees to an unseasonable high of eighty-one, as measured in Berkeley and Oakland, since San Francisco no longer had a functioning weather bureau. Friday was also unseasonably hot.[1]

THE FIRST SHOCK WAVES

At 5:12 A.M., give or take some seconds because not all timepieces were in accord, the rocks six to nine miles deep at a point south of Lake Merced in San Francisco and on or just off the northern San Mateo County coastline snapped like a thick elastic band stretched far beyond its normal level of endurance. A series of concentric seismic waves spread across the land and water at speeds of up to three miles per second.[2]

Among the first to encounter the shock waves was the captain of an inbound steamer, who thought the ship had struck a rock or a submerged wreck, although a casting of the lead showed plenty of water beneath the hull. The chief engineer of the *National City* reported: "The ship seemed to jump clear out of the water, the engines raced fearfully, as though the shaft or wheel had gone, and then a violent trembling fore and aft and sideways, reminding me of running full speed against a wall of ice." The crew aboard the nearby *Mackinaw,* loaded with coal, thought the vessel had struck bottom three times.[3]

On the Farallon Islands just west of the fault line, a hundred-pound rock slid downslope and a crack appeared across the front of the fireplace in the weather bureau's building on the main island.

Immediately to the north of the epicenter an early morning bather in the frigid waters off Ocean Beach quickly swam ashore amid a confused sea. He staggered to his clothes across the surface of the undulating beach. "Every step left a brilliant iridescent streak," the bather said. He had experienced a type of luminosity that accompanies some earthquakes.[4]

Undulating motions also passed through the paved city to the east of the displacement. "It was as if the waves of the ocean were coming towards me, and billowing as they came," said a police sergeant who was looking westward up Washington Street toward Russian Hill. Structures were left intact after the passage of the first waves. The first shock wave came moments later: "The ground seemed to twist under us like a top while it jerked this way and that, and up and down and every way," said the policeman, who was on patrol in the produce district.[5]

The bather in the water and the sailors on board the vessels were the closest humans to the epicenter and the focus of the earthquake. (The *focus* is the source of the tear within the mantle of the earth; the *epicenter* is the point on the surface directly above the focus.) There was no accurate way to immediately determine the epicenter since the rudimentary seismographs in the Bay Area were not sufficiently dampened to withstand a large shock; the styluses veered wildly off the graph paper.[6]

For years the epicenter was thought to have been at the head of Tomales Bay in Marin County, between Olema and Point Reyes Station on what is now known as Sir Francis Drake Boulevard. The greatest displacement of twenty feet was observed on the old roadway at a point just west of Highway 1. More careful studies in recent years have located the epicenter on or near Thornton State Beach in Daly City.

From a point off Cape Mendocino in Humboldt County to near Hollister in San Benito County—a total of 270 miles—the Pacific Plate moved suddenly in a northwesterly direction, leaving the landward North American Plate behind by varying offsets. The movement was mostly horizontal, there being only a small vertical displacement.[7]

It was a moderately large but not a truly great or megaquake such as those in Chile in 1960 and Alaska in 1964. Larger temblors had occurred in California during historic times, namely in rural southern California in 1857 and the distant Owens Valley in 1872. There were few deaths and little damage in those relatively unpopulated regions. Timing and location were everything. As a USGS scientist noted nearly one hundred years later: "Significantly, this stretch of the San Andreas fault also represents the only fault segment in the United States with a proved potential for a magnitude 7.8 earthquake that directly transects a major urban area."[8]

Along with magnitude, duration of the earthquake is another factor that determines the amount of damage, but scientists were unable to determine precisely how long the earthquake lasted. From forty to sixty-five seconds was the generally agreed duration. It seemed like a lifetime to some.[9]

HOUSES OF SAND

The people who were awake and working at 5:12 A.M. on that Wednesday morning were involved mostly with the buying and selling of food and with policing the produce district along Washington Street, which extended east from Sansome Street to the waterfront. One of them was Jesse B. Cook, the police sergeant who saw the waves rolling down Washington Street.

The sergeant, who was later to become police commissioner, ran for the shelter of a building on Davis Street. Right before Cook's startled eyes "a gaping trench that I think was about six feet deep and half full of water" opened in the street. He jumped the chasm but failed to reach the building before the front of the wooden structure leaned precariously across the street, its complete collapse halted only by stacks of produce.

As the ground heaved and revolved, a brick structure on the opposite corner of Davis and Washington streets crumbled "like a house of sand." Two fleeing men were crushed under six feet of bricks, oranges, and other assorted fruits disgorged from the Ivanovich Building, which housed the Bodwell brothers' wholesale food establishment.

The snapping of thick timbers, the crash of heavy walls, dust rising to obscure the scene, the cries of terrified people, and the frightened whinnying of horses filled the early morning air with the unholy cacophony of a major disaster. No longer was there permanence underfoot. Cook recrossed the street. The gap he had previously jumped was now seemingly sealed tight, but the first wagon and team to cross the street sank through the thin crust of granite paving stones that disguised the new crevasse.

Cook decided to head back to his police station at 5:30 A.M. On his way, he noticed a fire at a wholesale grocer's on Clay Street, just west of Davis— the first fire of which official notice was taken in the city. He thought the blaze was caused by electrical wires. The sergeant ran the block and a half to the fire station that was across the street from the Harbor Police Station, dodging falling bricks along the way.

The police station was intact, but the wall of an adjoining bag factory had fallen on the fire station. The firemen had managed to get their horse-drawn engine into the street, where they were waiting for the alarms and orders that were not issuing from the nonfunctioning alarm and telephone systems.

Cook gave the verbal alarm. When the firemen reached the grocery store, they found the blaze had already spread to an adjacent meatpacking company. A wall fell on a fireman, crushing his leg and forcing the leg's amputation a few days later. No water flowed in the distribution lines or the hydrants.

The sergeant set out again. "I went around inspecting conditions and looking for our patrols in the district north of Market Street," Cook said, "and I found scarcely one building undamaged." Fires were breaking out all over the area. One hour after the earthquake it was obvious to Cook, the ranking policeman on the street in his district, that nothing could stop the blazes from spreading.

Had the normal amount of water been available, there still would have been no hope of controlling the conflagrations, according to a postquake assessment by the National Board of Underwriters. These experts, who had also issued the prequake warning, concluded: "It is therefore quite certain that even without disablement of the supply the Fire Department would have found itself hampered for lack of water in the presence of even half a dozen simultaneous fires." There were more than fifty initial fires.

The rush of frightened people for the eastbound ferries at the partially damaged Ferry Building at the foot of Market Street had already begun. Cook was put in charge of directing the increasing flow of refugees. He noticed that people were dressed in odd ways, carried unusual objects, and were dry-eyed. Others commented on their silence.[10]

LIFE AND DEATH

Thomas A. Burns, a food broker, was in the brick building that Sergeant Cook had seen disintegrate at Davis and Washington streets. Burns was checking boxes of asparagus that he was considering purchasing for a cannery. They were stacked as high as a man.

The second violent shock had a sickening twisting motion. Burns ran between a narrow gap in the boxes and collided with a team of terrified horses that had bolted down the street. The food broker ricocheted off the galloping horses just as the walls on opposite sides of the street collapsed, meeting in the middle of Washington Street.

"At that moment," Burns said, "I believe I was beating every world's record running against time, and running every way at once. I did not know what had become of Mr. Bodwell and his clerk, and did not learn until some time later that they had been killed. Most people thought I was killed, too. Sergeant Jesse B. Cook was watching the collapse of Bodwell's and thought I was buried there. What I did see and did know was that the pavement of Washington Street opened and shut while I was dodging about on it."[11]

Officer H. C. Schmitt was also on Washington Street, standing inside a produce store, when he heard a sound like thunder. The policeman was almost buried by dust and falling debris but managed to work his way to the street. He touched something that felt like dog's hair, then discovered that it was the hair of an employee who had been killed instantly. The dead man was carried to the street, where the body was covered with copies of that morning's *Chronicle,* which carried accounts of the previous night's opera. The useless newspapers were appropriated from a passing newsboy, placed over the corpse, and anchored by fallen bricks.

Schmitt pulled the dead and injured from the wreckage, halted the looting of a cigar store that later burned, and dispatched injured horses with his pistol. He watched helplessly as a fireworks factory exploded in a series of spectacular pyrotechnic displays and then caught fire, then crossed Market Street and made his way to Mission and Front streets, where he was greeted by a scene straight out of the Wild West.

Mission Street was strewn with bricks, stone masonry, and the broken remnants of fancy cornices. Trolley, electrical, and telephone wires hung in disarray like naked decorations on a gaunt Christmas tree. Injured and dead cattle that had been driven by cowboys up Mission Street to the stockyards were entangled in the debris, their frenzied bawling echoing through the ruins.

"That had been a horrible mess while it lasted," said Schmitt. "Some of the long-horns were crushed through the sidewalk into the basement under Mission Street when the front of a warehouse fell on top of them near Fremont Street. Others ran amuck with fright and went chasing the refugees that were rushing about the streets after the shock."

Schmitt had been preceded at the morbid scene by a fellow officer, Harry F. Walsh, who witnessed the goring of a saloon owner.

At that moment I ran into John Moller, who owned the saloon at the southwest corner of Fremont and Mission streets. . . . I asked him had he any ammunition in his place and if so to let me have some quick. He was very scared and excited over the earthquake and everything; and when he saw the cattle coming along, charging and bellowing, he seemed to lose more nerve.

Anyhow there was no time to think. Two of the steers were charging right at us while I was asking him to help, and he started to run for his saloon.

I had to be quick about my part of the job, because with only a revolver as a weapon, I had to wait till the animal was quite close before I dared fire. Otherwise I would not have killed or stopped him.

As I shot down one of them, I saw the other charging after John Moller, who was then at the door of his saloon and apparently quite safe. But as I was looking at him and the steer, Moller turned and seemed to become paralyzed with fear. He held out both hands as if beseeching the beast to go back. But it charged on and ripped him before I could get near enough to fire.

Moller was killed. Crazed cattle were running or limping about. Walsh had no more ammunition.

A young Texan who knew cattle and was "a cool shot" ran up with an old Springfield rifle in hand. Walsh and the Texan alternated firing the rifle and killed about fifty or sixty head in an orgy of shooting. They were about to dispatch a half-buried horse that was held erect by bricks but discovered that it was "already stone dead."

During the killing spree Walsh had not noticed the growing number of fires. By the time Officer Schmitt had arrived at the scene, refugees were fleeing toward the ferries from the palatial Palace and Grand hotels on Market Street and the cheaper wooden hotels and rooming houses South of the Slot. The time was 7 A.M. "Fires were beginning to puff smoke out of windows in various directions," said Schmitt, "and half the crowd was distracted with fright."[12]

PHELAN TAKES CHARGE

James Phelan was awakened in the bedroom of his residence at the southwest corner of Valencia and Seventeenth streets. The combination gas and electric chandelier hung by a single electric cord and was oscillating wildly and emitting gas. All the chimneys had fallen into the garden of the Mission District residence.

Phelan took charge immediately. He was that kind of man. A former mayor and a U.S. senator-to-be, Phelan was to become the single most powerful individual in the city beginning on that Wednesday and extending through the aftermath of the earthquake. He roused the servants, turned off the gas, and gave orders not to attempt any cooking because of the faulty chimneys. It would be a few hours before a similar order would be issued citywide by Mayor Schmitz.

Phelan walked out the Valencia Street gate to see what was happening and met two women and three men, all of whom were weeping. He asked, "What is the matter?"

They pointed two blocks south to the Valencia Street Hotel, where the large four-story wooden structure had shrunk to one story. One of the passersby said, "Everyone is killed."

Phelan hastened to the hotel, between Eighteenth and Nineteenth streets. Seeing numerous people trapped beneath the heavy timbers, he returned home and gathered servants, axes, and saws and, his two automobiles being stored elsewhere, had the coachman harness two horses to the family carriage. He drove back to the wrecked hotel.

Phelan was familiar with the topography:

Knowing that the ground in that block was a "fill," a part of the old Willows [a small lake known previously as Laguna de Manatial or Laguna de los Dolores], I assumed that the disaster was local and that this building suffered on account of the foundation slipping from under it, which, doubtless, was true.

In the vacant lot adjoining, firemen and others, who had arrived earlier, had removed the wounded and dead, and were carrying them away to the Southern Pacific Hospital [at] the corner of 14th and Mission Streets; and, my carriage was, therefore, used for such purpose.

The saws seemed to be the only effective implements for releasing persons. I directed my attention particularly to one man, who said he was not hurt, but so bound that he could not help himself, and we got him out. Everyone seemed [aware] of the danger of a second shock throwing the remaining part of the building down, and worked with vigor and intelligence.

An assistant coroner came along and asked: "Don't you know that the whole city is wrecked and fires have broken out in different places?"

Phelan said, no, he didn't. The two men set off in Phelan's carriage for the damaged City Hall, leaving behind the site of the single largest number of fatalities in San Francisco.[13]

THE VALENCIA STREET HOTEL

Who would suffer most was preordained: there is no social or economic equality in an earthquake. One businessman whose firm was destroyed but whose home was saved during the fire was aware of the disparity. Horatio P. Livermore wrote of the poor "in whose quarters of labor and of living the destruction has been complete, sweeping them in an instant into unemployed suffering for the prime necessities of life, while the richer element of the population, though fearfully punished in all their business and financial interests in the main city, were spared in their homes, as the fires were prevented from getting west of Van Ness Avenue."

The crowded boarding houses on the filled land south of Market Street—the Valencia Street Hotel, the Brunswick House, the Nevada House, and others serving the industrial sector of the city—suffered far more damage and were the site of far more deaths than the middle- and upper-class homes at higher elevations and on more stable ground to the north. "The hills," said Livermore, who lived on Russian Hill, "came out of it decidedly better than the flat lands."[14]

Patrolman Henry N. Powell had the Valencia Street beat. Because the café in the Valencia Street Hotel was an all-night rendezvous for newspapermen, the officer had standing orders to check it. There were a few groups of men playing cards and drinking beer quietly at 5 A.M. The night clerk was about to begin making calls to roomers who had to go to work early or catch trains. Officer Powell was just leaving the hotel when the earthquake struck.

> The first quiver was strong enough, but it was not terrifying. As I stepped out to reach the middle of the street and safety from the falling glass and stuff that accompanies all earthquakes, the twister came, and for a few moments it baffled me.
>
> Valencia Street not only began to dance and rear and roll in waves like a rough sea in a squall; but it sank in places and then vomited up

its car tracks and the tunnels that carried the cables. These lifted themselves out of the pavement, and bent and snapped. It was impossible for a man to stand, or to realize just where he was trying to keep standing.

Houses were cracking and bending and breaking the same as the street itself and the car tracks.

The night clerk and one of the card players made it to the street with Powell, who continued the account:

As we ran we heard the hotel creak and roar and crash. I turned to look at it. It was then daylight and the dust of the falling buildings had not had time to rise. The hotel lurched forward as if the foundation were dragged backward from under it, and crumpled down over Valencia Street.

It did not fall to pieces and spray itself all over the place, but telescoped down on itself like a concertina.

This all took only a few seconds.

The people in the lobby and the café escaped. The residents on the fourth floor merely stepped out onto the street. It was the people in the two middle floors who were trapped or dead.

Fate, coincidence, God, or the gods ruled the day. The margin between a charmed life, a crippling injury, and death was infinitesimal. Who slept in which adjoining bed could make the difference. The owner of the Valencia was never found; his wife was uninjured. One of the owner's two sons was killed; the son's wife was only slightly injured. The other son's infant was found sucking a bottle, the father's shoulder was broken, and the mother was unhurt.

All day policemen, firemen, and volunteers pulled the living and the dead from the debris. The street filled with water from the broken water main that had shifted seven feet to the east. The toll was more than one hundred dead. Some died in the earthquake, and some were trapped alive and died in the fire that swept Valencia Street the next day.[15]

THE BAKER

There were approximately twenty cheap rooming houses on Sixth Street between Mission and Howard streets. At the five-story Nevada House most of the occupants died. William F. Stehr, a baker who lived on the top floor, was one of the few survivors. He later recounted his harrowing experience of being trapped in the rubble:

Then came another bump, very sudden and severe. The place fell in on top of me, the breath seemed to be knocked out of my body and I went unconscious.

When my senses came back I was buried and in complete darkness. I tried to feel myself all over, working my limbs as best I could, to find out if any bones were broken. But though I could feel that I was painfully bruised all over, I guessed that all my bones were intact.

Then I tried to raise myself, because when I came to I was lying flat; but the weight of the debris that covered my body was more than I could lift. My feet were pinned fast, so I ceased struggling and rested for a minute or so. While I was gasping for more breath for a second struggle I heard somebody running over the debris over me, so I shouted for help as loudly as I could.

No attention was paid to my calls; so I began to struggle again, and presently managed to release my feet. But I lost my left shoe. It was wedged in too tight, and it was by pulling my foot out of it that I escaped.

After that I began to grope and feel about me to find some way of escape. Then I began to hear other agonizing screams for help, and screams of "Fire!" And soon I began to smell smoke, and I fancied I could hear flames crackling sharply.

This made me struggle desperately, and soon I got my arms out over my head, and could feel an opening that led upwards on a slope. I worked my way along till I could see a little glimmer of light. I got to the crack in the debris and could see out; but I was in a very tight place and was very tired from the exertion, so I had to stop for a while. But I got a breath of fresh air which revived me, and I began to cough violently and spit out the dust and plaster with which my mouth and lungs seemed to be filled.

After resting for a minute or so, as well as I could judge, I began to pull away the laths and plaster that blocked the passage. It was hard work doing it in such a tight and narrow passage. But after a while I made a hole large enough to crawl through, and then I found that I was not at the end of my trouble. I had to turn on my back and crawl upward through a sort of chimney that was bristling with nails and splinters of laths and plaster that tore my sides and my clothes. But eventually I squeezed through and found myself sitting amidst the ruins nearly on a level with the street, and all around me was ruin and debris.

Blood from a gash in his scalp dripped into Stehr's eyes, and he tied a handkerchief around the wound. He looked at his watch; the time was 5:45 A.M. Stehr had been trapped for about half an hour. A stranger came by and gave the dazed baker a drink of whiskey, which revived him temporarily. Stehr rested, then struggled to his feet to help other rescuers dig toward cries for help in the rubble. By 7:15 A.M. six fires raged about him, three of them on Sixth Street. The smell of burned flesh filled the air.

Army troops arrived at 8 A.M. and told the civilians to clear out of the area. Stehr hobbled away on one shoe. Someone gave him a pair of socks and slippers. He was hungry, but there was no place to eat. While watching the Emporium department store burn on Market Street at 9:30 A.M., Stehr fainted. He woke up in the makeshift emergency hospital at the Mechanics' Pavilion. Stehr moved to Los Angeles three weeks later.[16]

TO THE RESCUE

The commander of the army's Pacific division, Major General Greely, had left San Francisco a few days earlier and had headed east on leave. Brigadier General Funston was the acting commander. Short, barrel-chested, neatly bearded, and much decorated (the Medal of Honor), the forty-year-old Funston bore the wounds and remnants of tropical diseases—souvenirs of an extremely active career as an explorer, adventurer, newspaperman, and army officer. Like Phelan, the general was a man of instant action.

Funston had risen through the ranks from Cuban mercenary to United States Army general in ten years. Although a Kansas farm boy, he was cut in the mold of his friend, and later commander-in-chief, Theodore Roosevelt. Funston returned to San Francisco from the Spanish-American War in 1902 a hero, malarial, a drinker, and no admirer of "bullet-headed Asians." The outspoken and swashbuckling general chafed under the restrictions of the peacetime army.[17]

From his home on Russian Hill, Funston had an excellent view of the downtown area. After the intense shaking, nothing seemed seriously amiss at first. He dressed quickly in his uniform and marched along Jones Street to California Street at the top of Nob Hill, where there was a commanding view of the city. Columns of smoke were rising from the produce and banking districts below him and from the rooming-house district to the south. As he walked down California to Sansome Street, he saw that there was no water available for firefighting.

Funston immediately realized that "a great conflagration was inevitable" and that "the police force of the city would be totally inadequate to maintain order and prevent looting and establish and hold the proper fire lines in order that the fire department might not be hampered in its work." This initial impression, voiced later in a magazine article and an official report, was the basis for the general's decision to call out all available regular army troops without martial law being declared. "Without warrant of law and without being requested to do so," Funston said, "I marched the troops into the city, merely to aid the municipal authorities and not to supersede them."[18]

What Funston unwittingly set in motion was the gathering on city streets of the largest peacetime military presence in this country's history. It was composed of elements of the army, navy, marines, California National Guard, and military cadets from the University of California. When General Greely returned some days after the earthquake, he would take exception to some of Funston's more precipitous acts. Greely later said, "It is against the public interest, against public policy to keep any large body of troops [on city streets]. It is contrary to our forms of government, and contrary to sound principles." Of course, what he would have done at the time is not known.[19]

Funston then faced the question of how to implement his decision. Telephones were not working, and none of the few automobiles that were now buzzing around the city on private errands would stop for the general. So Funston alternately ran and walked the one mile to the army stables. He arrived breathless and barely able to stand, let alone talk. The general scribbled in a notebook and tore out the page, then dispatched his carriage driver on a horse with the note to Colonel Charles Morris, commanding officer of the Presidio. He gave instructions to Captain M. L. Walker, who commanded Fort Mason, to report with all available troops to the chief of police at the Hall of Justice on Portsmouth Square. He asked a city policeman to inform the police chief of his decision.

Funston then walked leisurely back to the crest of Nob Hill. It was a beautiful, clear morning—the last such morning for many days. "The thing that at this time made the greatest impression on me," the general said, "was the strange and unearthly silence."[20]

For the next three days and on into the time of recovery, there was, in effect, a suspension of law. The sight of U.S. Army and California National Guard troops on the streets gave the distinct impression that martial law had been declared. It "existed de facto, if not de jure," wrote Henry Winthrop Ballantine in a 1913 *California Law Review* article titled "Military Dictatorship in California and West Virginia."[21]

Nearly everyone thought the city had been placed under martial law. The April 19 joint edition of the *Call-Chronicle-Examiner* declared on its front page: "At nine o'clock under a special message from President Roosevelt, the city was placed under martial law." On page four, under the headline "Martial Law Is Declared," the first paragraph in the story gave a different source for the declaration: "After a conference between Schmitz and Chief of Police Dinan, San Francisco was placed under martial law at 9 o'clock yesterday morning."[22]

Roosevelt sent no such message, the mayor and the police chief made no such proclamation, and Governor George C. Pardee did not request that martial law be declared or proclaim a state of insurrection, the legal requirement needed to activate the National Guard, which was then under state control. The governor did, however, order the militia to patrol the streets of San Francisco and three other cities. (Exactly one month after the earthquake, Pardee wrote a National Guard colonel: "Under a strict interpretation of the law, therefore, the Federal troops have no right to be in San Francisco. Yet their presence there has been and is greatly desired to prevent possible disturbances.")[23]

Three thousand miles away in New York, the April 19 edition of the *New York Times* stated unequivocally on its front page: "The city is under martial law, and all the downtown streets are patrolled by cavalry and infantry." When it was nearly over, William Randolph Hearst's *Examiner* proclaimed in a banner headline: "Funston Relaxes the Rigor of Martial Law." The end was signaled by a story in the April 27 *Examiner* headlined "Military Law Ends in the City by Funston's Orders."[24]

Troops also patrolled the streets of Santa Rosa, Oakland, and San Jose. Many people shared the sentiments of a woman in San Jose who wrote, nine days after the earthquake: "This town is under Military rule, and I think it a wise thing." The British consul general in San Francisco, whose consulate burned the first day, reported to the Foreign Office: "Martial law was declared at once, and looters and rioters were shot by the dozen." The wife of a San Francisco doctor was comforted by the presence the military and vigilantes: "We are under martial law, and we have a vigilance committee."[25]

The official explanations that came afterward were rather weak. Governor Pardee asked President Roosevelt on April 27 not to withdraw the federal troops. In the eyes of the War Department, the telegram removed "any doubt" about the legality of the situation. Pardee's request was apparently viewed as a retroactive declaration. Mayor Schmitz's view of the situation, sent in a telegram to President Roosevelt when questions arose about the status of troops one month later was that on the morning of April 18 "the U.S. troops stationed here were put under control of the municipal authorities by General Funston."[26]

A murky legal situation existed in the four cities. If there was martial law, then that meant there was no civil law; if there was civil law, then there was no martial law. In reality, there was both and neither. To put it more precisely, there was the law of the moment. Most of the orders the San Francisco mayor issued and the military authorities enforced, and sometimes initiated themselves, had no legality or legislative sanction. They recalled the era of the vigilantes. Afterward, any number of publications and high-ranking officials denied that martial law had ever been declared.

Speed and decisiveness were certainly necessities, and legal ambiguity fit the needs of the moment. But the window of officially sanctioned lawlessness caused the deaths and wounding of innocent and guilty alike, neither having had the opportunity for any type of hearing, let alone a trial. The summary justice that existed in San Francisco—and earlier in Chicago and Galveston, and to a lesser degree after September 11, 2001—illustrates the fragility of democracy and civil liberties in times of great peril, whether real or imagined.

One perceptive observer, Marion Osgood Hooker, a doctor and member of a prominent San Francisco family, privately voiced a minority opinion: "The division of authority between army and municipality brought some terrible results. . . . The military was called in to take partial command; the citizens did not know whom they were to obey, and certainly the military subordinates and guards were not made to understand the limits of their authority. The consequences were tragic." She concluded, "Preserve us from our preservers was the cry of many of us."[27]

When Phelan reached the new City Hall in his carriage, he realized the magnitude of the calamity. Showing his partiality to classical allusions, the banker-businessman wrote: "The City Hall was completely wrecked, large parts of the dome having fallen, leaving the cap in the air and the brick structure, on every side, ruined, with here and there a column standing, resembling the ruins of the Temple of the Dioscuri in the Forum in Rome."

He drove to the Phelan Building at the corner of Market and O'Farrell streets and found General Funston outside. The headquarters of the Pacific Division was on the fourth floor, and Phelan's office was on the fifth floor. The two men walked up the stairs to the fifth floor and entered Phelan's office. "At that moment," Phelan recalled, "there was a slight quiver of the earth, and General Funston said, 'This is no place for me!' and returned hurriedly to the street."

The general supervised the removal of the most important records from the fourth floor. He greeted and dispatched troops, the first having arrived at 7:45 A.M. after reporting to the mayor and the chief of police at the Hall of Justice. They had been directed by Mayor Schmitz, Funston said, "to guard the banking district and send patrols along Market Street to prevent looting."

At first the mayor did not think that the earthquake was very serious. Two men from the city attorney's office who had seen the remains of City Hall arrived at Schmitz's home at 2849 Fillmore Street in the Western Addition by automobile at 6 A.M. and told him of the damage elsewhere. "At that time," Schmitz said, "we could already see indications of a great fire somewhere in the downtown district." The mayor kissed his family good-bye, jumped into the car with the men, and headed east on Green Street to Van Ness Avenue, where they encountered two engineer companies under the command of Captain Walker from Fort Mason. Schmitz informed the captain that he was the mayor and that they should proceed to the Hall of Justice and await orders.

The mayor was driven to the new City Hall so that he could see the damage for himself. Then the party drove down Market Street to Kearny Street and then to the Hall of Justice, where they arrived at 6:45 A.M. The mayor later recounted his journey and his subsequent actions that day:

All along Market and Kearny Streets I saw signs of great destruction that had been caused by the earthquake shock of the early morning.

Numbers of people were out in the street and the buildings presented a pitiful appearance. The Hall of Justice had also been badly damaged, and the Chief of Police informed me that the tower of the building was about to fall.

I got all the officers and officials together, and immediately established quarters in the basement of the Hall of Justice.

A little while later Colonel Morris of the Presidio reported to me for duty. My orders to him were that he should take his men and distribute them over the city, but especially in the district that was burning, and that they should drive the people back from the burning houses and keep them away from the ruins of houses that had collapsed or been burned. Also to place a special guard around the City Hall, and especially to guard the vaults of the Treasurer's office in that building, which contained about $6,000,000.

Anticipating that looting would take place—I had already seen some of it on my trip down town—and realizing that we would have no place in which to keep prisoners if any were arrested, and that it was time for firm and decisive action, I told Colonel Morris and also the Captain that reported to me from General Funston, to let the news be widely spread that anyone caught looting should not be arrested but should be shot.

Colonel Morris asked me if I would be responsible for that order and I told him yes, that I would be responsible for that order; we would not take prisoners; we must stop looting, and therefore to shoot anyone caught looting. The same order was issued to the Police Department.

The next order I issued to the police and military authorities was to close all places where liquor was sold and to notify those who sold liquor that they should discontinue the sale. Also that they were to close their establishments and keep them closed, and that if any man were found disobeying that order, the liquor in his place should be confiscated and spilled into the street.[28]

THE EXTREME SOLUTION

The exaggerated concern about looting led to the extreme solution: to summarily kill suspects of any crime. It was one of the principal tragedies of the disaster. Schmitz set in motion one of the most infamous and illegal orders ever issued by a civil authority in this country's history.

All later accounts by both officials and private citizens emphasized that looting was minor or nonexistent. Of course, it could be argued that this was because troops were on the streets along with regular and special police. But the troops were also guilty of looting.

From available anecdotal evidence in newspaper stories and personal accounts, it appears that the shoot-to-kill order was carried out aggressively when the targets were poor people or ethnic minorities. One exception was the mistaken shooting of a member of the ruling citizens' committee. More words were devoted to this one incident than to all the others.

The upper classes were treated differently from most people. When "high railroad officials," "society people," "capitalists," and "reputable business-men" were caught pouring over the ruins of Chinatown in search of gold, the order given regular army troops was not to shoot to kill. Instead, shots were directed at nearby walls, and "the looters fled like so many sheep." The ruined mansions atop Nob Hill attracted the same type of looters, who went unpunished.[29]

In any case, how was looting to be defined? Citizens pillaging drug-stores for medical supplies for the injured? Others seeking food for hungry families from stores that were about to be burned? Well-dressed residents sifting through the ruins of the mansions and Chinatown? Or army troops pawing through boxes of shoes in the middle of the street? Price gouging of ordinary citizens, surely a form of looting, was not punished by instant death.

The determination was subjective and made in a moment. No one publicly questioned the order that substantially infringed upon the few civil liberties that existed at the time and cost the lives of an undetermined number of innocent citizens.

The infamous written order that followed the mayor's oral command came about in the following manner: A group of the mayor's advisers, including the lawyer Garret McEnerney agreed that such an order was necessary, although they recognized that it was not legal. (Many years later, in a moving tribute to McEnerney, who went on to a distinguished legal career, John Riordan termed the mayor's proclamation "dictatorial and unconstitutional.") McEnerney went looking for a printer. By this time it was late in the afternoon. Already, suspected looters had been shot without any warning.[30] Eventually, the lawyer found the Altvater Printing Company, run by the Altvater brothers, Edward and William, at Mission and Twenty-second streets. It was one of the few intact printing concerns remaining in the city.

McEnerney drafted the proclamation in longhand by the light of a coal-oil lamp. The brothers set the type in their union shop. With the aid of one helper and foot power, since there was no electricity, two job presses produced more than one hundred thousand copies of the proclamation over the next four nights. Edward Altvater later recalled, "They were taking them away from us as fast as we could print them."

The relevant section stated: "PROCLAMATION BY THE MAYOR: The Federal Troops, the members of the Regular Police Force and all Special Police Officers have been authorized by me to KILL any and all persons found engaged in Looting or in the Commission of Any Other Crime." Schmitz warned of the danger of fire from leaking gas lines or faulty chimneys and "requested" a darkness-to-dawn curfew.[31]

The mayor was asked in a court case following the disaster if he had issued the proclamation. Schmitz answered, "I issued orders in the morning to that effect, and they were adopted by the committee of citizens at 3 o'clock that afternoon." The hastily formed citizens' committee had no legal status.[32]

The news and rumors spread. A woman wrote her daughter from her place of refuge in Jefferson Park: "I presume you have heard the terrible news. Nearly the entire city is burned and we are under martial law. Men are being shot all over for stealing. I cannot describe the horror of it all." Another wrote a relative: "The city is under martial law, and they shoot a person for the slightest disobedience."[33]

FIREMEN

Meanwhile, the fire department was facing an impossible task. For the city's nearly six hundred firemen, the earthquake was an exercise in extreme futility. With no functioning fire alarm or telephone systems, communication was verbal and delivered by messengers on foot, on horseback, or in automobiles. Because the system of water pipes was fractured in numerous places, there was very little water with which to fight the blazes—a condition that "reduced the contest to a series of forlorn-hope stands on the part of the Fire Department, with more the character of a massacre than a battle."[34]

What to do? The answer was to use explosives. There seemed to be no alternative. No contingency plan could have anticipated the type and extent of all the problems, beginning with Chief Sullivan's critical injuries that led to his death.

The chief and his wife were asleep in their three-room apartment on the third floor of Engine Company No. 3 on Bush Street near Kearney Street when the heavy masonry wall and decorative cupola of the adjacent five-story California Hotel plummeted sixty feet. The heavy mass collapsed onto the fire station and drove a portion of the brick engine house into its basement. Neither Sullivan nor his wife was hit directly. The chief leaped to his feet, snatched a mattress to cover his wife in the adjoining room, and the couple fell into the yawning vortex and were buried under a mass of debris on the first floor.

The firemen in the second-floor dormitory had to use the circular staircase, as the brass pole they usually slid down in emergencies was badly bent. Barefoot and clad only in their underwear, they were at first stifled and blinded by the thick dust that rose about them. Then, aided by arriving policemen and other firemen, they uncovered their chief and his wife. The chief was seriously injured, but his wife's injuries were less serious because she had been wrapped in the mattress.

The assistant fire chief, John Dougherty, was named acting chief by the mayor. Sullivan survived long enough to hear the distant sound of explosives, indicating that the fire was extremely serious. He died in the Presidio hospital four days later. One other fireman and a policeman were also killed in the earthquake. A third fireman was killed while fighting a fire.[35]

The experiences of the nine firemen from Engine Company No. 2 at 22 O'Farrell Street were typical. Earlier in the evening the quelling of a large fire at a cannery had taken all the firefighting resources in the downtown area.[36] They returned from the cannery fire at 3:30 A.M. and put their equipment in order before tumbling into bed.

Nearly two hours later they had no difficulty harnessing their horses for the second time that night. Passing the nearby Engine Company No. 3, they saw the wreckage and stopped to help their colleagues dig out the chief and his wife. They then rushed to a fire at the corner of Market and Kearney streets. They tried all the hydrants in a one-block square area bounded by Market and Mission streets on the north and south. There was no water. Off they dashed to a fire at O'Farrell and Taylor streets. Again, no water, but they were able to extinguish the fire with sand from a nearby construction site.

The next stop was a large apartment house at Geary and Stockton streets that had collapsed in the earthquake and was now on fire. This time there was no water or sand. A stairway collapsed under the combined weight of firemen and residents, but there were no serious injuries. They dug out the residents trapped in the ruins and were cheered by a large number of bystanders.

By 7 A.M. fires were raging all about the men of Engine Company No. 2. They looked for water in a dozen places and failed to find it before finally locating a supply in an underground cistern at California and Montgomery streets. They linked hoses with another company to pump water to the nearest fire. As water reached the fire, the flames began to lessen. When the water gave out, the fire erupted again.

The firemen repeated the futile process at other locations, working continuously for fifty hours while snatching an hour of sleep here and there in doorways or on streets. They were fed snacks by grateful residents. Two firemen needed a six-hour rest in a hospital and then returned to duty. A stoker went to an emergency hospital and then home, where he chose to remain with a sprained ankle. The captain had his sprained ankle treated while he worked, and remained on duty.

The firemen could not change from their torn, dirty, wet clothing because their remaining gear had been destroyed when their firehouse was gutted. Some didn't know until later whether they had lost their homes, nor did they know the fate of their families. They didn't ask for a leave to determine what must have been weighing heavily on their minds, given all the destruction surrounding them.

Captain George F. Brown of Engine Company No. 2 concluded his report by stating the obvious: "They worked hard, faithfully, and conscientiously."

Other companies had similar experiences. Some worked steadily for forty-five hours, others for fifty-five, and one for seventy-five hours.

The paid firemen were aided by volunteers, one of whom was F. Edward Edwards, a publisher. Edwards crossed and recrossed the city on various errands for seventy-two hours. He had an encyclopedic memory of events. "As I walked along," Edwards recalled, "the thought came over my mind of the loneliness of the thing. I was walking through a deserted city, a city of silence lit by that great red monster, the all-devouring fire with which man's feeble efforts were unable to cope." At the end of three days, the firemen put Edwards, with badly burned feet, in a wagon and sent him home.

The intense heat, which reached temperatures above 2,000 degrees

Fahrenheit, scorched the fire hoses. It turned a solid stream of water into instant steam. It bent iron and steel into corkscrew shapes and melted glass. To protect themselves from the heat belching like dragon's breath from the innards of the firestorms, the firemen covered themselves with wet sacks and fashioned shields from doors.

Fireboats and other vessels supplied the fresh water needed to run the steam engines that pumped fresh and salt water onto the fires. The fresh water was hauled in buckets and brewery wagons. Fresh and salt water was also transported inland by linked hoses and pumpers positioned in hastily arranged combinations.

The firemen searched everywhere for water or a suitable substitute. Soda water siphons were used on small fires. For larger conflagrations, barrels of vinegar and wine were tapped. Abandoned wells yielded some scant supplies. Long-forgotten buried cisterns were searched. Water flowing from burst mains was dammed and then pumped. Sewer water was used where it could be found. In fact, anything available that was liquid and noncombustible was thrown on the flames. A constant refrain in the reports written by the various commanders of the engine companies was "no water."[37]

NO WATER

In the end, the firemen were betrayed, and the city was destroyed, by the shortage of water and by the use of explosives that spread, instead of halting, the fires.

The lack of water was not due to failure of the three large reservoirs immediately outside the city, reservoirs that were located either on or quite close to the San Andreas Fault. Two earth-filled dams bent but held. Nor was the immediate problem the broken conduits that carried the water from these three reservoirs to the nine distributing reservoirs and tanks within the city. The city's storage facilities had enough water to fight the initial fires.

The problem was the distribution mains that led from these reservoirs within the city to thousands of individual service pipes. About 300 distribution mains and 23,200 connecting pipes were fractured, mostly where the ground was soft or had been filled. On solid ground, most of the breaks were caused by dynamiting. The result, in the words of the chief engineer of the water company, was to cause "the water in the main pipe system to flow freely in tens of thousands of uncontrollable and inaccessible jets, large and small, into the accumulated debris of the burning buildings."

Valencia Street was a good example of the lack of water and the resulting loss of life. All types of material, including garbage, had been used to fill the original twenty-foot-deep swamp underneath the street. When shaken violently, the loose material liquefied and the surface dropped four or five feet. At Eighteenth Street, Valencia shifted seven feet horizontally to the east. The water, gas, and electrical lines snapped. These massive ruptures quickly emptied the College Hill Reservoir, which served that section of the city. Fire swept the street, and residents trapped in the wreckage of the hotel burned to death.

———

Upon discovering that there was no phone service, Herman Schussler, chief engineer of the water company since 1864, headed on foot for the pipe storage yard on Bryant Street. Schussler met the head foreman coming toward him in a buggy. Once at the yard, they organized the men in squads and dispatched them to assess damage. Schussler then set out for the reservoirs. Along the way he met an assistant who gave him the reports of the various pipeline walkers. What Schussler heard meant that there would be no water to immediately refill the drained city reservoirs.

The upper thirty-inch conduit from Pilarcitos Reservoir that connected to the partially damaged Lake Honda Distributing Reservoir in the western section of the city paralleled the San Andreas Fault. The pipeline was thrown sixty feet to the side, torn apart for over one hundred feet, and lay at right angles to its original position.

The middle-level conduit from San Andreas Reservoir was badly ruptured. Four large lugs that held the thirty-seven-inch iron pipeline in place were torn off like so many buttons on a blouse. This conduit supplied the College Hill Distributing Reservoir. It would not be repaired until May 20.

From the granite-faced Crystal Springs Dam, the forty-four inch conduit fed the lowest-level distribution reservoir in the city. It ruptured in seven places, the longest rupture being where the conduit crossed three swamps near the bay. The heavy iron pipeline was thrown into the air. When it dropped, it destroyed the wooden trestle on which it had rested.

Once the managers had a sense of the extent of the damage, the water company crews worked hard. By making temporary repairs by 9 P.M. of the first evening, a small amount of water could be supplied to the Western Addition; unfortunately that was where it was least needed.[38]

Natural gas and electrical lines were also badly damaged.

Gas had become popular for cooking and was still used for lighting the city. The city was rent with exploding gas mains after the earthquake, causing the deaths of many people. Four hundred miles of gas mains were ruptured, and since underground electrical conduits were frequently bundled with the gas mains, the resulting explosions severed electrical lines.

The twenty-four-inch trunk line between the Potrero and North Beach gas plants was cut in forty places. The trenches opened by the explosions served as handy dumping grounds for dead horses and other animals. The dead animals then had to be removed before repairs could be made. The burned district remained dark until May 12, when the gas street lights came on again.

Underground electrical cables were pulled apart by the earthquake, and poles carrying overhead lines toppled or were burned. Lines arced, igniting natural gas mains. The twelve-inch-thick concrete manholes used to gain access to underground utilities were shattered like eggshells. Water from broken distribution mains flooded both underground gas and electrical facilities, further complicating matters.[39]

THE EXTENSIVE USE OF EXPLOSIVES

Human nature demanded that *something* be done in the absence of water. Explosives were handy in the Bay Area; the immediate response was to use them. The idea was to blast firebreaks, a desperate maneuver that had achieved indifferent results during the London fire of 1666. (By World War II, German firefighters knew better than to use explosives when their cities were firebombed.)[40]

The dynamiting of the city has never received much attention. It adds significantly to the concept that San Francisco was the city that nearly destroyed itself.

The first detonation took place shortly after 9 A.M. on Wednesday morning, when a detachment of artillery corps troops under the command of Lt. Charles C. Pulis placed a large quantity of black powder in the basement of a building at the northeast corner of Sixth and Jessie streets (Jessie was a narrow street lying parallel to Market and Mission streets). They lit the fuse, but nothing happened. Police Sergeant John Lainsbury relates what occurred next:

> After waiting some time, and no explosion having occurred, the lieutenant and Captain Gleeson went to the place where the train was set. Just as they arrived at the door of the building the explosion took

place, throwing Captain Gleeson out into the street. He quickly freed himself from the debris and struggled to his feet; but he was blinded by the blood that was flowing from wounds all over his head and face. We ran forward to help him and assist him to an ambulance. But as I reached him he pushed me off and said, "John, go get him!" meaning the lieutenant. So I left him and, with the assistance of the soldiers, we lifted the debris off the lieutenant and pulled him free.

First aid was rendered on the spot. Lint and bandages were applied, and both were taken to the Mechanics' Pavilion which at that time was being used as an emergency hospital.[41]

The lieutenant had a fractured skull and later died. Captain Gleeson had glass shards in his head, one of which was removed two years later.

Battalion Chief John J. Conlon, who dynamited all the structures on Eighth Street between Market and Folsom streets, later questioned the effectiveness of the explosives. A Southern Pacific Railroad foreman who was working on a tunnel nearby offered Conlon a wagonload of explosives and his services. Conlon had never used dynamite before, so he accepted. They placed a case of dynamite on the east side of each floor of a three-story frame building but blew the flaming structure in the opposite direction from the cleared zone.

In another incident, a chain of pumpers was keeping a stream of water playing on the Valencia Street fire. The firemen were ordered away when it was decided to blast a firebreak. "The work of the wreckers was not successful, as the block burned up after being dynamited," said Battalion Chief W. D. Walton.

Captain T. J. Murphy recalled still another incident: "In the afternoon, we met civilians hauling boxes of dynamite and also fuses and caps in a buggy, and with this we attempted to check the progress of the fire by dynamiting both sides of Langton Street, between Folsom and Harrison streets. This also was unsuccessful, as we had no water to extinguish the flames which originated after dynamiting."

Part of the problem was that the dynamiters were using the wrong type of explosives. "Great harm was done during the first days of the fire by the indiscriminate use of black powder," the new fire chief explained afterward. "It developed that when black powder was exploded it threw off a combustion that ignited all woodwork with which it came in contact, thus starting additional fires." Black powder is gunpowder. This highly flammable explosive packs little punch compared to nitroglycerine and more modern compounds. "Giant powder [granular dynamite], made of nitroglycerine, was also used with the same results," the new fire chief said after the disaster. "On the third day at the conflagration 75 per cent dynamite, in stick form, was used with splendid results as there was no combustion and the buildings were leveled without danger." Gun cotton was also found to be acceptable.[42]

Too late they had determined the right types of explosives to employ. But even the right type could be used on the wrong target, meaning a structure such as a fireworks factory or a patent medicine plant that contained flammable materials.

<hr />

Miners who used explosives extensively, firemen who had never used them previously, and laypersons who simply observed their extremely flammable effects later expressed grave doubts about demolishing buildings in the immediate path of the flames. They thought the flames were being spread, not halted, by the use of explosives.

The criticism, expressed mostly privately at first, surfaced publicly in the *Mining and Scientific Press,* a respected technical journal that served the mining industry. Miners were adept at using discrete explosions to accomplish precise goals, exactly the type of expertise that was needed in San Francisco. In its first full postfire issue, there was one paragraph noting that explosive devices were used too timidly, too late, and often served only to spread the fire. Those opinions were expanded in a subsequent edition under the headline "The Misuse of Explosives," which gave a full account of the terrible mistakes that were made.

The use of high-grade explosives by people ignorant of their strength and proper application, was instrumental in destroying a vast amount of property without the result desired, and in many cases it actually spread the conflagration. The work was done by Dick, Tom and Harry, until the very end of the operations when the naval officers from Mare Island took a hand and directed affairs in a scientific manner. Before that the police, the militia and volunteer firemen used a box of dynamite where a pound would have sufficed, they blasted on the wrong side of walls and did such foolish things as placing a keg of black powder in the center of wooden buildings, with the result that they set them afire instead of bringing them to the ground. Spectators could see that the explosion threw up a lot of dust, to be followed forthwith by flame. They dynamited buildings already on fire and simply made an avenue for the spread of the conflagration instead of creating an obstacle to its advance. Under such conditions, the explosion scattered brands right and left. . . . It might be supposed that with so many experienced mining men in the community, it would have been possible to get their help in work which they understood and we can state that several of our friends did volunteer to give suggestions and to proffer systematic aid, but in vain. It is difficult to persuade a man that he does not understand what he is doing. San Francisco has reason to bitterly rue the misuse of the explosives that properly employed have proved so powerful an aid to the advancement of mining.[43]

The National Board of Fire Underwriters' postfire report stated that no explosives should be used to fight fires: "It is not surprising that men reduced to helplessness by the lack of water should have resorted to what has proved in all modern conflagrations to have been useless and, in the opinion of prominent fire chiefs and experts, even harmful."[44]

Many citizens who witnessed the dynamiting commented on it. Mathematician Eric Temple Bell was an investor in one of the city's telephone companies and was in the company's office trying to locate the safe. "We began to hunt for it," he said, "when suddenly there was a yell in the street, and we made out the word 'dynamite.' The way we got out of that building was nothing slow. Five minutes later it was a heap of bricks and scrap iron. The dynamiting seemed to do absolutely no good. Although there was no wind—it being a beautiful sunny day—the fearful heat just melted things a block away."[45]

Writing twenty years later from a wealth of primary source materials not available today, the anonymous narrator of the sixty-nine-part series on the disaster concluded in the *Argonaut,* a weekly San Francisco newspaper:

The dynamiters, it should be explained, worked bravely as dynamiters, but unintelligently as fire-fighters. They went ahead of the conflagration, blowing up buildings with feverish haste and using no water, because they had none, to extinguish sparks caused by the explosions, and damp down the ruins of the buildings they destroyed. They simply blew down walls that might have served as fire-breaks, and turned floors, beams, and other woodwork into bonfires of kindling wood ready for the flames as the conflagration steadily advanced.[46]

Who was responsible for the indiscriminate use of explosives?

Early on the first day, when it was determined that there was little water, acting fire chief Dougherty sent a message to the Presidio at 6:30 A.M. requesting "all available explosives." Forty-eight barrels of black powder were sent from the Presidio. That shipment was followed by more black powder, giant powder, and dynamite from other military stores, private powder works, and commercial suppliers in the Bay Area. Because of the recent war in Asia and the mining industry in the nearby mountains and deserts, there was no lack of explosives. Firms such as the Vulcan Powder Works, the Giant Powder Company, and the California Powder Works were located in the Bay Area.

Chances were taken with the explosives. In Portsmouth Square, Schmitz's temporary headquarters after he was forced out of the nearby Hall of Justice, the mayor sat on a case of dynamite and used another for a desk. A ton of dynamite surrounded him. Explosives were carried about the streets in fast cars commandeered from their civilian owners.

The military reported to the mayor, who gave orders for the use of explosives. Fearful of legal and political consequences, he stressed that explosives should not be used until the fire came close to the point where a void could be created. Oftentimes this was too late, as the intense heat could ignite buildings and their contents from a distance.

Confusion reigned on the first day. At one time Schmitz dispatched a fire commissioner, a battalion chief, and his principal aide, Abe Ruef, with instructions for the military. Others, both civilians and the military, made decisions on the spot, banging away with explosives at everything they were told to destroy or that seemed to make sense to remove. They found that wood-framed buildings were a lot easier to drop than steel-framed structures, which were nearly indestructible. The constant bedlam of warfare—artillery was even employed—echoed through the streets, further terrifying the residents.[47]

In its official report, the army papered over its mistakes by offering this explanation: "The authority for demolitions was in every case derived from the Mayor or his representative. During all of the 18th and until the afternoon of the 19th the city authorities withheld their permission to blow up any buildings, except those in immediate contact with others already ablaze. Consequently, although we were able to check the fire at certain points, it outflanked us time and again, and all our work had to begin over in front of the fire." The report said the soldiers tried to abstain from using black or giant powder, unless pressured by local authorities.[48]

In a letter to the *Argonaut* answering his few critics some months later, General Funston said that nothing was accomplished by the use of the black gunpowder on April 18 "and on the other hand no harm [was] done by it, despite the fact that a few buildings may have been set on fire, as all that portion of the city where gunpowder was used was doomed to destruction, and could have been saved only by the use of carloads of dynamite." Funston admitted that circumstances sometimes "made it necessary" for the military to act without civilian permission.[49]

A captain in the corps of engineers at Fort Mason wrote his family that even the dynamite, when it arrived, was of slight help. "A little after noon," said the officer, "we managed to get in a boat load of dynamite, but it was not used to much advantage. They worked too close to the fire and used no tamping so that little was accomplished except to splinter the buildings and make them burn quicker and to break all windows within a radius of 5 blocks."

Besides setting fires, the explosives showered debris on the streets. They ignited the sewer gas in the middle of the street, in one case hurling a manhole cover one hundred feet into the air "with a report like a cannon." Sewer gas exploded under a horse and cart, upsetting both.[50]

ALONE AND FEARFUL

San Francisco, a virtual island under the best of circumstances, was isolated from the remainder of the world for all of that first day. There were no newspapers, no telephones, no mail deliveries, and no telegraph messages. Along with fear, its handmaiden—wild rumors—circulated and served as news. New York, Los Angeles, and San Diego were destroyed by earthquakes; Portland was inundated by the Columbia River; Chicago was wiped out by a tidal wave; a tidal wave was about to inundate San Francisco; the city was under martial law; soldiers were shooting citizens; looting was general and widespread; dusky-hued men were chewing diamond earrings from the ears of dead women; others lopped off the fingers of the dead with knives to steal jewelry; ears and fingers along with the attached jewelry were stuffed into pockets.

Like cockroaches emerging from hibernation in a sewer and blinking in the new-found daylight, the usual ancient urban legends surfaced again.

A widespread account at the time was later formalized under the subhead

"Ghastly Tale of Ghouls" in a quickie book published in 1906 by James Russel Wilson. He quoted a Salt Lake City man who had fled to Los Angeles as stating:

> While I was walking about the streets I saw man after man shot down by troops. Most of these were ghouls. One man made the trooper believe that one of the dead bodies lying on a pile of rocks was his mother, and he was permitted to go up to the body. Apparently overcome by grief, he threw himself across the corpse. In another instant the soldiers discovered that he was chewing the diamond earrings from the ears of the dead woman.
>
> "Here is where you get what is coming to you," said one of the soldiers, and with that he put a bullet through the ghoul. The diamonds were found in the man's mouth afterwards.[51]

The ghouls were often depicted as cruel, grimacing Asians or a cross between African Americans and Italians in the illustrations for the sensational books that appeared shortly after the disaster.

H. Morse Stephens, a history professor at the University of California who had been given the task of compiling a history of the earthquake and fire, commented two years later: "Some of these legends are old friends which always crop up when any disaster befalls a city from sack or pillage, from fire or flood, such as the tale of the capture of ghouls with their pockets full of human fingers and human ears which had been cut off by brutal ruffians in search of rings and earrings." Stephens dated the legends back to the Middle Ages. He could not understand why anyone believed robbers held onto the appendages of their victims and thus risked being caught. It just didn't make sense. "Of course nothing of the kind occurred in San Francisco," he said.

After assessing a more complete record of the disaster than exists today, the professor came to the conclusion—as many others did at the time—that there was little looting. "The remarkable freedom of the city from crime is the next noteworthy feature of those days of crisis," he said.[52]

THE OTHER GOVERNMENT

The lawyer McEnerney and the millionaire J. Downey Harvey conceived the idea of crafting a citizens' committee that would take charge and displace the elected civil government. The mayor, guided by others, made the appointments to the committee. The chairmen of the subcommittees made their own appointments. It was a speedy process, designed to perpetuate a like-minded membership. "Thoughtful men of business, professional men, capitalists," was the description of the membership given by the committee's secretary.

The types of occupations and the specific names did not fit the labor-oriented roots of the Schmitz regime: Phelan, two Spreckels, Herrin of the Southern Pacific, the Jewish banker Hellman but not the Italian banker Giannini, a de Young, a Sutro, a Crocker, a Tobin, a Flood, a Gerstle, the requisite prominent clergymen, and others. It was called the Committee of Fifty, although there were more than fifty members.

James Phelan, who assumed control over the millions of dollars of donated funds, became the most powerful member—"The central figure at the policy-creation level for the relief of San Francisco," according to one of his biographers.

Phelan was not present when nominated to be chairman of the finance committee by McEnerney in the afternoon of April 18. That night he and his friend J. Downey Harvey drew up the membership list of the committee at Phelan's home. The finance committee acted independently of the Committee of Fifty and its successors. It later absorbed all the relief work, which was what remained of disaster-related activities once the elected and appointed officials were allowed back into power by the citizens' committee.[53]

Phelan, Rudolph Spreckels, and their Progressive friends had already begun the process of attempting to topple Schmitz and Ruef, who were suspected of graft. The mayor was tolerated and even praised by the city's capitalist elite during the crisis. (Like Rudolph Giuliani, the once-troubled mayor of New York City ninety-five years later, Schmitz emerged triumphant after the disaster, at least for a short time.)

The first members of the citizens' committee met under extremely trying conditions at the partially ruined Hall of Justice at 3 P.M. on the first day. Fires raged all around Portsmouth Square. Dynamite was being set off nearby, and one blast broke the windows in the meeting room. An aftershock jolted the tenuous structure. Someone ran in and announced the obvious: the building was unsafe. The members adjourned to the adjacent square. As flames closed in, they fled up Nob Hill to the new Fairmont Hotel.

The main committee planned to gather the next day at 10 A.M. at the Fairmont. The finance committee would meet in four days. McEnerney dashed off to get the "KILL" proclamation printed.[54]

In his contemporaneous history of San Francisco, John P. Young described the rise of the oligarchy:

> Although Eugene Schmitz as mayor had called the Committee of Fifty together, and presided at the subsequent meetings of the citizens' body, there was something like a complete abdication of their functions by the constituted municipal authorities. The mayor was to all intents and purposes merely a member of the organization over whose deliberations he presided, and, while the question of authority was not raised, it seemed to be tacitly assumed that he was to perform a duty analogous to that of the vice president of the United States when acting as president of the senate.[55]

THE GOVERNOR

If a city needed the immediate unity of its most powerful elements, then San Francisco possessed it to the nth degree. Decisions that otherwise might have been debated were executed immediately; there was no opposition.

Funston, Schmitz, Phelan, and the Committee of Fifty functioned harmoniously during the first three days and nights and for a short time thereafter. But the essentials of democracy—due process and representative government—were clearly lacking. The oligarchy did not serve all segments of the social order equally. It imposed its values unilaterally on others. And it froze out a very important player, one who has never been given his proper due: Governor George C. Pardee.

Pardee was the great coordinator, acting as the liaison between those on the torn streets of San Francisco, committee members in whatever temporary meeting place they could find, and the outside world from his headquarters in the Oakland mayor's office. From that mainland city Pardee was in telegraphic contact with the rest of the country and the world. The governor guided the flow of money, goods, and materials into the stricken city and had an overview of the needs of those in the shaken city and the goods and services being offered by providers and how they needed to be moved about.

Pardee lacked a glamorous frontline role, and he was criticized for not dashing about the flame-licked streets. With a large staff imported from Sacramento, the governor was the expediter of paper; in every great disaster there needs to be at least one such competent bureaucrat.

A graduate of the University of California at Berkeley and the University of Leipzig in Germany, Dr. Pardee was an ear, eye, and nose specialist; a resident of Oakland; a previous mayor of that city; and a Republican in the progressive mold. He was the first native-born governor and the only physician to hold that office. Like others in positions of power, he was completely unprepared for the disaster. The governor had been busy the previous day with such mundane matters as making notary public appointments and regulating the control of agricultural pests.[56]

Although Mayor Schmitz was widely praised for rising to the occasion, mainly because he acted unilaterally and in the interests of those persons surrounding him, the one-term governor was a less-dramatic match for the emergency. Among other vitally necessary tasks, Pardee was responsible for shaping the important special session of the state legislature that followed the disaster.

———

The cables that first morning flew back and forth between the White House and the state Capitol:

Hear rumors of great disaster through an earthquake in San Francisco but know nothing or the real facts call upon me for any assistance I can render.
Theodore Roosevelt, 12:51 P.M.

Pardee promptly replied from Sacramento:

Owing interruption of telegraph communications extent of disaster in San Francisco not well known here, but no doubt calamity very serious. People of California appreciate your prompt inquiry and offer of assistance. State troops doing patrol duty, and if Federal assistance is needed will call upon you.

Federal troops had been on the streets of San Francisco for at least five hours, a fact that neither Pardee nor Roosevelt was aware of. Pardee had already dispatched the state militia.

The president felt a special affinity for San Francisco. Roosevelt had received a rousing reception there three years earlier and had various political informants and like-minded Progressive contacts in the Bay Area. Roosevelt also recognized San Francisco's strategic importance in the recent conflict in the Philippines and the emerging military threat posed by Japan.

The president answered Pardee's telegram within the half hour:

It was difficult at first to credit the news of the calamity that had
befallen San Francisco. I feel the greatest concern and sympathy for
you and the people not only of San Francisco but of California in
the terrible disaster. You will let me know if there is anything that
the national government can do.

Theodore Roosevelt, 1:41 P.M.

It was like San Francisco was a vast void, invisible to the rest of the world,
which was waiting anxiously for news of the stricken city.

Governor Pardee took the 5:30 P.M. train to Oakland, arriving at 10 P.M.
He immediately went to the office of Mayor Frank K. Mott and began issuing handwritten passes for travel to San Francisco on any scrap of paper or
stationery that was handy. The requests for permission to travel to San
Francisco were voluminous and varied in the coming days. Eventually,
printed forms replaced the handwritten notes.

Pardee worked twenty-hour days. The house he owned was rented, so he
slept in Mott's office, a friend's house, or a hotel. He traveled back and forth
to meetings in San Francisco on April 21, 23, 26, and 27; to San Jose on
April 29; and to Santa Rosa on April 30.[57]

"I WANT TO GET OUT OF HERE . . ."

The last messages from the flaming city read like hurried missives desperately flung from a dying civilization, or firsthand accounts transmitted
from a sinking passenger liner.

The only instantaneous words and feelings that have been preserved
are in the form of telegraphic cables. Handwritten and printed words—
hundreds of thousands of them—came later. The telegrams were the equivalent of the televised images from the World Trade Center.

A sampling of direct and relayed bulletins from the various telegraphic
services in San Francisco follows:

To answer to query as to what caused damage, S.F. says the greatest
damage done by fire account no water. They are getting at it now,
as it has such headway can not control it. The damage by earthquake very severe, and considerable loss of life by falling buildings.

The Call Building is in full blaze now and it is only question of minutes for us in Postal here.

10:30 A.M.

San Francisco says fire within few doors now. They are going to move out right now.

11:05 A.M.

The city practically ruined by fire. It's within half block of us in the same block. The Call Building is burned out entirely, the Examiner Building just fell in a heap. Fire all around in every direction and way out in the residence district. Destruction by earthquake something frightful. The City Hall dome stripped and only the frame work standing. The St. Ignatius Church and College are burned to ground. The Emporium is gone, entire building, also the old Flood Building. Lots of new buildings just recently finished are completely destroyed. They are blowing standing buildings, that are in path of flames, up with dynamite. No Water. It's awful. There is no communication anywhere and entire phone system busted. I want to get out of here or [I will be] be blown up.

Chief Operator Postal Telegraph Office, San Francisco, Cal. 2:20 P.M.[58]

The news also trickled out by way of the Associated Press. The San Francisco superintendent of the newspaper wire service, Paul Cowles, later reported to the AP general manager:

I arrived at the office at about 5:45 after a rapid sprint through the streets. It took but a moment to ascertain the telegraph situation so far as the Western Union was concerned, so I went to the Postal [Telegraph Company] office a few blocks away. There Chief Operator Swayne was found tinkering with a feeble wire to Chicago. He held out a faint hope for a wire, so I wrote a bulletin and stood over him while he tested and manipulated. The Pacific cable office was in the same building, so I filed a cable bulletin addressed to you, to be sent across the Pacific around the world to New York. The cable operator declined to take the message, saying it was irregular and he did not know the rate. I offered to pay any rate that would be charged, but the cable man was confronted by an emergency that the cable company's rules had not provided for, and he declined to take the message. He did send a message to Honolulu, however.

Then I went back to Swayne and moved that Bulletin. Finally, there was a hopeful click and away went the news to Chicago.

Chief Operator Swayne fled his post at 2:20 P.M. The news then had to be ferried to Oakland. However, a new technology, the wireless radio, was still available.

Although the San Francisco wireless station had been knocked out, the naval wireless station on Yerba Buena Island remained in operation. From there bits of news flew north, east, and south on military frequencies and were plucked from the air and sent onward over civilian telegraph cables. Three large navy ships intercepted the radio messages. The flagship *Chicago* and the cruisers *Boston* and *Marblehead* altered course and steamed north from off Long Beach to San Francisco. Help was finally on the way.[59]

JAMES HOPPER GETS THE STORY

The irony of the media, which at the time consisted of scores of newspapers and magazines, was that fresh news of the night before could not have been more outdated. Florid descriptions of all that wealth gathered in one place to hear an opera were being hawked on the rubble-filled streets as the flames began to spread and devour the buildings of those great bastions of the San Francisco press: the *Call, Examiner,* and *Chronicle.* The impressive structures were grouped together on Market Street, as if needing each other to proclaim the collective power of the Fourth Estate.

The daily newspapers—including the lesser *Bulletin, Daily News,* and *Evening Post*—were pervasive elements in the life of the city. But to say that they ran the city would be to oversimplify their influence, which could at any one time be diffuse. To say that they set the civic agenda and portrayed those images of the city that were most beneficial to their health as profitable businesses, would be closer to the truth. The journalistic truth was a much more personal and vituperative matter one hundred years ago than it is today.

The first three days were unusual in many respects. With all the major newspaper offices destroyed on Wednesday, there was a vacuum of news and information until the papers could be printed elsewhere and distributed widely. In modern terms, the television screens went blank.

James Hopper of the *Call* had gone to bed at 3 A.M. thinking that

Caruso's performance in *Carmen* was "the summit of human emotions." Born in Paris, Hopper came to California at the age of ten and became a legendary football player at Berkeley. He studied law but became a writer. He was to become the only journalist whose prose came close to matching the immensity of the events.

Hopper slept fitfully and awoke to the earthquake, sensing immediately that this one was different from the others:

> Right away it was incredible—the violence of the quake. It started with a directness, a savage determination that left no doubt of its purpose. It pounced upon the earth as some sidereal bulldog, with a rattle of hungry eagerness. The earth was a rat, shaken in the grinding teeth, shaken, shaken, shaken, with periods of slight weariness followed by new bursts of vicious rage.

The length and the "sudden violence" impressed Hopper. At first he chose to die in bed; then curiosity got the better of the reporter. The window pane fell outward, and Hopper stuck his head outside his rooming house window. "Then I heard the roar of the bricks coming down in cataracts and the groaning and twisted girders all over the city, and at the same time I saw the moon, a calm, pale crescent in the green sky of dawn."

From three stories above Hopper, the back wall of his building came tumbling down. "I saw the mass pass across my vision swift as a shadow. It struck some little wooden houses in the alley below. I saw . . . the bricks pass through the roof as through tissue paper." The shaking stopped. He dressed, noting "the great silence. . . . This silence continued, and it was an awful thing. But now in the alley some one began to groan. It was a woman's groan, soft and low."

Hopper did what many others chose to do, almost automatically. He walked downtown not thinking about the danger of fire. "In the morning's garish light I saw many men and women with gray faces, but none spoke." The parade of people in dark clothes resembled a promenade of living specters. Hopper felt elated, a not uncommon feeling among surviving soldiers after battle.

As Hopper walked toward the newspaper, he went through the motions of reporting as a professional journalist. Yet he failed to observe the types of literal facts that were used to fill the columns of his publication. He collected random images, then dropped his observer role entirely to help the injured.

When Hopper eventually arrived at the Call Building (also known as the Spreckels Building) he found that the steel-framed structure was relatively intact. He was greeted by the acting city editor who told him to cover the collapse of the Brunswick House at Sixth and Howard streets, where more than one hundred were feared dead.

Hopper had just gone through danger himself. He had the sudden insight afforded by his experience that journalism was not about being there but about recording what happened after a meaningful event. There was a delay. "In spite of what we had already seen," he wrote later in *Everybody's Magazine,* "our power of realization was behind time as it was to be through the three days' progressive disaster."

Hopper stopped an auto driven by "one of the city's gilded youths" and offered him $50 to drive him around the city. They zoomed here and there. "From that time, I have only a vague kaleidoscopic vision of whirring at whistling speed through a city of the damned." South of the Slot was now ablaze. "The scarlet steeplechaser" had beaten them to the Brunswick House. "By that time we knew that the earthquake had been but a prologue, and that the tragedy was to be written in fire."

Circling, ever circling the outer limits of the fire, they came upon refugees on the move, carts and wheeled contrivances of every description, crowded emergency hospitals, the Valencia Street Hotel, again back to the edge of the fire and refugees who sat transfixed on their few rescued household items, and then back to the Call Building, now "glowing like a phosphorescent worm."

The ten-year-old filigreed Call Building, the city's tallest at 310 feet, was advertised as "constructed of marble and fire proof throughout." It was one of three iconic structures in the city, the Palace Hotel and the new City Hall being the other two. All were shaken by earthquake and destroyed by fire.

More circling. Hopper returned to his room. The door was open. Looters? No, his Chinese servant was cleaning the room that would soon disappear in flames. Off to the ruined City Hall, which was just catching fire, then back to find a newspaper office, any newspaper office, to give his circles within circles journalistic meaning.

The newspaper buildings and the nearby Palace Hotel were burning fiercely at 1 P.M. That end of the city "was one great flame which smacked in the wind like the stupendous silken flag of some cosmic anarchy."

What to do about all the news Hopper and the others had collected? The staffs of the *Call* and *Chronicle* met at 7 P.M. They decided to rendezvous at buildings that, unknown to them, would no longer be standing the next morning.

"All night the city burned with a copper glow," Hopper wrote, "and all night the dynamite of the fire fighters boomed at slow intervals, the pulse of the great city in its agony."[60]

One newspaper functioned fitfully in San Francisco on Wednesday. Earlier in the day the *Daily News,* located more than a mile from the newspaper giants on Market Street, managed to print two abbreviated extra editions. The first was printed on one side of a pink sheet of paper. "HUNDREDS DEAD!" proclaimed the headline; "City Seems Doomed for Lack of Water" was the subhead.

Meanwhile, arrangements were being made to print a combined Thursday edition of the *Call-Chronicle-Examiner* in Oakland to supply news and keep the tradition of not missing a day of publication intact. Representatives of the three newspapers drew lots to determine the order of the unprecedented title, and by chance it was alphabetical. The combined edition's banner headline proclaimed: "EARTHQUAKE AND FIRE: SAN FRANCISCO IN RUINS." The major factual error in the four-page edition was that San Francisco was under martial law. Forty thousand copies were printed: half were dispatched north and south and into the interior of the country, ten thousand went to Oakland, and ten thousand to San Francisco.

The newspapers were free, as were many essential services such as mail and transportation when they resumed. One of Hopper's colleagues described the mayhem surrounding their distribution:

> The people were crazy for them. Out in the park, crowded with refugees, a big chap got on our front [running] board and refused to get off. If we had stopped anywhere we would have been stripped of our papers. I leaned across Jimmy Hopper of the *Call,* who was with me in the tonneau, and socked Mr. Husky. We were running some and he spun like a top when he hit the macadam.

For Friday's editions, Hearst's *Examiner* went its separate way when it gained exclusive use of the *Oakland Tribune*'s printing plant. The ousted *Call* and *Chronicle* combined their efforts elsewhere in Oakland. The united effort had lasted only one night before the fierce competition between newspapers resumed.[61]

THE BURNING OF THE "FIREPROOF" PALACE

At the luxurious Palace Hotel, described by Hopper as "treasured perhaps above everything by San Franciscans," there was panic among the guests.

A newspaper reporter, Frank Ames, was walking past the Palace at 5:12 A.M. A carriage was waiting inside the *port cochere*. Inside, the bright lights looked inviting. Then the palms in the lighted lobby began to sway. "At first I thought it was an optical delusion [*sic*]," Ames said, "but then the ground felt as if it were sinking under my feet." Heavy cornices and bricks fell around him. The team that was hitched to the carriage bolted. "The beasts' eyes were big with terror and foam was coming from their nostrils," noted Ames. Frightened guests, clad in their nightclothes, fled from every doorway, then retreated inside when confronted by the extent of devastation around them.

Ames ran. The cobblestones of Market Street seemed alive, popping up and down like heated popcorn. The tops of the tall buildings nodded toward one another. Ames heard "a low grumbling like the roar of ten thousand lions." The ground heaved. Electric wires spit blue arcs. Women screamed. Soon there was the cry of "fire, fire!"

Inside the hotel large chunks of plaster fell, a fine dust rose, glass broke, heavy chandeliers dropped from the ceilings, guests were thrown from their beds, large timbers creaked, heavy bureaus toppled over, and the elevators ceased functioning.

The stairways were jammed with debris and people. "Order at that moment did not exist," said a guest. "Hurrying and scurrying every person sought only safety. Everybody was frightened. Some were dumb with fright; others were gabbing excitedly." Another guest, who said his hair was streaked with gray, swore that it had turned "completely white" when he next examined it in a mirror.

───────────

One of the Palace's frightened guests was Enrico Caruso. A fellow opera company member said: "He tore about in a frantic state, rejecting all attempts at consolation." A guest saw him "running about in the scantiest of attire, shouting excitedly and twirling at his mustaches with unconscious nervousness, jostling everybody and not knowing where to go."[62]

A light sleeper, Caruso had been hovering on the edge of wakefulness. He felt his bed rocking like an ocean liner and thought he was dreaming of returning "to my beautiful country." He walked to the window and raised the shade. "And what I see makes me tremble with fear. I see the buildings toppling over, big pieces of masonry falling, and from the street below I hear the cries and screams of men and women and children."

He called for his valet, Martino, who opened the door and said quite coolly, "It is nothing." Caruso dressed hastily and grabbed his jewelry. "Then I did what you call—skidoo," he told reporters on arriving in New York City a few days later.

His friend the baritone Antonio Scotti met him in the hall. He begged Caruso to slow down, "but he seemed half-crazed and only continued on his way down stairs."

The conductor of the Met's orchestra, Alfred Hertz, who, unlike Caruso, would return to San Francisco one day and become the conductor of the San Francisco Symphony Orchestra, had made his way downstairs, passing an elderly Chinese man who was calmly cleaning the chairs and carpets in the dust-filled lobby. "Caruso, standing in the lobby, embraced me hysterically," Hertz said, "and crying like a child, repeatedly insisted that we were doomed and all were about to die."

They went outside and stood, then went back inside. An aftershock struck. "Again I ran out into the street," Caruso said, "Oh, my poor heart—it was going now tum-tum-tum, very quick—like that."

Caruso's valet gathered up most of his belongings, and, along with other members of the company, they made their way toward the new St. Francis Hotel. The photographer Arnold Genthe spotted Caruso in Union Square with a fur coat over what Genthe thought was his pajamas. The great tenor was smoking a cigarette and muttering, "Ell of a place. I never come back here!"

Other members of the company had gathered in Union Square, unaware that the Grand Opera House, badly damaged in the earthquake, had burned by 9 A.M. The roof and the gas-lit crystal chandelier had crashed into the orchestra seating area, and the company's costumes and sets were now ashes.

Ernest Goerlitz, the acting manager, was responsible for the temperamental singers and others in the company. Speaking of their time in the square, Goerlitz said it was "a hard task to keep a cheerful countenance" when "surrounded by two hundred and thirty people, mostly all of them of an emotional character, condemned to inactivity, the conflagration spreading rapidly in all directions and apparently about to consume the entire city with no shelter for the night."

Some said that Caruso kept testing his voice. Caruso's friend Scotti said the tenor had a towel wrapped around his precious throat and was clutching the signed photograph of Theodore Roosevelt that the president had given him after the Washington performance. The resourceful Scotti went looking for a wagon and driver, finally finding one who for $300 would take the two singers, the valet, and Caruso's trunk to the home of a friend, Dr. Arthur Bachman. Caruso, perhaps reflecting the knowledge of ancient cultures with longer histories of earthquakes, chose to sleep outside that night.

Other members of the dazed company took refuge where they could find it, the soprano Marcella Sembrich sleeping on the beach at the Presidio and the conductor Hertz squeezed tightly into an abandoned streetcar with other refugees. Hertz was unable to sleep because of the clamor of fire engines, the blowing of automobile horns, the thud of dynamiting, and the frightened "roars and screams" of "wild beasts" in a nearby menagerie.

The company departed for Oakland the next morning, Caruso using the signed photo of the president to gain entrance onto the ferry boat. Their special train left Oakland on April 20, and all members of the company made it safely back to New York City. Of five hundred trunks with personal belongings, thirty survived. Costumes, props, and scenery for nineteen operas were destroyed.[63]

———————

Another hotel guest had a much more harrowing experience. Guion H. Dewey was a Virginian who represented a New York manufacturing firm. He was staying in the Palace annex, known as the Grand Hotel. Dewey returned to his room at 8 A.M. to gather some papers when an aftershock struck, dislodging the brick chimney above the fireplace in his room. He struggled from the room with a broken jaw and embarked upon an odyssey that sampled the highs and lows of human conduct on the streets of San Francisco. One week later Dewey wrote his mother from the safety of Fresno.

> I saw innocent men shot down by the irresponsible militia. I walked four miles to have my jaw set. A stranger tried to make me accept a $10 gold piece. I was threatened with death for trying to help a small girl drag a trunk from a burning house, where her mother and father had been killed. A strange man gave me raw eggs and milk, and offered me his own bed in his house, which had not been wrecked (this is the first food I had had for twenty-two hours). I saw a soldier

shoot a horse because its driver allowed it to drink at a fire hose which had burst. I had a Catholic priest kneel by me in the park as I lay on a bed of alfalfa hay, covered with a piece of carpet, and pray to the Holy Father for relief for my pain and ease to my body. I saw a poor woman, barefoot, told to "Go to Hell and be glad for it" for asking for a glass of milk at a dairyman's wagon; she had in her arms a baby with its legs broken. I gave her a dollar and walked with her to the hospital. I met a casual acquaintance on the street, and he went across the ferry to Oakland with me, and there we fell in with the ministering women, who, God bless them, poured attentions on us. I saw hundreds of men with bottles of whiskey tied up in the remnants of bed clothes, begging for food, and I saw men with the Red Cross on their arms looting stores.

I was pressed into service by an officer, who made me help to strike tents in front of the St. Francis Hotel, when the order was issued to dynamite all buildings in the vicinity to save the hotel. I liked him, and hope to meet him again. When he saw I was hurt, which I had not told him, not yet having been bandaged, he took me to his own tent and gave me water and brandy and a clean handkerchief.[64]

One hotel guest said afterward that she had been "oppressed with an impending sense of disaster." The writer Mary Austin left the claustrophobic Palace Hotel, where she had gone to meet her New York publisher's representative, and went to stay with friends on the night of April 17.

Austin was awakened in the morning by the "noise and confusion" of the earthquake, but there was little damage in the neighborhood. They went outside and bantered with the neighbors. Then the scene changed: "Almost before the dust or ruined walls had ceased rising, smoke began to go up against the sun, which, by nine o'clock, showed bloodshot through it as the eye of Disaster."[65]

At the fortresslike Palace Hotel the fire crept closer. No one had been killed in the hotel, which suffered only superficial damage from the earthquake. Some guests were cut by glass. Fire would be the chief agent of the hotel's destruction.

The Palace had its own water supply, derived from a private reservoir under the grand court and pumped to rooftop tanks and a hydrant at the corner of Market and New Montgomery streets. Bellboys and other hotel employees stood on the fire escapes and soaked the south and west sides, from which the fire was approaching.

It seemed the hotel was safe until city firemen attached a hose to the hydrant and ran into nearby Sansome Street to fight a blaze. The water pressure to the hotel dropped. When the pumping plant on Jessie Street burned, the water supply failed entirely. "Shortly after noon the Palace Hotel itself was ablaze," said a witness to its destruction, "and once the fire started the inside of the hotel went like tinder." There was much wood and rich brocade in the supposedly fireproof hotel on which the flames could feed.

In his book *Bonanza Inn,* Oscar Lewis wrote of the "last, sinister guest" of the famous hostelry: "Trailing his scarlet robe, he advanced inexorably, permeating every corner of the structure, silently at first, then more boisterously, until presently the grand court vibrated with an immense humming roar."[66]

THE MEN OF SCIENCE

In contrast to the guests at the Palace, the men of science were more composed, at least according to their own accounts. They had been looking forward to experiencing an earthquake, albeit a more benign one.

For twenty years Professor Alexander McAdie of the weather bureau had been in the habit of timing earthquakes, including the destructive Charleston, South Carolina, quake of 1886. Always laid out next to his bed were an open pocket watch, a notebook open to the date, a pencil, and an electric hand torch.

It took him "6 or more" seconds to react. McAdie lost his composure, or rather his footing, only once, and that was around the twenty-second mark, when he had trouble standing. "The end of the shock I did not get exactly, as I was watching the second-hand and the end came several seconds before I fully took in the fact that the motion had ceased." McAdie wrote in his notebook: "Severe lasted nearly 40 seconds."

He hurried to the weather bureau office on the tenth floor of the Mills Building. The American flag was raised on the roof at 6:40 A.M. Fires surrounded the structure at the corner of Montgomery and Bush streets, near the produce district. The bureau's seismograph, the instrument nearest the epicenter, had been partially disassembled at the time. The east-west component was working, and the pen was knocked off the sheet of paper. The office was vacated at 5:30 P.M., and all the records and instruments in the San Francisco and San Jose weather bureau offices were destroyed by fire.[67]

Although ever alert to earthquakes, McAdie was oblivious to the possibility of fire. Like many others in San Francisco that day, he did not comprehend that the city would soon burn and offices would be destroyed. Many businessmen, lawyers, bankers, and others walked to their offices and checked the seismic damage but did not react quickly enough to save what they valued from the approaching flames.

Grove Karl Gilbert of the USGS, the most knowledgeable of all geologists in the country about earthquakes, just happened to be sleeping in the Faculty Club at the University of California that morning. Gilbert was in California conducting a study of the effects of hydraulic gold mining. His presence would be science's gain.

Although volcanic eruptions generally await the arrival of the geologist, Gilbert noted, "the earthquake, unheralded and brief, may elude him through his entire lifetime." He had narrowly missed being present at the Owens Valley earthquake of 1872 and the southeast Alaska quake of 1899. "When, therefore," Gilbert wrote, "I was awakened in Berkeley on the eighteenth of April last by a tumult of motions and noises, it was with unalloyed pleasure that I became aware that a vigorous earthquake was in progress."

Gilbert took careful notice of the movements. "While they had many directions, the dominant factor was a swaying in the north-south direction, which caused me to roll slightly as I lay with my head toward the east." A suspended electric light swung in a north-south arc, and water from a pitcher spilled toward the south.

In another part of the club, the dominant motion was east-west. Gilbert concluded that the peculiarities of the redwood-frame structure on the edge of the Hayward Fault accounted for the differences, not the motions of the earth underneath it.

Two hours later the geologist learned of the disaster that had befallen San Francisco. "This information at once incited a tour of observation, and thus began, so far as I was personally concerned, the investigation of the earthquake." Although unable to enter San Francisco until Friday, Gilbert would play a key role in the compilation of the 1908 State Earthquake Investigation Commission report.[68]

American science was caught unprepared. All the seismographs in California were outdated, and none were sufficiently dampened to withstand the force of a magnitude 7.7–7.9 earthquake and give an adequate reading. Not until Professor Fusakichi Omori of Tokyo Imperial University arrived in San Francisco a few weeks later with a gift of a seismograph of his own design would there be a modern seismograph in this country. (Japan led the world in earthquake research at the time.)

The intensity of the earthquake was so great, however, that seismographs elsewhere throughout the world recorded the temblor. In Europe, Japan, and Washington, D.C., the first news of the earthquake arrived by way of seismograph. It took eleven and one-half minutes for the shock waves to travel across the Pacific Ocean to Japan and seven minutes to pass across this country and arrive in the nation's capital. Subsequent deductions about this earthquake have been formulated from the more reliable distant readings.[69]

What can't be measured with scientific accuracy, because they are almost impossible to catch in the act, are earthquake phenomena: the low rumbling sounds; the flickering, colored luminescence; the passage of waves that leave objects intact; the unusual animal behavior; and the fluctuations in water levels in underground bodies of water. There is enough historical evidence to confirm their occurrence. These phenomena, for which there are no adequate explanations, do not occur or are not observed all the time. Their inconstancy reflects the random, chaotic nature of earthquakes. Neither the long-term seismographic record nor the phenomena are reliable predictive tools.

The phenomena were present in the early morning hours of April 18. Along with the accounts printed in commercial publications, the State Earthquake Investigation Commission collected and published reports. There were doubters, however. David Starr Jordan, president of Stanford University, represented empirically minded scientists. In a satirical article published four months later in *Science,* Jordan called the academic author of a newspaper story about these phenomena a "professor of astronomy and geology in the University of the Sunday Supplement."[70]

WELLS FARGO AND THE BANK OF ITALY

The commercial sector was also unprepared. Businessmen had to literally think on their feet. Some did so better than others.

Two bankers commuted to work from the suburbs on Wednesday under unusual conditions. Before the day ended their different responses to the earthquake and fire would determine the fates of their respective institutions for years to come.

Frederick L. Lipman, the cashier and future president of Wells Fargo Nevada National Bank, was awakened in his Berkeley home by the noise of the brick chimney falling to the ground. Lipman's family went outside to check their neighbors' chimneys and then had breakfast at home, since they cooked on a gas stove that did not require a brick chimney.

Lipman went to work carrying his evening clothes in a suitcase for the opera that night. The plan was for Mrs. Lipman to join him in San Francisco for the performance of *Lohengrin* by the touring Metropolitan Opera Company. The banker saw nothing in Berkeley that would prevent his going to the opera. But on the ferry ride across the bay, plumes of dense smoke were visible over the distant city. After disembarking, the banker walked up California Street to the ornate bank building at Pine and Montgomery streets, skirting fires on his left and right but letting none of the blazes impede his steady progress with tuxedo in hand.

The bank opened at its regular time, 9 A.M. Most of its badly shaken employees had reported to work. The doors closed at 10:30. "As the fire got nearer and nearer," Lipman recalled, "we were chased out by the fire department." They threw everything of value they could lay their hands on into the massive vault on the first floor. "We had to quit and locked our vault." Lipman went home.

On Friday he returned to look at the ruins of the bank building. "Of course there was nothing there. All burnt off." The structure had also been dynamited. "There was no bank to go to," Lipman said forlornly, "no anyplace to go to."

A temporary office was established in a private home. Taking a lesson from the Chicago fire, the bankers at Wells Fargo waited two weeks to let the vault cool off before opening it; otherwise a rush of oxygen would have caused the spontaneous combustion of anything that might have remained unburned. Almost all the other banks in San Francisco had similar experiences to that of Wells Fargo.[71]

Meanwhile, a newcomer, the Bank of Italy, reacted more quickly than the other banks. Amadeo Peter Giannini, a wholesale grocer who dabbled in real estate, had founded the tiny bank two years earlier in one room of a leased three-story building at the corner of Columbus Avenue and Washington Street.

Giannini had roamed the streets in the Italian community of North Beach and advertised to attract business. The bank's loans, which exceeded deposits by $200,000 on March 31, 1906, were almost entirely in real estate. Conservative bankers representing more established institutions referred derogatorily to the newcomer as "the dago huckster seeking customers in much the same way as he had once sold pears and apples."

The earthquake had destroyed the chimney on Giannini's home, a wood-beam and brick Tudor-style structure in San Mateo called Seven Oaks because of the grove of trees on the grounds. On his seventeen-mile commute that normally took a half hour by train, Giannini was forced to walk and hitch rides because the tracks were twisted. He arrived at the bank at noon, having witnessed the destruction and the early stream of refugees fleeing the city along the way. The bank had been opened by two employees at 9 A.M.

"I figured we had about two hours to get out of there," Giannini recalled. "At the rate the fire was spreading, I realized that no place in San Francisco could be a safe storage spot for the money." He was correct. "I decided to take it home to San Mateo."

Giannini had certain advantages that the presidents of Wells Fargo and other more established banks did not posses. He had seen the extent of the disaster. The $80,000 in gold and silver that represented all the Bank of Italy's cash was a small enough amount to carry in two produce wagons, which he could easily borrow from his stepfather, the owner of the largest wholesale grocery business in the city. And he had a safe hiding place.

Giannini loaded bank records, office furniture, mattresses, and crates of oranges on top of the money in order to disguise it from possible robbers. (For weeks afterward the money smelled of orange juice.) At the nearby home of Giannini's brother-in-law, they waited for night, when the precious load would attract less attention. With the glow of the burning city behind them, Giannini, his brother-in-law, and the two employees set off for San Mateo, using a less-traveled route for part of the way. The harrowing journey took the entire night.

The banker stored the cash in the ash trap of his disabled living room fireplace, a much safer and a more accessible location than a vault. The four took turns guarding the money. On Friday, Giannini returned, as Lipman had, to the city and gazed upon the ruins of his new bank. At that point, the courses of the two bankers diverged.

Unlike Wells Fargo, the Italian banker chose to react aggressively to the disaster. Giannini's plan, devised over the next few days, was to begin lending money as soon as possible to his customers to rebuild. He had little choice, since most of the real estate on which he had loaned had been destroyed. Each customer, whose credit rating Giannini held in his head, would get half the money he requested in order not to deplete the bank's meager capital. Meanwhile, Giannini would attempt to increase assets by cajoling Italians to deposit their money in a safer location than hiding places in the refugee camps where many of them were now living.

He opened offices in his brother's Van Ness Avenue home and on a plank laid over two barrels on the Washington Street wharf. A bag of gold was prominently displayed on the plank, behind which was Giannini's desk. A nearby banner proclaimed the presence of the Bank of Italy. Either one of these temporary locations could be considered the future Bank of America's first branch.

Despite Governor George Pardee's declaration of a month-long bank holiday to avoid a run on banks, Giannini was quickly back in business as a full-service bank. Wells Fargo and a few other banks conducted business on a limited scale until they could recover the money in their vaults and reestablish their records.

Some twenty thousand Italians lost their homes in the fire. Six thousand new Italian immigrants arrived to help clean up and rebuild San Francisco. In 1930 the Bank of Italy became the Bank of America, which at its height in the post–World War II years became the state's, the nation's, and then the world's largest bank.

An interviewer asked Wells Fargo's Lipman in the mid-1930s if it was true that the Bank of Italy was the only bank to open for business after the earthquake. Lipman replied:

> That statement is not so greatly exaggerated. The fact of the matter was Giannini could have gone to his vault, taken all the contents out. He could do it, but the other banks couldn't do it. We couldn't do it. He made good use of the thing. . . . I think young Giannini, if he had an advantage over the other banks, had a right to use it. I think I would have used it myself.[72]

THE INJURED

The Central Emergency Hospital was located in the basement of the new City Hall, whose collapse was best described by the anonymous *Argonaut* writer: "In the space of a minute a building that was architecturally the largest and most pretentious in the State of California was shaken to the ground almost like a pack of cards. Its walls and pillars collapsed, its copper dome remained standing on its skeleton steel pillars above a chaos of destroyed masonry." There was also a police station inside City Hall. Remarkably, no one was killed. The day workers had not yet arrived in the massive structure.

Before completion of the $7 million edifice, there had been hints of graft.

People were quick to jump to the conclusion that shoddy construction had caused its collapse. The monstrous municipal building—shaped like a fully-rigged, top-heavy sailing vessel—was built on shaky ground that had once been swampland. (Other city hall buildings were destroyed or damaged in 1865, 1868, and 1989; it had become a San Francisco tradition.)

Police Officer E. F. Parquet was inside the emergency hospital, having just checked on the ward for the insane. "Then there was the roaring of the earthquake itself," Parquet said, "and the crashes and shocks and rumblings as we felt the walls and pillars of the City Hall bursting and breaking over our heads, and the dome came tumbling down in great lumps that crashed like new earthquakes and broke into pieces, bursting and banging against the doors and windows."

A huge piece of masonry fell on an empty bed; nearby, others were full. It was pitch dark and dusty. Both the mad and the sane shrieked and moaned. Every exit was blocked, and they thought they were entombed. Officer Parquet fired his pistol to attract attention. Digging from the outside and the inside, an opening was forged through which patients and medical equipment were passed.

The Mechanics' Pavilion, across Larkin Street, became the new emergency hospital. The huge barnlike structure, which served as the athletic arena and convention center of its time, had hosted a masked carnival and roller-skating contest the night before. Doctors, nurses, volunteers, and every type of conveyance, from hand cart to automobile, that could transport the injured and dead soon converged on the temporary emergency hospital.[73]

Dr. Tilton E. Tillman arrived at 6 A.M. in a neighbor's Pierce-Arrow. Other city-employed doctors, local doctors with private practices, and out-of-town doctors who were in the city to attend the April 19 California Medical Association convention made their way to the pavilion. Tillman said, "By the time I reached the pavilion affairs were still rather chaotic. New patients were arriving every moment and in all sorts of vehicles, and were being carried in on the doors or shutters or whatever other apologies [there were] for stretchers."

At the same time, parties with official badges, Red Cross armbands, uniformed officers, and official-looking faces and dress, or some combination of the above, were dispatched across the city to conduct some necessary medical looting. In one party there was an "energetic and enthusiastic" ex–Salvation Army woman. "When we arrived at a drug-store . . . she jumped out, and, finding the door locked," said James B. Stetson, the president of the cable car company who accompanied her, "seized a chair and raising it above her head smashed the glass doors in and helped herself to hot-water bags, bandages, and anything which would be useful in an emergency hospital. I continued in this work with my son Harry [an attorney] for a couple of hours."[74]

From drugstores, medical supply houses, bedding stores, grocery stores, hardware stores, hotels, and rooming houses, supplies and bedding were hauled back to the pavilion, mostly in commandeered or volunteered automobiles. In some cases, the foragers were helped by soldiers. (Perhaps one of these incidents accounts for Guion Dewey believing that Red Cross workers were looting stores.) Additional medical supplies came from the Southern Pacific Hospital.

The dead were brought there too, the bodies placed behind the seats that surrounded the floor space so as not to disturb the living. Tillman counted sixteen bodies. He thought the doctors and nurses had treated more than 150 injured. (More than twice that number of injured had to be moved later, according to another estimate.) The injuries included cuts from glass, broken limbs from falling or jumping, and crushed or burned bodies. Triage was practiced widely. The emergency hospital acted like a field station in war. Patients were patched up and sent elsewhere.[75]

Dr. Margaret Mahoney and a fellow woman physician arrived and offered their services. "As we entered a dead body was carried out in a wicker basket coffin. Within all was perfect order; the wounds of the injured bandaged; coffee being served; every attention given."

Sometime in midmorning the doctors and nurses began whispering among themselves: "The place is afire, we must get them out at once."[76] Sparks from the approaching flames fell on the wood-shingled roof. Around 11 A.M. the roof of the pavilion caught fire. One wall began to burn. The exodus of patients—again transported in any type of available stretcher and conveyance—began at a hurried pace. Most of the injured went to the hospitals at the Presidio, and the dead were taken to the morgue or to a park for temporary burial.

The vast room was cleared by 11:30 A.M. Dr. Tillman said, "[An ambulance driver] and I were the last to leave the Polk Street end of the pavilion, which was then completely cleared of patients and dead." Officer E. J. Plume thought he was the last to leave: "I know that when I left there was nobody in the front end of the building." Perhaps they left from different ends of the building. In any case, their conclusions were the same.

From whatever mental or emotional swamp where the vapors of rumors ferment, the stories rose and spread across the country that 350 of the patients were either shot by soldiers or chloroformed by doctors and nurses to prevent their painful deaths in the flames. The *New York Herald* published a much-copied account that attributed this story to an Omaha man who was a Red Cross worker.[77]

THE "DEVIL WAGONS"

Lucy Fisher was a nurse who had been working in the pavilion until it was evacuated. She was assigned to an automobile with two other nurses, and they were transported to the California Women's Hospital. It was a wild ride for the nurses. The young nurse thought they would surely be killed in the speeding vehicle after having survived earthquake and fire. Upon arriving safely, however, she praised the new form of transportation that had been much maligned in the popular press.

The Mobile Carriage Company was the first to volunteer its services, and its manager, William G. Harvey, was put in charge of the automobile rescue effort by Mayor Schmitz. "For three days," Harvey said, "our machines were engaged, first, in carrying loads of sick and wounded and then possibly the next load would be one of dynamite for the use of those engaged in fighting the fire, then possibly another load of sick and wounded, then a load of gasoline or lubricating oil for use at the headquarters of the garage, in fact, the machines did whatever was asked of them."

The earthquake and the fire were to prove to many that the automobile was more than just the play toy of the rich. "They were devil wagons turned into chariots of mercy," declared the *Chronicle,* which went on to state: "That the automobile played an all but indispensable part in the saving of the western part of San Francisco, and at the same time has proved invaluable in the serious business of governing the city through its greatest stress is conceded by everyman who has had his eyes open during the ten days or so that have elapsed after the earthquake."[78]

Rudimentary at the turn of the century, numbering in the tens in San Francisco, and mostly confined to trips to the beach or the park, the infernal machines were always breaking down or frightening people and horses. By 1906, more reliable autos could be rented in front of hotels and restaurants, and their presence had increased on city streets. Nonmotorists hated them, and onerous restrictions were placed on their use.

The injured, doctors, dynamite, dynamiters, ranking officials, and the fleeing rich were transported by the belching horseless carriages at speeds of up to thirty miles per hour, and sometimes more. "It was truly a glorious sight," enthused *Sunset* magazine, "this rush of the despised bauble of the wealthy, the vehicle which had been slurred and cursed, damned and deplored."

The availability of fuel was the key to their continued functioning. Gasoline was supplied free by the Standard Oil Company and the Southern Pacific. It was transported from Oakland and distributed free in a Knox truck. At one point, the truck stalled on one of San Francisco's steep hills, and a crowd helped push it over the top. "At any other time the crowd would have scoffed at the idea of helping a motorcar," commented a motorist.

Horses hauled loads until they dropped. They died by the thousands of heat and thirst. The autos were driven hard, too. They ran on the rims when tires frayed or burst on the hot pavement. "I saw four soldiers," a woman recounted, "in an automobile loaded with dynamite; one tire was punctured, and half of the wheel, and the auto bumped over every stone, but never slackened speed." The clanking and popping machines dropped by the side of the road, but not before they had done more at a faster pace than horses.

The owners of the vehicles were commanded, sometimes at gunpoint, to do the bidding of the military, civil authorities, or special police. Some two hundred autos were seized for various purposes. Many were commandeered, said Harvey, under false pretenses by people with fake credentials and stories of false emergencies who wanted to be driven outside the city. A counterfeit Red Cross badge was the most common scam.

Behavior varied, as it always does under such circumstances. Although some volunteered the services of their expensive machines, others used various ruses to keep their motor cars for their own purposes.[79]

One car dealer rose from obscurity to fame. Charles Howard, who owned a bicycle repair shop on Van Ness Avenue, repaired the automobiles of the wealthy who lived nearby on the wide avenue. He opened a Buick dealership with three autos, which went unsold. Then came the earthquake. The three cars were used for various emergency purposes, and Howard parlayed the newfound popularity of the auto into a successful automobile dealership and the eventual ownership of the racehorse Seabiscuit.[80]

Even a sober technical journal, the *Mining and Scientific Press,* gave its stamp of approval to the auto in its first postquake edition:

The value of a self-contained machine or complete unit is strikingly proved by the timely service given by the motor car during the conflagration. It is true there is many a wrecked automobile now lying in the streets of the ruined city, but the accident or damage that brought the activity of the machine to an end, did not take place until it had served a beneficent purpose, with wonderful efficiency. In removing wounded, in carrying doctors, in bringing dynamite for the blasting operations, in transporting food and, last of all, in aiding the escape of the terrified people, the motor car was of immense service. It was the only means of rapid locomotion.[81]

After the earthquake, the machines were increasingly used by military and civil authorities for emergency purposes. They had proved their worth on the broken streets of San Francisco.

THE PRESIDIO

The Presidio of San Francisco, where most of the injured were transported after the Mechanics' Pavilion burned, was a place of relative safety compared to the chaos on city streets. It was a bleak place, however. When General Funston, then a colonel, passed through along with eighty thousand troops on his way to the Philippines during the Spanish-American War, he commented: "Everything was sand, sand, sand, deep and fine, blowing into tents, getting into food." Others complained of the cold fog, biting winds, and numerous fleas.

By 1906, the tent cities Funston saw had mostly been replaced by wooden barracks and brick buildings, including the three-hundred-bed General Hospital that treated special cases from all over the United States. There were eleven doctors and thirty-nine nurses on the staff. A smaller Post Hospital handled more common ailments.

The peacetime troops, not only at the Presidio but also at other Army posts scattered about the Bay Area, were of poor quality. Desertion rates were high. An infantry colonel complained of the troops under his command, stating that they were of "inferior character, many being mere nomads." They were housed in poor accommodations and frequented the "low dives" outside the gates.

There were 1,499 enlisted men and 52 officers stationed at the Presidio the month before the earthquake. The military post was closer to the fault line than any other large grouping of buildings. Two adobe barracks collapsed, some brick buildings were extensively damaged, water pipes burst, electric lines were down, and communications with the outside world were temporarily lost. (It would cost $127,320 to repair the post.)[82]

The commander of the Post Hospital, Major William Stephenson, had experienced earthquakes in the Philippines. After the earthquake, he noticed "a strange silence in the gray dawn and a sky-line bereft of chimneys," including the shattered brick chimney on his two-story military residence. Stephenson warned his Chinese cook against using the stove, and thus risking a fire with a faulty chimney. Like many others in the city, the family began to cook outdoors.

At the small Post Hospital he found thirty injured soldiers, many of them cut by glass or with broken legs from having jumped from second stories. He watched the troops under the command of Colonel Morris march off toward downtown San Francisco.

Soon the crowds arrived seeking refuge and medical treatment, and, according to the major, "feeling safer under the protecting arms of Uncle Sam." The Post Hospital soon filled past capacity, with more than two hundred injured. "Patients on litters and mattresses lay everywhere in the halls, porches and, finally, under the sky alone," said Stephenson, "with its ominous glare cityward and flying cinders." The prison ward was reserved for maternity cases, births having seemingly increased after the ground shook.

The larger General Hospital had been extensively damaged by the earthquake, but it managed to open its doors to some two hundred injured civilians and patients from other hospitals either damaged or in the path of approaching flames. The injured were placed in the wards and overflowed into the halls, porches, and grounds.

The number of patients quickly leveled off at approximately 345 at the Post and General hospitals. The two military hospitals treated the largest number of injured of any hospital, with many patients coming from private hospitals and the city's five emergency hospitals.[83]

Among the patients taken to the General Hospital was a young woman named Anna G. Blake. Anna had been a patient at the Clara Barton Hospital and was suffering from a painful ear ailment.

Anna had also noticed "the most dreadful" silence immediately after the earthquake. The noise of fire and all that accompanied it broke the spell of silence. She was placed in an ambulance, and the horses galloped off to the army's General Hospital. "I can never forget that awful picture," she wrote. "The whole city burning, and the flames over two miles long and nearly a mile high sweeping from behind us. The heat was terrible. The streets were crowded and the men carrying me had hard work to get through."

The young woman woke up in a bed in temporary quarters and was soon transferred to Ward G. The plaster had fallen from the ceiling in which there were two large holes, the walls were cracked, and the windows wouldn't shut in the ward. She recalled:

The first week here was like a week in Libby Prison. Over a hundred of us were crowded together in one room of the barracks. There were rich women and poor women, white, yellow and black, from all quarters of the city. It was impossible to keep the place clean. There was no heat, scant food, and little water. We were allowed no communication with the outside and sentries guarded the place day and night, no one being allowed to enter but priests and nuns and wearers of the red cross.

"This is terrible," she managed to write her mother. The young woman wasn't getting proper medical attention, but she realized she was better off than other women in the ward:

There was one lady here with a young child. "Did your house burn?" I asked her. "Oh, yes, everything. But I don't mind that. But I've lost a little girl eight years old. We were dug out of the ruins, but they never found her."

There was a young girl here all alone. Her face was so badly cut that the scars will remain all her life. "I don't mind that," she said, "but my mother and I were sleeping in the same bed, and they dug me out, but no one has heard of her."

"Will, oh Willie, is that you?" another woman would scream all night until the night corpsman would say "Yes mother, it is Will." Her son was killed in the fire and his image was all that remained in her shattered mind.

I hear a child in the bed next to mine died and the notice on the door read: "Parents Unknown."

"Yes, I am one of the four survivors dragged from the ruins of the Brunswick Hotel," said another.

And yet through all the tragedies of the hospital scarcely anyone cried or complained, and the bravest women were those who had been the richest and had lost the most.

A badly frightened Anna Blake wrote her mother on another day:

Oh Momma we must all be vaccinated. Pestilence threatened. In my weak condition I am afraid to be vaccinated after a crowd of Italians and Irish etc. here. I'm awfully scared. They won't accept [my] vaccination mark. Army surgeons do it. Awfully afraid. Wish I could walk out. Please get in to see me. Get me moved quickly. I'm so helpless. It's a young Jew of [Mayor] Schmitz's health board who is going to do it.

Five minutes passed.

The deed is done, and I suppose I must accept that with the rest. I positively refused to have it on my arm like the rest so I have it on my leg. Carried my point for once.

A fire broke out adjacent to Ward G. The patients were awakened at 4 A.M. by bugles, running soldiers, the warning boom of a cannon, random shots by the sentries, and an officer shouting: "Shoot anyone caught looting" and "Get the patients out."

The patients thought it was a riot. They dressed and were readied for evacuation. The sky showed blood-red through the transoms. The fire was controlled, and the fearful patients went back to their beds—but not to sleep.[84]

LIFE AT THE CLUBS

From the Presidio, the vast columns of smoke and the thud of dynamite looked and sounded like a distant battle. With everything under control by 4 P.M., Major Stephenson hitched a ride in a returning automobile to the Bohemian Club, where he observed:

An ominous quiet pervaded the club, the precious paintings were down and in the halls ready for hasty removal, and occasionally some disheveled member would enter, more exhausted than he realized. At this time the fire had not overshadowed the earthquake, and comparisons with the historic shock of '68, and the shock-resisting strength of various constructions were in order among the old-timers and the architects respectively.[85]

Lunch was served at the various clubs under makeshift conditions and with the fire approaching. After two hours of gathering hospital supplies, James Stetson stopped at the Pacific Union Club at Stockton and Post streets for a quick cup of coffee and a sandwich. Then he was off again to walk through the fire zone.

General Funston and James Phelan also lunched at the Pacific Union. Phelan's chauffeur, James Mountford, finally found him there. Mountford had been on his way to Phelan's house in the morning when he and the car were impressed for ambulance service at the Mechanics' Pavilion.[86]

James W. Byrne had been staying at the Palace Hotel with his mother. He and a bellboy had hauled their three trunks to the street, where a cart carried them to the Pacific Union Club. He asked the manager to put the trunks in the cellar. Too late, Byrne realized that his mother's valuable jewels, which she had worn to the opera the night before, were in one of the trunks.

The club burned that night. Two weeks later Byrne returned. The building had been reduced to "some shapeless remnants of twisted steel beams and columns." As chairman of the building committee, Byrne knew the layout of the cellar. He hired a crew of men to dig, not telling them the purpose. It took seven days to find the trunks, which had been reduced to handles, hinges, and ashes. They scooped up all the ashes in the vicinity, sifted through them, and found the diamonds unharmed. The Pacific Union Club would later find a new home in the gutted Flood mansion across the street from the restored Fairmont Hotel.[87]

Earlier that morning, after being awakened by the earthquake, Jerome Barker Landfield made his way through the debris-covered streets to the Bohemian Club. Landfield was a socially connected world traveler who taught history at the University of California and headed the university's press. He met the *Examiner*'s drama critic, Ashton Stevens, and his wife on the sidewalk outside the Occidental Hotel, from which they had just escaped "with barely the clothes on their backs." Landfield went inside to get the couple rolls and coffee from the club while they waited outside.

Inside, the members were chatting about the earthquake and comparing it to earlier ones. One of the members invited Landfield to take a tour of the city in his car. Landfield accepted, rides in autos being rare and it being even rarer to drive through a postquake city. They toured the city, winding up at the St. Francis Hotel, the Bohemian Club being located just across Union Square from the hotel. Landfield climbed sixteen stories to the top of the hotel from where there was a commanding view:

Below us spread Chinatown. Suddenly there were blasts, followed by flames. Here was apparently the dynamiting that had been rumored.

To my experienced eye it was obvious that it was not dynamite but black powder that was being employed. As a result it was simply spreading the fire.

Landfield returned to the club in the late afternoon. A car drove up and out stepped an exhausted Frank Ainsworth, the chief surgeon at the Southern Pacific Hospital. The steaming car needed water. The members carried pitchers of water from the dining room tables, there being no running water in the pipes. The doctor collected his belongings in his room, stuffed them into pillowcases, and departed.

It was then nighttime, although the city was brightly lit by the flames. Most of the members had left. Landfield sat down with his friend Peter Robertson, and they played a game of dominoes for the fate of the Bohemian Club. "We played by the light of the fire down the street," Landfield recalled, "and the club lost!"

Tom Barbour, a longtime resident of the club, and Landfield took blankets, walked across the street to Union Square, and joined other refugees. Earlier in the day Funston had given Landfield a pass. Using the valuable piece of paper, Landfield passed back through the fire line to take one last look at the club where he "had spent so many happy hours."

Many paintings and drawings still remained on the walls, though a couple of truck-loads had been hauled out to Golden Gate Park for safety. With my pocket-knife I cut several choice ones from their frames, rolled them up, and carried them away. Among them were two priceless cartoons by Thomas Nast which he had made for the club, and an apron from a Lambs' Washing of the Lambs of New York, signed and illustrated by all the leading artists and actors of the day. They now adorn the walls of the present club. Flames had already broken through the ceiling of the Jinks Room on the upper floor when I left the club just before one o'clock, the last to leave the building. As I passed through the door to the street, seated on the steps was Omar, the faithful old club servant, weeping.[88]

CHINATOWN

Chinatown was at other end of the social, economic, and cultural spectrum from these private clubs. In fact, it is hard to imagine a people and a place further removed from the wealth and power of the white clubmen and their ornate surroundings.

The members, who employed Chinese house servants, moved easily about the city during the disaster. They obtained passes, badges, transportation, food, and temporary lodging from their relatives and friends who lived outside the fire zone. On the other hand, only two alternatives were open to the Chinese: they either escaped across the bay to Oakland or were herded like cattle through the streets of San Francisco.

There were, however, commonalities. Each culture sought comfort from its own gods.

Mass was being said at St. Ignatius Church when the earthquake hit, and a falling candlestick struck the Jesuit priest on his nose. The main altar, still filled with elaborate Easter decorations, was a shambles. Communion was extremely popular at all four masses throughout that day. Three hundred worshipers were present at the last mass as flames approached the Catholic church at Hayes Street and Van Ness Avenue.

The priests heard confessions continuously, "so eager were the terrified people to receive absolution." Said Father John P. Frieden, the head of St. Ignatius Church and College, "It was a solemn and distressingly pathetic sight."[89]

The Chinese feared the Earth Dragon, who in a fit of anger split the cobblestones that caged him. Erica Y. Z. Pan wrote:

> With such a belief in mind, a good portion of the Chinatown population swarmed to their different temples to offer incense and sacrifices to the deities. The faithful hurriedly confessed their sins and begged their gods to appease the anger of the Earth Dragon. . . . Before the Earth Dragon was soothed, however, the Fire Dragon got out of control. It spat flames in every direction of the city. . . . The foreboding that this was the end of the world spread feelings of fear and despair among the fleeing refugees.[90]

To the city policemen on duty in Chinatown, it did not appear that there were many casualties. "That several were lost in the cellars and basements was the current belief at the time; but the Chinese made no reports of these casualties," was the conclusion of the *Argonaut* narrator. Whatever the number of dead and injured and for whatever reason, few Asians were counted as victims. It was as if they did not exist. Two police officers saw only two casualties. Others saw more. "Yet," one said, "the place looked like it had been bombarded."

The Chinese crowded into Portsmouth Square, as did some Italians. To add to the confusion, a crazed steer that had made its way from Folsom Street caused panic among the Chinese, who looked upon the appearance of one of the four bulls who was supposedly holding up the world as a very bad omen.[91]

Chinese families fled. They reassembled in groups of family, friends, neighbors, or church members. Fifteen-year-old Hugh Kwong had lost his parents before the earthquake, and the older cousin to whom he had been entrusted by his father fled without his relative. As Young Kwong dragged his father's trunk with his belongings over San Francisco streets following the flow of other Chinese refugees away from the flames and toward the Presidio, he looked back from Nob Hill and saw all of Chinatown burning.[92]

The immediate cause of the burning was dynamite in its granular form and black powder, which does not mean that Chinatown would not have burned had no explosives been carelessly used. It just would not have burned as quickly.

From the top of the St. Francis Hotel, Jerome Landfield had seen the threat of the explosives-fed conflagration to Chinatown. Chinatown was a case study in how not to fight a fire with explosives.

Mayor Schmitz, Abe Ruef, a fire commissioner, and a battalion chief were involved in the decision to blast a firebreak along Kearny Street. Police Sergeant Maurice S. Behan was on the scene and described what happened: "By this time powder and dynamite were being used to blow up buildings with a view to arresting the march of the fire in various places, but the efforts along that line were not successful. In some places they helped to spread the blaze."

In its postdisaster reports, the army tended to blame city authorities for insisting that the more flammable explosives be used on the eastern flank of Chinatown. Raymond W. Briggs, an artillery lieutenant in charge of a squad of dynamiters, described the downfall of Chinatown:

> An attempt was made to put out this fire, but as there was no water to be obtained it was soon seen to be a vain endeavor. A building between the fire and Kearny Street was then blown down. Here the supply of stick dynamite gave out, some of that which arrived from Angel Island evidently having been sent to other points of the fire. A number of wagons came up loaded with giant powder—dynamite in granular form—but I hesitated to use this, knowing that its combustion was a matter of flame and that any building destroyed by it would, in addi-

tion, be set on fire, as would also result if black powder were used. I was urged as a last resort to use it, however, and consequently I destroyed a building on the west of Kearny on the corner of Clay and also the one adjacent. Both immediately caught on fire, and in the second, which had been a cheap lodging house, bits of clothing, etc., which had become ignited at the combustion were thrown across Kearny to the west side, and soon that block was on fire.

A battalion chief continued the story:

In a short time this place was a roaring furnace and the firemen were forced to back away on account of the heat and the flames. This as near as I can judge was about 6 o'clock. Our water supply had given out about 11 o'clock, so we were forced to retreat. . . . In the meantime Lieutenant Briggs was ahead of us, dynamiting all the time. Here is where I came to the conclusion that dynamiting is all right provided you have plenty of water to cool off the ruins, but it is almost useless without it, as it only makes kindling wood of the buildings for the flames to feed upon.

The Chinese were slow to leave their ghetto. For where would they go? Where would they be welcome?

By 2 A.M. on Thursday, the second day, "Chinatown was all ablaze and the last of its inhabitants that we could find had been cleared out," said Sergeant Behan.[93]

REFUGEES

The refugees made their way east to the ferries, west to the Presidio and Golden Gate Park, and south into San Mateo County by way of bumpy and torn city streets. The dominant noise of the otherwise silent exodus of people was the sound of trunks scraping over the pavement. A common sight was parrots and canaries in cages being held aloft by their owners. The birds were popular pets at the time for city dwellers, a pet store having just received a large shipment. Rather than letting the birds die in the flames, the owner of Robinson's Pet Shop handed them out to anyone who wanted one.

From a lawn near her apartment on Pacific Avenue, Dr. Mahoney watched the migration westward:

From the lower section of the town the mass of people were already moving westward. All that day and all that night they passed, the inhabitants of a cosmopolitan city: French, Spanish, Italians, the dark children of African origin; Oriental, Chinese, and Japanese. They came pushing trunks, wheeling baby carriages full of household goods, carrying babies, carrying canaries in cages, carrying parrots; pushing sewing machines and trunks until the sickening sound of grating on the concrete entered so deep into my brain that I think it will never leave it.[94]

The heat, smoke, and ashes were hard on clothes. Many men and women appeared bulkier than usual because they were clothed in multiple layers of their best clothing. Some women managed to wear three suits and three skirts. Wool suits were worn over silk suits to provide protection from hot ashes.

Postal worker Roland L. Roche watched the stream of refugees trudging along Market Street in late afternoon from a hillside at Laguna Street that became known as Camp Lake. He left a memorable description of an urban population on the move during a great disaster:

It was an amazing spectacle, a living kaleidoscope: Small boys leading their dogs, men and boys on bicycles, single and double teams of horses, men and women dragging trunks at the ends of hay ropes or clothes lines, trucks laden with household goods, scavenger wagons piled high with costly furniture, express wagons, drays, hay-wagons, small carts drawn by men, or sometimes by women, baby carriages loaded to the bending point, official vehicles that whizzed by, or buggies speeding along with Red Cross workers.

In nearly every case each of these autos and buggies carried one or two soldiers, at the sight of whom the densest crowd promptly divided to give the party a passage.

But it was not an angry or sullen or shouting mob that so divided. Everybody seemed to be looking at the emergency in a manner of fact sort of way, each person bent upon saving all he could, and at the same time lending a helping hand when occasion required or saying a cheery word to his neighbor.

Roche noticed an African American man passing with a rat trap in one hand and a sack of flour on his shoulder. A woman carried a healthy young girl who screamed and kicked under one arm and a canary cage in the other.

Pets were high on the priority list. One woman had put a cat in a bird cage, while the cage's usual occupant, a parrot, perched on her other hand. Another carried a full goldfish bowl.[95]

Paul Shinsheimer, the assistant telegraph editor of the *Call*, had taken refuge with relatives in the 1400 block of Franklin Street. People passed in the lurid glow of the fire Wednesday night asking the same two questions over and over again: "Will the fire reach us?" "Will there be another earthquake?" Shinsheimer gave innocuous answers to the questions, which no one could answer.[96]

The sound of things being dragged remained with people for years afterward. One woman said, "I shall never forget that sound of dragging trunks, all night long." Another said, "The noise of these scraping boxes, the casters of the beds and couches, and chairs as they were dragged along the street is one that I can still hear."[97]

JACK AND CHARMIAN LONDON

While most people were fleeing San Francisco on Wednesday, a few were attempting to enter the city. Unless they had passes, most were turned back from the Oakland side.

Two young friends who were seeking to return home were told that only medical personnel were being allowed on the ferries. Herb Peck, an uncle of actor Gregory Peck, and Etoile Millar dressed as a doctor and nurse. They scribbled a note that stated: "Pass Dr. Peck and Nurse Millar." The signature was indecipherable; the ruse worked.[98]

From Marin County, there were no restrictions. People were going to work, returning home, seeking friends and relatives, offering their skills, or just sightseeing. Jack and Charmian London were in the latter category.

In 1906, London was at the height of his powers and fame as an author. The couple had just been married. They rode horses together, boxed, wrote and typed as a team, and called each other "mate." Their brief experience in San Francisco would solidify them further.

The earthquake shook the Londons awake in Sonoma County's Valley of the Moon. They ran to the barn, where their horses, "still quivering and skittish," had broken loose. By 6 A.M. they were in the saddle and on their way from Glen Ellen to their "Beauty Ranch," where they found the two-foot-thick walls of their half-built barn cracked. On they went to the crest of Sonoma Mountain, from where they could see smoke rising in the directions of San Francisco and Santa Rosa.

They returned quickly, breakfasted, and caught the train to Santa Rosa. They passed water tanks knocked off their foundations. "Awful ruins," said Charmian of the seat of county government. "Santa Rosa got it worse than San Francisco," said Jack. They were among the few people to see both cities on the day of the earthquake.

The Londons took the train to Sausalito and from there took the ferry to the city in the afternoon. Jack watched the firestorm develop:

At that time I watched the vast conflagration from out on the bay. It was dead calm. Not a flicker of wind stirred. Yet from every side wind was pouring in upon the city. East, west, north, and south, strong winds were blowing upon the doomed city. The heated air rising made an enormous suck. Thus did the fire of itself build its own colossal chimney through the atmosphere. Day and night this dead calm continued, and yet, near to the flames, the wind was often half a gale, so mighty was the suck.

After he landed near the damaged Ferry Building and wandered the city's streets that night, London concluded: "All the shrewd contrivances and safeguards of man had been thrown out of gear by thirty seconds' twitching of the earth-crust." He looked about him and wrote a few days later: "Not in history has a modern imperial city been so completely destroyed. San Francisco is gone." All that remained was "the fringe of dwelling-houses on the outskirts of what was once San Francisco."

The couple walked along desolate Broadway and Market streets, halted at the intersection of Kearny and Market streets, and stood in Union Square with fires raging on three sides. Charmian praised her "mate's cool judgment" in escaping the flames.

Both noted the "gracious" and courteous stream of refugees "from the labor ghetto," and, of course, the numerous trunks. "Everywhere were trunks," said London, "with across them lying their exhausted owners, men and women." The city was quiet, except for the muffled blasts of dynamite. "Surrender was complete."[99]

Jack's feet were blistered, and Charmian's ankles were sore. "Mate and I spent night in burning streets. . . . Terrific experience. Napped on a doorstep till dawn," Charmian scribbled in her diary. Jack was proud of his new wife's endurance and strength. He later wrote a woman friend: "Mrs.

London, by the way, stood with me that night at Kearny and Market, and was with me through all that 'red hell.' Remember, always, when you think of her, that she is a man's woman, and my woman."

Jack and Charmian left San Francisco early the next morning and arrived in Oakland at 9 o'clock. They checked on Jack's Oakland house, which had lost two chimneys, and were in bed by noon. They returned to Glen Ellen on Friday: "Blessed country. Long sleep. So tired," wrote Charmian.[100]

ORDINARY PEOPLE

The Londons were celebrities. It was the experiences of more ordinary people that encompassed the full dimensions of the disaster. A sampling follows:

Hundreds of Masons were gathered in the city for the fifty-second annual convocation of the fraternal organization. They were staying at hotels scattered about the downtown district. Most left town immediately after the earthquake, but about forty of them struggled to the wrecked Masonic Temple at Montgomery and Post streets at 10 A.M. for the hasty election of officers. T. F. Griswold from southern California walked past the damaged portraits of past grand masters. "It gave me a feeling of sadness to feel that even the glory of having been a Grand Master could not save one's picture from such destruction."[101]

Most slaughterhouses were located in Butchertown, which extended on a pier into the bay from the foot of Potrero Hill. On one side of the pier were the slaughterhouses; on the other were the stables for the horses that pulled the meat wagons. The stables sank into the mud, the tide rose, and two hundred frantic animals were about to drown. Men climbed into the stables and held the horses' heads above water until they could be released. Most swam to shore.[102]

Almira Hall Eddy described the devastation: "We walked through the town all day Wednesday, before the flames crossed Market Street. They make light of the effects of the earthquake, but so far as we wandered the business portion of the town was a ruin before the fire completed the annihilation. One must see it to believe it,—the devastation of earthquake, fire, and dynamite is not to be told."[103]

In letters written at the time, people struggled to find the words to match the horror of what they experienced. Most settled for "awful."

Father Henry D. Whittle, of the Society of Jesus, escaped from St. Ignatius Church and took refuge in the Holy Family Convent at Hayes and

Fillmore streets. He wrote that day: "The fire is creeping up towards the convent. It seems that this place too will go. The City seems a sea of fire." Four sisters and Father Whittle remained to guard the convent. The last sentence in his diary for April 18 reads: "If the Sisters cannot sleep, I can; I shall need strength for tomorrow and so in God's name after this fearful day, I shall go to sleep on a lounge in the Bishop's parlor."[104]

Two acquaintances encountered each other on Post Street. One said to the other, "Come along with me. I have something I want to show you." They walked to Market and Bush streets. "What do you want to show me?" asked the second man. In front of them was a store with a sign stating "M. Roth & Co, Wholesale Liquor." "There are barrels and barrels of the finest whiskey in the State of California and it's going to make one damn fine fire," said the first.[105]

Josephine Fearon Baxter, who lived in comfortable circumstances in the Western Addition, totaled up her losses:

The broken things are too numerous to mention, but I do not care as long as we are saved. And, then we fared so much better than most of the people. In the bedroom the chiffonier, dresser and everything was out of place. The globes were all smashed—it was a wonder they did not fall on Baby. You ought to have seen the kitchen and pantry. My Jap had not come and I had the clothes in the boiler for him. The water was all over the floor. In the pantry, so many things are on the floor, but not so many were broken.[106]

The photographer Ansel Adams, whose father had built a home farther out in the sand dunes of the Western Addition, was a curious four-year-old at the time. He later recalled: "It was fun for me, but not for anyone else. I was exploring in the garden when my mother called me to breakfast and I came trotting. At the moment a severe aftershock hit and threw me off balance. I tumbled against a low brick garden wall, my nose making violent contact with quite a bloody effect. The nosebleed stopped after an hour, but my beauty was marred forever—the septum was thoroughly broken." Although only a child and living far from the center of the city, the earthquake remained his "closest experience with profound human suffering."[107]

"Did you ever see a dog shake a rat?" asked Warren Olney. "We were like rats in a dog's mouth. Old Mother Earth appeared to be trying to shake us off her face."[108]

"There is nothing a man can feel, see or hear that will so impress the mind with the power of Nature as did that earthquake," said D. G. Doubleday.[109]

THE FIRST SEVENTEEN HOURS

If order can be made out of these scenes—as others have made sense of chaotic battles—then it could be said that by midnight of the first day rubble lay strewn on city streets, an uncounted number of people were injured and dead, and the fires that began in the produce district and South of the Slot were joined in a pincer movement by a third and more dangerous conflagration that originated in Hayes Valley.[110]

The fire that began when someone tried to cook in a stove to which a faulty chimney was attached at Hayes and Gough streets has been dubbed the "ham-and-eggs-fire," on the assumption it was breakfast fare that was being cooked at 10 A.M. The name, like the cow that supposedly kicked over the lantern in Mrs. O'Leary's Chicago barn, has a working-class connotation to which blame, unjustly, was attached. Again a woman—this time an unidentified cook—was blamed for a fire.

The real cause of this devastating fire does not matter; what matters is that there was no water available to fight it. Battalion Chief W. D. Waters reported: "I next drove to Hayes Valley where I found a fire starting at the corner of Hayes and Gough Sts. Engine #19 was on hand, but as no water could be obtained the fire gained rapid headway." The fire department's overall report on the three days of fire stated: "Had there been but the slightest quantity of water obtainable when this latter fire was discovered it could have easily been extinguished, but we were compelled to watch it burn and spread."[111]

The fitful winds were blowing in opposite directions. Beginning at 10 A.M., the Hayes Valley fire spread eastward and southward, while the other two fires took a westward course. It was the Hayes Valley fire that swept over St. Ignatius Church and College, the ruined City Hall, and the Mechanics' Pavilion.

The first day of fire consumed the largest acreage and most valuable real estate. The burned area included what is now the Financial District; the downtown hotel, theater, and shopping districts; and Chinatown. The perimeter lay, in a clockwise direction, from just west of the Embarcadero (then called East Street) to Powell Street and north to Washington Street; south of Market in a bowl shape from the Ferry Building on the east to as far south as Townsend Street, to Twelfth Street on the west; and the wedge-shaped Civic Center area from Eddy Street and Golden Gate Avenue west as far as Octavia Street and south to Market.

The wharves bordering the Embarcadero were fortunately unharmed, allowing access by the ferries and larger vessels, which provided a lifeline to the world. The crews from a navy destroyer and tugboat and two state fireboats kept watch on the docks and pumped fresh and salt water to the nearby fire engines. There was little else to be thankful for. The *Argonaut* narrator commented on the status of the fire at the end of the first day: "There was absolutely no apparatus or any other means whereby this fire could be arrested."[112]

THURSDAY, APRIL 19, 1906

The next day the clouds of smoke rolled skyward to a height of two miles, their lower layers dark, but the topmost billows sunlit and splendid. As evening came, a wind from the southwest blew the smoke over the Bay toward Mt. Tamalpais; the sun, like a red ball, threw a crimson light over the waters and there was more suggestion of horror than at any time. That night the big wooden houses in the residence portion were burning luridly; so that the flames rose high to heaven and glowing clouds pierced a starlit sky; the sight was one of desolating splendor.

MINING AND SCIENTIFIC PRESS,
April 28, 1906

A CHECK FALLS FROM THE SKY

Wednesday night and early Thursday morning were unseasonably warm. James Phelan left the windows open in his bedroom as a precaution against escaping gas from the broken light fixtures. His sister and three friends from Los Angeles, who had been staying at the Palace Hotel, chose to sleep outside, as they were nervous about the recurring tremors.

In San Jose, where he had extensive real estate holdings, Phelan's death had been reported in the newspaper. Evidently, someone had seen a body being transported in his automobile, which had been commandeered the previous day in San Francisco.

Phelan owned two automobiles but had the use of only one, an older Renault. He had loaned his new Mercedes to Herman Schussler of the water company to inspect the water lines outside the city. Phelan had asked Schussler to take it easy on the car, "but, with destructive obstinacy, he forced the car over impossible roads, where it finally had to be abandoned and towed back to the City for repair."

He was uncertain about the fate of the Phelan Building on that warm spring morning of the second day. He walked into the garden and asked his sister's maid if she had heard anything. No, she hadn't. She leaned down at that moment to pick up a piece of paper at Phelan's feet. She handed it to him. It was one of his cancelled checks, slightly scorched and four years old. "The building has been destroyed," said Phelan.

"How do you know?" she asked.

"Here is a messenger from the skies."

Phelan was a pack rat. Each year's cancelled checks had been kept in wooden boxes stored in the topmost floor of the Phelan Building, some two and one-half miles distant. Pieces of the millionaire's cancelled checks had rained down upon San Francisco that night.

With his chauffeur, Phelan attempted to drive downtown, but the car could not get past obstructions in the road at Mission and Sixth streets, so they turned back. Massive explosions were occurring at Twelfth and Mission. "Dynamite was being used to blow up buildings in the path of the flames," Phelan noted, "but the dynamiting was done too close to the actual fire, and the wreckage, caused by the dynamite, soon ignited, and the fire went on."

Returning home, Phelan organized a caravan consisting of his sister, her house guests, the servants, various pieces of furniture, and personal possessions, all packed into one auto, two carriages, a buggy, and a dog cart. Previously, Phelan had arranged for two wagon loads of household goods to be hauled away at the exorbitant cost of $60 (although he purchased a can of milk that day at the normal price). The caravan proceeded to Golden Gate Park, where Phelan found the entourage a camping spot located between the Japanese Tea Garden and the museum.

He returned to his home near the old mission just in time to see the cypress trees that formed a protective barrier around the grounds ignite in flames. Wind-driven brands fell on the house and grounds. Paintings and other valuable items stored in the yard went up in flames. Phelan later regretted that he hadn't buried them.

He returned to the park with a marquee tent that was used for entertaining. After making sure the party was relatively comfortable, Phelan set out to find the newly formed citizens' committee. He found it in Franklin Hall, on Fillmore near Bush Street, where it had moved from the Fairmont Hotel when the fire edged up Nob Hill.

That second night and for the next few days Phelan slept in the home of his friend J. Downey Harvey, who was also a member of the committee. Other members of the citizens' committee, such as Garret McEnerney, also found refuge there. Harvey's wife was in Europe, and his daughters had fled south to Burlingame. The male power brokers had much to talk about.[1]

RUEF'S ODYSSEY

On the other side of the political and religious spectrum was Abe Ruef, the mayor's chief aide. Less is known about his whereabouts during the three days, but some of his movements can be traced from the accounts of others.

Having been excluded from the original citizens' committee, Ruef seems to have concentrated his activities during those three days of fire mainly on ordering and advising what should be dynamited. But first, like many others, he had to find a bed.

Alice Gerstle Levison told the story of Ruef's homeless wanderings. The wife of Jacob B. Levison, the future president of Fireman's Fund Insurance Company, Mrs. Levison, her three children, and servants had fled to their country home in San Rafael on a tug boat chartered by her husband. Meanwhile, a Levison relative met Ruef on the street. Hearing that Ruef had no place to stay for the night, the relative invited him to the Levison home.

Before the earthquake, Jacob Levison had been working with James Phelan and Rudolph Spreckels to oust the prolabor Schmitz regime. Levison came home and discovered Ruef in his bed. "I came in," his wife recalled him saying, "and I saw that big nose sticking up out of my bed, and there was Abe Ruef, the man that I was fighting tooth and nail, sleeping in my bed."

Jacob Levison made brief visits to his family in the country but remained in the city most of the time. "His duty was first to watch his own property," Mrs. Levison said. "At certain hours of the evening, these men who had never held a pistol in their hand (my husband hadn't) had to act as police and watch for people looting the empty houses. He did his duty that way."

As a young woman, Alice Levison had known Ruef. "I didn't particularly like him, but he was one of the young men that I knew," she said later. Mrs. Levison said her husband fought Ruef "with vigor and integrity." The Jewish community was split on Ruef. Members of the community either abhorred him and sought to distance themselves from him or they came to his defense. What they had in common during the disaster, and for a short time afterward, was the need to help one another.[2]

Ruef used his considerable influence to direct efforts to save his commercial properties as well as his home. The *Argonaut* narrator wrote: "The Commercial Hotel, on the northeast corner of Kearney Street and Montgomery Avenue, was owned by Mr. Ruef, and particular efforts were made to stop the flames before they reached it."[3] Ruef's family home was at 422 Lombard Street. A woman neighbor vividly described in a handwritten note the attempt to save the homes on Lombard, which Ruef must have witnessed on Thursday night:

By this time the wall of fire, which fighting a north wind had been advancing at the rate of four to four and [one] half hours to a block, had reached Lombard St; barrels and vats of wine had been taken to the corner, carpets had been suspended from roofs of buildings on north side of street and men and women worked might & main to prevent the fire crossing the street, buckets of wine were poured from the roofs and with sacks dipped in wine they beat the walls, only suspending their efforts for a moment when a shout warned them a building on south side was falling; lower down on Lombard St two streams of water were playing on Mr. Ruef's property; thanks to these stupendous efforts the fire was checked on the south side of Lombard St. When turning away from Lombard St, I saw a man struck to the ground by a soldier, as he arose cut & bleeding and staggered to his feet, he was struck a second time to the ground, whether injured or not, I do not know.[4]

Despite his efforts to save them, Ruef lost his commercial properties on Market Street and Grant Avenue as well as the family home. But as well as using his power to save his own properties, Ruef used it to save others.

Jerome Landfield, the last to leave the Bohemian Club, was taken in by his close friend Frank Deering, who lived on Russian Hill. Landfield filled a leadership vacuum in the neighborhood and organized the residents to fight the fire.

Seeing flames approaching and black powder being used just in advance of the fire and thereby spreading it, Landfield became alarmed. He located Mayor Schmitz and a group of officials who were standing nearby.

Landfield recalled: "The greatness of the disaster seemed to have unnerved them. I went up to Schmitz and begged him to stop the dynamiting. I told him we had the fire under control and stopped at Greenwich Street, and that further dynamiting would imperil the rest of Russian Hill, which was now safe. But he would not listen."

Schmitz and the men around him were tense. A man from a prominent San Francisco family, and wearing one of the thousands of special police badges handed out by the mayor and police, rushed up to the group and pointed out that one particular building needed to be dynamited. The mayor told him to mind his own business. When the man wrote down the badge number of the regular policeman who pushed him aside in front of the mayor, Schmitz ordered that the man's star to be taken from him. The man was given a second push and sent sprawling from the group.

Landfield conferred with Deering and another friend. Under the impression that the city was ruled by martial law, the two men sought out General Funston at nearby Fort Mason. Funston was sympathetic but said he was powerless, since the mayor was in control. William F. Herrin, the chief Southern Pacific attorney and political operative for the railroad in California, overheard their request. "When he heard the story," Landfield wrote, "he pointed out that the one man that could handle Schmitz was Abe Ruef, the political boss of San Francisco. As luck would have it, Ruef came in while they were talking," Landfield said. "Quickly the situation was explained to him. Without a moment's delay he called his car, drove to the mayor, and stopped the dynamiting."

Ruef's action and the efforts of the residents saved the top of Russian Hill that day.[5]

THE BATTLE FOR VAN NESS AVENUE

On Wednesday night and early Thursday morning, the fire spread onward toward Van Ness Avenue. It engulfed Nob Hill and swept westward, destroying everything south of Washington Street. A number of eyewitnesses penned accounts of the westward-spreading conflagration. Marion Hooker wrote from the family's Washington Street home on Thursday:

> I never passed such a night, and I hope I never shall again. The constant apprehension of a fresh earthquake, the frequent dynamite explosions, the red sky that made the rooms all light, the fear of the approach of the fire to the old house that has been home to its occupants practically all their lives, and held the dear treasures of Aunt Bess and Uncle Osgood, the constant passing of the people of the region—the streets were crammed with people of all sorts and nationalities, many from the burned parts, many sleeping outside from fear of another demolishing shock to the houses. The Squares—Portsmouth, Union, Jefferson—were crowded with wan, apprehensive people, mostly encamped on their trunks or possessions tied up in sheets. The children and little babies were pitiful. People were passing up and

down dragging trunks, carrying baggage of all sorts, automobiles tearing here and there under police direction. The Chinese in our region were particularly numerous, scared out of their quarters by the approaching flames, which were now often accompanied with the explosions of stores of Chinese fireworks.[6]

Not all the Chinese fled immediately. Ah Wing had been a servant in the Leland Stanford mansion for nearly a quarter-century. The home on Nob Hill had withstood the earthquake fairly well. Statues and vases had fallen to the floor, but the paintings remained on the walls. On Wednesday Ah Wing had cooked his meals in the mansion, which was unoccupied except for the servants. (Leland Stanford had died in 1893, and Jane Stanford, in 1905.) The wind drove the fire toward the mansion "like a tiger" on Thursday, said Ah Wing.

About one o'clock in the night Ah Young [another servant] went out and left me alone in the house. About three o'clock he came back and asked me to leave the house. But I was unwilling. I went out and called the watchman and gardener in to watch the house with me. I saw a fire start up in the art gallery, and called the watchman to put it out. About half an hour later, a place over the front door again caught fire. I was in the house. The gardener, John, rang the bell and called me to go out. I told him that there was a fire upstairs, and I called the watchman to put it out. The watchman said that there was no water all over town. I told him that there were three buckets of water upstairs. It was put out in ten minutes.

Firemen arrived in the neighborhood, found water in an underground cistern, and directed it toward the nearby Hopkins mansion, San Francisco's first cultural center held in trust by the University of California for the San Francisco Art Institute (and now the site of the Mark Hopkins Hotel). The Mark Hopkins Institute of Art had caught fire from the heat of the nearby flames that also threatened the Stanford mansion.

"We then played a stream on the Mark Hopkins Institute," said a fire captain, "and the surrounding buildings until the supply in that cistern was exhausted." The mayor visited the engine company and exhorted them to save the institute and its treasures. They tried. "We continued working until the fire surrounded us in a very threatening manner, and to save our apparatus we had to leave there."

When the firemen left, Ah Wing packed a few personal possessions, closed the door, and departed. He was tearful and looked back to see the Stanford mansion in flames.

Ah Wing found a friend, and they camped in a vegetable garden for three days. It rained on Sunday night, and he began to feel ill. On Monday he walked to the train station at Valencia Street and departed for Palo Alto. The Stanford home in the university town was partially wrecked, but Ah Wing was employed at the Stanford museum at the same salary as before. He was grateful for the job and the fact that Mrs. Stanford had left him $1,000 in her will. But the ruins of the Stanford residences in the city and Palo Alto were too much for Ah Wing. He departed shortly thereafter for China, after leaving flowers on Mrs. Stanford's tomb.[7]

A woman of modest means who signed her letter Aunt Bertha wrote that the threat of the fire in San Francisco on Thursday had escalated greatly.

The fire had got within a block of the house by noon and the militia ordered all persons out of the houses along Hyde Street as they intended to dynamite the buildings from there to Van Ness Ave in the hope of checking the fire there. Van Ness is a very wide and beautiful street where all the fashionables live & where some of the most costly and beautiful residences of the west coast were to be seen. So at the last moment I picked up some of my little trinkets and filled my dresscase. What victuals I had I put into a little telescope [a small folding satchel] and with that slung over my shoulder like all the rest, rich and poor alike, I trudged up the street toward a hill 3 or 4 blocks beyond Van Ness where there were almost no houses at all.[8]

Twelve hours later Eleanor Watkins, whose husband Jim was a Red Cross surgeon, stood on another hill and gazed down upon the full-fledged battle being waged for Van Ness:

We staid [sic] there until after midnight, watching; by this time, the soldiers had adopted the plan of dynamiting every house that caught fire and the houses around it. The concussion of the dynamite explosions was like a slap on one's cheek. We saw the dynamite loaded into the automobiles, and the dynamited houses collapse. I saw a man take up a box of dynamite, run down a hill, and put it into a house next to the flames. I saw four soldiers in an automobile loaded with dynamite; one tire was punctured, and half of the wheel, and the automobile bumped over every stone, but never slackened speed. . . . No words could describe what we saw from that hill. Flames as far as eye could reach, on three sides a roaring inferno of fire. Where the fire was almost burned out, the squares and houses were outlined by creeping things. The sky was a horrid glare around; round us on the grass were the refugees, mostly asleep, within a square of the flames, trusting to the soldiers to tell them to move on.[9]

The breeze was light early that morning. Then an unusual east wind from the high pressure system that was pushing hot, dry desert air into the Bay Area picked up. This was good news for the unburned portions of the business and industrial sections of the city to the east but bad news for the remaining residential areas of the city to the west.[10]

The chief of the Department of Electricity toured the area between O'Farrell Street and Van Ness Avenue that morning "in the hope that there might be some cessation of the awful conditions, but there was nothing save the terrifying roar of a vast, tremendous furnace."[11]

The flames were indiscriminate. Hotels with the names of St. Francis and Fairmont; mansions of mining, sugar, and railroad families by the names of Flood, Spreckels, Crocker, Stanford, and Hopkins; places of worship named Old St. Mary's, Grace Church, and Temple Emanu-El; rooming houses, single-family homes—none were spared.

The fire worked its way down the backside of Nob Hill and headed toward Van Ness. The fire department—hampered by a lack of water, poor communications, and fatigue brought on by a second day of continuous labor—could not hold back the flames.

There was a breakout. The fire crossed Van Ness in the five blocks between Sutter and Clay streets and began to surge westward in a flanking movement. Major Stephenson, who was on his way to the Bohemian Club, watched the intense heat jump the broad avenue and ignite structures on the opposite side:

About 4 P.M. I saw the flames leap the avenue opposite two churches whose tall frontage threw a maximum of heat across. Then I saw St. Luke's church and three adjacent frame residences blown up. In one case only did it seem a total success. The large houses seemed to raise a trifle and then collapse, leaving their large chimneys looming up like spires.[12]

According to General Funston, "the fire department seemed powerless." Captain Le Vert Coleman of the artillery corps, who was in direct charge, agreed: "The fire department at this place and time was utterly helpless and unable to meet the situation."

The military went into action with a scorched-earth policy based on destroying structures far enough in advance of the flames to create an effective firebreak. Both officers emphasized in their official reports that they acted under the "general authority for demolitions" issued by the mayor.[13] The army used massive amounts of explosives. "I doubt if anyone will ever know the amount of dynamite and guncotton used in blowing up buildings," said Funston, "but it must have been tremendous, as there were times when the explosions were so continuous as to resemble a bombardment."[14]

Captain Coleman and his troops worked quickly with the proper type of dynamite on the west side of Van Ness. "Time and again the fire outflanked my small party and we were importuned by numerous property owners looking after their own interests," he said. "But the work as outlined was carried out successfully, and by getting ahead of the fire on Franklin and demolishing houses between Franklin and Van Ness on the north side of Sutter, the fire was finally stopped."[15]

The troops dragged artillery to Van Ness Avenue with horses and brought the guns to bear on targets. J. C. Cunningham, a car dealer, described how one cannon was aimed and fired by a partially blinded gunner:

I was ordered to take an army surgeon in my car to the assistance of one of the gunners from Mare Island who had been sent over with a cannon to blow up some of the buildings and stop the flames on Van Ness Avenue. The principal man had gotten his face burned, and he was suffering with his eyes. He had ceased handling the gun when we appeared, but as others were doing such poor execution it was really necessary for this poor fellow to go to his post again.

Several times I saw this man carried to his gun—he was unable to walk—aim it and fire and then fall from the concussion and exhaustion combined. The soldiers would move the gun to the next stand and then carry the brave fellow and stand him in position. He would open his eyes, take a survey of the scene and sight the gun and give the signal. Boom! A great sheet of flame and smoke was belched forth. I could see a bunch of fire sailing toward the house. In it went; then there was a great explosion and the house collapsed.[16]

One version of the battle for Van Ness Avenue was told by James Stetson, the owner of the cable car company who helped liberate medical supplies on Wednesday. The seventy-four-year-old widower watched the oncoming flames from his three-story Victorian home at the northwest corner of Van Ness and Clay streets. Built of wood with bay windows, the house had marble steps that ascended from street level to tall doors. It was one of many impressive structures on the avenue. Stetson was precise, tracking the fire with his watch and carefully assessing the damage to his home. By 2:30 P.M. the fire was approaching Van Ness.

I was in my front room watching with my field glass, and house after house took fire along the line of blaze, as I have just described. I saw many pigeons flying wildly about, seeking some place of safety. . . . At 3 o'clock the soldiers drove the people north on Van Ness and west up to Franklin Street, saying that they were going to dynamite the east side of Van Ness. From my window I watched the movements of the fire-fighters and dynamiters. They first set fire to every house on the east side of Van Ness Avenue, between Washington and Bush, and by 3:30 nearly every house was on fire. Their method was about as follows: A soldier, with a vessel resembling the form of a fruit-dish, containing some inflammable stuff, would climb to the second floor, enter the house, go to the front window, open it, pull down the shade and curtain, and set fire to the contents of his dish, and in a short time the shades and the curtain would be in a blaze. When the fire started slowly they would, in order to give it a draught, throw bricks and stones up to the windows to break the glass. From 4 to 4:30 St. Luke's Church, the Presbyterian Church, and all the houses from Bush to Washington streets, were on fire. At about this time they began dynamiting. This was called "back-firing," and as the line of fire was at Polk Street, the idea was to meet the flames and not allow them to cross Van Ness Avenue. The explosions of dynamite were felt fearfully in my house; each explosion within two blocks of my house would jar and shake the house violently and break the windows, and at the same time set off the burglar alarm. As the windows would break it tore the shades and curtains, covered the floor with glass, and cracked the walls. After it was over I found that it had demolished in my house twelve plates and fifty-four crystal sheets, each measuring about thirty by fifty inches.

"Get out of this house!" a soldier ordered the prominent businessman at 4:45 P.M. He had a bayonet mounted on the end of his rifle.

"But this is my house and I have a right to stay here if I choose," said Stetson.

"Get out damned quick and make no talk about it either."

The soldier marched Stetson two blocks west to Gough Street. Stetson watched his home, expecting to see it burst into flames any minute. As the intense heat drove the soldiers away, the old man, shielding his face from the heat with his hat and pulling his coat collar up to protect his neck, ran back to his home, arriving at 5:40 P.M.

The ravages of dynamite and fire had created a clear space around his house. Stetson thought that the house might survive the holocaust. But soon another tongue of flame threatened the residence.

The Clay Street danger began at about 7:30 P.M. At 8:15 the whole frontage . . . was blazing and at its full height. My windows were so hot that I could not put my hand on them. I opened one window and felt of the woodwork, which was equally hot. I had a bucket of water in the front and rear rooms, with an improvised swab, ready to put out any small fire which would be within my reach. I watched the situation for an hour, and as the flames died down a little I had hope, and at 10 P.M. I felt satisfied that it would not cross Van Ness Avenue, and neither would it cross Clay Street.

A small flame sprouted on the outside of the adjacent Clay Street house. Stetson offered three men, one of whom was an artilleryman in Captain Coleman's detachment, $10 to climb up and extinguish it. They did. The two civilians declined the reward, but the soldier accepted it. Stetson thought if the fire had not been put out, it would have swept westward.

At midnight, Stetson saw smoke coming from the Claus Spreckels mansion across Clay Street. An hour and a half later flames erupted from the upper stories. "I feel quite sure," Stetson said, "that if anyone had been on guard inside with a bucket of water the fire could have been put out."

The army believed its efforts were responsible for saving the Western Addition. Stetson credited the northwest wind, which providentially reasserted itself.[17]

THE NANKERVIS FAMILY

Elizabeth Nankervis and her family heard the dynamiting along Van Ness Avenue that night while huddled in a freight car in South San Francisco. "At first we did not know what it was," she said. "There would be a fearful commotion, a rumble, then severe shaking which was terrible frightening." Elizabeth also suffered from the constant glare of the fire. For the rest of her life she had to sleep in a completely darkened room, or not be able to sleep at all.

They slept that night on hard grain sacks in the freight car. It had been a taxing two days, as it had been for tens of thousands of other refugees.

Elizabeth, her husband, Will, and their five-year-old son, Will Jr., lived in a district of modest homes on Rincon Hill. Will's mother and brother lived in a house nearby. Both residences suffered minor damage in the earthquake.

As the fire swept southward, the family decided to flee. Because the previous Sunday had been Easter, they wore their new outfits: "Will, a light gray suit, myself a tailored gray suit, Will Jr., two suits, one a blue sailor suit and the other a dark red Russian blouse outfit." For the same reason the exodus consisted, for the most part, of exceedingly well-dressed refugees.

They began their trek south. Will carried a suitcase strapped to his back, Will Jr. pushed his new bike, and Elizabeth clutched a package of food and her silver knives and forks. Uncle Chris carried a heavy music roll that Elizabeth could not bear to leave behind.

Elizabeth had an advantage over other refugees. She had chosen outer garments that were made of heavy wool because she had been reading a popular novel about the Chicago fire, titled *Barriers Burned Away*. The light cotton clothes worn by the heroine in the book had forced her into the uncompromising position of having to tear off her light outer clothing in order to avoid the risk of catching fire from "the sparks that were driven about like fiery hail." The wisdom of her choice was confirmed. Elizabeth carried her new Easter hat in a paper bag. The bag burst into flames, destroying the flimsy chapeau.

"We took the straightest road away from the fire," Elizabeth recalled, "but the fire seemed to be following us, ah so swiftly, so we went on." They came to the open country of South San Francisco. The fire pursued them. As hot ashes fell on Sausalito to the northwest, so they fell far to the south.

An elderly woman of means whom Elizabeth knew slightly had become separated from her family. Someone had given her a chair, and she was sitting beside the road when the Nankervis family walked by. She joined them, with her chair.

They found the freight car and remained there for a few nights, the chair providing the only comfortable place to sit. They listened to the distant explosions and gazed in awe and fear at the crimson sky.[18]

A TRICKLE OF HELP, WHICH WILL BECOME A FLOOD, ARRIVES

For individuals and families like the Nankervis clan, it wouldn't be long before massive amounts of food, clothing, and shelter arrived. A tidal wave of goods and money, first in the form of promises and then in freight cars and hard currency, descended upon Governor Pardee in Oakland, from where it was funneled to San Francisco. At the same time, Americans were donating to the victims of the eruption of Vesuvius in Italy and a Chilean earthquake. For a short time, it seemed as if the world were falling apart.

Across the bay in Oakland, toward which most of the refugees fled, Pardee and his staff were fielding requests in the City Hall from persons seeking lost relatives. They were also responding to a flood of telegrams offering aid from across the country.

Mrs. Edgar Hobart sent a handwritten note to the governor, who was dispensing passes for transportation into the city: "My little girl is in S.F. I have just arrived from Los Angeles and must go over and find her. How can I get there?"

Colonel Horace D. Ranlett wired from Boston: "For old times sake governor, please try and locate and succor my wife who was alone at eleven twenty six Valencia St." The address was in a particularly hard-hit section of the city. Pardee replied: "Number killed and injured much smaller than at first supposed. Have no doubt Mrs. Ranlett is safe with friends."

The first telegrams offering help arrived on Thursday. Among them were the following:

George E. Chamberlain, governor of Oregon: "Twenty six cars supplies leave Portland tonight also car nurses and Doctors. Twenty six cars supplies again tomorrow. All blankets and mattresses in Portland. Train load bread and provisions every day following. Two cars potatoes one car bread leave Salem in the morning."

E. J. McGanney, president of the California Society of New York: "Californians everywhere share the agony of the awful disaster that has overtaken our state and its people. The California Society of New York will do all in its power to be of some assistance. Let us know how we can help."

California Senator Frank P. Flint, 11:48 A.M.: "Please wire me if in your opinion Congress should make an appropriation for the purpose of relief of people of our state by reason of great calamity and in what amount."

Senator Flint, 3:05 P.M.: "Congress appropriated one million dollars for relief of the people of your state."

John Weaver, mayor of Philadelphia: "Philadelphia citizens permanent relief committee authorize you and such relief committee as shall be appointed to draw on Drexel & Co. Philadelphia for any amount up to twenty five thousand dollars for relief of sufferers by earthquake." The next day Mayor Weaver increased the amount to $75,000. Four days later the total donated by the Philadelphia City Council and the Permanent Relief Committee stood at $350,000.

The first offers of help also came from the governors of Indiana and North Carolina; city officials in Wenatchee, Wisconsin, and hurricane-stricken Galveston, Texas; private businesses; the Kansas City Fruit and Produce Exchange; and the Savannah Cotton Exchange.

George C. Houghton, secretary, New England Shoe Association: "Is the need so great and the circumstances such and taking distance into account that in your opinion contributions of boots and shoes from New England would be timely and acceptable?" Governor Pardee: "Answering inquiry it will be necessary to supply footwear to many poor people whose shoes were destroyed in walking over cinders in the streets. Therefore, your proposed gift would be acceptable. Thanks."

John Sparks, governor of Nevada: "Nevada tenders condolences to California in hour of affliction. Money and provisions being raised in all parts of the state. You may depend on the sagebrush for liberal assistance. Wire us what you need in the way of emergency supplies." Governor Pardee: "You have our sincere thanks. Things needed are tents, bedding, food supplies. Also disinfectants, drugs, hospital materials. Forward everything to Relief Committee care Mayor Schmitz, San Francisco."[19]

A mass meeting was held in Los Angeles City Hall, and a general relief committee and subcommittees were organized within the chamber of commerce. The executive committee met on Thursday and pledged an immediate $100,000 to San Francisco, the money having been diverted from the Mount Vesuvius fund.

Ever-generous Philadelphia, reading of Los Angeles's demise in the same earthquake, wired if the southern California city needed help. No, it didn't, was the testy reply.[20]

Upon being awakened in New York City with news of an earthquake in San Francisco, William Randolph Hearst cautioned his eastern editors not to overplay the story. "They have earthquakes often in California," said the native of the Bay Area. A late riser, Hearst then went back to sleep. The Examiner Building at Market and Third streets was on fire by 3 P.M., eastern time.

Hearst soon discovered the seriousness of this earthquake and issued orders to his far-flung empire, which included papers in New York, Los Angeles, and San Francisco. With his usual mixture of humanitarianism and self-aggrandizement, the Chief quickly dispatched a special train from Los Angeles with forty doctors, seventy nurses, and assorted journalists. Wednesday night, while chugging north, they decided to call themselves "The Los Angeles Examiner Relief Corps."

The train arrived in Oakland shortly after noon on Thursday. A ferry boat, placed at their disposal by the Southern Pacific, quickly took them to the damaged Ferry Building at the end of Market Street, where, said one of the members of the corps, we "looked upon the scene of indescribable desolation where San Francisco had stood a few hours ago." Among those they met, they scotched rumors that Long Beach had slipped into the sea and Los Angeles was destroyed.[21]

One of the corps's young nurses, Nellie May Brown, wrote frequent notes and postcards to her mother in Los Angeles. She was afraid, "anxious" in her words; bothered by her menstrual period; and worried about her brother, Ralph, who was somewhere in the city. (Ralph wrote their mother that he was "in fairly good condition.")

"Words cannot describe the horror of the scene—people are leaving everything & are crowding the ferries & every other transport which will carry them out of it," Nellie wrote on Thursday. "The whole city will eventually be swept away completely."

The following day the young nurse was more in control of herself.

How about me. I am perfectly well and am working in the thick of the suffering—at last experiencing the horrors of the field hospital. I was in the first squad sent out & am at one of the forts—well protected & well fed. We are threatened with an epidemic of measles & smallpox & of course in the latter case, will not be able to get any mail out of the city so, if you don't hear for some time, that will be the case. . . . The city is being consumed—I have the experience of a lifetime to relate when I get home.

A pall was cast over the *Examiner* relief corps when one of the doctors fell down some stairs and the loaded revolver he carried in his pocket discharged, killing him instantly. The resilient Nellie felt "splendid," however, after a bath and a good night's sleep.[22]

<hr>

Until the promised food arrived in the next few days from outside the Bay Area, residents and refugees had to rely on what they had stored, liberated from fire-threatened stores, procured from local bakeries that still functioned, or obtained in rations from military stores that had not been destroyed by fire.

General Funston wired the secretary of war: "We need thousands of tents and all rations that can be sent. Business portion of city destroyed and about 100,000 people homeless. Fire still raging; troops all on duty assisting police. Loss of life probably 1,000. Best part of residence district not yet burned."

The Vancouver and Seattle barracks were immediately told to purchase and ship rations to San Francisco. "Greatest urgency. Have stores rushed forward without delay," ordered the commissary general in Washington, D.C.

The few military food supplies that were unburned in San Francisco, and bread from the remaining bakeries in the city, Berkeley, and Oakland were distributed on Thursday. Food was scrounged from private warehouses, hauled away by military wagons, and given to the homeless. "The gathering of food," stated the official military report, "continued until the factories and warehouses were destroyed and the men driven out by the fire."[23]

Among the immediate beneficiaries was the Nankervis family, which was living in the freight car. "Soon food began to be distributed—one package to each person," Elizabeth recalled. "We joined the line we saw forming and most of us got packaged breakfast food precooked. We ate it from the box and thankful to have it."

In order to have plates on which to eat the food, she rooted through the still-warm ruins of a pottery factory. The resourceful Elizabeth found a large dinner platter, a smaller platter, a dinner plate, and a luncheon plate to go with the silverware she had saved. "What a find! Now we could pour out our dry food on a plate and feel more civilized."[24]

THE ARRIVAL OF MORE MILITARY UNITS

The military poured into the city and, along with the paramilitary, established a massive presence on the streets and in the harbor.

The destroyer *Preble,* the fire tug *Leslie,* and the tug *Active* had steamed south from Mare Island Navy Yard. The sailors—along with a small detachment of marines, the army tug *Slocum,* the revenue cutter *Golden Gate,* and two state fire boats—concentrated their efforts on saving the waterfront and keeping that vital transportation link open.

Fire lines were run as far as one mile inland, and salt water was pumped onto flaming buildings to no avail. Firemen and sailors were hampered by frequent breaks in the hoses and the fact that the federal and municipal standards for hoses and couplings differed.

Steaming north from off southern California, the *Chicago,* the flagship of the Pacific Squadron, and the *Marblehead* arrived Thursday night. The crews of the smaller vessels that had been fighting the fires were dizzy from fatigue, many having had no sleep or food in two days. Their feet were blistered from the heat. "Our men were now on the verge of collapse and were approaching hysteria," said one officer.[25]

Infantry troops from Alcatraz Island and Angel Island and artillery troops from Fort Baker in Marin County swelled the ranks of regular army troops in the city on Thursday. General Funston, who could no longer call the Phelan Building his headquarters, established his base of operations at Fort Mason. More regular army troops would arrive from the Vancouver Barracks and the Presidio of Monterey. The number of federal troops was close to two thousand.

Even before the official orders were issued by the state's adjutant general, and without the governor ever having declared an emergency, National Guard and California Naval Militia troops were in uniform, armed, and on the streets of San Francisco. Eventually there were some fifteen hundred militia in San Francisco. National Guard companies in Oakland, Alameda,

Santa Rosa, San Jose, and Santa Cruz patrolled the streets in their respective cities. Eventually, all but one of the state's National Guard units and the Naval Militia were activated.

With regular army and state militia troops, uniformed University of California cadets, regular police, two special police forces, and neighborhood vigilante groups on the streets, the result was confusion. It was a commander's nightmare. "The National Guard had been called into service and had acted independently so far," Funston said, "with the result that regular troops, militia, and police were scattered indiscriminately over the city."[26]

The state university's greatest contribution was its uniformed students. The Berkeley campus had sustained little damage, certainly nothing to compare to the ruins at Stanford University, which was closer to the fault line. Some books fell from the shelves in the library, a few chimneys toppled, and some fragile equipment broke in the chemistry building.

The earthquake occurred on the morning of the annual inspection of the Corps of Cadets. By noon a rumor spread that the cadets would be going to San Francisco. There was a run on local stores for supplies. For the first time, the cadets were issued live ammunition; each cadet received five cartridges.

Four hundred and fifty cadets left at 9 P.M., and another 150 embarked on Thursday. On the way over they joked—until they saw the flames.

With no tents, few blankets, and little food or water, the students began the boring routine of four hours on and four hours off of guard duty. They patrolled within an eight-by-twenty-six-block area in the Western Addition that was not threatened by fire. The cadets scrounged candy bars and cookies from shuttered grocery stores. Some drank thick cream and were sick. A few fortunate students slept in the homes of fellow cadets.[27]

The cadets returned to the university, where classes had been cancelled, three days later. They left behind one cadet who had been shot and wounded by a drunken regular army soldier.

After pulling guard duty early Thursday, Corporal Irvine P. Aten of D Company and his college roommate walked a dozen blocks to watch the fire making its way toward Van Ness Avenue. A regular army soldier who was busy keeping citizens from entering their homes by cursing and pointing his gun at them asked the two cadets to clear out the grocery store–saloon at Polk and Eddy streets.

Aten and his roommate were armed only with bayonets and were hesitant to plunge into "the howling, drunken, fighting, mob" until they were joined by two other cadets armed with revolvers. The four pushed their way into the saloon and hustled the men toward the door, leaving the women and children who were seeking groceries. Aten heard a shot. As he reached the door he was hit in the thigh by a second shot.

Several more shots were fired into the ceiling of the store. "There was no excuse whatever for this shooting," Aten said. "We Cadets were clearing the store without having to resort to strong measures. No material resistance was being offered, and a random shot into such a crowd of men, women and children could not be justified." A civilian was also wounded.

Aten was taken to the Presidio Hospital, where there were two other victims of gunshot wounds: "One of these was a Chinaman who had been a prisoner and tried to escape. He was shot through the head and subsequently died from the wound. Another was a Japanese that ran away when a soldier challenged him, and was shot through the hand, the head, and the shoulder. He recovered." There was an unconfirmed report that a patient in the woman's surgical ward had been hit by a stray bullet. Aten almost lost his leg, but he eventually recovered.[28]

The six hundred regular police officers on the streets were augmented by the Special Police and the Citizens' Special Police. Both were throwbacks to the days of gold rush vigilantes. On Wednesday, under the auspices of the civil government, two thousand Special Police were appointed. One thousand badges were handed out on Thursday by the citizens' committee, which had no legal status, to their Citizens' Special Police. A Civil War veteran and retired National Guard colonel was in charge of screening the volunteers.

There also were informal neighborhood groups. "Vigilantes Are Doing Their Duty: First of Its Kind Since Early Fifties at Work" read the headline over the approving *Examiner* story about one volunteer unit whose commander had fought in the French army and served in the U.S. Navy.

The neighborhood groups patrolled the area just east of the Presidio under the constraints of General Orders No. 1, which included the following advice: "A rash display of arms is absolutely forbidden, all guards being particularly cautioned not to show their weapons unless it is imperative and their use only resorted to when there is an absolute necessity." The group's outstanding accomplishment was the arrest of a drunken regular army soldier, who was handed over to military authorities at Fort Mason.

The main qualifications for the special police were that applicants had to know somebody or seem to be somebody, preferably reputable. Ironically, considering that there was a great fear of syndicalism, one of the best accounts of Citizens' Special Police activities was written by a union organizer, Charles Ross.

For Charles Ross, the earthquake was a lark. The Nova Scotian was an organizer for the pressman's union and a Jack London wannabe. He lived with his brother on Fillmore Street in the Western Addition.

Ross had literary aspirations. He had left Nova Scotia "to get literary color," "to broaden my mental horizon," and "to seek adventure." He wrote a friend in Toledo, Ohio: "I could not ask for more. And I like it all—the excitement, the uncertainty, the danger, the adventure." The earthquake had given him an appreciation for "the tremendous forces of Nature." Ross first served in the vigilante group commanded by the veteran of the French army.

In our immediate district we formed the first <u>Vigilanté</u> that has been formed in San Francisco for 50 years, and I was among the first to enlist. We named our band "Golden Gate Vigilant Committee." We received permission to carry arms and patrol the district. The city is nominally but not actually under martial law. It is our duty to halt all suspicious persons and if necessary arrest and march them to the military provost guard; to see that all lights (only candles are used) are out at a stated hour—8 o'clock at first while the city was burning, and 10 o'clock now; to see that everyone digs closet and garbage vaults in their yards as the house closets cannot be used owing to lack of water; and to arrest or <u>shoot</u> anyone caught setting fire to buildings. . . . Many men have been shot in the last few days for stealing from the vacated houses and for attacking women.

The union man was proud that he was chosen from the ranks of the vigilantes to be one of the Citizens' Special Police. Two thousand men were personally examined by the retired colonel. "One thousand men were sworn in [by a superior court judge] as special police, and the last 40 of the number were taken from our Committee ranks. I was one of the 40, together with my brother and nephew."

Alas, Ross faced no dangers. He patrolled from 2:30 A.M. to 5 A.M. without serious incident. Ross expected even "greater lessons" from life in the future and was fatalistic about the present: "We are here today—where tomorrow? Kismet! Well, so be it."[29]

"KILL"

The military and quasi-military forces shot and killed an undetermined number of people beyond the officially declared totals. To civilians it was difficult to tell one uniform from another, but those in uniform knew the difference. The regular army tended to blame the militia in those cases that received public attention. The citizen soldiers were clearly to blame in some instances, but so were the regular army troops in others.

The stories of witnesses who were not prone to exaggerate and who did not write for publication tell of an undetermined number of bodies that were dumped in the bay or disposed of in the fire.[30] The exact number, or even an approximate tally, of citizens killed by the military and the overall total number of fatalities is unknown. It was, as Charles Ross said, "impossible yet to estimate the number of the dead, and perhaps the true number will never be known."[31]

Ross and others estimated that "many men" were shot. General Funston waffled when he stated that there was no "well-authenticated case" of a single person being killed by regular army troops. Two men, he said, were shot by the state militia. General Greely, in his official report, said nine men died violent deaths, two having been shot by the National Guard and one by a marine. (There were more, as letters and news accounts indicate. One researcher placed the number at 490. I doubt if the number exceeded 50 or 75 such murders, which was no small amount.)[32]

The best-documented death involved a member of the citizens' committee. It was extensively documented because, like a similar incident in Chicago, the victim was of some importance in the community. The shooting deaths of ordinary people received little or no attention.

Heber C. Tilden, a businessman working for the Red Cross, was returning at midnight from Palo Alto in a car marked with a Red Cross flag. With him were his military escort, Lieutenant R. B. Seaman, and another man.

Tilden was driving the car on Guerrero Street when it encountered a roadblock set up by volunteer guards at Twenty-second Street. As he had at other roadblocks, the lieutenant yelled, "Red Cross." The car proceeded onward. A warning shot was fired into the air. Other shots followed from the group of men.

The car swerved left and stopped. Seaman jumped on the running board and returned the shots with his revolver. Tilden, staggered out of the car and fell across the curb. He died a few minutes later.

Three vigilantes, judged to be men of "good character," were arrested. Their rifles were still warm. At the September trial, they said the car failed to stop, so they fired, thinking the occupants were looters. Their defense was that they were following orders from a National Guard colonel and had heard that looters were using autos. They thought martial law was in effect.

Superior Court Judge Carroll Cook, in his charge to the jury, said that "mere orders and proclamations" from civil or military authorities did not make laws. Martial law was not in force; civil law was. Judge Cook explained the confused situation that existed at the time.

> As a matter of history—and the Court and the jury must take cognizance of history—everything was greatly disturbed after the fire. It is also a matter of history that the entire community believed on the afternoon of the 18th and the morning of the 19th that martial law had been declared.
>
> Therefore, if the defendants honestly believed, and circumstances were such as to lead them to believe that they were under martial law, and if the evidence proves that the mistake removes any criminal intent, then the defendants were incapable of committing a crime.

The jury took eighteen minutes to return a verdict of not guilty.

Other fatal shootings of people involved marines, regular army, and National Guard troops. Stray dogs were also shot, and some citizens believed that they, and not the dogs, were the targets of the poor marksmen.[33]

A Mormon journal published a private account that provides an example of what was not reported, what did not go to trial, and what was not officially documented. The Mormon leadership in California, which was then headquartered in San Francisco, was camped in Jefferson Park on Thursday. Walking back to their camp, they passed a large grocery store that was about to be destroyed by fire. The police gave them permission to enter and take what they needed. They filled their pockets and arms, took the supplies back to the camp, and returned for more.

"Inside, Elders Gardner and Franklin Badger froze when an armed officer first ordered everyone out and then shot and killed the man standing beside them," according to their account of the incident. "Dropping their baskets and raising both hands over their heads, the elders rushed out, 'glad to get out with our lives,' Elder Gardner said." It was then they discovered that they had entered a different store.[34]

The story of another unreported incident was related years later by Ernest W. Cleary, an orthopedic surgeon who in 1906 had been a member of the university's cadet corps. He carried a Springfield rifle, and his greatest fear was that he might have to use it to shoot someone. His orders were "to shoot and shoot to kill" suspected looters.

A crowd, armed with sacks, was poised in front of a liquor store. Cleary prodded them with his bayonet, and they dispersed. A woman ran up to the young cadet and said, "I just saw something awful. A man saw that the fire was coming and opened his grocery and told us to 'help ourselves.' A man came out with his arms full of groceries, and a soldier ran up and stabbed that poor man with his bayonet."

Free liquor was available not only to civilians but also to soldiers. Cleary was patrolling on a steep cobblestone street. "Down the middle of this hill staggered and stumbled a soldier in regular uniform. His tin cup was jingling at his belt. As he approached me he said, 'I kin hear everything jingle but money.'"

The family of National Guardsman Elmer E. Enewold hoped he didn't have to shoot anyone. The San Francisco guardsman, who believed that martial law was in effect, wrote his family that he had had only one such experience.

> One evening during guard duty over the ruins at the end of 3rd St., I saw a man about a quarter of a block away from me bending over something on the ground. I yelled at him to get out but he paid no attention to me, so I up and fired at him. I missed, of course, but the shot must have scared him for he started to run. I was just getting ready to shoot again, when a shot was fired from across the street and the fellow toppled over. This was fired by a regular who had seen him run after my shot was fired. When the two of us reached the fallen man we found he had been shot through the neck and was stone dead. It proved to be a Negro. An officer came along and ordered us to throw the body into the still burning ruins, so in it went.

Price gouging exacted a lighter sentence than suspected looting. While on guard duty in the Panhandle, the long thin portion of greenery extending eastward from Golden Gate Park, Enewold saw the driver of a bakery wagon charging fifty cents for a loaf of bread.

Of course, this was outrageous and the poor people could never afford a price like this, although one or two had bought being they wanted it so bad. But I knew that the majority would have to go without so I leveled my gun at the driver and told the people to line up and get a loaf apiece. Well, Pa, we cleaned that wagon out in a couple of minutes and the crowd thought I was just o.k.[35]

A number of accounts told of soldiers, both regular army and National Guard, engaged in looting.

Charles D. McArron, who was twenty-five years old and lived on Twelfth Street in Vernal Heights, was ordered by a soldier to come with him. There was no choice, said McArron, as the soldier carried a rifle on which was mounted a bayonet.

The soldier entered stores that sold firearms and helped himself to the guns. He gave McArron a .22-caliber rifle to carry for him. The soldier entered a glove factory and, with the owner standing by helplessly, took an expensive pair of gloves. He told McArron to help himself, but the young man said he had no use for gloves.

A French bakery was churning out bread day and night. The soldier apparently felt some compulsion to guard it. He ordered McArron to stand guard with the rifle and to prod the crowd with the bayonet while he napped. "After all this work, I was given a couple of loaves and then released," said McArron.[36]

A soldier in a hospital unit wrote to his mother: "One of the soldiers quit his guard and broke into a jewelry store and stole $2,000 in money and about $1,000 worth of diamonds, but the other soldiers caught him and put him in the guard house."[37]

The military also sanctioned several cases of what might be termed benign looting. On the second day the troops were getting ready to dynamite the businesses and homes near Polk and Sutter streets. An army officer told some kids to help themselves to the goods in Blum's Candy Store.

"This was a dream come true," said Sol Lesser, then sixteen years old. "All that good candy!" A dozen youngsters piled boxes of candy on the sidewalk. They loaded them onto the caboose of a Sutter Street cable car, pushed the disabled caboose to the top of a hill, and coasted down to the corner of Laguna and Sutter streets, where they distributed it to the neighborhood. "Some took the candy doubtfully," said Lesser. "Others didn't quite understand and didn't take any, so we got stuck with a lot of it."[38]

Meanwhile, a young woman was going through an experience that would enable her to dine out with ease in the famous salons of Paris and to entertain the likes of Picasso, Matisse, and Braque with stories of the earthquake and fire.

Harriet Levy had graduated from the University of California at a time when few women went to college. She was a drama critic for the *Call*. Her next-door neighbor on O'Farrell Street was Alice B. Toklas. Another neighbor was Sarah Samuels, who married Michael Stein, brother of Leo and Gertrude Stein. Sarah and Michael Stein moved to Paris in 1903.

Levy and Toklas were close friends. A subdued Toklas served as the housekeeper for her grandfather's all-male household at 922 O'Farrell Street. Once a year she escaped the confines of her dull existence in San Francisco and sampled the bohemian lifestyle in Monterey and Carmel. Levy accompanied her friend on one of those jaunts.

Levy and her mother lost their home at 920 O'Farrell in the fire. They spent a night in a hotel where members of the Metropolitan Opera Company had taken refuge. Levy recalled a German baritone, who was wearing the coat of a Japanese emperor. The semicostumed singer looked up to the sky and declaimed: "Gott in Himmel was ist denn." The drama critic in Levy thought the scene was appropriate under the circumstances.

It was stories such as this that Levy and Toklas took with them to Paris in 1907 when they visited the Steins. At first they felt uncomfortable among the couple's artist friends. Levy recalled:

> The next night when we went to dinner at the Mike Stein's one of the guests asked me where I came from. I said San Francisco. All faces turned to me with curiosity and interest.
>
> "Were you there during . . . during the earthquake?"
>
> When I said yes, questions awoke in all the eyes.
>
> "You were in San Francisco at the time of the earthquake?"
>
> Yes, we said, we were there.
>
> In a moment we had become guests of importance. Everybody listened to us. We had something to say that interested them. Our knowledge of the recent earthquake was an accomplishment. We knew something that everybody wanted to know about.
>
> Suddenly we were at home.

At once we became "friends of the Steins who had been through the earthquake in San Francisco."

Any sense of inadequacy, of being in an intellectual world beyond our background, left us.

The two women realized that they could dine out on these stories only so long and considered embroidering them. Then an earthquake in Messina diverted attention from their experiences. Gertrude was attracted to Alice, and Harriet returned home, to a city she had difficulty recognizing in 1910.[39]

STANFORD UNIVERSITY

The world's attention was riveted on San Francisco, but intense dramas were also unfolding to the south at Stanford University and Agnews State Hospital, in San Jose, and in isolated communities in the Santa Cruz Mountains; to the north in Santa Rosa the story was much the same. The immensity of the disaster in these communities was proportionately greater and more noticeable because, unlike San Francisco, they were small, isolated, and cohesive.

As the noted psychologist and philosopher William James, brother of the novelist Henry James, was preparing to embark for a year at Stanford University the previous December, a Harvard University colleague remarked: "I hope they'll give you a touch of earthquake while you're there, so that you may also become acquainted with *that* Californian institution."

Some people, like James, are turned on by earthquakes. He was one of the founders of the philosophy of pragmatism, which held that the meaning of an event lay in its observable and practical consequences.

When the earthquake hit, all the chimneys in the house where the Jameses were staying were knocked down, and the living room was filled with bricks. James ran into his wife's bedroom, declaring: "This is an earthquake. Are you frightened? I am not, and I am not nauseated either." Perhaps the most intellectually acute mind to experience and later write about the earthquake, William James said he felt no fear.

In my case, sensation and emotion were so strong that little thought, and no reflection or volition, were possible in the short time consumed by the phenomenon.

The emotion consisted wholly of glee and admiration; glee at the vividness which such an abstract idea or verbal term as "earthquake" could put on when translated into sensible reality and verified concretely; and admiration at the way in which the frail little wooden house could hold itself together in spite of such a shaking. I felt no trace whatever of fear; it was pure delight and welcome.

James gave the earthquake a threatening human form and believed that others did, too. It was the very earthquake his colleague had predicted. It "stole in behind my back, and once inside the room, had me all to itself, and could manifest itself convincingly." Others, to whom James spoke, agreed. It was aimed at them, they thought.

But what was "it"? To some "it" was a demonic power, to James "it" was his colleague's earthquake, and to others "it" was "a living agent" of destruction. To science, James said, earthquakes were "simply the collective *name* of all the cracks and shakings and disturbances that happen."

James drew a distinction between earthquake myths and science, siding with the former. "I realize now better than ever how inevitable were men's earlier mythological versions of such catastrophes, and how artificial and against the grain of our spontaneous perceiving are the later habits into which science educates us."

Mrs. James walked to the Stanford quad and Encina Hall to view the damage. When she returned home, she found her husband cleaning up the mess.

The philosopher visited San Francisco by automobile late Wednesday. He was interested in observing human behavior, not material ruins. "The faces, although somewhat tense and set and grave, were inexpressive of emotion," James observed. "Physical fatigue and *seriousness* were the only inner states that one could read on countenances."

Mrs. James was worried about her husband. "All night at intervals came the booming of the buildings in San Francisco which they were dynamiting to stop the fires. William did not get back until nearly 11 o'clock. I had spent a day of great anxiety about him and a certain loneliness on my own account," she wrote relatives in the East.

James returned to the city eight days later and was struck by two impressions: "the rapidity of the improvisation of order out of chaos" and a "universal equanimity." The "natural ordermakers," like James Phelan, had immediately come to the fore. Although there was suffering, James detected "a steadfastness of tone" that did not degenerate into complaints. He thought that might be due to the nature of California, which makes "all possible recuperations easier." In a poorer land "the outlook on the future would be much darker."

James posed some interesting hypotheses, which represented the height of public discourse on this event. (In comparison, the Lisbon earthquake of 1755 engaged the minds of Rousseau, Voltaire, Kant, and Goethe.) Viewed from a distance, James theorized, "mental pathos and anguish" seem greater. "At the place of action, where all are concerned together, healthy animal insensibility and heartiness take their place."

Mrs. James wrote friends and family that there was good news. Both were well. They had an oil stove, so they could cook. The term had ended precipitously, and William was "jubilant at getting through his lectures." They would be returning home soon.[40]

The Stanford students had no such Jamesian musings.

Fearing another earthquake, most of the students and faculty slept outside. "The vocal babble of early-waking girls and boys from the gardens of the campus," James observed, "mingling with the birds' songs and the exquisite weather, was for three or four days a delightful sunrise phenomenon." In the midst of a glorious spring, the students were happy to be alive.

The campus thirty miles south of San Francisco had been isolated from the world on Wednesday. Smoke had obscured the sun, and all that night a red glow was visible to the north. Reliable news was just beginning to seep south on Thursday.

University administrators assessed the damage. Only one student and one university employee were killed at Stanford, where newly constructed buildings and architectural embellishments lay in huge heaps of native sandstone. A student observed: "Just imagine if it had come later in the morning and we had been in classes." On Easter Sunday 2,500 students and faculty had been crowded into the now ruined Memorial Church.

While the University of California across the bay at Berkeley sustained damage to income-producing properties in San Francisco, the damage at Stanford was to the gleaming new physical plant of the fifteen-year-old university. The loss of income and loss of structures evened out the harm done to the two institutions.

To a sophomore sleeping in Encina Hall, where the student was killed,

"The most noticeable part was the noise of falling buildings. They roared in an astonishing fashion. I remember seeing the new library and the church spire go. They didn't fall exactly, they just settled as if they had been made of sand." The 150-foot stone chimney on the university's power plant fell, killing a fireman inside.

The church spire, modeled after the one at Trinity Church in Boston, was a grave aesthetic and engineering mistake for a Mediterranean-style structure in earthquake country. A dome of Spanish design would replace the spire, said Stanford president David Starr Jordan. The president referred derisively in his private correspondence and conversations to the insistence of the Stanfords on beautiful structures to the detriment of educational priorities. He referred to the architectural era dominated by the Stanfords as the university's "Stone Age."

A reporter talked to faculty members unhappy about the emphasis on grandiose architecture and then wrote that corners had been cut in the newest buildings "in an effort to erect pretentious but in reality cheap and gingerbread structures."

Jordan answered the criticism: "I suppose it was a mistake not to consider the possibility of an earthquake in drawing the plans for the construction of the university buildings, but we all supposed that this section of the country was immune from temblors."

Jordan was not only a teacher and administrator but also a writer published widely in various disciplines, including geology. He vowed, "Everything in the future will be, so far as it may be, earthquake proof." (Stanford's buildings were damaged again in the moderate 1989 Loma Prieta earthquake.)

Privately, Jordan told a confidant that "not every ruin demands respect. Some of ours do, and some do not." The church, whose mosaics, stained glass, and organ were still intact, was an "exquisite ruin." He added, "But the new Library, Gymnasium, and Museum Annex, crushed like a pie set on edge, we have no feeling for. They have kept us impoverished for long tedious years."

While most classrooms and core educational facilities were intact, the newest "showy buildings" (Jordan's term) suffered the greatest damage. Charles Derleth Jr., an associate professor of engineering at the University of California, surveyed structural damage all along the fault line. "Considering earthquakes," Derleth wrote in a book edited by Jordan, "I do not think the main type of structure at Stanford was happily chosen." The buildings were too rigid, too high, and lacked "unity and coherence of frame." An architect and two civil engineers reported to the Board of Trustees that most of the $1.8 million damage was the "direct result of the disregard of simple constructive principles, both of design and workmanship."

Besides Memorial Church, the Memorial Arch, the art museum, the new geology building, the new gymnasium, and the unfinished library building were wrecked. The brick Stanford residence on the campus was heavily damaged. One of the more telling touches of the earthquake was the headfirst plunge of the statue of the famed Harvard geologist, Louis Agassiz, into the ground so that it rested like an arrow that had been shot into the air. Existing geological knowledge had, in effect, been turned on its head.[41]

Alumni and potential donors were given a much less bleak assessment. The university was young. Discouragement was unknown in California. Stanford alumni would be loyal. "Daring and forceful spirits in the East will flock to a university where things happen and the very rocks are alive with energy," Jordan predicted. The university reopened in August for the new academic year.

Jordan remained at Stanford, although he had been offered the presidency of "one of the great institutions of the East" and had been asked if he was interested in heading the Smithsonian Institution. He wanted to put Stanford on a firmer foundation. "I shall stay with the poppies, the perfect sunshine, and the shadow of the great Temblor," he said.

One of the advantages of the earthquake cited by Jordan was that the nearby fault would serve as an excellent teaching and research tool. Two high school students took advantage of the proximity of the San Andreas Fault.[42]

Olaf P. Jenkins, who lived with his family on the Stanford campus, and his friend George Branner bicycled over the coastal hills to the San Andreas Fault in Portola Valley. (Jenkins would one day head up the California agency that investigated earthquakes. Young Branner was the son of John Casper Branner, the chairman of Stanford's Geology Department and the successor to Jordan as president.)

They found an oak tree split in two. The branches of other oak trees had swept the ground around them when they rose, fell, and twisted as the seismic waves passed underneath. The youngsters passed the displaced and telescoped water mains leading from Crystal Springs Reservoir to San Francisco. "Very few people at that time had given a single thought to earthquakes," Jenkins wrote seventy-five years later, "and even now it takes a lot of explaining to get the fact across."[43]

The mentally disturbed patients at nearby Agnews State Hospital were not as fortunate as the students at Stanford University. At Agnews, the design and construction of the structures were a matter of criminal negligence.

The imposing hospital, known as "the great asylum for the insane," was opened on 276 acres of land five miles north of San Jose in 1888. Shaped in the form of a cross, two three-story ward buildings protruded transept-like from the four-story administration building. The architectural goal—besides adding useless ornamentation and a grandiosity that was not warranted—was to house "the largest number of inmates at the least possible expense." All the structures were constructed of brick or stone. Enoch A. Van Dalsem was the builder.

Most of the deaths occurred in the soaring great hall in the administration building. A total of 112 persons died: 101 patients (out of a total of 1,103) and 11 members of the staff. They were killed when the flimsily constructed brick buildings that lacked mortar collapsed. Three of the four turrets that served as ornamentation and passageways between floors buckled. The deaths at Agnews constituted the largest verified number at a single location.[44]

The screams of the injured patients, numbering between 125 and 150, were horrific. It took rescuers days to dig through the rubble. The living were mixed with the dead. There was this description of the first day:

> The sight that met their eyes was one to make strong men weep. The buildings, so imposing in their magnitude, were razed to the ground, and in the gray light of the early morning hundreds of terror-stricken unfortunates were seen huddled in little groups beneath the palm trees. Awful consternation prevailed and the survivors seemed paralyzed with the terror the calamity had struck to their hearts. The four floors of the Administration building crashed in a mass to the basement and from the ruins arose the cries of the injured that were pinioned beneath the weight of the timbers. The stillness that followed the rumble and roar of the earthquake was broken only by the moans of the wounded—those who escaped were dumb with fear.

Patients shimmied to the ground on knotted sheets. One raised a ladder so that the hospital's superintendent, Dr. Leonard Stocking, and his family could climb down from the second floor. Temporary operating tables were placed under trees for the injured. County sheriffs from around the state, who were meeting in San Jose, and students at nearby Santa Clara College (now the University of Santa Clara) rushed to the scene along with others to render aid. The county morgue and local undertaking parlors were filled to overflowing with bodies.[45]

Rescue efforts began almost immediately and achieved some successes. Angelina Kell, a sister of the county coroner, had fallen from the fourth floor. After some hours, she managed to attract the attention of rescuers by waving one free hand. They dug and found her lying beneath four dead bodies. For days after the earthquake, rescuers heard a strange noise in the ruins of the administration building. They dug and dug. Each day the sound became weaker. Finally, on April 23 they reached the dying victim, a parrot in a cage; the parrot recovered quickly.

A San Jose newspaper reporter visited the hospital grounds on Friday. "The scene of the inmates on the park grounds is heartrending," he wrote. "Tents to shelter all have not been secured and many are provided only with blankets and mattresses." There was cooked food now, but there had been none earlier. "The violently insane have been confined in an enclosure where their cries add to the terror that still envelops the place." Earlier, they been chained to trees.[46]

The remaining administrative staff had set up a headquarters under a large tree on the lawn of the hospital. They were besieged for information by worried relatives and friends of the patients.

Stanford history instructor Payson J. Treat and a dozen students arrived on Saturday to help.

> As soon as we saw the buildings we realized what a catastrophe we had escaped at Stanford. The main building was a four story brick building several hundred feet long. In places the back of this building had fallen in. Almost all of the roof had fallen in on the top story. Corners had fallen out. One of the large pavilions detached from the main building was wrecked. Can you imagine the scenes at this asylum on that morning?
>
> It was 5:13 o'clock. Light had come but the sun was not up. The place must have been a veritable hell with the shrieks of the insane, the cries of the wounded and dying, the wild rush of every one for safety. The attendants who escaped injury had to aid the injured, capture the violent and even protect themselves from the persons they would rescue. So people who were there that day say the attendants

acted as if dazed. They made no effort to rescue the insane but worked frantically to dig out the physicians and attendants who were pinned under the debris. The maniacs were herded in one place and guards were prepared to shoot any who tried to break away—whether any were shot I cannot tell. The women who grew violent were hand-cuffed to posts and trees.

One hundred of the most violent patients were transported by armed guards on special railroad cars to Stockton State Hospital. The less violent were released to their relatives. A dozen sheriff's deputies patrolled outside the grounds.[47]

Superintendent Stocking reported, "All the brick buildings of this Hospital are so badly damaged that they can not be occupied." Only one-fourth of the once-grand administration building stood, and it had "yawning cracks from top to bottom." The engineers prowled through the wreckage, looking for answers. A report by Grove Karl Gilbert of the USGS noted:

Perhaps the worst example of poor design, bad workmanship, and poor materials in the earthquake territory, except in the city of San Francisco, is the insane asylum at Agnews, about 6 miles northwest of San Jose, consisting of a main building surrounded by a number of others—all flimsily constructed brick structures with timber frames. The construction of these buildings, with their thin walls (in many places devoid of mortar) and light, insufficient wooden framing, indicates a criminal negligence that is appalling.

Charles Derleth, the engineering professor, also visited Agnews. He commented:

Of all the destruction that I saw, and I visited the whole disturbed area, this cluster of buildings exhibited the most complete earthquake destruction, with the possible exception of the City Hall buildings in San Francisco. They are both public structures. Is it not time for California seriously to realize the situation?[48]

The worst example of journalistic misinformation—in fact, a case of outright fabrication—was committed by a correspondent for the *Seattle Times*. Three hundred inmates at Agnews rioted, R. W. Boyce wrote, and killed eleven guards and attendants. Hospital officials retaliated with rifles and revolvers. Boyce wrote:

> None but the leaders—brutes among the unfortunates—were singled out, but picked they were, and at every explosion some frenzied, fear stricken patient fell. There were 300 insane men and women, the mild among the violent thrown out of prison walls in the twinkling of an eye. One among them beat out the brains of a fellow patient, and the sight of blood, the screams of terror and the horror of it combined to make such a bedlam as the pen of history is seldom called upon to record.

Governor George Pardee, who had a temper, responded heatedly: "Boyce's lying account of the mythical horrors at Agnews is, however, the masterpiece of this unconscionable and absolutely indecent liar."[49]

Dr. Stocking reported to the governor on April 26 that he had the situation "fully in hand and all is going orderly and well." Stocking was being optimistic. The superintendent sought to curry favor with the governor, but he rebuffed Pardee on one matter. Stocking desperately needed more staff. When Pardee recommended that Stocking hire a qualified woman physician for one of the many vacancies, the superintendent told the applicant: "There will be no appointment of a woman physician to this Hospital for an indefinite time to come." Stocking was evidently being protective. A woman doctor had perished in the earthquake.[50]

SAN JOSE

The nearby downtown district of San Jose, in what is now the heart of Silicon Valley, was a shambles. It had been crowded with visitors the night before the earthquake. The annual convention of California county supervisors and a meeting of state sheriffs were under way in the small city of twenty-one thousand inhabitants.

Whole sides and fronts of stone retail and office buildings collapsed. In the center of town on First Street, a row of a half dozen buildings teetered to one side. Most of these commercial structures were occupied by stores with large windows; upper stories were supported by no more than stilts. Government buildings, public schools, and churches fared no better. Ninety percent of the chimneys in town were knocked down.

Fire swept the downtown area, spreading north and south and engulfing San Jose's tallest building, the five-story Dougherty Building, and other structures. There was water in the hydrants, however, and the blaze was soon brought under control.

A dentist was killed in the Phelan Building, where two women—including the dentist's wife—were pulled from the wreckage with minor injuries. The Phelan Estate suffered the most extensive damage of any single property owner. Nine Phelan buildings were destroyed.

The annex of the Vendome Hotel collapsed, pinning fourteen people in the ruins. All but one were pulled free. A former state senator recalled: "My room was up on the second floor, but when I picked myself up, I was in the basement of the building. I crawled up and out over the debris and escaped through a window on a level with the ground. After getting out I found this was one of the third story windows." His experience was similar to those who escaped from the Valencia Street Hotel in San Francisco.

Outside the commercial area, a lamp fell during the earthquake, igniting a rooming house at Locust and Santa Clara streets. Seven roomers, including one family of four with two children and another couple with a baby, were trapped and burned to death. A total of nineteen were killed in San Jose, and there were many injuries.[51]

When Derleth visited San Jose, he found the same design and construction flaws that he had witnessed elsewhere. "Again we find cheap construction with lime mortar, weak framing and insufficient anchoring for floors and roofs." The conclusions of the USGS were similar.[52]

San Jose quickly adopted a fortress mentality. The local militia company was called out shortly after the earthquake by the clanging bell in the fire tower. Martial law was declared, the newspapers said, but who declared it was never announced, and it is very doubtful that it had been done in a legal manner.[53]

The warnings to potential looters were more severe in San Jose than anywhere else. Flyers were posted to deter the mobs of San Franciscans thought to be headed south. They stated: "WARNING!: NOTICE IS GIVEN that any person found Pilfering, Stealing, Robbing, or committing any act of Lawless Violence will be summarily HANGED. VIGILENCE COMMITTEE." Another proclamation was posted by the mayor, setting a 7:30 P.M. curfew and warning: "All lawlessness will be repressed with a heavy hand." There was "practically no vandalism" in San Jose, the *San Jose Daily Mercury* later reported.[54]

A mass meeting was called by the chamber of commerce and the merchants' association. Most of the discussion centered on whether San Jose should welcome or repel refugees from San Francisco. The discussion at the meeting proceeded thus:

E. K. Johnson said: "This accommodation of outsiders is a very serious matter. We must look to ourselves. What about sufficient supplies of meat and bread, after the two weeks' of meat and bread which Mr. Doerr guarantees? I would ask the Southern Pacific, if possible, to keep the people of San Francisco away. There are 200,000 people homeless in San Francisco. I know that some of them are coming here. We must look out for ourselves.

"Now, I want to give this meeting a cheerful message from ex-Mayor Phelan. I met him in San Francisco, told him of our condition here and he said: 'We must stand together to build up San Jose. Look out for this crowd [referring to the refugees]. They are not bad, but they are hungry.'"

"I am willing to share my first loaf with them," said Sam G. Thompson.

"That is all right, but don't invite them here," said Mr. Johnson.

"Let us not advertise that we will take care of them," said Sam Rucker.

The chair: "Let us provide ways and means for whatever necessity may arise, but first let us take care of ourselves."

The discussion continued. A county supervisor said that thirty thousand refugees, most of whom were walking, were on their way to San Jose. "If they come here, they will eat us out of house and home in three days," he said. Ralph Hersey, the chairman, said his brother was at that very moment in an automobile determining the number of people who were descending on San Jose. One man suggested that the refugees be routed to Stockton, although Stockton had its own reservations about accepting outsiders.

Besides the militia, the town was adequately protected. One of the organizers of the meeting pointed out: "A [vigilante] committee of about 350 has already been formed that will hang any person caught in the act of robbery." There were loud cheers. He continued, "The Mayor, Chief of Police and Sheriff are with us. We will also post placards around town giving warning to that effect."[55]

In the remote Santa Cruz Mountains to the west there was silence. Then the word spread about what the shaking earth could do to tall trees, steep hillsides, and fragile humans. Along Hinkley Creek, twelve miles northeast of Santa Cruz, "the mountains are said to have come together," reported the local newspaper. At first, seventeen lives were thought to be lost.

Landslides cut the inhabitants of Boulder Creek off from the remainder of the world. A high school teacher recalled: "A wave of terror swept over the little town as we realized that we were virtually trapped in our narrow canyon."

The tops of redwood trees and chimneys alike snapped and collapsed. To the north, in the direction of distant San Francisco, a huge plume of smoke rose in the air. The chill of isolation swept over the mountain community.

A small hill, thickly wooded, had slipped into the creek, carrying trees with it. Only a few intrepid horseback riders could cross the landslide to summon help from Santa Cruz.

Elsewhere in the mountains the roar of the churning avalanches of earth and huge trees and boulders descending in a solid wall fifty or sixty feet high sent sleeping loggers running for the hillsides in their BVDs. Some made it; others did not.

One observer described a landslide in the following manner: "Hundreds of great redwoods were swept down, crushed, broken and buried in the pathway as if they were mere twigs. Below the [ridges] that were swept away a canyon or gulch of timber was encountered and this was filled over a hundred feet deep with the debris and the remainder passed over it with a resistless sweep."

On Deer Creek, nine miles northeast of Boulder Creek, two men were killed by falling redwood trees. The bodies were carried into town and laid out in the Elks Hall, there being no undertakers in Boulder Creek.

The rumors of deaths persisted. A runner rushed into town and said that a landslide had buried sixteen or twenty loggers while they were sleeping in their tents near a sawmill.

Six days after the earthquake the millwright of the Loma Prieta lumber mill, located twelve miles northeast of Santa Cruz on Hinkley Creek, arrived in San Jose with more precise news of the rumored tragedy. He brought with him two small boys, sons of the mill's master mechanic, who had been killed in the landslide that claimed eight of his coworkers. The terrified boys had been spending their Easter vacation with their father in the mountains.

The millwright described the landslide to a reporter: "The speed of the landslide was extraordinary. It slid to the bottom of the mountain and filled the gulch with a mass of debris. . . . The mountainside where the land fell was swept bare of vegetation. Massive redwoods and pines were jammed on top of the mill in the gulch below." The deadly slide dropped five hundred feet, covered twenty-five acres, and was three hundred feet deep where it came to rest in the bottom of the canyon.

The nine men were sleeping in the cookhouse and three cabins. Two men who also slept in the cabins had left minutes earlier to start the fires in the mill's donkey engines. They were unharmed.

Forty remaining mill employees dug frantically. The bodies of a man, thought to be the foreman, and his dog were found standing upright in the river of mud. They were frozen in the act of running from the massive slide. A redwood tree over one hundred feet tall moved with the mass of material. It stood erect, like a stately monument, marking the buried logging camp.

Loma Prieta, a nearby prominent landmark, was also the name given to the 1989 earthquake that rocked the Bay Area. The epicenter of the 1865 earthquake experienced by Mark Twain in San Francisco was also in the same general area. Loma Prieta means "dark hill." [56]

SANTA ROSA

For years before 1906, wrote Santa Rosa newspaper columnist and historian Gaye LeBaron eighty years later, "promotion-minded" newspaper editors had minimized or neglected to mention the existence of earthquakes in the City of Roses. [57]

Like San Francisco to the south, Santa Rosa was ravaged twice—first by earthquake and then by fire. The shoddily constructed buildings in the business district sat on an alluvial plain twenty miles from the fault line. It was a recipe for a disaster that was proportionately greater than what occurred in San Francisco.

Charles Derleth, who traveled the entire break, said that while the events in San Francisco greatly overshadowed Santa Rosa's plight, "in my judgment, proportionately speaking, Santa Rosa's loss was greater than that of San Francisco." He attributed the widespread destruction to the poor quality of mortar, which crumbled to the consistency of sand when squeezed, and to the placing of brick buildings with little internal bracing and no firm attachments to foundations atop shaky soil.

"At Santa Rosa," said Grove Karl Gilbert of the USGS, "the destruction was greater than in any other section affected by the earthquake, and the fire that followed completely wiped out the business section of the town, which suffered a greater proportionate total loss than San Francisco."[58]

J. Edgar Ross, who published a pamphlet of dramatic photos of the Santa Rosa disaster, was more plainspoken. The deaths, he said, resulted from "the great American passion—a desire to get the largest possible returns from the smallest possible investment." Within a minute, Ross wrote, the earthquake "converted the beautiful City of Roses into the City of Ruins."[59]

Two quite different men who had visited both cities agreed on the relative degrees of destruction. They were Motley Hewes Flint, grand master of the Masonic order in California, and Jack London. Flint focused on the relative extent of losses to merchants in both cities and the greater proportionate loss in Santa Rosa. London believed simply that Santa Rosa "got it worse" than San Francisco.[60]

Devastating fires followed the shaking, and there was no water to fight the flames. As in San Francisco, Santa Rosa's resident hotels (the Occidental, the Grand, and the St. Rose) and the large public structures (the Sonoma County Courthouse, the Hall of Records, and the Free Public Library) were in ruins. Stories of ghouls stripping rings off the dead and biting ears to loosen earrings circulated.

There were, however, major differences between the two cities. Little notice was taken of Santa Rosa's plight outside the immediate area, it being a city of merely some ten thousand inhabitants. The flames consumed mainly rubble after the earthquake had caused most of the damage in Santa Rosa. No explosives were used to halt the fire.

The descriptions were quite graphic. The *Santa Rosa Press Democrat* managed to print a two-page newspaper on Thursday. "A Dreadful Catastrophe Visits Santa Rosa" was the headline over the story, which began:

A frightful disaster overtook Santa Rosa yesterday. Just as dawn was breaking, a mighty earthquake struck the city. It came with awful force and suddenness, hurling many people from their beds. Before the terrified community could realize what had happened, the entire business section was a maze of ruins, every residence had been more or less damaged, some being completely wrecked, and approximately half a hundred or more people had been swept into eternity. Flames immediately broke out in all directions and lent additional horror to the scene.[61]

J. W. Brown rushed outside when he felt the first movements. He heard a "great noise" to the west and saw treetops waving. As the noise and movements approached, he grabbed a small tree only to have it torn from his grasp. The ground undulated in a series of two-foot waves. The dome on the nearby courthouse lurched three times, then collapsed.[62]

In a series of descriptive letters to her two sisters in Sacramento, Jessie Loranger Lamont imparted a sense of human pathos. With her family, she walked through the downtown area on Wednesday morning.

The sight that met our eyes was terrible. Fire was raging in a half a dozen different places. Men were digging and chopping in the ruins of what had been hotels and lodging houses trying to get out those buried beneath the falling timbers and debris. As we went down B Street at Mrs. D. N. Canther's, the body of a man lay on a door covered with a sheet on the lawn near the gate. Women were crowded everywhere crying and everyone near the fire had household goods packed to go as soon as the flames got nearer. Although men worked with all their might the water pipes were broken and a very small amount of water was available. Chas., in helping with the hose, got his eyelashes burned off. The heat was overpowering and all that saved [the remainder of] the town was the absence of wind.

Later that day they began to hear rumors that San Francisco was on fire and that a huge tidal wave had destroyed the city. They verified the fire when a "lurid red" and smoke were seen on the horizon to the south. Jessie wrote her sisters on Thursday:

Santa Rosa is totally destroyed and no one knows how many lives are lost. The business houses are all destroyed—nothing left of Fourth St. and the adjoining streets. The earthquake threw down all the large buildings and they are a mass of debris—what did not burn. . . . Miles Peerman [a former constable] was burned to death in the Carither's block when they nearly had him saved. His sister escaped. . . . The courthouse is down. You can't realize it until you see it. Everyone here are living in tents. . . . Pa and Ma lost all they had in the store and it will pretty near ruin them. . . . Our real estate is worth nothing here now. You couldn't give it away to many people. Oh, I can never feel the same here. The horror of it is beyond description. . . . It is very warm here and I am afraid the conditions will be very bad if they do not get the bodies out but it seems they can't make much impression. I can hear the axes chopping as I sit here writing. . . . If the earthquake had occurred a little later a great many more would have been killed, but as it is the death list keeps growing. I saw dead men covered with sheets lying on sidewalks and lawns where they carried them at first. Now the Christian Church is turned into a morgue. . . . The list of the dead is now 68, but there are still lots missing and the hospitals are full of wounded.[63]

An account of the man burned in the wreckage and the quandary faced by his potential rescuers was also given by Monroe H. Alexander:

A man by the name of [Peerman] was held down by wreckage in the Carither's building in plain view of the people. They did their best to dig him out, but the heat of the raging fire became so intense that they could no longer stay by him. He then begged them to shoot him. So he was burned to death fully conscious of his approaching fate.

The total of fatalities was officially listed as sixty-one, although, like San Francisco, that was a minimum number. The death toll was probably around one hundred. Besides the missing, Alexander referred to others not brought to the coroner's attention, such as "a poor Chinaman or an Italian whom nobody seemed to know."[64]

The residents thought, mistakenly, that Santa Rosa was under martial law. The troops from a Petaluma National Guard unit patrolled the city. Immediate aid came from the surrounding towns: Petaluma, Ukiah, and Sebastopol. Later, Philadelphia and Pittsburgh diverted a small portion of their money to Santa Rosa, whose relief committee eventually collected $60,000.[65]

Martin Read, who lived on a ranch five miles north of Santa Rosa, brought thirty-six dozen eggs to town to sell on April 24. The dead bodies that had not been recovered were beginning to smell. "Santa Rosa is a pitiful looking sight at present, 4th st is nothing but a mass of brick and broken timber. Martial law prevails, and several more have been shot for robbing the dead." Read sold the eggs on credit for twelve cents a dozen.

Jessie Lamont and Martin Read were grateful to be alive. "We are a lucky family to be saved," said Jessie, who was bothered afterward by earthquake nightmares. "We are very thankful to be in the land of the living," said Martin.[66]

THE SECOND TWENTY-FOUR HOURS

Back in San Francisco the fire was halted at Van Ness Avenue late Thursday. Three personal accounts of separate fire fronts that very long day are particularly vivid.

Episcopal Bishop William F. Nichols began the day with a church, then lost it. Grace Church had recently been strengthened. It had withstood the earthquake with little damage, but the fire destroyed the church and diocesan house at California and Stockton streets. Little was saved except the costly communion service dating back to 1856 and the parish records.

Bishop Nichols fled to Lafayette Park, just west of Van Ness. It was "almost black with people." There was an elevated view of the fire immediately to the east, and from his balcony seat, he described the dramatic scene:

> We sat there hour after hour saying little, but awed by the almost incredible panorama before our eyes. There was nearly a semi-circle of furious flame, and a sky of smoke receding from the immediate foreground as far as the eye could reach. Over there on the hill a cloud of flame would swoop down with cyclonic force upon a whole block of frame buildings and engulf them as in a furnace. On the far horizon, darting masses of fire would throw radiance against the sky with startling searchlight effect. Just below us there would be periodical detonations of dynamite, followed by snapshots of burning timbers and sparks, as the fierce battle to keep back the fire went on.[67]

After the fire, Nichols journeyed to New York City to confer with the Crocker heirs. It took them twenty minutes on board their steam yacht *Elsa II* to decide to donate the land on which the ruined Crocker Mansion had stood. The new Grace Cathedral would rise to the west of the old Grace Church on the crest of Nob Hill.

Another thrust of the fire was halted that night to the southwest, near Mission Dolores. The squat mission in the Spanish style, completed in 1791, had withstood the shaking. The four-foot-thick adobe walls and the tile roof supported by redwood logs remain in place to this day. But the soaring Gothic church constructed of bricks in 1876 adjacent to the mission was a total loss.[68]

It had been a hectic day for James Phelan. After taking his sister and her maid from Golden Gate Park to the greater safety and comfort of the Burlingame Country Club on the peninsula, Phelan and his chauffeur returned to the burning city Thursday night. The road was brilliantly lit by the glow of the flames. It was bright enough to read a newspaper.

A fireman rushed from the sidewalk and attempted to commandeer the car. Phelan explained that he was a member of the citizens' committee, showed his special police badge, and asked for what purpose the car was needed. To haul dynamite, he was told.

My chauffeur nudged me not to consent, but I said, "Get aboard. We will bring the load for you as it seems to be important. So he stepped in the tonneau, and, when we arrived at the [trolley] car barns, without a word, somebody began, as though they were waiting for the car, to load it with sticks of dynamite—all in silence, and the fireman took his position on top of the load.

I told him I was not familiar with dynamite, and asked whether there was not a danger of it exploding, in case the auto was wrecked. He said he thought not, and, holding aloft the dynamite caps said, "These are the only things that can explode it, and I will hold on to them." The care with which my chauffeur drove the car over the rough roads was extraordinary for him. He seemed to be going over velvet streets.

We heard the explosion of firearms, and I asked old "Charon" who sat on the "sticks" whether a rifle or pistol shot would explode the dynamite. He said, "Possibly."

We arrived at a point—21st Street near Dolores—at the head of the fire, and a crowd gathered around us to ask what the news was. I said that we had a load of dynamite, pointing to it, and the crowd scattered.

The dynamite was carefully unloaded, and the fire was actually stopped at, or in, that neighborhood, due to the blowing up and destruction of all inflammable matter in its path. When the fireman asked me to return for another load, I said, "No, commandeer another car. I have other work to perform," feeling that I had fulfilled my part of the original bargain of transportation. I had no zeal for the work. I did not get to bed until after two A.M.[69]

Phelan would not discover until later Friday morning that his home near the mission had been destroyed by the flames.

———

Typing amid the ruins and crosses marking the hastily buried dead in Portsmouth Square, Henry Anderson Lafler, an editor on the *Argonaut*, described the view he had seen earlier from the crest of Russian Hill:

Evening came, and again the city flowered in terrible red gorgeousness. About eight o'clock I stood on the balcony of one of the seven or eight houses that lie scattered on the very crest of Russian Hill. Only a few persons have been so adventurous as to build there. There are trees, and shrubbery, and grassy spaces. From the balcony there is, on any day, a magnificent view of the gray city, the blue shimmering Bay, and the green Berkeley hills beyond. That night—last night— the line of flame made an almost perfect running V, its easternmost corner south of Telegraph Hill, its point due south of Russian Hill, its other side touching Hyde, near Sutter. Chinatown and the district south of it was burned clean away. The white asphalt streets running through the black squares whereon flickered little green, blue (copper and lead, perhaps?) and red flames, made the effect of some great strange, sinister plaid, wrought upon the loom of the earth.[70]

FRIDAY, APRIL 20, 1906

On the day following the fire had pretty well exhausted itself and a dark murk of drifting smoke hid the ruins of the proud city of the Argonauts. But it was a quiet clear day, one of California's best; the sun that had set in a mist red as blood, rose resplendent and full of life-giving promise. Already with the unconquered energy of a people that has developed a continent, the inhabitants began to talk of the re-building that was to give them another and a more beautiful San Francisco.

MINING AND SCIENTIFIC PRESS,
April 28, 1906

THE BATTLE FOR RUSSIAN HILL

The fire persisted through the third day and into the early morning hours of Saturday. Dynamite, once again, was the match that ignited a new fire that burned eastward from Van Ness Avenue, over Russian Hill, and to the waterfront on the northeast edge of the city on Friday. This last major fire was the product of human ignorance and foolishness.

Like tufts of hair atop a bald head, two small groupings of structures would survive within the fire zone because of the actions of residents and employees. As the fire swept eastward on Friday, the first patch, atop Russian Hill, was saved by the residents of that exclusive enclave and their friends.[1]

As of noon Friday, it seemed that the fires had ended. Jerome Landfield believed the neighborhood was safe from the flames, the firefighters having beaten them back on the south side of Russian Hill.

Then the unexpected happened. I was standing in a garden, looking down on Van Ness Avenue. Suddenly I heard a dull explosion, followed by a cloud of dust and debris just below me. Then came a fresh burst of flame. I went down at once to investigate. It appeared that the authorities had turned again to dynamiting and were using black powder. With this they had blown up the plant of the Viavi Company, a patent medicine concern, and in doing this had ignited thousands of gallons of alcohol that were stored there.[2]

The Viavi Company complex was located on the corner of Van Ness Avenue and Green Street. Firebrands shot into the air and ignited homes to the north and east. A strong west wind, prayed for the two previous days as the fire ate its way westward, fanned the flames in an easterly direction that would, in the next eighteen hours, consume fifty blocks in the northern sections of the city.

For a time the fire threatened Fort Mason, where General Funston had his headquarters. "I directed that fences and a number of outbuildings be torn down and that men be stationed on the roofs of buildings," said Funston. But the fire did not reach the fort.

A detachment of artillery corps troops had been responsible for dynamiting the firebreak along Van Ness Avenue. But no single entity—either military or civilian—took responsibility for the destruction of the Viavi plant. It was as if the incident never officially happened.[3]

Choking smoke, falling cinders, and the crackling of fresh flames once again filled the thick air with a miasmic stew. The fearful residents believed a fiery plague had descended upon them. They made their way in small, stark knots or as lone silhouetted figures past blackened ruins and through the buckled streets that by then bore no familiar landmarks.

The sweetly cloying stench of corpses, charred building materials, and personal belongings stuck to live bodies and frayed garments that had not been washed in days. Mary Austin described the scent as "a strange, hot sickish smell."[4]

Some of the residents who lived on the crest of Russian Hill, like the prominent Livermore family, remained to fight the fire. Time and again the residents were driven by threat or gunpoint from their homes, but they managed to sneak back and continue their efforts. "The stories have but one beginning and one end," wrote Lafler. "They begin with the criminal idiocy of the military; they end with the surmounting heroism of the citizen."[5]

Katherine Hooker's brothers, Osgood and Edward Putnam, fought the fires on and around Russian Hill. Hooker was critical of the firemen: "No doubt the firemen worked. Perhaps some of them wisely, but the limp intelligence of a good many the moment the hose gave out seems to have been a feature of the occasion."

A fire captain, stung by the criticism of his department's performance, offered a defense: "In order to correct the erroneous impression that our Fire Department was not up to the standard of efficiency," Captain T. J. Murphy of Engine Company No. 29 said in his written report, "I would state that had it been possible to obtain water we would have been in a position to extinguish the fires that had originated immediately after the earthquake." That was a debatable point.[6]

The firemen were confronted by an impossible situation. Their chief was dying, they had little or no water, they had lost most of their firehouses and much of their equipment, they had no alarm system, they had little communication between the separate units, they were inexperienced in the use of explosives that spread the flames, they worried about their families and homes, and they were exhausted.[7]

The military were also criticized for their actions on Russian Hill. They threatened to dynamite the few houses. Another member of the Hooker family, Marion, wrote:

> Norman Livermore and Mr. Meyers were fighting fire at the back of their house, where their outbuildings and parts of their fences were already burning down, a supply of coal there adding to the danger. Norman was threatened by the military again and again, but each time he was forced to give way he eluded them and after keeping out of sight for a time returned, stealing up and extinguishing tongues of flame which had started, and finally stamping out the burning grass that was on fire ten inches from the wooden walls of his home! Thus only by persistent disobedience to the authorities was the group of houses saved in the end.
>
> Why these same authorities wished to dynamite this little settlement, separated by cliffs and green slopes from the surrounding streets, is one of the many unsolved questions of the time.[8]

Seventy-year-old Horatio Putnam Livermore and his son Norman B. Livermore were ordered to leave the family home at 1023 Vallejo Street twice by soldiers. They returned the third time, the soldiers having fled.

With the help of water from a lily pond in the garden and a rainwater cistern in a nearby empty lot, they managed, with the aid of Meyers (an employee), and some local boys to beat back the flames. They saved not only their homes but also the houses of their neighbors who had fled. The climax came when the agile boys, "with a wonderful disregard of heat and danger," said the elder Livermore, climbed out on the roof of the family home with wet sacks and extinguished a burning cornice.

There was a lesson to be learned, said Livermore, who had surveyed the damage elsewhere. "It was inconceivable how houses like the Floods [and] the Crockers, which stood in their wide gardens, so remote from contact with others, should have been destroyed and the conclusion is irresistible that it was because they were abandoned after their roofs ignited. Had they been patrolled by a small band of fearless, active, cool headed fighters, like those who saved our hill, I am confident they could have been saved."[9]

Attorney Osgood Putnam was critical of the peremptory manner of the authorities and the decisions they made. "I myself," he said, "am no approver of the sentimental optimism that prevailed during the weeks after the fire in praise of everybody and everything. In my opinion, there was practically no danger of anyone being burned to death by being permitted to enter his own residence or office."

Another attorney, Frank Hittell, cited examples of soldiers looting homes and prohibiting citizen volunteers from helping exhausted firefighters. In one attempt to cross a line to help, Hittell was struck on the side of his head with a gun barrel. On Russian Hill a marine and an army soldier were caught looting separate homes by the occupants, but they were not arrested by their colleagues.[10]

At least in one case on Russian Hill, however, the military distinguished itself. E. A. Dakin, a Civil War veteran who lived at 1654 Taylor Street, had a large collection of American flags. Before fleeing the onrushing flames, he hoisted his largest flag and dipped it in a farewell salute three times.

A company of the Twentieth Infantry, just arrived in San Francisco, saw the flag dip and rushed to the house. They lathered window frames with wet mud. One spot under the eaves continued to smolder. Four soldiers held a comrade by his legs while he leaned over and doused the hot spot with a charged bottle of soda water, thus saving the four-story house.[11]

From the vantage point of the crest of the hill, Marion Hooker was among the residents watching the city burn. She wrote:

As well as they could for the blinding smoke they watched the last act of the drama from this spot. The fire tore over Hyde Street ridge, swept down the hills, crossed the plain below, and met the conflagration on Telegraph Hill—the whole progress one wild swirling rush. All the valley north of Russian Hill was now on fire at once, and it burned all night till everything inflammable was consumed.[12]

SAVING THE POST OFFICE AND THE WHISKEY

One of the other undisturbed patches of ground in the fire zone was the two blocks bordered by Montgomery, Jackson, Battery, and Washington streets. The commercial prize that *everyone* sought to save was the A. P. Hotaling & Company whiskey warehouse adjacent to the Appraiser's Building within this rectangle.

The narrator of the *Argonaut* series credited the saving of three thousand barrels of whiskey to the management of Hotaling, who "were strong-minded and influential enough to persuade the military to allow them to save that property." He continued:

> There can be little doubt that had more latitude been allowed by the military to competent citizens in various places and at various stages of the fire an immense amount of property that was abandoned under compulsion by orders of the soldiers might have been saved. The inflexibility of military discipline, however, prevented the intelligent exercise of any such latitude except in the case of the Hotaling property. Thus it happened that while millions of dollars worth of normally non-inflammable material was reduced to ashes, some three thousand barrels of highly inflammable whiskey were preserved intact in the very heart of the tremendous holocaust.

Saving structures took not only individual initiative in defiance of the authorities, but also cooperation with them. The military and federal employees cooperated with each other at the main post office, the U.S. Mint, and the Appraiser's Building, which resulted in those governmental structures being saved.

Of the three federal buildings, the gleaming new granite Post Office at Seventh and Mission streets, which also housed law courts and other government agencies, has had the most lives. Cosmetically but not structurally damaged by the earthquake—the warped cobblestone streets outside bearing mute testimony to the force of the seismic waves—refugees temporarily sought rest on the lawn behind the building.

Fire licked at the beaux arts structure, seeking entrance through the windows. Soldiers ordered the postal employees out. Ten remained. They dipped canvas mail sacks into an indoor water tank and beat the burning woodwork. The intense heat blew tin cans into the air, fractured marble slabs, and cracked the recently completed mosaic ceilings and tile walls. By nightfall on the first day, they had saved the building.

The main post office was back doing limited business on Friday. Anything, whether with or without postage, that had an address on it was forwarded, including, in the words of a postal employee, "bits of cardboard, cuffs, pieces of wrapping paper, bits of newspapers with an address on the margin, pages of books, and sticks of wood."

Three days later, after surviving earthquake and firestorms, the post office nearly succumbed to human foolishness when the civil and military authorities began dynamiting partially standing structures in the immediate vicinity. Warned ahead of time, only a handful of employees remained at work as salvo after salvo reverberated through the neighborhood.

Every remaining pane of glass in the post office was shattered, marble cornices tumbled, doors were torn from their hinges, and law books were blown from shelves. The damage from explosives added $100,000 to the total cost of a half million dollars needed to repair the building. (The structure was damaged again in the 1989 Loma Prieta earthquake. Renovated and seismically retrofitted, the building is now the home of the United States Court of Appeals for the Ninth District, the most liberal and controversial such court in the country.)

The saving of Hotaling also involved cooperation, but the impetus behind the effort differed. Besides the obvious appeal in saving the whiskey, which piqued the interest of the military, the firm had an extremely competent and innovative manager.

Edward M. Lind, the firm's cashier and manager, arrived at the combined office and warehouse early Wednesday morning and immediately took charge. Meanwhile, dynamite—furnished by the president of the California Powder Works, John Bermingham, who was also the U.S. inspector of steam vessels and had an office in the nearby Appraiser's Building— "exploded with unfortunate and unexpected results," said Lind. "Instantly thereafter the adjacent buildings burst into flames, and the conflagration, apparently lashed into greater fury by the explosion, swept westward along the low roofs of buildings until it reached the east wall of the Montgomery Block." Bermingham, who set other explosions that day, was later said to be drunk.[13]

Water from a cistern was played on the whiskey warehouse. Some of the cornices caught fire, but a fireman climbed to the roof and chopped them off, thus saving Hotaling's on the first day.

The military arrived on Thursday with orders to save the federal buildings "at all hazards" and to dynamite the Hotaling structure, if necessary. Lind and the business manager took their case to Captain Orrin R. Wolfe. They argued: "On account of the large stock of whiskey in the warehouse, the consequences of a dynamite explosion would be the immediate combustion of all this vast amount of highly inflammable spirit, which would flow all over the place in a liquid wave of flame, and be virtually certain to destroy instead of save the adjacent Appraiser's Building."

The alternative, to which the captain agreed, was to move all the stock two blocks to a vacant lot. The waterfront was scoured for men who would work for $1 an hour. To roll barrels of Old Kirk whiskey and be paid for the effort was an attractive proposal. Eighty men, termed a "mixed lot," were hired. They included at least one safecracker, who later opened the company safe.

The company's more reliable employees were armed with pistols, furnished by the army, to serve as a deterrent to looting. Armed guards were placed around the barrels stored at Jackson and Battery streets. They were paid $25 for the night and were instructed by the army to shoot to kill anyone attempting to steal the whiskey.

Shortly after midnight the area was threatened for a second time. By then twelve hundred barrels had been moved. By linking hoses from a navy tug, water was obtained, and the whiskey was again saved.

The wind shifted on Friday, and the Viavi fire approached. "This was a bad fire," said Lind. "The shacks went like tinder, and a whole block would be destroyed in thirty minutes." More barrels were rolled to the vacant lot. Ropes and pulleys were used to lower the heavy casks. Two broke.

There wasn't time to eat, but there was time to drink. Despite the mayor's prohibition against the sale or distribution of liquor, the barrel rollers were given ale and stout "for their sustenance," said Lind. "In this way our force was maintained intact and enthusiastic."

By noon another thousand barrels had been moved. The fire was bearing down on the warehouse. The nearby Barbary Coast, normally the scene of much debauchery, was an inferno. The barrel rollers were extremely nervous and refused to enter the warehouse, which they thought might explode. The barrels were rolled outside to them by braver employees.

The management gave up. The iron shutters were closed, and the building was abandoned. Hotaling employees walked to the Appraiser's Building to give the military a hand. Government clerks were removing records as cinders fell all about them.

Suddenly the wind shifted and hope was reborn. Lind and the others had an idea. They obtained two wine pumps, dropped the ends into a sewer and salt water seep in a construction site, and pumped "a *compote* of the sewage and seepage" onto the stored casks.

A bucket brigade was formed to carry the potent mixture to the Hotaling building. The sludge was accidentally dropped on Lind. "It was horrible," he said. There was no time to bathe and change clothes. "One side of Jackson Street was a roaring fury of flame," said Lind, "with walls toppling and smoke choking people." The buckets kept coming, and "the evil-smelling stuff made a steam that was suffocating as it evaporated on the roasting woodwork."

The warehouse was saved by the application of the foul concoction on Friday night, and the next day the whiskey was rolled back. All other stocks of whiskey in the city had been destroyed. The company turned a preacher's words about the burning of the sinful city into an advertisement for its product.

> If, as they say, God spanked the town
> Because it was so frisky,
> Why did he burn the churches down,
> And save Hotaling's whiskey?[14]

A REAL HERO

If there was a hero, it was neither General Funston nor Mayor Schmitz, both of whom were praised lavishly but both of whom colluded in the disastrous dynamiting that spread the fire and in the shooting of unarmed citizens. If there was a single hero, it was Navy Lieutenant Frederick N. Freeman.

For three days Freeman was decisive, organized, and tireless. Freeman and his men were chiefly responsible for saving the four unburned areas on the east side of the city: the produce and factory district on the east and south sides of Telegraph Hill; the federal Appraiser's Building and other buildings within the enclave that also housed Hotaling's whiskey; the warehouses, factories, and residences south of Howard, east of Main, and north of Townsend streets; and the waterfront along East Street, as the Embarcadero was then known. They lost the residential area on Rincon Hill because they were unable to recruit enough volunteers.

Additionally, the navy forces under Freeman's command managed to pump water and operate linked hoses as far as one mile inland, furnish salt water to city firemen to douse flames, deliver fresh water for the boilers of the firemen's pumpers, quench the thirst of civilians, establish an emergency hospital, and patrol the waterfront in the almost total absence of the police.

Saving the waterfront was a remarkable achievement in itself. Had the waterfront gone up in flames, escape and the landing of supplies would have had to be shifted to more remote and less-developed sites to the north and south of the central city. There would have been no departures from the Ferry Building and other nearby slips. The walk through and around the flames would have been longer, and the death toll would have been higher.

Supplying fresh water to people who were "piteously crying" for a drink was also no small matter. The heat generated by the unseasonably hot weather combined with the high temperatures of the flames caused intense suffering.[15]

Praise for his efforts was heaped upon Freeman in letters to his superiors after the fire. The president of the State Board of Harbor Commissioners wrote of the efforts of Freeman and his men: "Had it not been for their great assistance, we would never have been able to have present almost intact the entire waterfront of San Francisco." An executive of Hotaling wrote, "We believe to him [Freeman] is due the saving of this block." Nine prominent businessmen, headed by P. S. Rossi, president of Italian-Swiss Colony, credited Freeman with saving their properties at the base of Telegraph Hill.[16]

Freeman had certain advantages over others. The wall of flames to the west isolated him from higher-ranking military commanders and civic officials. He was the virtual general and mayor of the waterfront from 10:30 A.M. on Wednesday, when he arrived off San Francisco in command of a small flotilla from Mare Island Navy Yard, to when his force was relieved on Monday. And Freeman had water, which was lacking elsewhere in the city.

A photo of Freeman depicts a craggy man with a lean, angular face and a lithe body that seems poised to jump out of his chair. Midshipman John Pond later said of his commander:

> Lieutenant Freeman had no instructions with regard to his position as far as preserving order was concerned, but he was not a man who would wait for instructions before taking action in an emergency. He was a born leader of men, a skipper whose men would go to Hell and back for him. I can hear him now, "Come on, men, sock it to 'em!" and they did.

In the absence of uniformed police, Lieutenant Freeman assumed complete control of the entire waterfront district. His orders were instantly obeyed and his authority was recognized without question by all, officials and civilians alike. Even his superiors refrained from interfering, and gave him a free hand, recognizing him as the man for the job.

Freeman's command presence was such that he ordered the powerful Southern Pacific to halt ferry service from Oakland at a time when too many sightseers were arriving to interfere with firefighting efforts. "So strictly was this order obeyed," said Pond, "that for a time passes issued by higher authority were not honored until countersigned by Lieutenant Freeman—and Freeman was a mighty hard man to find."

As the flotilla drew near the city that had been burning for five hours on Wednesday morning, the scene was overwhelming. "As we approached the waterfront," said Pond, "we were appalled by the immensity of the holocaust and began to realize our insignificance compared to the task lying before us."

Freeman immediately saw that he had dual tasks: to fight the fires and to establish order. He explained his situation in his official report written twelve days later: "I had had no instructions with regard to my position as far as preserving order was concerned, but from rumors which reached me I learned that the military was in control, and in the absence of police I assumed control of the water front with the handful of men I had, and issued orders to arrest all stragglers in uniform."

Various fire department records attest to Freeman's ubiquitous presence and the fact that government tugs were furnishing fresh and salt water. The fire department presence along the waterfront was minimal on Friday. At the critical time when the waterfront was saved, Freeman said only one member of the fire department was present.

As the Viavi fire approached, Freeman and his men were isolated from the remainder of the city. They were exhausted and badly needed help. He wrote:

Had fresh men been available to man the *Active* and *Leslie* on Friday morning, April 20th, there is no doubt in my mind but that much more property would have been saved, as my men were thoroughly exhausted from that time on and could not work with stamina. During all of that day, the men of my command were not only fighting fire, but also policing the territory in which they worked.

Great trouble was experienced in controlling matters on East St. People hysterically endeavoring to escape the flames drove down East Street at frantic speed over the hose lines, bursting the overworked hose at frequent intervals. It was finally necessary to station sentries at all corners with orders to shoot down horses whose owners drove over hose faster than a walk.

At this point my men were too weak to handle the hose, having been without sleep and very little food except what could be commandeered for seventy hours.

Freeman was in bad shape, too, said Pond: "He looked all in, with the sweat streaking down through the grime on his weather-beaten face onto the dirty white handkerchief he had tied around his neck, and he seemed discouraged at the unfavorable turn of events. So far as I know, he had not been off his feet since we landed, Wednesday morning."

New men were desperately needed, and Freeman dispatched Pond to the *Chicago*. Admiral C. F. Goodrich, the commander of the Pacific Squadron, assigned fresh crews to the navy tugs and fireboats at 2 A.M. on Saturday. The original crews returned to their vessels twelve hours later.

Policing was an added duty. Trouble had erupted on Thursday. "The crowds rushed saloon after saloon and looted the stock," Freeman said, "becoming intoxicated early in the day. In my opinion great loss of life resulted from men and women becoming stupefied by liquor and being too tired and exhausted to get out of the way of the fire."

By Friday, Freeman had established order along the waterfront. Armed first with only a few revolvers carried by officers, then given twenty unimposing rifles, and finally armed with intimidating shotguns appropriated from a sporting goods store on Broadway, Freeman established an impromptu shore patrol.

Volunteers were hard to find South of Market. Freeman could not recruit able-bodied men to help fight the blaze that swept the residential district on Rincon Hill in a half hour. Men wanted to be paid more than the prevailing wage for laborers. As a result, the sick, the infirm, and others died on the hill from which the Nankervis family had fled.

"If there was any great loss of life in any one place during the fire," said

Pond, "it must have been in that inferno. We were told afterwards that the heat had been so intense in this area as to cause the cobbles of the streets to pop like pop-corn." Freeman lamented, "If I had had two hundred men at this time to aid in leading out hose and rescuing invalids and the aged, much more property and a great many more lives would have been saved."

There were also problems with the special police. Pond recalled: "Many men, wearing special police badges issued by authority of San Francisco's Mayor, had already been passed inside our fire lines; but finding some of them bent more on looting stores than on helping us fight fire or preserve order, we had to cease recognizing their authority and keep them out with the rest."

There were bright spots in the otherwise dark picture. The chief electrician on board the *Pike*, a submarine based at Mare Island, helped the National Guard dynamite some buildings. Then J. Curtin, as the electrician was identified in Freeman's report, turned constructive.

Having nothing to do, Curtin seized the initiative and established an emergency hospital in a church near Market Street. "He organized this institution," said Freeman, "getting doctors and nurses together, impressed automobiles into service, and supplied the hospital with medicines and food; and at the end of a day or so had a first class relief station in operation."

Freeman was present at the one last flare-up in the early morning hours of Saturday.

> The hardest fight we had during the fire was at this point. A sulphur works was burning, the wind was blowing a gale, and showers of cinders, some three or four inches square, made this spot a purgatory. We succeeded in gaining about ten feet on the fire in half an hour, and then practically had the fire under control. Large quantities of water, thrown on the air by the monitors of the fire tugs, were carried as spray down the docks to the roofs of the shed and over the piers, and acted as a blanket for the cinders, thus saving the waterfront.[17]

Except for brief eruptions of hot spots, the fires, which had little else to burn, petered out at the Belvedere ferry slips at about 6 A.M. on Saturday. They had burned, in various incarnations and forms, for approximately seventy-two hours. Then it rained—a cold, driving rain that was too late to dampen the flames but right on time to cause health problems for the refugees.[18]

As people fled the city on Friday, a deluge of money and supplies began to flow in to it. The politics of who would control the largesse, and the governing of the city, began in earnest. The Committee of Fifty organized. Subcommittees were formed that either duplicated municipal functions or determined when they could resume. The groups included Resumption of Civil Government, Resumption of the Judiciary, Transportation, Light and Telephone, Water, Housing, Medical Supplies, Relief of Sick and Wounded, Relief of Chinese, and, most important, the finance committee, headed by James Phelan.

Phelan began to solicit funds from San Franciscans, not anticipating the outpouring of millions of dollars from elsewhere. "The work of collecting from the men whose fortunes were all apparently broken was not a cheerful task," Phelan said. He eventually gathered $413,000 from 131 local donors.

The chairman informed the committee of the names of those whom he had appointed to his subcommittee. Most members of the finance subcommittee were drawn from the main committee. It was the largest subcommittee. To be appointed to the finance committee was perceived as not only an opportunity to aid San Francisco in a time of extreme duress but also as being anointed as one of the city's principal movers and shakers.

The finance committee members included Phelan's business partner and fellow Progressive, Rudolph Spreckels; the attorney and the chief political operative for the Southern Pacific Railroad (and their supposed nemesis), William F. Herrin; the banker, I. W. Hellman Jr.; the publisher of the *Chronicle,* M. H. de Young; Phelan's friend and host, J. Downey Harvey, who was secretary of the committee; a federal judge and the regional representative of the Red Cross, William W. Morrow; and others with such prominent last names as McEnerney, Flood, Sutro, and Tobin.

Phelan gave a description of how the finance committee functioned in relationship to the mayor and the main citizens' committee in a court deposition after the disaster. He said that the finance committee, which recognized the "general authority" of the mayor, functioned independently from the Citizens' Committee of Fifty.

Was the committee guided by any law? No, it was guided by "the general sense of equity, considering all the circumstances and the confusion of the times," Phelan said. What was equitable was a subjective matter.[19]

By Friday the main and auxiliary committees were meeting outside the reach of the flames at Franklin Hall in the Western Addition. Members of the main citizens' committee met at 10 A.M. and again at 8 P.M., despite having to take care of personal matters.

Police, Fire, Restoration and Resumption of Retail Trade, and Permanent Location (meaning relocation) of Chinatown committees were added to the roster. Abe Ruef was appointed chairman of the Chinatown subcommittee.

Members of the Committee of Relief of the Hungry were delegated to investigate the advisability of setting up a refugee camp in Golden Gate Park. Obtaining food was the first priority, it was decided, because empty stomachs bred unease.

The fear of social and political unrest was ever present. The chairman of the food committee, Rabbi Jacob Voorsanger, said: "Above all, the people must be fed. Hunger is the worst anarchist in existence. The insanity of thirst and empty stomachs creates infinitely more mischief than the wrath of the earthquake or the fury of fire."

The main committee asked the mayor to seize food supplies and place them under guard. Transportation was to be arranged for flour to be shipped from elsewhere in the Bay Area to the city. Certain bakeries were to be allowed to bake under strict fire regulations. A loaf of bread would cost no more than ten cents. A single refugee would be limited to a maximum of five loaves.

Calling himself "the biggest thief in the United States," Rabbi Voorsanger set off to find food.

> I commandeered store after store, with a police officer's badge on my clerical coat, and the Mayor's authorization in my pocket. I emptied grocery stores, drug stores, butcher shops, hardware establishments— and at four o'clock that great and glorious day (the Jewish Sabbath), I was able to report to the Mayor that the people were being fed and that to the best of my knowledge there was not a hungry soul in San Francisco.[20]

The Committee on Housing and the Homeless reported that two thousand people were camped in Golden Gate Park. Twenty-five wagons had been impressed to distribute food with the help of the Young Men's Hebrew Association. Word was received that Congress had appropriated $1 million. Other cities had begun accepting refugees, with transportation furnished free by the railroads. Trainloads of donated food and supplies were piling up in Oakland. The dynamiting of dangerous walls would begin on Monday.

Leaders of the Catholic, Jewish, and Protestant faiths represented on the committee called for open-air services in the public parks to "express thanksgiving for the many mercies of preservation and of faith in Almighty God to give our people faith for all that lies before them."[21]

The Committee of Fifty's secretary, Rufus P. Jennings, wrote a glowing description of the committee's operation:

> Men prominent in business and social life, regardless of their personal affairs, came in throngs to the headquarters eagerly volunteering their services in the relief work. There seemed to be no demand for service in any special line, but that the right man to render that service was at hand, this one for this task, that one for that—the assignments fell with decision and judgment. Men of thought and of action, who had been accustomed to plan and to do, found themselves undaunted in this sudden and unexpected crisis and rose to meet it with all the mental and physical alertness born of the stimulus of emergency.[22]

THE CONTROL OF NEWS

The newspapers molded public opinion in accordance with the wishes of the citizens' committee at a time when any news was an extremely precious commodity.

Besides individual San Francisco newspapers, many of which were represented on the citizens' committee by their publishers or editors, the Associated Press wire service, composed of member newspapers, supplied news to the Bay Area and the nation. Wire service dispatches from San Francisco were copied and relayed around the world.

One of the first acts of the Citizens' Committee of Fifty was to appoint a Press Committee. The purpose of the Press Committee was to distribute "official news and otherwise assist in ameliorating the conditions already produced by the temblor and then being aggravated by fire." The chairman of the Press Committee was Paul Cowles, superintendent of the western division of the Associated Press. A businessman and the city editor of the *Chronicle* were also members of the committee.

An emergency news bureau was formed, consisting of one representative from each San Francisco daily newspaper and the entire staff of the Associated Press. Western Union telegraphed the bureau's dispatches free of charge.

The Press Committee appointed a subcommittee to write "an official report containing a consensus of the actions" of the Citizens' Committee of Fifty and its various subcommittees. The membership of the subcommittee included representatives from two newspapers and an attorney, Garret McEnerney.

There was little doubt that the role of the press was to uncritically applaud the decisions of the citizens' committee. In his history *Journalism in California,* John P. Young of the *Chronicle* wrote: "Had there been no press to record the heroic utterances of the members of the Committee of Fifty and to applaud and assist in the dissemination of their plans their efforts must have been in vain."[23]

Much of the news that was generated was related to relief efforts. Some news was manufactured.

One day when there was a light rain falling and donations were lagging, Phelan was talking to Paul Cowles in Franklin Hall. Run a story about a big storm, was Cowles's idea. "The good people of other States," Phelan said later, "had their pity and solicitude increased by the thought of the fire sufferers sleeping in public places and parks without shelter during 'the storm' and funds again began to flow in as copiously as the tears of the sympathetic."

The press committees ceased to operate on May 5. The Citizens' Committee of Fifty thanked them for "disseminating reports of a reliable nature regarding the recent catastrophe."[24]

"DO NOT SEND DESTITUTE"

Tens of thousands sought refuge in the parks or fled the city. There may have been as many as 200,000 or 250,000 refugees—numbers that represented half or more than half the population of San Francisco. The army estimated that there were 70,000 to 90,000 homeless in other northern California communities. Like the number of injured and dead, no accurate count of the homeless was (or is) possible.[25]

The refugees who were pouring out of the city received a mixed reception elsewhere. People wanted to open their hearts, their homes, and their communities, but they were fearful of who they might get—people with yellow or brown skins, drunkards, criminals, and prostitutes. San Francisco was paying for its reputation—whether deserved or not—as a fun-loving, sinful bohemian city.

Governor Pardee sent a telegram to hundreds of communities in the West. "How many people from San Francisco can you take care of in your community," he asked. "The need is great. Take care of as many as you can. Answer immediately."

The authorities in San Mateo County, San Francisco's neighbor to the south, panicked and telegraphed the governor: "Tremendous crowd from San Francisco here and on the way. We lack arms and ammunition to preserve order. Please send immediately one hundred guns and ammunition and any other help and relief you can. Answer important."

Other Bay Area communities reacted similarly. Pardee wrote a constituent: "Several towns in the neighborhood of the Bay were terrorized by rumors that armed bodies of desperadoes were advancing on them; and I was several times appealed to for military protection."

The reaction of the city of Stockton in the San Joaquin Valley was typical—on the one hand open and generous and on the other guarded against the fear of city crime invading the hinterlands. The sheriff swore in one hundred additional deputies and established twenty-four-hour patrols, and the mayor closed all liquor outlets.

Elsewhere in the state and the West, the replies were mixed.

Tiny Hanford, already sending daily shipments of dressed beef, could take five hundred refugees: "Wire time of departure."

"Do not send entirely destitute," replied a Highland minister. "Send desirable element, such as can be accepted in best homes."

On receiving Pardee's telegram, residents of Santa Paula were directed to their respective churches to debate and reach a decision. Santa Paula voted not to take any refugees, as "San Francisco is unloading all her worst elements on neighboring towns."

San Rafael and San Jose—the latter displaying unusual generosity—volunteered to take San Francisco's prisoners, there no longer being a functioning city jail in San Francisco. An asylum in Washington, D.C., offered to take between two hundred and three hundred "insane" patients from Agnews.

Portland, the closest major city to the north, received thirty-five hundred refugees. They were given "meals, baths, clothing, lodgings, and employment, where wanted."

To the east, jobs were available in Salt Lake City, wired the thrifty Mormons, indicating that there would be no free handouts in that city. There were openings for one thousand house servants and between two hundred and three hundred hotel and restaurant employees.[26]

To the south, the response of Los Angeles was like that of Stockton: generous and guarded. The day after the quake, the city shipped seventeen railroad carloads and six steamer loads of supplies that Pardee said were needed. The city prided itself on being the first to respond.

The Los Angeles Chamber of Commerce's Citizens' Relief Committee prepared for the expected inflow of refugees. Its report noted:

By this time a great flood of refugees had begun to pour into Los Angeles and sub-committees were appointed to care for them. A lodging camp was established in Agricultural Park and a detention camp, called Camp Sepulveda, was established between Tropico and Glendale. The latter was based upon the supposition that a horde of undesirable characters would descend upon Los Angeles, and also on account of the possible appearance of smallpox.

The fears as to smallpox happily proved to be for the most part unfounded, while the precautions taken had the effect of deterring undesirable characters from approaching Los Angeles and in consequence the detention camp was soon abandoned.[27]

The general manager of the Southern Pacific telephoned the governor on Friday with a report. He suggested that Oakland was becoming too crowded with refugees. They should be transshipped to other California cities on the railroad's lines.

THE REFUGEES FIND A HOME IN OAKLAND

The largest number of refugees descended upon Governor Pardee's hometown of Oakland. San Franciscans looked down on Oakland much like New Yorkers did on Brooklyn at the time. But the smaller city across the bay rode to the rescue of its haughty cousin. The *New York Times* made the following comparison:

Imagine New York from the Battery to Central Park wiped out by earthquake and fire with the exception of a small part of a residence district and, say, East Broadway, with one or two adjoining streets. Imagine some few of the business houses, great stores, lawyers, bankers, and stock brokers locating in clothing shops and eating houses in East Broadway, and the rest establishing themselves in Fulton Street, Brooklyn.

Referring to Oakland residents as "these cheerful, warm-hearted, careless, rather lazy people of the Pacific Coast," the anonymous *Times* reporter, who regarded the West Coast with the same disdain as he did Brooklyn, said that but for the generosity of Oakland, San Francisco would have been "a hundred times worse off."

Oakland provided a refuge for the homeless and hungry, a place where the relief effort could be organized, a communications and transportation hub in all directions, and a temporary location for charitable organizations, insurance offices, and businesses.[28]

The first response of Mayor Frank Mott was to worry about looting. The entire police department was alerted, and the mayor asked the governor for two companies of National Guard troops. They were augmented by regular army forces. There were few arrests.

The first refugees squatted in vacant lots. In the following weeks, most of the refugees were concentrated at Adams Point on the north shore of Lake Merritt. Some Chinese had a separate camp under willow trees on the shore of Lake Merritt. "Special care was taken of thousands of Chinese, Japanese and other exceptional peoples," according to the Oakland Relief Committee's report. "It was not possible," the report stated, to merge the Willows Camp with the Adams Point Camp.

It rained the Sunday night following the earthquake. The *Oakland Tribune* reported: "Those most exposed to last night's rain were the Chinese camped under the willows at Lake Merritt. Their comforters this morning are soaking wet, and prospects for tonight's lodgment are not of the brightest." The whites camped at Adams Point, the Oakland racetrack, and Shell Mound and Idora parks were given shelter. The Chinese on the lakefront were marched at 3 A.M. to a garage.

Most of the twenty thousand Chinese who had fled San Francisco were crowded into Oakland's tiny Chinatown at Ninth and Webster streets. Chinatown was "overflowing with Chinese refugees who are said to be worse off for food and lodging than Americans," commented the newspaper.[29]

At one time there were twenty camps housing sixty thousand refugees, overseen by the relief committee. In addition, the Salvation Army, various religious organizations, and private citizens housed the homeless. Among others, there were the W. R. Hearst Relief Camp, the Piedmont Skating Rink Camp, the John D. Rockefeller Camp, the Spanish War Veterans Camp, the Elks Camp, and the Druid Relief Camp.

Oakland's population swelled. Civic leaders had been attempting to lure San Francisco businesses eastward for years. Now it was happening, but some landlords were charging exorbitant rents and demanding long leases. The *Tribune* cited the "greed of certain property owners and real estate agents who are taking advantage of the deplorable condition."

Not all the refugees remained in Oakland. Thousands passed through the city daily, pausing only for a meal or a brief rest at the rail hub before hurrying on to other destinations.[30]

Some Oakland residents were not particularly happy about the large influx of refugees. Alice Hutchinson wrote her mother: "'Home Sweet Home.' It is too dreadful here, everything and everybody is upset both as a result of the earthquake damage here in Oakland and because thousands and thousands of homeless, hungry, forlorn people are coming to Oakland." The young woman registered survivors at the First Methodist Church at Fourteenth and Clay streets before they were treated for injuries, fed, and given a place to sleep. "Some were too tired and shaken to give their names," she said, "and I never saw so many hungry people in my life."[31]

Edward N. Ewer was the city's health officer and chairman of the relief committee's health subcommittee. He left a full account of his activities.

> 1st day: All ferry boats filled with refugees. That night many slept on the grass of the City Hall park, 14th and San Pablo. Churches were thrown open and seats were filled with sleepers.
>
> 2nd day: People began making shelters of packing cases, pieces of canvas, tents, if available, roofing papers, etc., etc., on vacant lots all over Oakland. The Health Department began to realize it had a job to do. Information came in that 10,000 Chinese had located on a spot on Lake Merritt called The Willows. It was located on the shore between 15th and 18th Streets. Of course, the number was exaggerated but the area seemed pretty well covered with Chinamen. They had to be supplied with water and sewage facilities, so I as health officer asked Mr. Turner, the city engineer, to supply them. He said it would cost $300 and he had no funds for that purpose. So we went in to see Frank Mott, the mayor. I told him there was danger of a typhoid epidemic unless proper toilet facilities were provided. His remark to Turner was that if that happened the Health Department would be blamed for it and so we best do what that department advised. Where will we get the money? Oh hell, do the job today and we'll get the money later. The Chinamen had water and toilets before night.

Ewer got all the funds he needed for health purposes from the Finance Subcommittee of the Oakland Relief Committee. Sufficient quantities of medical supplies were shipped in from elsewhere, but Oakland did not have enough hospital space. The county hospital was in San Lorenzo, and there were no ambulances to transport the sick and injured arriving on the ferries from San Francisco. The city health officer found a temporary space in Oakland for an emergency hospital, and it was furnished with relief funds.

William Randolph Hearst opened a maternity hospital in a large rented house on Broadway. Hearst said he would present each baby born there with $100. Pregnant women, not all of them refugees, flocked to the W. R. Hearst Maternity and Children's Hospital. "A few babies were born," said Ewer, "but he soon got tired of dishing out the hundred per and closed the place up."

The Hearst tent city on Adams Point was a problem for the health officer. One shelter was unknowingly built over an abandoned sewer, and for a time, the Hearst people would not move it. The camp remained open for about two weeks and was then abandoned. "It seems that projects like the Hearst Maternity and Relief Camp have an advertising value which sinks to nil in about two weeks," commented Ewer.

Twenty cases of smallpox were isolated. When the army's cavalry arrived to take charge of relief work at the Adams Point camp, their horses brought flies with them that bothered the smallpox patients and the staff. Ewer thought that the two Australian nurses who were there at the time took better care of the smallpox patients than had the dozen American nurses who had returned to Chicago.

Overall, Oakland did the best job of sheltering the most refugees. Writing in the *Los Angeles Examiner*, Benjamin Fay Mills, a member of the Hearst expedition, said: "I would say, parenthetically, that Oakland has cared for more than one-fourth the population of San Francisco and that, in my opinion, the most efficient work about the bay has been rendered by the Oakland Relief Committee."[32]

THE WORLD OPENS ITS HEART AND PURSE TO SAN FRANCISCO

It was easier to send supplies and money than to receive refugees. As in the tale of the Sorcerer's Apprentice, for a time there was no turning off the flood of material goods and cash. The world opened its heart and purse to San Francisco.

More than one hundred carloads of supplies were on their way immediately to Oakland from Philadelphia, Portland, Los Angeles, and Sacramento. Much more was being assembled. The first supplies from the outside world began to arrive on Friday. At first confusion reigned. Then the army and National Guard, the remnants of city government, and the citizens' committee began to impose order on the process of moving the supplies to needy recipients.

From nearly every state in the Union, goods that arrived by ship and rail first went to two military depots in San Francisco, where they were sorted. The city was eventually divided into seven relief districts, each with subsections and a military officer and civilian in charge. The idea, which did not always work in practice, was to ship the goods to where they were most needed.

Some of the food, clothing, medicine, and household items was of good quality; some was of poor quality.

Meat could be fresh or putrid, depending on its original condition and the adequacy of refrigeration in the railroad cars. Clothing could be clean and wearable, or dirty and ragged castoffs. Toys for children could be functioning, or lacking essential parts. The army contributed 84,002 pairs of outdated boots that had once been destined for soldiers in the Philippines. Some forty thousand grateful residents were shod in these brown "ammunition boots" for months.[33]

Pardee's staff in the Oakland mayor's office attempted to keep a running total of donations beginning on Friday. A sampling of initial donors of supplies follows: two railroad cars of food and supplies from Aberdeen, Washington; $1,000 worth of provisions from Bellingham, Washington; seven carloads of medicines and provisions from Butte, Montana; 464 loaves of bread, forty-two biscuits, and one sack of doughnuts from the Women's Christian Temperance Union of Brawley, California; 46,413 pounds of potatoes from Colville, Washington; thirty-nine carloads of assorted provisions and medicines from Denver, Colorado; ten carloads of flour from Great Falls, Montana; twenty cars of bedding, bottled water, shoes, and so forth from Kansas City, Missouri; thirty carloads of flour from Minneapolis, Minnesota; three carloads of food from Ogden, Utah; eighty head of cattle from Prescott, Arizona; eight carloads of bread, flour, and condensed milk from Salt Lake City, Utah; fifteen hundred pairs of shoes and blankets from Stockton, California; and thirty-one carloads of flour and cornmeal, two carloads of cured beef, and one carload of potatoes from Topeka, Kansas.

The largest donations of cash came from the East, and New York City in particular. Nearly $3 million was raised in the city within a few days, with $755,000 coming from the chamber of commerce, $700,000 from the mayor's and Red Cross funds, and $150,000 from the New York Stock Exchange.

In that era of Rooseveltian trust-busting, the "tainted" money of prominent capitalists was gratefully accepted. John D. Rockefeller of Standard Oil Company in New York City funded a relief camp in Oakland, furnished free gasoline, and wrote a check for $100,000. Edward H. Harriman—who controlled the Union Pacific, the Southern Pacific, and Wells Fargo Express—put all the resources of his extensive transportation empire at the disposal of the city and the refugees. He contributed $200,000 and then rushed across the continent to personally oversee relief efforts. (Harriman and others were later partially reimbursed for services rendered to the federal government.)

Wealthy New Yorkers like Jay Gould and Andrew Carnegie dug deep and came up with $100,000 apiece. Before he departed for his native city of San Francisco, William Randolph Hearst, a New York congressman, sponsored legislation providing funds for San Francisco and arranged public benefits. He distributed highly publicized amounts of cash and conducted fund drives in his New York City, Boston, Chicago, and Los Angeles newspapers.

There were many smaller contributions. A chorus girl sold smiles for $5, and a debutante who sold her trousseau said, "It seems these fine things mock me." Organized efforts by private citizens throughout the United States asked for amounts as low as ten cents from each person. The money was often generated by a chain letter. [34]

The federal government and foreign governments, along with state and municipal governments, were large contributors. Congress donated a total of $2.5 million, and foreign governments gave $312,000. President Roosevelt preferred that donations from foreign governments not be sent from one government to another, so they were funneled through relief organizations such as the Red Cross. The president felt that the contributions of United States citizens were sufficient, and he didn't want the United States to be obligated to foreign governments.

More than $400,000 was forthcoming from various Philadelphia municipal and relief sources. Large contributions came from the state of Massachusetts and Boston. From the mining town of Cripple Creek, Colorado, came $4,000 in gold. The City of Fargo, North Dakota, contributed $1,117.85.

The totals were impressive. Nearly $10 million in 1906 dollars was collected and spent on relief. Slightly different totals for supplies were offered by the two organizations involved in the effort. According to the Red Cross, 1,850 carloads of food and 150 carloads of bedding, clothing, and tents were shipped to the stricken city. The army counted 1,702 carloads and five steamship loads. A total of fifty thousand tons of relief supplies was received by July 20. At the height of the operation, 150 railroad carloads arrived daily.

In the nine days after the earthquake, the Southern Pacific Railroad transported three hundred thousand people on their ferries and trains, nearly eighty thousand of them beyond Oakland. Most of this movement was on April 19 and 20. Within that same nine days, the railroad handled 1,409 freight cars—or the equivalent of a train ten miles long. Relief trains had the right-of-way over all other traffic. Not included in these figures was the contribution of the smaller Santa Fe Railroad.

Taking monetary inflation and increased costs into account, the relief effort was—and remains—without precedence in this country's history.[35]

THE LAST SEVENTY-TWO HOURS

As the smoke lifted on Saturday, the residents of San Francisco were stunned by the sight of the black desert that surrounded them. The scale of the destruction was beyond what any American city or region has experienced. The damage and loss of lives were not limited to just San Francisco, however, but occurred on and off the fault line in northern California.

The statistics give the illusion of hard-edged reality, but they are not exact. The Subcommittee on Statistics, which operated under the jurisdiction of the Committee on Reconstruction, produced the final statistical report on the disaster. The subcommittee depended on volunteers and a budget of $225, and it admitted the data were "not as extensive as is desirable." The numbers adequately portray the scale if not the precise dimensions of the disaster.

An area of 4.7 square miles, or 508 city blocks, was blackened. (This is equivalent to 20 percent of the borough of Manhattan.) The fire front, meaning the boundaries of the fire, extended for 9.3 miles. This area encompassed the heart of the city's commercial and residential districts and represented about three-fourths of the developed landscape. The National Board of Fire Underwriters estimated the burned area at 2,831 acres.

A total of 28,188 structures burned, 24,671 of them wooden. Forty-two of fifty-four so-called fireproof buildings, of which there were five types (among them steel-framed, reinforced concrete, and brick-walled), were damaged extensively. To indicate the extent of the loss of infrastructure, a partial list of ruined public buildings follows: the City Hall; the Hall of Justice; the Hall of Records; the county jail; five police stations'; twenty-seven firehouses; three emergency hospitals; thirty-one schools, serving nearly forty thousand pupils; and the main library and two branches, including the Phelan Branch.

The assessed value of the lost property was placed at $52.5 million (the assessed value was generally 50 percent of the market value, meaning the market value was $105 million). That figure did not include the thirty-nine churches of all major denominations and the many public buildings that were not assessed for tax purposes. The city's estimate of the total property loss was $250 million.

These figures do not account for the value of the contents and furnishings. For instance, the Bancroft Library, about to be transferred to the University of California across the bay, was the only major private library that survived in San Francisco. There was no value placed on the tens of thousands of books lost in the other libraries. Nor, at the opposite end of the scale of values, was any dollar amount placed on the 30 million gallons of well-aged premium wine that had been stored in San Francisco. (Another 5 to 10 million gallons were lost in Sonoma and Napa counties.)[36]

A committee representing thirty-five insurance companies put the total loss, which it said "will probably never be actually known," at $1 billion. Approximately one-fifth of that amount was paid out in insurance claims. Writing in the *Political Science Quarterly* five years later, Thomas Magee placed the total loss at between $500 million and $1 billion. Needless to say, an equivalent disaster today would mean many billions of dollars in losses.[37] (For the difficulty in determining the equivalency of money between then and now, see the Author's Note, page 346.)

Estimates of the numbers of the dead and injured were also published.

About one thousand people were hospitalized, some four hundred with serious injuries. This estimate was sent to President Roosevelt on April 26 by Commerce Secretary Victor H. Metcalf. The eyewitness accounts of others during the three days seem to confirm the small number of injuries. Dr. Margaret Mahoney, who had visited hospitals and walked the streets, said: "In passing I must remark that after it was all over it was marvelous how few were seen on the streets with bandages. Most of those who escaped with their lives were uninjured."

A careful relief survey done by a foundation after the fire put the number of seriously injured at 415. The report by the Russell Sage Foundation stated: "Most of the hospitals stood outside the burned section, and though some of them suffered heavy damage by the earthquake, no demand had to be made for hospital facilities that could not be met fairly adequately."

The rule of thumb for large-scale disasters is a ratio of injuries to deaths of approximately three hospitalized patients per death. That would mean— if the rule was valid in this case—some 140 deaths in 1906. There were many more. Using a low estimate of 3,000 deaths yields a number of 9,000 seriously injured victims who would have required hospitalization or extensive emergency treatment in a hospital. There are four possibilities for the discrepancy: the extraordinary nature of the disaster—meaning an earthquake followed immediately by a swift, hot fire—left relatively few hospitalized but many dead; the number of seriously injured was underestimated; the current estimate of deaths is too high; or the rule of thumb is faulty in this particular case.[38]

At the beginning, the count of the dead was quite low. The subcommittee on statistics, whose report was issued one year after the earthquake, stated that there were 674 persons either dead or missing. The overall number was broken down in the following manner: Of the 322 "known dead," 315 died in the earthquake or fire, 6 were shot "for crime," and 1 was shot "by mistake." The "reported missing and not accounted for" category totaled 352 persons.

Suspicions immediately arose that these numbers were too low. The report by the six members of the subcommittee added: "There are many who have stated to the Sub-Committee that the loss of life was greater, but such statements are founded on belief and not fact. The Sub-Committee, therefore, does not feel justified in going beyond the figures above given."

The number of fatalities was determined by those deaths that came to the attention of the coroner. There was no aggressive search for victims such as took place at the World Trade Center. To a great extent, racial minorities were undercounted. There is no evidence that numbers were deliberately manipulated. Let the official count stand was the thinking and the practice at the time.

Besides, such a policy served the perceived needs of the city. Eastern money markets were being asked to invest heavily in San Francisco, and there was no need to worry potential investors unduly. The California Promotional Committee, a business-backed organization formed to advertise California's attractions, assured outsiders: "The loss of life was comparatively small, many a minor catastrophe in recent history having resulted much more disastrously in this respect."

The city's *Municipal Reports* of 1908, which covered the events of 1906, listed 478 dead, which was an increase over the 322 known dead cited by the subcommittee the previous year. General Greely said there were 498 deaths, and the State Board of Health put the number at 503. These differences were small enough to account for minor errors or discrepancies in determining what constituted a disaster-related death.[39]

By 1911 the number of dead had slipped to 450 on the list sent by the coroner to the Catholic Archbishop. The deaths included 158 John Does, 25 Jane Does, 24 of unknown gender, and 15 listed as human bones. There were a few Chinese, Japanese, and Italian names—no more than a dozen in each case. Two families lost four members apiece. Five babies had died. Twenty-four victims had perished in hospitals.[40]

The numbers remained at those approximate levels until 1980, when San Francisco City Archivist Gladys Hansen became curious. Library patrons asked her for a list of the dead. She determined that there was none. So she searched San Francisco and Oakland newspapers between April 18 and May 19, 1906, when the newspapers stopped listing persons directly killed by the disaster. She compiled a list of 549 fatalities.

Hansen was joined in the search by retired registrar of voters Frank R. Quinn. They continued to dig through records of the San Francisco Board of Health, the coroner's office, and the emergency hospitals and looked at inheritance tax and orphan's records. They obtained additional names from gravestones at the Presidio National Cemetery. The toll rose to 826 in 1984.

The team then sent a letter to more than one thousand historical and genealogical societies throughout the country asking for evidence of deaths in San Francisco. They arrived at a total number of 1,498 documented San Francisco deaths. Hansen published her only article on the basis of those figures in 1989. Taken from official records, the causes of death were, in order of decreasing numbers, broken down as follows: burns, those crushed to death, asphyxiations, other (includes shootings, explosions, and drownings), exposure, suicides, heart problems, and those killed in the earthquake.

On the list were six dead with Japanese and twenty-two dead with Chinese surnames, which were disproportionately small numbers. The total did not include those who died outside of the city. The National Archives in Washington, D.C., the regional Federal Archives and Record Center in San Bruno, and the records of San Francisco funeral homes doing business in 1906 were not searched. Over time Hansen's estimate has risen to 3,000 on the basis of information contained in letters she has received.

As more recent information is volunteered, mainly through e-mail, Hansen believes there may have been as many as 4,000 deaths in San Francisco. If deaths outside the city—at Agnews Hospital, Santa Rosa, and throughout northern California—were included, the number would rise to between 4,000 and 5,000.

Bruce A. Bolt, professor emeritus of seismology and former director of the Seismographic Stations at the University of California at Berkeley, placed the figure at 2,500 in San Francisco. Adding in deaths elsewhere, the approximate total would then be 3,000. "The correct number will no doubt remain controversial," Bolt wrote.

There is no doubt that the number of dead was higher than the official count but lower than the current highest estimates. Two pieces of evidence indicate that a conservative estimate might yield the most accurate results. First, the number of injured was relatively small. Second, there was at least one group that could serve as an indicator cohort. Of the 584 uniformed firemen on duty in the city's forty-four stations or sleeping at homes scattered throughout the city and elsewhere, only two died as a result of the earthquake. One died while fighting the fire.

I would place the estimate of deaths in northern California at between 3,000 and 5,000, which does not include those who died of such disaster-related diseases as typhoid, smallpox, and the plague. Despite Hansen's commendable efforts, an exhaustive study has yet to be made.[41]

An earthquake fissure near Olema in Marin County.
The Bancroft Library, University of California, Berkeley.

The first fires engulf the produce district,
beyond the spire of Old St. Mary's Church on California Street.
The Bancroft Library, University of California, Berkeley.

As firemen and soldiers stand by helplessly,
smoke and flames erupt from within the Call Building.
The Bancroft Library, University of California, Berkeley.

Winds generated by the firestorms spread the flames.
The Bancroft Library, University of California, Berkeley.

One of the many victims who were incinerated by the heat.
Arnold Genthe, Fine Arts Museums of San Francisco.

The Valencia Street Hotel (on the left), where more than one hundred residents died
when the poorly compacted soil liquefied and three of the four stories sank
below ground level. The neighborhood was subsequently scorched by flames.
The Bancroft Library, University of California, Berkeley.

The ruins of the newly completed City Hall
after being toppled by the earthquake and then gutted by fire.
The Bancroft Library, University of California, Berkeley.

Regular army troops, who were massed on city streets
without martial law being declared, await orders.

The Bancroft Library, University of California, Berkeley.

One of the irregular policemen and vigilantes
who armed themselves and shot others.
The Bancroft Library, University of California, Berkeley.

The large conduits carrying water from Crystal Springs Reservoir
to the city snapped like matchsticks.

The Bancroft Library, University of California, Berkeley.

Ruins in Santa Rosa, which suffered the most damage relative to its size of any city.
The Bancroft Library, University of California, Berkeley.

More than one hundred patients and staff died in poorly constructed
Agnews State Hospital near San Jose.

The Bancroft Library, University of California, Berkeley.

The Memorial Church at Stanford University.
Fortunately no one was in the church when the ceiling collapsed.
The Bancroft Library, University of California, Berkeley.

Jack and Charmian London. The Londons walked San Francisco streets
the first night, and Jack later wrote about what they saw.
The Bancroft Library, University of California, Berkeley.

Brigadier General Frederick Funston confers with an
automobile driver who served as a messenger.
San Francisco Public Library.

Mayor Eugene Schmitz. Although nominally in charge,
in fact the mayor shared power with Phelan and Funston.
San Francisco Public Library.

Governor George C. Pardee. The governor was San Francisco's
primary contact with the outside world.

San Francisco Public Library.

III

AFTER

THE RELIEF EFFORT

BENEATH THE SURFACE

The physical destruction caused by the natural forces of earthquake and fire was followed by an unparalleled period of racial, political, and social strife. The human fabric that tenuously held the city of Saint Francis together was rent. The forces of nature shaped the subsequent culture and its history. Violence in the landscape begat violence in the human history that followed.

There is academic, journalistic, and anecdotal documentation for these observations. The entry for "disasters" in the *International Encyclopedia of the Social Sciences* defines the linkages between the "during" and the "after" periods:

> Viewed in this way, a disaster is an event that disturbs the vital func-
> tioning of a society. It affects the system of *biological survival* (subsis-
> tence, shelter, health, reproduction), the system of *order* (division of
> labor, authority patterns, cultural norms, social roles), the system of
> *meaning* (values, shared definitions of reality, communication mech-
> anisms), and the *motivation* of the actors within all of these systems.[1]

The unnamed *New York Times* correspondent had a clear view of the sig-
nificance of what was transpiring. In a long article entitled "Beneath the Surface in San Francisco," published in June 1907, the reporter wrote that the earthquake and fire were the "psychological events" that unleashed what followed.[2]

Carl Gundlach, a wine merchant, testified to the lasting impact of the three days on a personal level, as did the University of California students thirteen years later. Gundlach wrote in an April 22, 1906, letter:

This is Sunday—the Lord's day of rest! His week's work is ended and He did it well. The doom of San Francisco has been branded with unrelenting and uncompromising ferocity on the face of the darkest history of all mankind. I am so utterly physically and mentally unstrung that my mind and body refuse to act. The use of a pen is a hardship for me. Living the last four days and experiencing and seeing what we had to encounter before our hastened flight from the city of hell and devastation has left its indelible imprints of despair on everybody's vision, haunting him to the rest of his days.[3]

Gundlach was describing a condition that has since become known as post-traumatic stress disorder. (Unfortunately, many people have experienced it, including my wife and I when our home burned in 1988 and we lost all our possessions.) Its symptoms can transcend anxiety and depression. "Like the four horsemen of the apocalypse, fear, despair, rage, and guilt follow disaster, and in intense or prolonged forms may lead to the diagnosis of mental disorder," according to one study. Researchers from the National Academies of Science have identified four postdisaster stages: first, a passive depression; second, altruism and gratitude for help received; third, identification with the needs of the community and participation in rehabilitation measures; and fourth, a relapse into criticism and complaints. The stages and the durations of each vary with individuals.[4]

San Francisco went through four recovery stages: the immediate emergency period, when regular army troops patrolled the streets of San Francisco, ended on July 1; the relief effort was over by mid-1908; the physical reconstruction of the city was completed in 1910; and the official return of San Francisco to normalcy was celebrated at the Panama-Pacific International Exposition of 1915.[5]

In the immediate aftermath of the catastrophe no single narrative strand dominates. Rather, separate threads gradually fade as they coalesce and again become the rope of history. This account of the aftermath conforms, as it must, to the separate histories of relief, reconstruction, attempts to understand the history and science, cultural impacts, racial conflicts, political upheaval, and attempted closure.

A STAGGERING ACCOMPLISHMENT

What San Francisco achieved in terms of almost immediately easing the harshness of life for its citizens and rebuilding the city was staggering in its size, speed, and complexity. Americans deal with such events by moving past them as quickly as possible and then exorcising the harsh realities. San Francisco set records on both scores.[6]

The city had no significant history of relief work. No system of relief was in place, nor was there any general relief organization in early 1906. There were a few scattered charities and some youth centers, but few had offices where applications for help could be accepted, let alone processed. The prevailing concept was that relief wasn't given, it was earned.[7]

The "upbuilding," as the physical reconstruction of San Francisco was called, proceeded with great speed, without any plan, and with only slight regard for the congestion and shoddy building practices that magnified the scale of the natural disaster. Recovery was eventually gained, but at great cost to forests, horses, people, democracy, and future public safety.

In the end, what San Francisco achieved was very little, for the city quickly reverted to the status of its gold rush origins—highly vulnerable to natural disasters. The long view, however, was never San Francisco's, or California's, forte.

THE ASCENT OF PHELAN

San Francisco and James Phelan were very much concerned with the here and now, not the future, on Saturday, April 21. As the days lengthened toward the solstice and the months slowly progressed beyond the immediate trauma, Phelan—so prominent within the state and the leading citizen in the city—inexorably accumulated more power and visibility on a national scale.

It was an amazing achievement for a man who held no public office. He reversed a key decision by President Roosevelt, faced down railroad magnate Edward H. Harriman, sponsored the only plan for reconstruction, and, through the chairmanship of one committee, controlled the entire relief effort and dispersed funds for virtually the full panoply of civic functions. At the same time he rebuilt his personal fortune.

His presence extended in decisive ways to other phases of the postdisaster era. For instance, in the name of good government—or one that fit his personal needs more closely—Phelan was, along with a few other fellow

Progressives, responsible for prosecuting scores of his fellow citizens on graft charges and sending one of them to jail. His views on the "unassimilable races" mirrored and reinforced the prevailing racial attitudes during this period. As a result of all these activities, there was a Phelan boomlet for governor. He would settle for U.S. senator.

Phelan immediately plunged into a grueling round of intense public meetings while privately bemoaning his personal property losses in the late spring of 1906.

Following an evening meeting while San Francisco was still burning, Phelan attended meetings of the Committee of Fifty and his finance committee on Saturday morning. Unknown to others, his pockets were stuffed with valuables. For the next two months, until the bank vaults were considered safe, Phelan would carry in his pockets the jewels his sister had worn to Caruso's performance, barely four days and what now seemed like a lifetime earlier.

The finance committee engaged the Herrick accounting firm on Saturday. Phelan then hurried to a meeting with Mayor Schmitz, Governor Pardee, and General Funston at Fort Mason. He continued on to a meeting of fellow bankers and two later meetings.

That same day he loaned his car and chauffeur to a committee member who was collecting money for relief and had to travel to San Mateo to pick up a check for $100,000 from John D. Rockefeller's attorney. With help from the clerk of his finance committee, Phelan answered twenty-five telegrams from around the country asking what was needed.

Sunday was much the same: more meetings. Phelan obtained a special permit to keep the lights on all night at the Harvey residence where he was staying. As well as being banned by edict, soldiers were shooting at the windows of homes where the lights were not extinguished at 8 P.M. To protect himself and the jewels he was carrying during this perilous time, Phelan also obtained a permit to carry a pistol.

Monday brought more meetings, again with Schmitz, Funston, bankers, and others. Meetings, meetings, and more meetings loomed in the days, weeks, and months ahead. No scrap of paper—and there are many—hints at exhaustion or loss of the steely control he exerted on himself and others who were close to him.[8]

Phelan's emphasis, and the priority of others on the Committee of Fifty and the finance committee, was on the quick recovery of business, which was viewed as being synonymous with the well-being of the population as a whole.

To Sir Thomas Lipton in London, he confided, "Personally, I sustained heavy losses, but will make my occasional trips abroad." A "large dependent class" had been thrust upon "us," Phelan said, but already after one month, "I see evidences on all sides of the resumption of normal business conditions."

Phelan elaborated on his "dependent class" theme to Secretary of War William H. Taft. There was a need for laborers to restore commercial ventures. He floated an idea that would require women and children to suffer in order that business might prosper. "By limiting rations to women and children as a measure of restoring business, the men will be required to seek work of which there is much of rough character in cleaning up the city and preparing it for reconstruction."[9] Fortunately that scheme was not implemented.

To relatives and friends, the news was mixed. "I have suffered severe property losses, including my building and residence, but the town is being rapidly rebuilt with temporary structures that pay good rent." Phelan lost all his income property in San Francisco and half in San Jose. His extensive library was gone. He was living "in a state of siege," but there was an upside: in two or three years "San Francisco will be quite a busy and hospitable place again."

He was harried. "It is night and day with me without an hour for my private business." Phelan took on additional civic duties. He was chairman of the Chile Relief Committee; the committee raised $18,400 for the relief of earthquake victims in Valparaiso. Finally, one year later, as labor riots engulfed the city and lives were again being lost, Phelan admitted: "We are living in strenuous times."[10]

As if all this were not enough, Phelan had a nagging personal problem. He had a difficult mistress to contend with.

Before the earthquake, Florence Ellon had been asking for more hush money, specifically a $50,000 balloon payment. If the money was not forthcoming, she threatened to disclose all, and spare "neither you nor your lady friends." She hinted strongly at pregnancy and said she was ready to go to court. Phelan gave her $16,800, which was in addition to her monthly payments.

From Paris, Ellon hurried to New York City, where she addressed a letter on May 19 to Phelan, in care of the "Formerly Phelan Building." Marked "Personal," it was delivered to Phelan at Harvey's house. "Jimmy dear!" it began, "I am so anxiously awaiting news from you. Have wired and written." She asked if he had saved the "beautiful pictures" in his office; she said she would return to San Francisco in June; and she added: "Will you be glad to see me and forgive? You see my pride is humbled and I am at your feet."

There was a reunion in San Francisco, followed by a gift of property from Phelan, shared memories of Phelan giving her a tour of the upstairs floor of his former home, broad hints of other men asking if they could be "of service" to her, gossip, and idle chitchat while Phelan contended with all the serious aspects of the aftermath of a major disaster.

Ellon departed a few months later, writing to Phelan on the train to Chicago: "I did enjoy, so much, my short visit. You were so good in every way! Toujours à Toi, Firenze." From Europe she sent this busy man of public probity "naughty papers" wrapped in a newspaper.[11]

At the same time, Phelan emerged as the most visible spokesperson for the rebirth of San Francisco. His public discourse bent the reality of the near past to fit the perceived needs of the moment. Earthquakes were not dangerous. Fire, not the "exaggerated" stories about the earthquake, was to blame, said Phelan.

Phelan echoed the dominant litany put forward by organized real estate interests. It was the more-predictable and less-feared phenomenon of fire—the losses for which insurers might more readily reimburse and lenders might more readily loan reconstruction money—that was the real demon, not the earthquake. "But fire is the fiend we know and is common to us all," wrote Phelan. The earthquake was "a mere settlement of the soil at a point many miles distant."

California was perfect, said Phelan in an article in a national magazine. "Its perfections shall be perpetuated." The recent disaster was really nothing. "The burning of San Francisco, caused indirectly by earthquake shock, was merely a tragedy which will subsequently serve to make the history of California interesting."

To President Roosevelt, Phelan confided: "I fear Eastern capitalists may say when we apply that they can't insure against earthquakes." He then pleaded for more federal aid. (The $2.5 million eventually voted by Congress was for federal expenses. It was not until 1950 that the public would benefit from a federal disaster relief program.)[12]

Phelan was the orator of the day on July 4. He preached working for the common good without regard to race or religion. "A great calamity of this kind imparts a philosophy of its own," he told the crowd. "The people now know the insignificance of the individual, the meaning of brotherhood, and the uses of democracy." Phelan did not point out that there was precious little democracy being practiced in San Francisco at the time.

San Franciscans, he said, were morally impelled to rebuild, and rebuild quickly using "the utility of the Beautiful" as their guide.

Power flowed to the able and energetic Phelan, and he also worked hard at accruing it.

The citizens' committee, acting as a representative body at its first meeting in the damaged Hall of Justice on April 18, had authorized the mayor to take charge of relief efforts. Schmitz was fully occupied in trying to save the city from the fire. The finance committee quickly filled the void and took over the job of handling the relief funds.

Phelan was unchallenged until the arrival on Monday, April 23, of Edward T. Devine, who was representing Secretary of War Taft and was the national president of the American Red Cross. Dr. Devine was a highly qualified and politically attuned director of relief.[13]

The San Francisco earthquake and fire was the first test of a rejuvenated and reorganized Red Cross. An aging Clara Barton had been the imperious leader of the Red Cross for more than twenty years. The organization badly needed to become more public-service oriented, more national in its representation, and more businesslike in its practices.

The Red Cross went through a bitter internal power struggle in 1903. Mabel Boardman took over, and Barton was ousted. Instead of one person dominating the organization, the Red Cross was then led by "the born or self-made leaders of American society, with emphasis on wealth and social prestige." President Roosevelt backed Boardman. A new charter was passed by Congress in 1905 giving the president a strong hand in Red Cross matters.

The Red Cross was still in the process of reorganization when the earth moved violently in California. The organization was suddenly faced with "one of the worst disasters and largest relief funds" in its short history, wrote a historian of the charitable society. Suddenly, there were many possibilities to stumble. Roosevelt warned Boardman: "We have to remember that when once the emergency is over there will be plenty of fools and plenty of knaves to make accusations against us, and plenty of good people who will believe them."[14]

The president was the first to stub his toe, as was his wont. With little thought for local sensibilities, capabilities, and politics, President Roosevelt issued a proclamation designating the Red Cross as the only conduit for receiving monetary donations. An immediate furor arose in San Francisco among the members of the oligarchy, who saw it as an end run around themselves and a reflection on their honesty. Phelan said, "The Finance

Committee's administration of affairs is beyond reproach, and we believe some mistaken report has been sent the President."

There were two possible explanations for Roosevelt's precipitous action, other than his natural impulsiveness and the Red Cross's mandate to assume such a role. First, Roosevelt was aware of charges of graft in the municipal government and may not have wanted these funds to fall into tainted hands. He was quietly supporting the effort, initiated by Phelan and Spreckels before the earthquake, to subvert the Schmitz regime.

Second, the *Chronicle* publicly speculated that Roosevelt was aware of the "wild rumors of improper or inadequate treatment" of the Chinese, and for this reason did not want to put the relief money into the hands of prejudiced locals. Phelan had, in fact, been one of the first to make the suggestion that the Chinese be moved south to a permanent settlement at Hunter's Point.

The day after Devine's arrival, a summit meeting of the finance committee was held at Fort Mason. Among others who attended the rancorous meeting were Devine and Judge Morrow, the two top representatives of the Red Cross (Judge Morrow headed the California chapter); Greely and Funston from the military; and Phelan and Schmitz, representing the two factions of civic government.

Eventually, those present agreed on a course of action. Rather than confront Roosevelt's well-known sensitivity, Edward Harriman of the Southern Pacific suggested that they not send a telegram directly to the president but rather have Devine and Greely wire Taft with the suggestion that the local finance committee was capable of handling the funds. Roosevelt reversed himself and issued a second proclamation naming Phelan as the sole recipient for relief funds. While Roosevelt did not want the government to accept monetary donations from foreign governments and individuals, he had no problem with such funds being sent to private or local relief committees like the one headed by Phelan.[15]

Following the Fort Mason gathering, the *Chronicle* reported: "Mr. Phelan carried off Dr. Devine to luncheon—out of cans—and the best of feeling prevailed among all those party to the meeting."

Phelan faced two more challenges to his dominance.

Edward Harriman was not an easy man to get along with. At the next day's meeting at Fort Mason, Harriman seemed to be cooperating, Phelan noticed, until the railroad magnate "lost his temper and abused Rufus Jennings," secretary to the Committee of Fifty. Harriman berated Jennings for commandeering one of his Southern Pacific ferry boats to carry refugees.

"His assumption of proprietary rights was very ill tempered," Phelan observed in his personal notes. Jennings had only been doing what the committee had ordered and the railroad had offered.

The tension was building between the two independent-minded capitalists from different coasts. It came to a head at a conference meeting of the finance committee's executive committee on May 5. This small group effectively conducted most of the committee's business and was dominated by Phelan. Harriman and others who were not on the executive committee had been invited to attend the meeting to discuss how to distribute the relief money. William Herrin, the Southern Pacific's general counsel, was present along with I. W. Hellman Sr. and Jr., father and son, whose Wells Fargo bank was intertwined with Harriman's enterprises. It was the father's first meeting.

With no warning, the subject shifted to selection of a treasurer and where to bank the rapidly accumulating funds. Harriman said that he preferred that a banker be named to the treasurer's position and that the funds be deposited in banks throughout the country. After his boss spoke, Herrin immediately nominated Isaias Hellman Sr. to the treasurer's job.

Both actions would have robbed Phelan of his power. He neatly deflected them. "I will have to rule a motion of that kind out of order," he said. "This is a mere conference [on] the proper plan to dispose of our money and ultimate relief. If you bring that up in executive session, it will be in order."

"I was presiding," Phelan later recalled, "and seeing that it was obviously a prearranged plan to get possession of the funds, I ruled the motion out of order." Harriman and his party stormed out of the meeting room.

Benjamin Ide Wheeler, president of the University of California, told Phelan that it had been a mistake to offend "so good a friend of the community." Phelan hurried after Harriman. He caught up with him outside. Harriman was "scowling and black with a hostile expression on his face," said Phelan.

Phelan explained the procedure for having the matter brought up for a vote. He also said that the president had made him the custodian of the funds, and that they could not be released to a treasurer without Phelan's permission. Phelan pointed out that he, too, was a banker. Harriman, according to Phelan's account, relented and blamed his advisers for not making him aware of these facts. He said that he also was a friend of the president and that they frequently talked on the telephone.

Harriman invited Phelan to dine with him in his private railroad car at the Oakland Mole, but Phelan said he had another engagement and declined. Phelan was later told: "This was the first time anyone ever crossed

E. H. Harriman and got away with it!" The money remained in Phelan's possession.[16]

The last attempt to bypass Phelan originated with Mayor Schmitz and the supervisors in early June. The mayor invited the finance committee to his home for an elaborate lunch. "He then said," according to Phelan, "that the supervisors had complained that the Citizens' Committee had, during all these weeks, usurped their functions, and now that the work was practically done it would be well to turn over the funds to their custody, as they were the elected representatives of the people of the City of San Francisco." Phelan and the other committee members refused this request.

It so happened that Phelan, along with the mayor and others, was scheduled to leave the next morning for Washington, D.C., where they would lobby Congress for funds to rebuild the city. Phelan was worried that if he left, "something would be attempted in the way of turning over the funds to the Board of Supervisors, whose integrity was seriously questioned."

Phelan wrote the mayor a two-page letter with a number of transparent excuses for not being able to make the trip. One excuse was that "our Eastern friends would regard my absence from San Francisco, in view of the large fund on hand, as a mistake and that it might, therefore, reflect upon the mission of the Committee."

Following these efforts to limit his power, Phelan said that "no attempt was made to question the authority of the Citizens' Committee to collect and administer the fund to the end, which was done."

The Finance Committee of the Citizens' Committee of Fifty changed its name to reflect its association with the Red Cross. It became the Finance Committee of the Relief and Red Cross Funds. Phelan reported to, but took no orders from, the umbrella committee and its successor—the Committee of Forty—or the national Red Cross. After Governor Pardee and General Funston turned over the funds they had received, Phelan's committee effectively held all the relief monies.[17]

In a 483-page survey of the San Francisco relief effort, the Russell Sage Foundation concluded a few years later that, from the start, Phelan's finance committee was "the committee of power."[18]

RESTORING BUSINESS COMES FIRST

Given the social and economic prominence of the Red Cross officials, top military commanders, and the members of the citizens' committee, there could be little doubt that the relief effort would be incredibly efficient, relatively honest, and blind to the needs of the poor and minorities. With the suspension of the democratically elected government, remarkable harmony prevailed on how to deal with such potentially controversial issues as the homeless.

Three entities constituted the relief triumvirate: the Red Cross had the expertise, the army had the manpower, and Phelan had the money. Their primary goal, and the perceived panacea for a wrecked society, was the rapid restoration of business. It also happened to be a self-serving solution.

Following the Fort Mason meeting, there was harmony within the triad. Outsiders like Governor Pardee and his National Guard were discouraged from participating in the process.

The mayor and the citizens' committee politely asked the National Guard to leave the city on April 23. The guardsmen, it was thought, were implicated in a number of shootings of stray dogs and seemingly errant people, although regular army troops were also guilty of similar activities. Guardsmen had been seen looting the ruins of Chinatown and were overly zealous in grabbing the wrong prominent citizens and putting them to work clearing the rubble.

The issue of the guard's behavior was discussed at the daily meeting at Fort Mason on April 26. Pardee, a member of the state militia for nearly thirty-five years, was "testy and profane," said Phelan. He refused to order the guard out of the city.[19]

Mayor Schmitz then wrote the commanding general of the National Guard asking that his men act merely as sentinels. "There is no martial law, and never has been since the earthquake," he said. A National Guard colonel wrote Governor Pardee that "had martial law been declared, all these difficulties which are now arising would not have occurred."

The special police and vigilantes were disbanded, the University of California cadets had already returned to Berkeley, and the fifteen-hundred-member state militia, twenty-five hundred army troops, and the police were given specific districts to patrol. The last of the National Guard troops left San Francisco on May 31.[20]

The military situation was thus simplified. The seven relief districts were put under the control of the regular army. As with any large-scale, hastily organized relief effort, this one was plagued by too much of one thing (flour), not enough of another (suitable clothes), and delays in getting food and clothing into the hands of needy refugees. Perhaps two hundred thousand persons received donated clothing, much of it of poor quality. A survey of the relief effort determined:

Much of the clothing donated bore the well-known mark of the charity gift in kind. The second hand clothing in many cases was, to repeat General Greely's comment, "more or less of a burden on the Red Cross." Some was useless; some required to be cleaned and disinfected. The new clothing was, in the words of Captain Bradley, who had charge of its distribution, "of old and dead stock of mediocre and poor quality." Part of the shoes and articles of clothing supplied from the Army stores and charged against the appropriation from Congress were of obsolete pattern. The same criticism was made of some of the household goods donated. A large number of the cots, for instance, were worthless or of poor quality.[21]

Given the confusion and the army's need to organize in the army's distinctive way, delays in deliveries of stores already on hand were inevitable. People then helped themselves—looted and robbed in the eyes of the military—to goods in railroad cars that sat overlong on Southern Pacific tracks in San Francisco. The narrator of the *Argonaut* series described the dilemma thus:

> Among quartermasters, commissaries and the like, such stores are relatively more inviolable than were the Vestal Virgins to the Romans or the Ark of the Covenant to the Hebrews. When relief supplies began to pour into San Francisco, however, the hungering refugees in many cases refused to realize that once such supplies have passed into military control they become Quartermaster's stores and thus become sacred. On the other hand they believed that because the supplies had been sent to the relief of the afflicted, each person that felt afflicted would be justified in helping himself to anything he felt that he needed and which, by pilfering or otherwise, he could secure.[22]

Acute food shortages arose, and heroic attempts were made to alleviate them.

National Guard Chaplain Charles D. Miel wrote his superior about the urgent need in Golden Gate Park and local orphanages for milk for infants as well as blankets, mattresses, tents, and shoes. "For God's sake, try your best to obtain the necessaries asked for herein," he pleaded.[23]

The chaplain's superior officer said that Miel's name "should be written in letters of gold." He stated in his report to the state's adjutant general:

We secured a fresh supply of milk from one of the outside dairies, and every morning it was a heart rending sight to see the distribution of the supply of milk we received among mothers and children at Chaplain Miel's tent. There was only so much milk, and it could only go so far and some had to go hungry. The shock of the earthquake had affected many women who were nursing their babies and they were unable to give nourishment to their little ones, so milk was very precious.[24]

The chaplain obtained food for a nearby Catholic orphanage, a "colored" orphanage, and a hospital. In a deserted corner of the Panhandle near the park, Miel rescued a ninety-two-year-old grandmother, her daughter, and granddaughter who were huddling under a sheet.

Two weeks after the earthquake, 267,967 persons were fed in a single day.

More than 70,000 others had either fled during the three days of fire or departed during the immediate aftermath to seek work elsewhere. Their occupations provide an insight into what jobs were superfluous under the trying conditions: jewelers, inventors, masseuses, hairdressers, artists, acrobats, barkeepers (liquor was banned), teachers (schools were closed), bakers, grocers, apartment managers, tailors, dressmakers, milliners, printers, and nurses and doctors whose offices had been destroyed and whose patients had departed.[25]

GOVERNMENT BY COMMITTEE

The Committee of Fifty took over almost every function of city government. The California Promotional Committee referred to the citizens' committee as "this provisional government by committee."[26]

The meetings in Franklin Hall dealt mainly with reports, announcements, discussions, and the working out of differences between subcommittees. Decisions were mostly made at the subcommittee level and then reported to the general membership.

One major concern was inspecting and repairing chimneys so that homeowners would no longer have to cook in makeshift kitchens on the streets. On the first Tuesday after the earthquake, Jeremiah Deenen, chairman of the Restoration of Fires in Dwellings Committee, reported that insurance underwriters had approved the committee's plans for inspecting and repairing chimneys. More than one thousand bricklayers were at work on chimneys that day, he said.

Rudolph Spreckels, who was chairman of the Committee on Restoration of Lights, differed with the opinion of the members of the Committee on the Resumption of Transportation that immediate service could begin on the Fillmore Street trolley line. Loose wires could still be dangerous. His argument carried the day. (Not stated was the fact that Spreckels and Phelan had plans to replace the operator of the line.)[27]

Since the finance committee controlled the money, it set the policy for the dispersal of relief funds. A great deal of social engineering was involved. "Worthiness" was the deciding factor on who got what. Able-bodied men would not receive aid but would be forced to work. As one committee member said, "The object is to look after the destitute, and only the destitute. Let us do nothing that individuals can do for themselves."

Weighing the ability of an able-bodied head of a family to find work against the particular needs of his family required the wisdom of Solomon. "Demoralizing and pauperizing the poor" was to be avoided. The managers of the various relief stations met on May 12. Devine reported to the committee that they were alert "to the necessity of not pauperizing and cutting off everybody possible and not doing anything dangerous to family life." One solution was to give the mother and children, but not the healthy husband, rations.

"Of all the methods of relief," General Greely said, "that which most commends itself to me from a careful consideration of this question is that advanced by Dr. E. T. Devine, and known under the general term of rehabilitation. There is no better way of rehabilitating a man than by allowing him to earn a living salary."[28]

The activities of the Committee for Housing and the Homeless, which began its work the day after the earthquake, were a good example of government by committee. The housing committee was not motivated by altruism. The homeless were to be given shelter so that they could work on reconstructing the city. In a recapitulation of its activities before being merged with another committee in early May, the committee stated:

One of the first steps taken after the organization of the Committee, was the formation of a plan to construct semi-permanent camps for the shelter of citizens and their families.

It was the opinion of the Committee, that much of the work of reconstructing the city would be performed by those who had been rendered homeless, and consequently the Committee intended, from the very inception of [its] work, to provide such accommodations for the workmen as would prove adequate during the continuance of the work of reconstruction.

From the start, the strategy of the committee, and of the army, was to encourage refugees living on the streets and in vacant lots, squares, and small city parks to settle in the few semipermanent camps, two of which were to be erected in Golden Gate Park. Providing sanitation, food, housing, clothing, and medical care and exercising overall control would thereby become easier. General Greely explained to the finance committee the enticements that were being offered refugees to move:

The story has gone out that the Army is going down there to shoot them if they do not get into other camps. But I said, "We offer you certain things, and all you have got to do is to be clean, decent and orderly." I have given them a little more feed. I have shut them off of coffee. I am not permitted to use anything but persuasion. We cannot accomplish anything that goes beyond that. But the mayor can say, "You have got to get out of here." When Dr. Devine and the [Citizens'] Committee agree and they come to me, I will say to them, "If you will not come in here under military supervision and regulation and keep the camp in order, I will stop your supplies."

The Red Cross cut off food supplies to an encampment of eight hundred people on the San Bruno Road because of the cost of transportation to that outlying area. Devine explained the situation to the finance committee: "The only way the military can control the matter is not to issue food supplies. I understand that general relief was to be extended to the Jewish families on the San Bruno Road by transferring them to where the others are that came from the same part of town, in other words, to the permanent camp at the Park."[29]

The policy of containment was only partially successful. The more sympathetic police refused to move refugees from the impromptu camps, which were constructed from any materials that were handy. As of mid-June there were 43,000 homeless, of which 18,000 were in twenty-one camps run by the military and another 25,000 were scattered throughout the city.

The "official" or "permanent" camps were in Golden Gate Park, the Presidio, Fort Mason, Harbor View (the present-day Marina District), and city squares and parks. The structures consisted of barracks, tents on wooden platforms, and small shacks, called "earthquake cottages."[30]

While the army and Red Cross cajoled, the carpenters constructed. Where so much could go wrong, there was an almost perfect meshing of military and civilian functions in the building of the camps. Under the aegis of the committee, they constructed two camps and other structures in Golden Gate Park within a few days.

Military engineers, aided by a local architect and a contractor, laid out the camps in rigid patterns. Civilian relief workers purchased the lumber, found the teams and wagons, and employed the carpenters, who were given donated tools.

The hauling of lumber began on Friday while the city burned. In some cases one side of the lumberyard was on fire while wagons hauled lumber from the other side. Not all cooperated immediately. Some lumberyard owners, teamsters, and carpenters held out until they were assured that they would be reimbursed by the finance committee.

Eighty thousand feet of lumber was delivered on average every day to the construction sites in the park. A force of 110 men loaded and unloaded the boards. The first lumber was used to construct seventy outhouses, extending from the Baker Street entrance to the park to the boathouse at Stow Lake. They were completed in three days.

The number of carpenters working on the structures grew from 20 on Saturday to 257 on Monday. The first barracks were ready for occupancy by twelve hundred homeless people in eight days. Each barrack was 160 feet long and 20 feet wide and was divided into sixteen apartments. Each apartment had two ten-foot-square rooms separated by an eight-foot-high partition and one window and one door. Laundry, bathing, and toilets were communal.

The camps in the park were veritable cites within a city. The barracks were followed by dispensaries, headquarters buildings, commissaries, warehouses, more latrines, men's and women's bathhouses, laundries, tents on wooden platforms for housing, tents on wooden platforms for schools, a contagious disease complex, and other miscellaneous facilities. In the first two weeks, 1,134,000 million feet of lumber was used to construct housing for 7,500 people at a cost of $51,706. The committee reported: "They have been provided with many things, such as cooking ranges and cooking utensils, and other necessities. . . . In other words, they have been liberally housed, and the houses partially furnished."

The camps had drawbacks, however. They were located on low ground and could not be connected to the city sewer system. Filthy ponds formed when it rained. Additional work had to be done to make the barracks less drafty and to provide greater privacy. The crowding was demoralizing.

The committee's attempt to temporarily locate refugees in vacant and unfurnished houses without the owners' consent was not successful. The Committee for Housing the Homeless granted the "right" to occupy these structures. Few took advantage of this offer "either from fear of earth-quakes or from joy of camp life," the committee reported.

Work also needed to be done distributing the essentials of life such as clothing, tents, blankets, and shoes. That effort was more successful.

The report was very clear on one matter: "No distinction was made in furnishing relief on account of the color, race, or religion of any individual; Chinese, Japanese and Negroes were cared for without any discrimination being made. The Chairman of this Committee spent much time among the Italians, quieting their fears and seeing that their wants were supplied." In fact, this effort was far less successful than that statement would indicate.[31]

SEPARATE AND UNEQUAL

The leveling of racial, religious, social, and economic barriers—termed "earthquake love"—was a common, though mistaken concept, believed by many to have been achieved. The actual housing policy in the official camps was, in effect, separate but equal facilities and supplies. The Chinese were shunted to the edge of the Pacific Ocean. The few Japanese and African Americans melted into the crowds, sought safety by themselves, or fled the city entirely. The poor white refugees who did not seek housing in the official camps received little help.

The focus of the relief efforts was to the north of Market Street, while the need was greatest South of the Slot and in the Mission District, where the loss of residences had been greatest and the population was the poorest. Some poor people went to Golden Gate Park and other semipermanent camps. Many "instinctively clung to their own section of the city. . . . They had no facilities for escaping across the bay as had those who were on the northern side of the city," noted the *Argonaut*.

These poorer residents (along with the Italians, Chinese, Japanese, and the few African Americans) were and are—because their accounts were never written or preserved—the forgotten majority of the city's population. The words of others hint at what their individual stories might have been.

They preferred to live in temporary shelters on vacant land in or near their old neighborhoods and shunned the empty houses that were offered as refuges. Because of their isolation and the neglect by civilian and military organizations, a few individuals launched relief efforts within the Mission and South of Market districts.

For instance, in the more middle-class Mission District, James Rolph, who would serve five terms as mayor and be known as "Sunny Jim," called a meeting in his barn at Twenty-fifth and Guerrero streets to organize relief. By Monday, twelve thousand people were standing in line for bread outside the barn.

Informal generosity played a leading role in feeding the poor. Meat wagons from the slaughterhouses near Potrero Hill dumped a few hundred pounds of beef on street corners. Grocery stores that remained intact gave away food to the needy. Nearby coalyards donated fuel. Dairy owners on the peninsula who brought milk to the city left cans for women and children. But hunger and cold, especially when it rained, were the predominant conditions in these places.

The official relief effort was marked by great disparity of aid given to the middle class and the poor. One week after the earthquake, relief stations had been established in the Mission and South of Market districts. Red tape held up the delivery of food. By the time it finally arrived, half of the stations reported feeding forty thousand persons, which was more than five times the number being fed in Golden Gate Park.

In an attempt to reduce the number of repeat eaters, the concept of mass eating practiced in construction camps was introduced throughout the city, except in the Mission District, where there were angry objections to being stigmatized as poor by the soup kitchen image. Rolph managed to get an exception for the Mission, and thus launched a lengthy political career that would take him to the governorship.

Although also originally objecting, the South of Market refugees who were camped to the east of Eighteenth Street acceded to the soup kitchen concept. These poorer residents of the city—mostly Irish, Russian Jews, and a few Germans—were hungry. They had to make do without donated raw food during the interim period, as they had few cooking facilities. There was one small square in which to camp; otherwise they lived in hovels.

National Guard Captain E. F. Peckham lived in the area and was detailed to guard a cannery there. Peckham met Frank McLeod, the foreman of a hauling company. The two opened a shelter in the company's stable at Eleventh and Bryant streets. To feed people, they went foraging for food.

Peckham was arrested for being absent without leave, but he was released so that he could continue his unofficial relief work. The captain described the refugees: "They were absolutely destitute and consisted of the poorest classes of all the people in the city. They were hungry, barefooted, and ragged."

Peckham and McLeod used the horses and wagons of the drayage company to haul food from various unofficial sources such as the Western Meat Company and the California Baking Company. The food was distributed at the stable.

The civilian in charge of the relief district that encompassed the South of Market area described the makeshift housing.

No sooner had the fire died out than the people began to fashion rude dwellings out of the corrugated iron roofing left in the ruins. These shacks were of the most miserable kind, some so low and squatty that it was necessary to get on one's hands and knees to enter. The ventilation was bad and in a few days the filth and vermin was beyond description. The earthquake had left the sewers and water mains in a badly-battered condition and sanitation was impossible.

When the rains came, there were few tents and little clothing. Less-destitute sections of the city had a surplus of both. Requisitions for lumber by the relief workers assigned to the area went unfilled. A relief worker recalled:

I distinctly remember one Sunday morning when I saw two old ladies who cowered in a shack where they had piled up all their worldly belongings on a couple of boxes. The shack itself was flooded, its floor was muddy slop, and these two old ladies had climbed up and perched themselves on top of their property waiting for the water to subside. But they took it all with the best good nature, and said they were thankful that their plight was not worse.[32]

Who spoke for the poor? There was no question who spoke for the Irish-Catholic working class, the largest bloc of voters, whose religion dominated the city. Father Peter C. Yorke was chancellor to the archbishop, editor of the official church newspaper and his own labor-oriented newspaper, the *Leader*, and a harsh critic of James Phelan. Yorke took over the front page of the *Leader*'s first postquake edition. His was not a happy message.[33]

The wrath of God had visited San Francisco, and the city had deserved what it got, said the outspoken and militant priest. Saying that "there has been no town in the world in modern times or ancient in which vice was so naked and so unashamed," Yorke continued:

> No doubt we deserved it all. We had grown proud and insolent and had put our trust in our ownselves and boasted how we had harnessed the powers of nature; we gave way to the evil desires of our souls; we gratified every lust and every vanity, and we took the reins from our tongues and we exalted our pride in the face of the God of Heaven, and the God of Heaven lifted His little finger and behold, we are not.

Yorke was unable to obtain cots for old ladies who were sleeping on the floor, although the army possessed them. Aid to the people who needed it most, the elderly and the poor, was being held up by "the serpent of red tape, which, like the serpent of Laocoon appears to be strangling the giant of American Charity." The need for supplies was then, not the following week or the following year.

Yorke preached humility instead of pridefulness in the rebuilding effort. "We have no sympathy with the newspaper talk of building up a bigger and a greater San Francisco by the material aid, and the great corporations, the big business houses and the men of money. We have built up such a city already and it is no more."[34]

THE COMMITTEES BEGIN TO DISBAND

Outside the South of Market area, a degree of postquake normality was established within a couple of weeks. By the end of April much of the policymaking and relief and reconstruction work had been set in motion, and a number of the subcommittees began going out of business of their own volition. The army would then be handling relief matters. The prominent citizens had their own affairs to attend to. The board of supervisors was anxious to resume governing.

On May 1 Abe Ruef offered a motion that "an advisory committee of forty, to be known as the Committee on the Reconstruction of the City" be appointed by the mayor. The Committee of Forty, as it came to be known, would advise an official advisory committee of seven to be appointed by the board of supervisors. In this manner, the citizens' committee would be distanced from actual power.

The resolution passed unanimously. Not noted publicly was the fact that the finance committee retained its considerable power, derived mainly from President Roosevelt. By having the funds available to finance municipal government functions—the property tax base having been greatly reduced—and charitable endeavors, Phelan retained his power.[35]

The break from an oligarchic form of government and a return to a functioning democracy was not absolute. Those citizens' subcommittee activities and municipal functions the finance committee chose to underwrite—such as housing, hospital care, garbage disposal, contagious disease control—had to be conducted in accordance with the dictates of Phelan's committee. Those functions remained outside the control of city government, as did the millions of donated dollars.

On May 15 Spreckels, who had been appointed to three of the new subcommittees, announced his intention to resign from the Committee of Forty. He said he could do more as a private citizen. There was too much talk and not enough action, he said, and the new committee, which came into existence in the same manner as the first one, "has no legal standing."[36]

Spreckels, however, remained chairman of the Camps Department, which constructed, operated, and eventually disposed of the small green earthquake cottages that became scattered throughout the city. The department operated under Phelan's financial control.

The two- and three-room cottages (some exist to this day in greatly modified form) were a short but successful experiment in self-sufficiency for the less affluent. A nominal rent was charged and could be applied toward ownership. The money was refunded if the occupants rented lots to which the cottages could be moved.

Like the barracks, the cottages were squeezed together tightly. "The compact housing of people meant that in some cases respectable people were compelled to associate to a certain extent with the less desirable," stated a report. "On the whole, however, the general moral conditions were not bad."

By the middle of 1907 Spreckels, Phelan, and those citizens who had permanent housing wanted their parks back. There was also concern about creating a permanent "pauper class." The image of San Francisco, it was thought, was not enhanced by the continued presence of refugees in tents.

The newspapers concurred, and Spreckels led the campaign to close all the camps and relocate the cottages, causing great hardship to some. Resistance to moving developed within the encampments, but Spreckels ordered all camps closed by the end of the year. There was a rush to relocate. "Many people were injured and cottages and belongings damaged in hurried moves," wrote a historian of the period.[37]

Life as a refugee, which was not without its droll moments and camaraderie, was not one of never-ending joy in living the outdoor life as it was portrayed in crisp official reports and upbeat stories in newspapers and magazines.

The remainder of April and May 1906 were unusually stormy months, so much so, in fact, that people began to wonder if the earthquake had not altered the weather. Longtime residents noted that most storm winds then came from the north, rather than the southeast. The astronomer in charge of the seismographs on the University of California campus assured the public that although little was known about earthquakes, they "are never influenced by the weather, nor do they affect weather conditions in any way."[38]

The unusual weather was mentioned in the description of life in a refugee camp written by a San Francisco woman:

> The discomforts of living, in spite of adequate relief, are very great. Wind and fog—for the weather has been unusually cold for a month, dust unspeakable, cooking out of doors in camps and streets, lack of water for toilet appliances, the incessant boiling of water and milk for fear of fever, absence of light and means of transportation for some time—in short, the total uprooting of all ordinary habits of life, is bearing more and more heavily on the women and children.[39]

Men did not necessarily have an easy time either, as this account indicates:

> For the following week I dead-headed all my meals from different churches and benevolent societies. The only people that turned me down were the Masons and the Native Sons. These probably had enough of their own folk to look after. Anyhow, they questioned me, and when I stated I did not belong to either order, I had to go elsewhere for my grub.
>
> I slept in churches and furniture stores. One night I slept in the First Presbyterian Church where the announcement was made that "anyone refusing to do work when called upon by the committee will be arrested."
>
> Soldiers were on the spot to arrest the recalcitrants.
>
> I was one of the persons called upon to do work next morning. My

instructions were to climb up into the steeple of the church and fix the bell there so that it would ring.

I climbed up as directed, but could find nothing the matter with the bell; nothing that I could see wrong anyhow. So I came down and so reported.[40]

Children's stories are told through the classified ad sections of the *Chronicle* and the *Examiner*:

WILL someone of 1206 Market st., San Francisco, inform me of the safety of my children. MRS. ALICE MCINNIS and WILLIAM MCINNIS. Direct care I.O.O.F. Hall, Oakland.

FOUND—Italian boy, Louis Monte Porpolini, 5 years old, from Lombard st., North Beach district. Communicate with Fruitvale Relief Committee.

WANTED—Information regarding children of DR. RAMON CORRAL, vice president of Mexico. They lived with Miss Petronila Valasco, 1214 217A Mason st. Notify F. E. MONTEVERDE, JR., care Union Savings Bank, Oakland.[41]

Cooking on curbside stoves hauled outside from homes with wrecked chimneys was a trying experience made bearable, for a short time, by the novelty, the sharing with neighbors and friends, and the challenge of making a palatable meal from the miscellaneous raw ingredients obtained from relief stations. This recipe for "refugee stew" is from *The Refugee's Cookbook*.

Take three pounds of round of beef cut in medium sized pieces; take two good sized onions and fry brown in beef dripping; fry meat after sprinkling with flour in the onions very brown turning frequently; put it in a stew kettle and cover with boiling water; let cook very slowly three hours, adding boiling water as it cooks down; an hour before serving add three carrots, three turnips, potatoes, parsnip, parsley, bay leaf; thicken it with one-half cup of flour and teaspoon of caromel [*sic*]; be very careful not to burn; don't use cold water or too much grease.

The cookbook was filled with helpful hints. To rid a tent or home of flies, put a tablespoon of cayenne pepper in a pan and let it burn over a fire. Then open the doors or windows and the flies "will soon all disappear." To make a water filter, take a tomato can and perforate the bottom. Cover the bottom with a layer of cotton batting and place five or six tablespoons of pulverized charcoal on top of the cotton. Pour boiling water in and the sediment will be leached out.[42]

The poor used humor to ward off the discomforts. An unsigned handwritten note stated: "After the earthquake, among the little shacks made of anything at hand, where people cooked out of doors, was one rather pretentious shack, and on it the sign 'The Occidental' [a large hotel that burned]. Next to it was a little wild bird's nest of a shack, and it had the label 'The Accidental.'"

The upper classes had friends or relatives with large homes in the Western Addition or elsewhere in the Bay Area to which they could escape. The *Examiner's* society column, "What Society Is Doing" by The Chaperone, reported in the April 30 issue:

Mr. and Mrs. O. C. Stine went to San Jose the morning of the earthquake, never dreaming that the fire would reach the Cecil, where they were stopping, and so they lost everything.

The George Knights are at Belvedere.

The Leonard Chenerys were burned out and lost all of their effects, which were valuable. They are with friends on Pacific avenue, near Buchanan street.

The Jack Wilson house on Pacific avenue has been turned over to the Bohemian Club for its headquarters.

Many of our former prominent society women, girls who have been used to the luxury of maids, are cooking and even washing their own clothes. I always knew that our San Francisco girls could stand the test.

Dr. Humphrey J. Stewart and his daughter are in Ross. They lost everything in the fire.

Dr. Arnold Genthe has taken some excellent photographs of our poor distracted-looking city. I met him the other day and he, cheerful under the circumstances, said that he had lost all of his plates, his films, his library—in fact, every treasure that he possessed in the world. He, too, is prepared to commence all over again. Dr. Genthe is at present at the home of the Cowderys, corner of Maple and Jackson streets.

Harry Pendleton didn't save anything. My! But he is bright and jolly. He is at present on Divisadero street with friends.[43]

Sightseers from around the Bay Area flocked to the city, and gradually a few tourists returned. A local hotel offered an automobile tour, departing at 2 P.M. each day and costing $1.50 per person. Under the headline of "See San Francisco in Ruins: On the Trail of the Greatest Fire in the World's History" the descriptive literature read: "A two hour's ride through the most interesting parts of the burned district, which covers 460 blocks. A guide accompanies each trip, delivering enroute a complete descriptive lecture of the great fire."[44]

Time passed. One year later Anna Blake, who had been hospitalized during the fire, wrote her grandmother:

> This week—the anniversary of the earthquake and fire—has been a very busy one and a very serious occasion throughout the city. On the evening of the 17th, Wednesday evening, our church held a banquet, in the parlors, to which the members of the Plymouth Congregational Church were invited. The room is now carpeted and tinted and electric-lighted, and the evening was very bright and pleasant. There were after-dinner speeches, and a gentleman read a poem entitled "B.Q." (Before the Quake). It seemed so strange to step out of a brightly lighted room into the dark, to pick our way in the middle of the streets past all those ghostly moon-lighted ruins.[45]

CRITICISM OF THE RELIEF EFFORT

Criticism of the relief effort and evidence of the prevalence of disease during the aftermath of the earthquake and fire received scant mention in the press. The emphasis was on good or manufactured news. One example of the latter was "paper buildings," whose imminent construction was announced. A few materialized, but many were never built—at least in the form and at the time that had been indicated.[46]

As the novelty wore off, tempers shortened, inequities were noted, and critics emerged.

The camp administrators did not appreciate the complaints of the United Refugees, an organized group whose leaders gave speeches in the camps. Their criticisms were labeled "socialistic."

Dr. René Bine, who was in charge of the largest refugee camp at the west end of Harbor View, referred to the speakers as "the Agitators" or "chronic kickers." But he did admit that they had some justification for their complaints. "No mattresses, tatters for clothes, soleless shoes, no place to wash in and no underwear to wash were the laundry there, and $6,000,000 [the amount of donations cited] in the newspapers—it is not all surprising this socialistic organization."[47]

A leaflet circulated throughout the city accusing Phelan and Devine of misappropriating and squandering funds "for personal purposes rather than helping 'the refugees and sufferers.'" The broadside, signed "People of San Francisco," added: "General Greely says we are a lot of paupers. The finance committee is attempting to form another grafting corporation to build houses for the refugees."

The United Refugees devised a strategy of contacting donors to the relief effort with their complaints. The group met with representatives of the Massachusetts Association for the Relief of California while they were in San Francisco. The association referred to United Refugees in its favorable report on the handling of funds by Phelan's finance committee:

> They are undoubtedly well intentioned and perfectly honest in many cases, but in our opinion, their plans are visionary and often socialistic, their ideals harmful in making others badly enough off now, in all conscience, discontented with their lot. It does harm, not good. It complicates a sufficiently complicated situation and unjustifiably throws discredit upon and renders more difficult and less successful the work of capable efficient public benefactors, who are doing their utmost to serve their people.

According to the Massachusetts association's representatives who looked into the situation, most refugees wanted a per capita sharing of the donated relief funds, not discretionary handouts by the finance committee. "In fact," stated the association's report to its donors, "the almost universal feeling among the refugees is that they are part owners of a fund poured out by a generous public, to help make good their losses, and they are entitled to their share; that the Committee is wrongfully withholding it from them."[48]

After describing what she saw and heard while working and living among the refugees, Dr. Margaret Mahoney wrote: "Now comes the saddest chapter in the history of our disaster." She thought the professional charity workers from New York, Boston, and Chicago and the local relief workers had made a key mistake. "Charity methods should not be applied to urgent relief distribution," said Mahoney. The charity workers were conditioned to believing that poverty was the result of irresponsible behavior, not a natural disaster.

The doctor, who tended the injured and slept in a tent with her family in the Presidio, voiced the most revealing criticisms. She concluded her privately printed account: "May all other stricken communities be spared the combination of Red Cross, trained charity workers and a relief committee composed of wealthy men." The consequence of this socially narrow combination was:

> Being in the habit of dealing with paupers they undertook to pauperize a self-respecting community. Hoard was the keynote of their system, hoard supplies, hoard money, humiliate and insult the people so as to drive them from the bread lines. The cry was raised that there was work for all—remember that at that time the insurance companies prevented debris being cleared in the burned district. . . . Remember that at that time those who did obtain work were paid not in cash but in paper and that the savings banks were not open for business.

A relief official in her district told Mahoney, "Put them on their mettle. Make it hard for them." The doctor wondered, "Who were the people to be so treated? Human beings who had been through a most dreadful calamity, so dreadful that their faces bear the stamp that is probably indelible."[49]

DISEASE

Disease was another nonevent, but it, too, existed in lethal forms and could not be dismissed.

The number of cases of typhoid increased alarmingly, spread by flies that came in contact with feces, garbage, sewage, and thousands of dead horses and other animals. The city health officer reported: "The squares, public parks and vacant lots were packed with the stricken multitude, and without sanitary conveniences of any kind. . . . Sick and well were confusedly packed together; water supply cut off; sewers broken and no protection from the elements, which were unusually severe for this time of the year."

The doctor in charge of the South of Market relief district said that there were "so many millions of flies that it was impossible to find any habitation that was not filled with them."

By midsummer, 30 cases of typhoid had been reported within one month. The monthly average before the earthquake for hospital admissions of typhoid cases had been 12. For the two-month period dating from the earthquake, the army counted 95 cases, of which 17 resulted in death—a high mortality rate, according to an Army Medical Department report. By mid-1907 there had been 1,279 reported cases of typhoid and 228 deaths.

In the two months following the earthquake there was also an unusually high incidence of smallpox, with 123 reported cases and 11 deaths.[50]

San Francisco health officials asked San Jose relief officials for all the smallpox vaccine they could spare. None was available for San Francisco, they were told, because San Jose might need it. The chairman of the San Jose Relief Committee then offered advice on how to handle the public when there are alarmist reports:

> Assuming that it might be true, why tell the people about it? The only way to stamp it out would be not to tell the people about it and work quietly. At this time the people at large must be treated quietly, smoothly and carefully and gotten back to their normal condition as soon as possible.
>
> I appreciate the fact that you are anxious to be among the first to obtain your supply and commend you for your efforts but suggest that you do first missionary work with the newspapers and attempt to get a more cheerful aspect put on conditions as they exist at present. Talk against smallpox instead of for it and publish pictures of new buildings that are to be, rather than the ruins of the old ones.[51]

In 1907 another plague epidemic struck San Francisco, the first having been in 1900. "Social turmoil, in other words, had already been generated by the quake," wrote Susan Craddock in her book about diseases and poverty in San Francisco. "A plague epidemic merely exacerbated the chaos even as it altered its focus." The most cases occurred in the tightly packed earthquake cottages in Lobos Square (now the Moscone playground in the Marina District). Festering garbage throughout the city was blamed.

By this time it was known that the Black Death, as it was called, was caused by fleas carried by the rats that proliferated because of offal, the same refuse available to the flies that caused the typhoid. The city board of health reported: "All through the burned district there were vast accumulations of rubbish in which rats could breed; the sewers were broken and freely accessible to rats almost everywhere." Garbage was dumped on the ground, and the shacks attracted vermin.

In the two plague epidemics (the first two on the North American

Continent), a total of 285 people died, and 401 were sick. "It [the 1907 episode] was a broader and swifter outbreak, more democratic in its choice of victims, but less deadly than the smoldering plague of 1900," Marilyn Chase wrote in *The Barbary Plague.* "That earlier episode in Chinatown took a narrower aim on the Chinese, and case for case, it was far more lethal."[52]

This time rats throughout the city—not just those in Chinatown— were the targets of the campaign of eradication. Tens of thousands of rat traps and pieces of poisoned bait were set out. During the first four months of the epidemic, 16,494 rats were trapped or killed. Testing on a hit-or-miss basis revealed that 34 were infected. A plague hospital was quickly constructed. It was surrounded by a rat-proof iron fence. (In 1900, the whole of Chinatown had been cordoned off for the same purpose.)

The health campaign was almost completely ignored by the press and merchant organizations because of fears of the loss of business and the further stigma that might attach itself to San Francisco. The annual report of the board of health noted: "A very serious obstacle to [prevention] efforts, however, was encountered in the attitude of the press, which with one notable exception, either did not print any news on the subject at all or was openly antagonistic to the efforts of the Health authorities, using all means at their disposal to try to convince the people that there was no necessity for any radical improvements." Health authorities also attempted to "enlist the interest of the more important commercial organizations," but "very little success . . . was obtained in this direction."[53]

As with the death toll from the three days of earthquake and fire, deaths from diseases seem to have been vastly underestimated at the time. Writing fifty years later in *California Medicine,* Dr. William W. Stiles revealed a different set of statistics. The number of known typhoid cases existing on April 18 was 7. In the next few weeks there were 547 known deaths from typhoid and "probably an even greater number because reporting was far from complete." Such a number would have been of major epidemic proportions.

Dr. Stiles's article, which drew on city and state health and sanitation records, was first given as an address at a symposium on civil defense and disasters at the height of the cold war. He added that conditions in San Francisco "were as primitive as the military battlefields of the day," where the ratio of deaths from disease to battle injuries was ten to one. Using a very low "official" death toll of 463 from the earthquake and fire, Stiles estimated that there could have been 5,000 deaths from disease, a figure that seems excessive and which would certainly have attracted some attention at the time.[54]

THE END OF THE RELIEF ERA

The many facets of the relief effort ended at different times and in different ways.

The army withdrew its troops to their posts on June 30. The withdrawal ended seventy-three days of military occupation of San Francisco, a record for any American city.

Writing two decades later, General Greely grossly exaggerated his role, manipulated the truth, and rewrote history. It was a breathtaking achievement in self-aggrandizement. He claimed that he was at the apex of the civilian and military command structure, that no regular soldier had killed anyone and that there had been only one complaint of misconduct, that he had commanded the largest peacetime military force, and that there had been no murders, no riots, no epidemics, no formal criticism, and no one had gone hungry.[55]

One year after the earthquake approximately twelve thousand people were living in temporary tents and shacks, mostly South of Market.

Individual grants from the relief committee ended on July 1, 1907. About $1 million was held in reserve, mostly by the Red Cross, for final expenses. Nearly $185,000 was handed over by Phelan to various civic and religious charities, with the bulk going to those representing northern European populations and the Catholic religion. No Asian groups were listed as recipients.

The Japanese had contributed nearly $250,000 and the Chinese $40,000 to the relief effort yet very little money went to these two minorities. The Russell Sage Foundation stated in its report: "The Japanese asked for very little relief, in part because many had difficulty in speaking English, but more generally because all were aware of the anti-Japanese feeling of a small but aggressive part of the community. . . . Like the Japanese, and for the same reasons, [the Chinese] did not ask for much."

Phelan was lauded for his efforts. "Of the members of the San Francisco Committee from Mr. Phelan down," the *Overland Monthly* stated, "it must be said that the selection could not have been improved upon, for they are men of ability and integrity." The publication estimated that the committee in its various incarnations had distributed $9.2 million, of which $2.5 million had come from Congress and covered military expenses and

$312,000 had come from foreign donations. Operating expenses of less than 4 percent were reported.

The last official refugee camp was closed on June 30, 1908. The civic agenda thereafter emphasized public celebrations designed to send the message to the nation and the world that San Francisco was back bigger and better and more beautiful than ever.[56]

THE UPBUILDING OF SAN FRANCISCO

SPEED OVER BEAUTY

Relief was about caring for people. Reconstruction, or upbuilding, was about raising structures, preferably safe ones, in a planned manner.

The opportunity to create a beautiful new city seemed either heaven-sent or a great coincidence. An extensive urban landscape had been leveled, and, miraculously, there was a freshly minted plan on hand for its resurrection, a plan drafted by one of the world's great urban planners.

The obstacles to speedy reconstruction were the plan itself, known as the Burnham Plan; a lack of money, whose flow was hindered by tardy, partial, or nonexistent insurance settlements and the national financial panic of 1907; and new building requirements that would deter future fire and earthquake damage. One way or another, these impediments would be either swept aside or quickly dealt with in the rush to reconstruct.

The plan had been created shortly before the earthquake to beautify San Francisco. But in a city radically disfigured by earthquake and fire, market forces, not beauty, would determine the shape of modern San Francisco.

Dislocations are inevitable after a great disaster. San Francisco became more stratified—physically, socially, and economically. Inequities made this worse, as a study of the reconstruction process pointed out: "At one end of the spectrum, upper-class districts and individuals stabilized rapidly, whereas unskilled workers at the low end of the spectrum were still in motion five years after the disaster."

Besides an overall loss of numbers at the lower income levels, there were now more adult males and fewer children, Latinos, Italians, and Asian-Americans. Persons of English, Irish, Jewish, German, and French descent remained stable. Middle-class sales, service, and clerical jobs increased. Working-class manufacturing jobs declined, factories having located elsewhere in the Bay Area.

The major money institutions—the banks, the stock exchange, and the big insurance companies—located in what became known as the Financial District. The businesses that fed off them, such as department stores and large hotels, clustered around this core area. Higher-income housing moved westward into the unburned district. Lower-income housing, when it eventually became available, was pushed farther south. After the earthquake, the physical gap between rich and poor and the distance traveled for blue collar workers from home to job became greater.

Whereas San Francisco had been the statewide leader in growth in the nineteenth century, the rate of population increase in the first decade of the twentieth century was lower than elsewhere in the Bay Area and throughout the state. Tourism seemed like the solution to economic stagnation, and San Francisco began its long slide toward becoming an imitation of itself for outsiders.

In the boom years that immediately preceded the earthquake, the West Coast cities of Los Angeles, Portland, and Seattle had begun to challenge San Francisco's dominance. The desire to revitalize the city was one reason why James Phelan went in search of a grand plan and hired Daniel Burnham of Chicago to put it together.

Phelan had formed the Association for the Improvement and Adornment of San Francisco in 1904. Burnham and his associates went to work, designing a San Francisco that would be a Paris, Berlin, or Washington, D.C. The key to the plan was a great semicircular civic center *place* at Van Ness Avenue and Market Street from which nine broad arterial boulevards would radiate outward to meet inner and outer rings of concentric streets. (In later years the extensions of two freeways were, in effect, the pincers of the outer ring. They were torn down after the 1989 Loma Prieta earthquake.) Widening and creating new streets was the key to the plan, which meant that property owners had to relinquish their land, either voluntarily or through forced sale.

One characteristic of postdisaster cities is that they tend to replicate their former selves. This was true of London after the disastrous fire of 1666; Lisbon after the even greater damage and loss of life caused by earthquake, tsunami, and fire in 1755; Chicago after the fire and Galveston after the hurricane; and European cities after World War II. The instinct of New York City after the destruction of the World Trade Center was to build tall towers, which would again be prime targets for terrorists.

Other characteristics are that property rights remain sacrosanct, the tax base is restored as quickly as possible, and the speed of reconstruction becomes a mania. Additionally in the case of San Francisco, city records, including titles to property, had been destroyed. A means had to be devised to restore property lines before streets could be widened or pushed into new areas.

All these factors contributed to the demise of the Burnham Plan. As Charles Moore, Burnham's biographer and successor in the City Beautiful movement, commented: "It was the worst time to talk about beautification. The people were thrown back to a consideration as to how again they would live and thrive."[1]

For a brief moment after the disaster, however, there was hope that the plan could be implemented. Phelan wrote a correspondent on April 30: "San Francisco's calamity will enable us now to proceed to rebuild the city on the lines of the Burnham Plan." He wired Burnham in a telegram marked "Official" two days later: "Glad to hear you are coming. Sooner the better for us. Please advise immediately by letter on rebuilding Chicago [after the 1871 fire]. What new laws we need, long leases and other ideas."[2]

Burnham had written Phelan on the day before the earthquake that bound copies of the plan would be ready in a week or ten days. The Chicago planner rushed to San Francisco in mid-May. The publicity for the plan was extremely favorable. Burnham informed Phelan that an article in *Collier's*, a national news magazine, "is the best thing yet written on the new plan and should be sent broadcast. Every San Franciscan should read it."[3]

What was needed on the ground in San Francisco was a technocrat who was versed in the minutiae of city laws that covered the widening of streets versus property rights and was knowledgeable about how to get the proposal before the voters. That person, much to Phelan's chagrin, was Abe Ruef. On the one hand, Phelan wanted Ruef and Mayor Schmitz out of office; on the other, he desperately wanted his treasured plan to become a reality. His strategy was to do nothing, which contributed to the plan's demise.

Ruef dominated the long technical discussions dealing with the plan and other city matters in a series of May hearings conducted by the Committee of Forty's subcommittee on the special session of the state legislature. (It would be this committee, rather than the elected board of supervisors, that would forward the city's recommendations to the legislature for enactment.) Ruef's strategy, which the committee endorsed and the legislature placed on the statewide ballot, was a constitutional amendment that would allow the city to acquire land for street purposes by trading property, since the city then had little money.[4]

The counselor's activities demonstrated to members of the oligarchy that planning meant power. They were suspicious of power in Ruef's hands and not their own. "It was Ruef who came to personify civic concern in the crucial months from June through November, 1906, while Phelan stood aside and let private interests reassert themselves," wrote Judd Kahn in *Imperial San Francisco.* "James D. Phelan, the leading advocate of planning, sat on his hands while California voters defeated Ruef's cherished amendment."[5]

Another reason for its defeat was that downtown business leaders, of whom Phelan was one, opposed the plan. It soon became clear that implementation of the plan would delay reconstruction considerably and would be detrimental to the commercial interests of these property owners. Publisher M. H. de Young of the *Chronicle,* chairman of the Downtown Property Owners' Association, led the opposition. The downtown, meaning the Market Street area, was facing early competition from unburned Fillmore Street and Van Ness Avenue, where businesses temporarily located after the fire.[6]

De Young said the plan's recommendations, written by "men who simply sit down and work on theory," appeared "ridiculous" to practical businessmen. He added, "The plans as a whole for the business district would mean the loss of too much land to suit most of us. We have lost enough already by fire and earthquake, and I for one am not in favor of parting with any more of my holdings."

Kahn summed up the opposition's argument: "In San Francisco, a strong commitment to private property rights prevented the expansion of public authority." Phelan foresaw that Burnham's plan was doomed. He wrote to an official in the American Civic Association: "Of course, there is a sentiment here that resumption of business is the first consideration and an indisposition to make changes that will cost money."

There were historic parallels for this attitude. Christopher Wren's visionary, imperial, and impractical plan for rebuilding London after the fire of 1666 was defeated by "the merchants, brokers, and tradesmen [who] wanted the life of the city to resume just as quickly as possible," wrote Simon Schama.[7]

The only part of the master plan for San Francisco that eventually became a reality was the Civic Center, located three blocks north of the proposed *place.* A few years later voters approved construction of the new Civic Center as part of the beautification effort for the Panama-Pacific International Exposition of 1915, which trumpeted San Francisco's recovery to the world.[8]

The earthquake and fire disrupted the normal flow of money, which in California at that time meant coins rather than paper dollars. The banks closed to avoid a run on money stored in locked vaults, which were best left unopened for the time being. The fate of depositors' records was also unknown.

The leading banker in the state was Isaias Hellman Sr., who was the owner of banks and businesses in San Francisco and Los Angeles. Hellman had recently acquired the banking business of Wells Fargo & Company, while railroader Edward H. Harriman had taken over the venerable company's express business. Through Harriman, the California banker could tap the eastern money markets and have unlimited credit for the emergency, two sources of reserves that most California banks lacked.

Bankers from around the country and Europe contacted Hellman in the immediate aftermath, offering their sympathy and help. Hellman kept in close touch with the managers of his Los Angeles banks. His correspondence is a gauge of the pulse of money in an extreme emergency.

The fire had come within one block of Hellman's San Francisco home. Like many others, Hellman had no cash for personal expenses, but he had banks in Los Angeles and asked one of his managers to send him $5,000.

He advised this Los Angeles manager to keep a lot of cash on hand and to "make no loans for the present, except to regular clients & in moderate amounts." He thought the money and valuables in the vault of the ruined Wells Fargo National Bank in San Francisco were intact, as they later proved to be.

A letter was sent to customers, and reprinted in the press, assuring them that all was well, but privately bank officials fretted. There was "considerable excitement" in Los Angeles, but very little money was withdrawn, at first. The Los Angeles bankers were receiving telegrams from other cities whose money men thought Los Angeles had also been leveled by the earthquake. "We have done everything to correct that impression possible," Hellman was told by the bank manager, who drew on his "imagination" for an interview with a reporter to impart that message.

Although not observed in Los Angeles, a statewide banking holiday was declared by the governor. The purpose, which succeeded, was to avoid a run on banks in San Francisco. Withdrawals were limited to $500, although larger sums were given surreptitiously to favored customers.

Five days after the earthquake the manager of the Los Angeles bank panicked: "The demand for money from outside points here is simply tremendous. I fear if the San Francisco banks stay closed for thirty days that Los Angeles will be squeezed dry of coin. Just as we had to send money to you, every depositor we have got is sending money to some friend in San Francisco. . . . Our merchants are overwhelmed with orders from all over the Coast and will be absolutely sold out of goods very shortly."

Two days later the situation had eased.

On April 26 Hellman wrote the Los Angeles bank manager that Harriman was doing much to restore confidence. "Everything is being done by the strong to help the weak and no one is doing more than your friend I. W. H. to accomplish that. I think my liberal acts towards my neighbors and the assistance that I am rendering is being commented upon." There was a feeling of "the most confidence" in San Francisco, said Hellman, ever since "the insurance companies, big and little, have published notices that the insurance will be paid speedily."[9]

"THE GREAT FIRE"

For various reasons, insurance money was not immediately forthcoming. This was partially because of the verbal smokescreen erected by the very interests that needed the money as quickly as possible in order to reconstruct buildings. Once again San Francisco had harmed its own cause.

At a meeting in temporary quarters in the Calvary Church attended by a record number of members, the San Francisco Real Estate Board declared, six days after the earthquake, that there had been no earthquake. The *Chronicle* reported: "It was agreed that the calamity should be spoken of as 'the great fire,' and not as 'the great earthquake.'" In this manner the *e* word was effectively banished from public discourse.[10]

From across the bay, the *Oakland Tribune* editorialized: "How futile are such resolutions! No set of men can prescribe the terms which shall be applied to a catastrophe having few parallels in history. The fire and the earthquake are inseparably associated, and will forever remain so in men's minds." To guard against such calamities in the future "there is no need to play the ostrich and try to hide that which all the world must see."[11]

The underlying motives for the ban on mentioning the seismic event that triggered the massive fires in 1906 were explained later by two noted geologists.

Geology Professor John Casper Branner of Stanford University, who was one of the founders of the Seismological Society of America, said:

Another and more serious obstacle is the attitude of many persons, organizations, and commercial interests toward earthquakes in general. The idea back of this false position—for it is a false one—is that earthquakes are detrimental to the good repute of the west coast, and that they are likely to keep away business and capital, and therefore the less said about them the better. This theory has led to the deliberate suppression of news about earthquakes, and even of the simple mention of them. Shortly after the earthquake of April 1906 there was a general disposition that almost amounted to concerted action for the purpose of suppressing all mention of that catastrophe.[12]

Grove Karl Gilbert gave a major address before a scientific audience in Baltimore three years later, when he was at the apex of his profession. Quoting Josiah Whitney's comment following the 1868 earthquake that Californians had adopted a policy of "assumed indifference" to the danger of earthquakes, the USGS geologist said:

This policy of assumed indifference, which is probably not shared by any other earthquake district in the world, has continued to the present time and is accompanied by a policy of concealment. It is feared that if the ground of California has a reputation for instability, the flow of immigration will be checked, capital will go elsewhere, and business activity will be impaired.[13]

A curious reversal has occurred in recent years. For a long time the emphasis was placed on "the fire," but it has now become "the earthquake." Why? Charles Scawthorn, an earthquake engineer who is knowledgeable about fires, wrote in 2003: "Earthquakes historically have been the professional concern of seismologists and structural engineers, who, as a class of professionals, are largely uninformed about fire."

Earthquake-oriented seismologists, geologists, and structural engineers, most of whom are located in the Bay Area, are affiliated with universities, public agencies, consulting firms, and professional organizations that push seismic-related agendas. Science reporters cover their activities. Fires are regarded as one-time events, not as the subject of a discipline. Except for a few retired firemen who run an obscure museum in San Francisco that has a small display of earthquake items, little attention has been paid to the fire aspects of the disaster. The original sin of omission has, in effect, been compounded.[14]

After the earthquake and firestorms, insurers sent adjusters into the field who looked carefully and suspiciously at each claim, thus delaying settlements. Since earthquake insurance was nonexistent, claims were settled on the basis of fire damage.

The president of a midwestern insurance company dispatched a letter to Governor Pardee, who sent copies to Mayor Schmitz and two members of the citizens' committee:

> From the best information we can gather, it appears to me that your people are making a great mistake in minimizing the earthquake damage. I can understand why this is being done, but it immediately puts the Insurance Companies on the defensive. This whole thing is too serious a matter for the Insurance Companies, as well as your people, to justify any unfair methods on either side.[15]

John R. Freeman, an engineer and an insurance company executive, wrote a quarter-century later: "There seems to have been a local attempt to suppress information about earthquakes, lest it hurt California business, and rumors of this suppression have reacted unfavorably, by increasing the apprehension of Eastern underwriters."[16]

Samuel Weed, a gold rush–era fireman, left San Francisco to become an insurance underwriter in New York City. He returned in January 1908 to address the annual meeting of the Pacific Coast Underwriters' Association in San Francisco.

> I cannot doubt that you are aware that there is still a fear in the minds of underwriters in the East, as in Europe, that the earthquake danger is not over and the old saying that "what has once happened may happen twice" still lingers. I have heard this remark in underwriting circles one hundred times within eighteen months. The lesson for San Francisco is to relax no efforts to make your city safe. . . . But in all kindness permit me to say you cannot persuade underwriters at a distance that, if the losses were caused by fire, that the fire itself was not the result of an earthquake.[17]

Weed accurately stated the nub of the insurance industry's argument. That position led directly to the following conclusion in a San Francisco Chamber of Commerce report on insurance settlements: "So much money in controversy has caused an overstrain on human nature on both sides."[18]

By insurance standards, there was nothing to compare with this catastrophe. "The magnitude of the conflagration dealt a stunning blow to both insured and insurers. Conditions arose which had never existed before in the history of fire insurance," according to a report by the National Association of Credit Men. "Never had such a conflagration occurred since the origin of fire insurance," stated a history of fire insurance.

The complications were staggering. The fire was inextricably mixed with an earthquake "for whose direct effects the companies were not responsible," said the Fire Underwriters Association of the Pacific. Furthermore, the evidence of damage by the earthquake had been destroyed by the fire and extensive dynamiting. City property records and insurance policies in the San Francisco offices of the insurers and the homes and businesses of the insured had also been destroyed.[19]

AN INSURANCE MADHOUSE

For the first few months after the earthquake and fire San Francisco was an insurance madhouse. Between three hundred and four hundred adjusters from across the country, most of whom were unfamiliar with the city and were based in Oakland at first, fanned out across the blackened ruins or sat behind makeshift desks and began to collect and generate massive amounts of paperwork. Long lines of exhausted, frustrated, and angry policyholders formed in front of these temporary offices. One adjuster recalled: "The nervous strain of day after day meeting a constant stream of claimants, and the incessant call for good temper, courtesy, and tact, soon told upon all who were actively engaged in this business."[20]

The adjusters represented some 100 insurance companies authorized to do business in California, one-third of which were foreign. An additional 125 companies, both foreign and domestic, wrote insurance on San Francisco structures from outside the state, insured the insurers, or were small companies.

All 225 firms (except for one dozen that went bankrupt or fled California immediately in order not to have to pay any claims) processed nearly one hundred thousand claims. Between $220 and $250 million was paid on insured structures, whose prequake values were between $315 million and

$350 million. The payout was 80 percent of the face value of the amount insured, compared to 50 percent in Chicago and 90 percent in the 1904 Baltimore fire, neither of which involved an earthquake.

The seven-story Palace Hotel, once a palatial structure that occupied a whole block, was a brick and steel skeleton whose entire interior had been gutted. The hotel was the largest single insurance loss that had ever been adjusted in the United States. Its prequake value was $1.8 million. The insurance paid $1.26 million.[21]

The insurance money was important because it was that money and local private capital that helped rebuild San Francisco. The newspapers, in their attempt to hype the upbuilding of San Francisco, carried exaggerated accounts about eastern consortiums headed by the likes of the Harrimans, Rockefellers, and Morgans that were poised to pump massive amounts of money ($100 million in one story) into rebuilding the city. Phelan, city officials, and their congressional representatives submitted various proposals for federal funding that went beyond disaster relief. None were enacted.[22]

The poor were at a disadvantage in dealing with the insurance companies. Those people who needed cash immediately, did not know how the system worked, and were unable to exert political and legal pressure received the lowest returns on their policies.

Some companies employed "thoroughly disgraceful methods in dealing with their claimants" who were "poor" and "timid." In their defense, many adjusters arrived in San Francisco thinking—as early newspaper accounts indicated—that the earthquake had done most of the damage. They were also under pressure from their home offices to keep payments low. But this did not excuse the "intimidation and discourtesy" employed by some insurance adjusters. According to the chamber of commerce,

> reports of such gross incivilities very naturally found their way into the newspapers; as did likewise reports of many of the early settlements which as a matter of fact were much lower on the average than they were later, some of the companies which began paying early offering only forty and fifty per cent, while others definitely denied liability altogether.[23]

The insurance companies met frequently through May and early June but were unable to agree on a common formula, some opting to honor their commitments fully and others wanting to pay only 75 percent of the insured loss. A standard 25 percent deduction would cover whatever had been damaged by the earthquake, the thinking went. The split divided the firms in the public's mind into "dollar-for-dollar" (full value) and "six-bit" (75 cents or 75 percent) companies. The publication of names resulted in magically transforming some of the latter into the former.[24]

The governor and the mayor stepped into the fray and sent a telegram to all home offices, stating that "the insurance condition here is intolerable." They minimized the earthquake damage, said that "certain agents" were wringing "unfair settlements from a stricken people," and appealed to the companies' "manhood, business integrity, and sense of justice." The replies from the insurance companies included statements that the situation was unique, that each loss would be settled on its merits, that all legal liabilities would be met, or that partial settlement was better than no payment and bankruptcy.[25]

As the summer wore on, the insurance situation improved, with more claims being paid.

One of the companies was the Atlas Assurance Company of London, whose activities provide an example of how one of the more responsible firms dealt with the emergency. The manager of the company's U.S. operations was in New York City. The manager of its San Francisco office was F. J. Devlin.

On April 19 London telegraphed New York: "We cannot get reply from Devlin. Try to ascertain if they and Office records are safe." New York replied: "We have no news from Devlin. We very much fear Office destroyed." Both offices sent additional wires to Devlin, to which there was no immediate reply.

The next day, as the fires continued to burn in San Francisco, the manager of the New York office wrote a long "situation" memorandum to the home office. The gist of it was that, with other insurance companies greatly weakened or put out of business, Atlas's strong position would enable it to profit greatly. "The Chicago fire in 1871 rendered bankrupt a large proportion of the Companies which were doing business in that day," he wrote. "Those that were left in business, even though of but the weakest standing, reaped a rich harvest, some of the strongest institutions in America today dating their strength from that conflagration." The manager went on to urge quick action to take advantage of the opportunity.

> If the intention be, as I assume it is, to recoup ourselves for the terrible blow which has been encountered in San Francisco, we should act with promptness to take the full advantage of the next few weeks, when there will be the re-adjustment of business from bankrupt and weak Companies to those of demonstrated strength. The situation is likely to be that never in our history has there been a time when conditions will be so much upon our own terms, as to what we should write, and where, and at what rate as at present. We are likely to be importuned by the best of agents and the best of clients to force upon us the classes of business which we have for years been patiently cultivating, and it will be a position of such strength as to make itself felt in profit for years to come.

The manager, whose views paralleled others in the insurance industry, recalled the statement in the previous year's report of the National Board of Fire Underwriters that "San Francisco has violated all underwriting traditions and precedent by not burning up." He added, "Hence it is not really the unexpected which has happened there." A great opportunity was presented to the industry. "This conflagration will check adverse legislation, it will advance rates, it will reduce competition, it will stimulate demands for insurance . . . it will give us all the conditions which make for profit."

To demonstrate the company's solvency and goodwill, the manager requested that all payments be made from London, rather than New York. He asked the home office to reassure and encourage its American agents and policyholders. London replied: "Convey to all Agents our sympathy with them as American citizens. In California disaster Atlas will meet all obligations promptly and honorably by drafts on London."

On the same day, Saturday, April 22, London notified the New York office to donate $5,000 to the San Francisco relief fund. Four days later the New York manager was told: "We can, I know, depend on your getting the full advertising value, to which naturally our shareholders are entitled, in exchange for this contribution."

London finally received word from its San Francisco agent that the office had been destroyed but that the records were in a safe that had not yet been opened. Devlin moved the Atlas office to Oakland. The home office expressed its sympathy and distress but noted a silver lining: "We may look with confidence to this set-back to be followed by a period of exceptional prosperity from which we may hope to recoup to a large extent the payments we have now to face."

The company sent additional Atlas employees to San Francisco from New York, Chicago, and Canada. The London office urged caution: "We wish of course to be prompt in dealing with claims but naturally we do not wish to settle any without proper investigation, both as to liability and as to amount." Devlin estimated a $2 million loss for Atlas. The New York manager thought that was too high. In fact, it would be much too low.

On May 2, Devlin was advised by London not to pay any claims based on earthquake damage alone, for quake-damaged buildings that subsequently burned, or for buildings that were destroyed by dynamite. Devlin was to advise all agents of British companies of this position, which was taken by that country's insurance industry.

By mid-May, Devlin was the San Francisco policy coordinator for all British companies that had written a sizable amount of insurance on the ruined portions of the city. London urged him to act in concert with American companies. The New York manager reported the split among companies, stating that "the majority are all at sixes and sevens." He correctly foresaw the result of delay, which would be "public clamor and resentment . . . aroused by the urgent need for the insurance money, while the Companies so far are making no headway towards a point where money can be paid." Interminable litigation would be a public relations disaster, he said.

Atlas began settling. By August, the prospect of reaping great profits from the disaster was not encouraging. As opposed to the Chicago fire, far fewer companies had failed, some strong companies were not involved at all, others had successfully reorganized, and Atlas's increase in rates was meeting with "serious opposition in some quarters." The New York manager reported a "serious element of competition" had arisen in San Francisco, and it was "meeting with a certain measure of success."[26]

The Atlas Assurance Company was one of thirty-one insurance firms that would be named by a committee of the National Association of Credit Men to the "roll of honor" of companies involved in the disaster. Atlas settled its claims in full, less a 1 or 2 percent discount for cash. Its total gross loss was $4.7 million. Only five other companies on the honor roll had the same or higher losses. Three companies—Aetna, Continental, and the Queen Insurance Company of America—received "high praise" for settling without a cash discount. Although the Hartford had a 2 percent discount, its losses of $10 million earned it the "highest commendation."[27]

As other companies began settling with large clients in the second half of 1906 and early 1907, the pace of reconstruction became torrid.[28]

THE ENGINEERS PROBE FOR ANSWERS

What had stood? What had fallen? And why? What had been destroyed by the earthquake or fire or both? These were the questions engineers and others sought answers to as they probed the ruins. The answers, it was thought, would result in the design and construction of safer buildings. But that was not to be the case. In the rush to rebuild, San Francisco was denied a safer future.

One answer to why buildings tumbled had been known for forty-one years and then conveniently forgotten. They were built in the wrong places. After the first sizable earthquake struck San Francisco in 1865, the city's leading newspaper at the time, the *Daily Alta California,* noted: "The 'made land' part of the city, east of Montgomery Street, and the flats south of Market Street seem to have felt the effects the most severely."

Three years later, greater damage from an even stronger earthquake, centered on the Hayward Fault to the east, occurred in the same area of "made land" (where San Francisco's tallest buildings now stand). Each time, the proposed solution was to build bigger, better, and higher in the same places. Proper design and good construction techniques would defeat earthquakes, it was thought. One respected member of the engineering profession voiced a cautionary note: "Obviously, earthquakes may and do occur which will wreck any structure known to Man."[29]

In 1907, Gilbert pointed out the obvious in a government report: "It has long been known that buildings and other structures on ground of certain kinds are more susceptible to earthquake injury than on ground of other kinds, and these differences were strikingly illustrated in San Francisco. The general fact appears to be that the amplitude of vibration and the acceleration are greater in loose, unconsolidated formations than in solid rock."[30]

The investigators were limited in their determinations by the narrowness of their respective disciplines and the multiplicity of destructive forces: shaking, flames, and explosives. Earthquake engineers, whose profession evolved from the wreckage of 1906, believed the problems and the solutions lay in the design and construction of structures. Geologists looked for answers in the nature of the land. For many of the ruins there was no definitive way to separate one destructive force from another.[31]

A 1907 report by the American Society of Civil Engineers concluded that workmanship was a factor in earthquake damage, as was design. Elasticity was a necessity, and wood- and steel-framed buildings provided the necessary movement. Brick and stone walls, without interior frames, were "completely discredited." As for fire damage, all materials failed, including brick, tile, granite, marble, sandstone, steel, cast iron, concrete, plaster, cement, and wood.

The fire destroyed up to 90 percent of the twenty-four thousand ruined structures, leaving perhaps some twenty-four hundred damaged by the earthquake alone or some combination of the three destructive forces. No building was fireproof. Fire slithered like a snake through small openings, devoured vulnerable interiors, and left modern steel and brick buildings blackened shells. "Unless one has been an eye-witness, it is difficult to realize how all materials that men make into the shape of buildings can be so utterly destroyed in a general conflagration," the engineering report stated.[32]

Lead sash weights and window glass ran together in rivulets, unprotected cast-iron and steel columns resembled pretzels, and wooden barrels containing nails in hardware stores burned, leaving their contents, which had dropped through a number of floors, a mass of welded metal. The trim around windows, ornamental woodwork, and furnishings provided the fuel in what had been previously regarded as "fireproof" structures. Over 80 percent of so-called fireproof safes and vaults failed because they were too thin to withstand the intense heat and their contents vaporized.[33]

Two of San Francisco's iconic structures, the massive City Hall and the towering Call (or Claus Spreckels) Building, provided excellent examples of what happened to poorly constructed public buildings and well-designed private structures respectively. Both failed, but for different reasons.

The City Hall and adjoining Hall of Records were located at Larkin and McAllister streets (near the present monumental city hall that was damaged in the 1989 earthquake). It was built on top of the Mission Bay swamplands and the Yerba Buena Cemetery. The sandy, remote cemetery site was selected following extensive damage to the existing city hall in the 1868 quake. The project progressed in fits and starts, beginning in 1871 and taking more than twenty years to complete. James Phelan was the first mayor to occupy the building in 1900.

Estimated originally to cost $1.8 million, the new City Hall would end up costing nearly four times as much. The scandal-ridden project was designed and built by a series of architects and contractors. Supposedly solid-brick walls were filled with rubble, and one wing missed connecting with the main building by one foot.

What took years to build fell in seconds. The earthquake toppled large portions of the City Hall while the Hall of Records, built first, held steady. Fire then swept both buildings.

Countless photographs of the municipal ruins standing in a bombed and fire-blitzed wasteland came to symbolize the destruction of San Francisco. An engineering publication called it "perhaps the most spectacular ruin in the world." The *Mining and Scientific Press* editorialized:

> It is a sorry sight: the big dome has been stripped of its stone, leaving a bird-cage of steel trusses, the roof has fallen and the walls have crumbled; it looks like the disheveled remains of a doll's house, shaken to pieces. The building that housed the City's administration and should have been an example of architectural skill and artistic taste, has collapsed miserably, because every stone of it was laid in putrid politics; it is a disgraceful ruin, the great dome is stripped of its veneer of stone as thoroughly as the iniquity of the builders stands plain to every beholder.[34]

Geologists and engineers poured over the ruins looking for answers. The City Hall was a brick building with steel floor beams and iron arches and columns. An exterior covering of stucco was tinted to resemble the gray sandstone used in many San Francisco buildings. The unsupported and poorly mortared brickwork shook loose, the massive columns broke into pieces, and the iron arches softened and buckled. The geologists' report concluded: "The building was a monument of bad design and poor materials and workmanship, and was not, therefore, of such a character that it could be expected to resist successfully the effect of earthquake or fire."

The design and construction of the Call Building and its performance during the earthquake was widely praised because it was the prototype for the future. The future, it was hoped, would be an entire business district of such tall steel-framed structures, known as class A buildings. Then, the thinking went, one building would not fall upon another and fires would not spread.

The Call Building, the city's towering symbol of private enterprise, was believed to be the best-designed and best-constructed steel-framed building in the country. Twenty-one stories including a dome, the city's premier office building rested on a wider twenty-five-foot deep steel foundation embedded in a still wider concrete block.

Marble tiling in the corridors fell, as did the poorly fastened ceilings, which would have been deadly to any occupants at a later hour. Some minor structural problems could be found in the upper stories, but the steel framing remained plumb. According to the USGS, "the general behavior of the structure demonstrates that high buildings subject to earthquake can be erected with safety even on sand foundations."

The problem—and it was no small one—was the fireproofing of such structures. "Had the building been as well designed to resist fire as to resist earthquake, it is probable that the total damage would have been very much less than it was," said the government report.

How did demon fire—intense enough to bend steel and scorch reinforced concrete—enter this modern, supposedly fireproof structure?

The entryway was a tunnel leading from the powerhouse across the street. The fire was then sucked up the elevator shaft, which acted as an enormous chimney, and smoke and flames erupted from the lanternlike cupola, which resembled an Olympic torch. Wooden floors, ornaments, furnishings, and office contents burned. Glass windows and metal trim melted. The USGS report concluded: "The lessons taught by the great Chicago and Baltimore fires had been applied by but few of the architects of San Francisco, on account of cost restrictions insisted on by owners, and very much of the damage inflicted on these high-class structures during the conflagration is directly traceable to the imperfect fireproofing put in, or to the entire absence of fireproofing."[35]

What to do? For those in charge of the rebuilding effort, the answer was obvious: little or nothing should be done so the city could be rebuilt as quickly and as cheaply as possible.

An insider who witnessed the decision-making process left a stunning record of the thinking of those in the ruling class. John Debo Galloway was a leading civil engineer who had designed a number of the modern steel-framed buildings. After the disaster he was retained to report on the performance of structures at Stanford University, at Agnews State Hospital, and in San Jose and San Francisco. Galloway was also a member of the citizens' committee charged with revising the city's building code, and he was chairman of the American Society of Civil Engineer's Committee on Fire and Earthquake Damage to Buildings.

A fascinating dialogue took place between Galloway and one of his colleagues, J. K. Freitag. Freitag was also a civil engineer who was critical of Galloway's committee report that advocated the least expensive approach to rebuilding the city. Freitag advanced the radical position that the safety of the community must be considered over the rights of property owners. "A building which proves a menace to neighbors cannot be erected," Freitag argued, "and the responsibility of the individual as affecting the community is even carried so far in some localities of Europe that the owner of property causing fire damage to neighbors is held financially responsible for such loss."

Galloway took issue with Freitag's ideas. In the process, he revealed the thinking of members of the oligarchy, which eventually prevailed. His reply is testimony to the triumph of private gain over public responsibility:

> In the altruistic days after the fire the writer was a member of the Committee engaged in rewriting the building laws. When the subject of fire-limits came up, [Freitag] brought in a plan for a certain zone within the fire-limits which should contain nothing but incombustible buildings, about as outlined above. This brought out unanimous protest in the Committee, and from others, and the subject was dropped. The distant observer will ask why, with virgin ground before it, the city did not cut avenues, widen streets, and build nothing but incombustible buildings. Such comment is most superficial. The city had suffered from the greatest fire in history. Most of her industries were wiped out of existence, all business buildings were destroyed, goods burned, streets wrecked and filled with debris, sewers broken, the water supply badly crippled, and the transportation system destroyed. Comment on civic responsibility, in the face of such conditions, is mere froth. What San Francisco needs is the cheapest building possible in which business can be done, to insure the community enough to eat. The other subjects can wait.[36]

THE RIGHT ANSWERS ARE IGNORED

By the time the scientists of the USGS, the engineers of the American Society of Civil Engineers, and the various experts on the State Earthquake Investigation Commission had published their reports in 1907 and 1908, the policy of full speed ahead with no impediments had already been established. The reports were barely noted because the information was "too cumbersome, too technical, and too late to have much impact."

The executive director of the national Society of Building Commissioners visited San Francisco and correctly predicted: "The old San Francisco ordinance was a veritable hodge-podge. The people now in charge of the revisions will hardly do much better."

Efforts to upgrade the building code were defeated. There were a few minor adjustments, later retractions, and a general weakening of standards. An auxiliary water system (that failed in the 1989 quake) was built, mainly to lower insurance rates. The well-known San Francisco architect Willis Polk warned in 1907 that "many buildings are now being constructed in a manner that will court certain destruction in case of another earthquake."[37]

Nearly ninety years later, architectural historian Stephen Tobriner wrote:

> What had the citizens of the phoenix city learned from the worst single urban disaster in the history of the United States? Interestingly, the people did not respond as we might expect. The fire district of incombustible buildings was not significantly enlarged in San Francisco, nor was the building code greatly strengthened to insure that so-called "fireproof" structures might survive a similar conflagration. Just after the earthquake some seismic precautions entered the building codes, but within three years these were modified. Rather than being prescribed by law, individual architects, engineers and their clients acted on their own either to include or exclude safety features in the new structures being built in San Francisco.[38]

One of those persons acting on his own initiative was James Phelan, whose wealth was tied up in real estate. The prices of building materials and labor were rising, as were interest rates, in the summer of 1906. Phelan decided to rebuild the Phelan Building in December. It would be steel framed and ten stories high. In 1907 labor unrest caused delays in construction. Four years after the quake the building had still not been completed. As it neared completion, Phelan desperately sought tenants, among them the army.

Finally, the Phelan Building was completed, on a triangular lot at Market and O'Farrell streets. "An Entirely New Modern Class 'A' Office Building *and* a San Francisco Landmark," proclaimed Phelan's advertising. The structure was of "battle-ship construction." Phelan was so convinced of the building's stability that he asked the mortgage holder, the Metropolitan Life Insurance Company, to forgo the requirement for earthquake insurance.[39]

THE DEPLETION OF NATURAL RESOURCES
TO REBUILD SAN FRANCISCO

One consequence of the speedy rebuilding was the lowering of safety standards in the buildings that were constructed. Another was the depletion of natural resources elsewhere in the West in order to rebuild the city.

Despite the newfound popularity of the automobile, San Francisco was rebuilt by old-fashioned horse power. The death of fifteen thousand horses was celebrated as a necessity in order to rebuild San Francisco in a *Harper's Weekly* article by Rufus M. Steele. He wrote, "Into the foundations of the new city is going the life-blood of fifteen thousand superb horses in order that the paint-brush may begin its final coating in two years. Deliberately fifteen thousand draught-horses are being worked to death. Their lives are a sacrifice to an exigency of the times."

The horses were used to haul debris, excavate foundations, and deliver building materials. Where four horses were used before the earthquake, two were used after it, and still they were in short supply. The search for more and more horses went beyond the corrals in California and neighboring Nevada and Oregon to the Rocky Mountain states. There was even a plan to import mules from Missouri.

Contractors were awarded more money if they finished ahead of schedule. "The contractor reaps the premium," wrote Steele, "by driving his horses to death. It is willful murder in a just cause, for no city might readily summon horses enough for a task like San Francisco."

The cost of hay and grain was high, so the horses were starved. An unusually wet winter resulted in mud and potholes that crippled many. But the horses' owners, many of whom had left their ranches to make quick money, were getting rich.

As the horses died while pulling wagons loaded with lumber, the forests on the West Coast were being stripped in order to replace the twenty-four thousand ruined structures, most of which had been built of wood.[40]

A few days after the fire, the banker A. P. Giannini contacted a number of ship captains in San Francisco Bay and loaned them the money to sail to Oregon and Washington in order to buy lumber. "Get all the lumber you can," he said. "It will soon be in greater demand than anything else." Ships, dispatched by Giannini and others, sped northward.

In 1900 the forests of the Pacific Northwest were the last remaining timber frontier in the country. From Puget Sound south to Monterey Bay, spruce, cedar, hemlock, pine, and redwood trees grew, all easily available for shipment by water. Steam-driven vessels, with oversized decks to hold large cargoes of lumber, and steam-driven engines in the woods had transformed a cottage industry dominated by sail and the axe to one of mass production. Capitalists with names like Weyerhauser took over from small entrepreneurs.

These were boom times for the timber industry. With the boom came crime. The frenzied drive to acquire more timberlands in Oregon resulted in land fraud. William J. Burns, on loan to the Department of the Interior from the Secret Service, and Francis J. Heney, a federal prosecutor, joined forces in a number of high profile cases that brought them to the attention of President Roosevelt and others. They were dispatched south after the quake to investigate and prosecute San Francisco's graft cases.

Production significantly spiked upward in that year of earthquake and fire when many temporary structures were hastily thrown together. "The year 1906 will go down into history as the record breaker, both in the output of lumber and price obtained," reported the *Timberman,* the trade journal for the West Coast lumber industry. Records were broken despite a strike of sailors on steam-driven vessels and a shortage of railroad cars.

It was not the first time, nor would it be the last that San Francisco reached out after a catastrophe to rebuild itself by importing natural resources from elsewhere. The redwood trees just to the south in San Mateo County—where the name of Redwood City had once signified tall, stately trees rather than flat suburbs—had been cut to rebuild the city after its early disastrous fires. The earthquake provided the impetus for importing water from Yosemite National Park.

The difference in procuring natural resources this time was that San Francisco had to reach farther. There was this postdisaster assessment from Seattle: "Already the lumber mills of Washington and Oregon are running to their fullest capacity, and notwithstanding the great quantities of lumber which they are turning out daily, they are unable to supply the increased demand. The result will be a very active lumber market for many years to come . . . with a corresponding trade throughout the whole Northwest."

The most sustained boom occurred closer to San Francisco in the redwood forests of northwest California. Fire-resistant redwood was in great demand. Loggers worked unceasingly during daylight hours. Mills operated on "full double-time." The amount of redwood shipped to San Francisco in October 1906 was double that of the same month in the previous year, which had also been a record month.

For a time the use of lumber was indiscriminate. A San Francisco correspondent for the *Timberman* wrote:

Every one of these merchants, manufacturers and small tradesmen wanted to get their [stores] first: they were all to be of wood, and the consequence was that the demand was something phenomenal—anything in the shape of wood went. Flooring was used that could not have been over a week from the saw, No. 3 merchantable being run into T. and G. and used for ceiling. At the same time, people had to have some kind of habitations, repairs to houses had to be made, and this increased the demand.

The panic of 1907 put a dent in West Coast lumber production, but the demand in San Francisco remained high. Production rose again to match the quickened pace of construction that corresponded with the finalization of plans and distribution of insurance money that made it possible to build more permanent structures in the last years of the decade.[41]

THE SEARCH FOR UNDERSTANDING

THE MISSING HISTORY COLLECTION

The search for historic and scientific understanding of the unprecedented events that occurred in the cities and surrounding countryside led to two organized efforts. One was an astounding failure and the other a magnificent success. Both efforts were initiated at the University of California, barely thirty-seven years old in 1906. An even younger Stanford University was too busy attempting to physically rehabilitate itself to play a major role in these enterprises.

First, the failure. How did the single largest repository of historical information slip through the willing fingers of the university and become lost, probably forever?

One week after the earthquake the citizens' committee began a concerted drive to gather material for a history. At a Fort Mason meeting attended by all the major players on April 25, Judge Morrow moved—and all those present agreed—to form a Committee on History. The committee's job was "to collect information and all available data relating to the events connected with the earthquake and fire for the purpose of preparing a full and correct historical narrative of the events."

Mayor Schmitz appointed four prominent San Franciscans to the committee. The chairman was John S. Drum, who was an attorney, a friend of Phelan's, and an insider among the oligarchy. He would later become president of the Mercantile Trust Company of San Francisco and the American Banker's Association. The offspring of a pioneer family, he had a lifelong interest in California history and art.[1]

A fifth member was added later. H. Morse Stephens, a professor of history at the University of California, had already approached Governor Pardee in Oakland with the idea of a history. Knowing of Stephens's interest, university president Benjamin Ide Wheeler, a member of the citizens' committee, proposed his name to Mayor Schmitz. Wheeler had also instructed Stephens to organize "a small group of young historians" to compile a history of the university's role in the Berkeley relief effort. That chore was given to a graduate student.

Stephens was one of the faculty's stars. He had been recruited four years earlier from Cornell University, where he and Wheeler had been colleagues. The first Sather Professor of History at Berkeley, Stephens's specialty was European history. He had played a key role in acquiring Hubert H. Bancroft's library for the university in 1905.

The bearded, absent-minded Stephens was a bachelor, an enthusiastic member of the Bohemian Club, and an educator beloved by his students. He was the first director of the University of California Extension and traveled widely by train throughout northern California as its sole faculty member. He was also chairman of the history department and would become dean of the College of Letters and Science. His busy schedule included four days on the road, two days teaching at Berkeley, and dinner at the Wheelers on Sundays.[2]

The history committee immediately printed a handbill and letter entitled "We Want All the Facts" that was distributed throughout the city. The committee, the notice declared, "is preparing for publication by the War Department a complete history of the recent earthquake and fire in San Francisco." A series of questions was asked. The committee sought original municipal proclamations and military orders. The press publicized the plea for information.[3]

Stephens recruited two graduate students, Lawrence J. Kennedy and John D. Fletcher, who would later write their master's degree theses on the fire and the Berkeley relief effort. The students were paid $25 a month for their efforts. They made trips to San Jose, Santa Rosa, and Fort Bragg to collect information.

Stephens submitted expense accounts for travel, books, office supplies, and express services through 1908. He received a small amount of money from Wheeler, a number of $100 and $200 donations from Drum, and most of the funding, $3,864 in 1910, from Phelan's finance committee by way of the history committee. The amount did not cover publication of the report, which was "still in abeyance," according to Phelan at that time.[4]

Meanwhile, Stephens had been promising great things. In the university's 1908 yearbook he said that he had been contemplating a history from the very first jolt, and "the compilation of a record has been the chief business of the writer." On the second anniversary of the earthquake and fire, Stephens wrote in an *Examiner* article: "Never before has such an attempt been made at the collection of historical material on [as] large a scale for the record of a contemporary historic event."

The work that had been accomplished by April 19, 1908, was truly mind-boggling in its extent and thoroughness.

Three thousand written narratives were collected while memories were fresh. The "conspicuous actors" in the drama were interviewed, some more than once, and a court reporter compiled verbatim transcripts. Statements from firemen, policemen, and school teachers were also gathered.

The committee met regularly for lunch or dinner and invited busy guests, who did not have the time to sit for long interviews, to "throw light from personal knowledge and experience" on aspects of the events. "In this fashion," said Stephens, "hardly a prominent man or woman went uninterrogated." Stephens, who had written two books on the French Revolution and knew his European history, boasted: "No such attempt to obtain prompt personal narratives from participants and observers in a great historical crisis has ever been made before."

The committee sought information on governance and obtained voluminous records of the two citizens' committees and their many subcommittees, along with army and municipal records. Mayor Schmitz, Governor Pardee, General Greely, and Phelan were "always ready to give information and assistance," said Stephens.

Newspapers proved a valuable source of information, and again Stephens thought he was breaking new ground. Issues of eight hundred papers from April 18 to May 31, weighing "more than a ton," yielded some thirty-six thousand articles. All the news stories sent from San Francisco by the Associated Press were obtained. Stephens said, "Never was time, money or labor better expended."

All the historical materials, weighing one and three-quarter tons, were assembled in Berkeley. A staff of eleven undergraduates was employed to index and file. The material fell into four categories: the earthquake, the fire, the citizens' committees, and the relief effort.

Legend needed to be separated from fact: no fight occurred between Chinese and Italians in Portsmouth Square, the Cliff House did not slide into the ocean, few suspected looters were shot, and fingers and ears laden with jewelry and stuffed into the pockets of ghouls were the material of medieval legends. The committee members felt that the number of dead had been greatly exaggerated.

Given two years to gain some distance from the event, certain things became obvious "after prolonged study and meditation." Stephens's assessment, like others at the time, erred on the bright side. "Every great disaster that has overwhelmed or nearly overwhelmed a great city has been accompanied by or immediately followed by at least one and generally by all three of the following afflictions: a great outbreak of disease, a great outbreak of crime and a great financial and commercial crisis. None of these things occurred in San Francisco." The professor overlooked the financial panic of 1907, an outbreak of plague, labor riots, race riots, and the graft trials that were in progress at the time.

He also erred on another matter. Stephens believed that the committee was headed toward producing a published history in April 1908. "The time had come," he said, "to write and to close the work of collecting material." He outlined subchapters in "the forthcoming book of the Earthquake History Committee."

At the same time the professor noticed a coolness toward the project. "Both organizations and individuals grew weary of being reminded of April, 1906, and a reaction showed itself from the glad readiness with which the first advances of the committee had been met. The general public got interested in other things and wished to forget the earthquake and fire."[5]

The nearly two tons of historical materials—consisting of forty full file boxes, two full vertical filing cabinets, twelve trays of index cards, a box of notebooks and account books, a vast pile of newspapers, and a few reports having to do with relief work—languished. It remained in Stephens's possession until his death in 1919.[6]

Stephens died of a heart attack two days short of the thirteenth anniversary of the disaster. He was returning from San Francisco after attending the funeral of Phoebe Apperson Hearst, the great patron of the university. In the eulogies and press notices of his death no mention was made of the earthquake project. Phelan, at the time a U.S. senator, represented the state and federal governments at Stephens's funeral.[7]

The historian's will left all his property to the regents of the university. The earthquake collection was not mentioned in the will, indicating its lack of importance to Stephens, who at heart was a Europeanist. Stephens's beloved Bancroft Library was not named as the beneficiary of any materials. The earthquake collection went, by default, to the university library. Had it gone to the Bancroft, which specialized in California history, there was a far better chance that it would have survived, since its value would have been more readily recognized.

Stephens's personal papers, class notes, manuscripts, books, and the bulky mass of the earthquake materials were stored at first in the private office of the university librarian, then in a room on the library's fourth floor, and finally in the reserved book room in the stacks. The university librarian, Harold L. Leupp, kept badgering Farnham P. Griffiths, a former student and close friend of Stephens, to cull the mass of material. "We are anxious to get everything possible off the shelves at an early date," said Leupp in 1924, "as this year we shall be put to our trumps to find the necessary space to accommodate books received."

Griffiths had been a student secretary to Wheeler and was then a San Francisco lawyer with close ties to the university. He would later lecture at the law school and serve as a university regent. Griffiths emerged as the middleman between Leupp, who wanted to get rid of the bulky earthquake collection, and John Drum, who wanted to put it to some use.

Drum was peremptory in his desire to posses the collection, Griffiths was the expediter, and Leupp was meekly subservient. Leupp wanted to do nothing that would "irritate Mr. Drum and cause him to suppose that the Library has been negligent." Griffiths sent Drum copies of Leupp's letters "to relive Mr. Leupp of any criticism."

From the start, Drum asserted a proprietary interest. Replying to Drum's insistence that the earthquake collection be shipped to him, Griffiths, who had handled Stephens's estate, explained on January 6, 1925, why he had first placed it in the main library.

> My own first thought was that you would probably desire to have these papers and documents deposited and indexed in the Bancroft Library . . . where they would be conveniently accessible to historical scholars; and partly for this reason and partly because I wanted them safely placed in a fireproof building until I could have your instructions, I put them in temporary custody of the University of California librarian.

Griffiths explained to Leupp that Drum was the president of the Mercantile Trust Company and had been the chairman of the history committee. Griffiths would instruct Leupp when the collection was to be shipped to Drum. Leupp, who wanted to get rid of the huge collection, was amenable to the plan.

The earthquake collection was transported to Drum on April Fool's Day, 1925. Eight days later Drum thanked Griffiths for his efforts. It was all very civil.[8]

The headline over a notice on page twelve of the April 24, 1926, edition of the *Argonaut* proclaimed: "The Story of the Great Fire of 1906 Begins in the Argonaut Next Week." (Interestingly, twenty years later the disaster remained "The Great Fire.") The text of the ad stated:

> Professor Stephens died before he could take up the work of weaving together the wealth of material he had collected. Now, twenty years after destruction descended upon San Francisco, the *Argonaut* has been given access to his records of the earthquake and fire. From them has been written the *first full and authentic* account of the disaster, the first detailed, intimate record of the experiences of men and women and children under the catastrophe.

The series would begin on May 1, the weekly newspaper promised, and run for one year. Actually, the sixty-nine-part series ran weekly until August 1927.[9] It seems that Drum, desiring some type of publication, had given the collection to the newspaper.

The articles, a mix of narration and partial verbatim accounts, used only a small portion of the available material. A few of the accounts, of which multiple copies were made, survive in their entirety in the Bancroft and California Historical Society libraries, where they can be compared to what the newspaper printed. The *Argonaut* series—a mere shadow of the mother lode of lost primary documents—is the single best source on the topic.[10]

After the series ended, the collection vanished. Those who had contributed to Stephens's effort were mystified. Marion Hooker wrote a memoir that she was seeking to get published. In 1950 she wrote her attorney, who was acting as her literary agent:

> Not long after the earthquake, someone connected with the University of California was asking for personal records in the catastrophe (the name of Morse Stevens (?spelling) has been in my mind, but I am not at all sure it was he), and we hoped a record would be assembled for future interest. The man died a few years later and we never

heard anything more of the collection—if he had been able to make one nor where what he had assembled had been kept. If there still exists such a collection on the U.C. records, this could eventually join it.[11]

The irony is that Hooker's unpublished manuscript is in the Bancroft Library, but the extremely valuable collection is not.

The Society of California Pioneers purchased the John Drum collection of paintings, etchings, lithographs, prints, and photographs in 1942. Some of the works of art had been badly damaged in storage. The society also received Drum's books that remained following a sale at the Park Bernet Gallery in 1947. In the assessment of the offering to the society and in the gallery's sale catalogue, no mention was made of the earthquake collection.[12]

I could find no trace of the Stephens collection in any likely Bay Area repository. My guess is that it was dumped by Drum's heirs, who were in arrears in storage fees and wanted to sell only what seemed like the most valuable portions of their inheritance.

A GREAT SCIENTIFIC ACCOMPLISHMENT

The second major effort to gather information on the events of April 1906 was mounted not by historians but by scientists. And unlike the first effort, it was an unqualified scientific accomplishment that had little effect on public policy at the time.

Like Stephens, Andrew Lawson, a geologist at the University of California, lost no time in contacting Governor Pardee. The difference in their respective efforts lay in the fact that the earthquake was not peripheral but was central to Lawson's academic specialty. Lawson had been the first to publish a description of a small portion of the San Andreas Fault in the previous decade.

While Stephens used graduate students, Lawson enlisted the foremost scientists of his time. The result was one of the most comprehensive, lucid, and readable scientific reports ever written.

The story of the report's preparation, publication, poor initial reception, and eventual timelessness revolves around one man. Through the late 1890s Lawson was active in building his personal reputation and the university's standing in the field of geology. He published frequently, focusing on the geology of the California coastline, and founded the university's first scientific journal. In 1899 he became a full professor. When Joseph LeConte died in 1901, Lawson was named chairman of the Department of Geology.

The professor collected paintings and wrote poems and the lyrics for such popular songs as "Love's Refrain." Lawson had a bushy mustache and piercing eyes and was described as "stimulating," "provocative," "friendly," "crusty," "kindly," and "irascible." When asked what his religion was, his wife replied, "He is a geologist." In 1904 Lawson thought there was no danger of damaging earthquakes in the Bay Area. After the 1906 event, he sold his older Berkeley home and built a new more quakeproof and fireproof residence.

Lawson was ambitious and had a quick tongue. Charles Richter, the famed Caltech seismologist and one of his students, remembered Lawson's "vitriolic personality." But in dealing with the eight members of the earthquake commission; twenty-five geologists, seismologists, geodesists, biologists, and engineers; and some three hundred others who contributed to the massive report, he was the model of diplomacy.

Lawson was, in effect, the perfect manager. He was firm, he cajoled, and he pleaded that they get their work done on time. In this manner, the commission was able to get a preliminary report published on May 31, 1906. The first volume of the final report was published two years later, when the history committee was still collecting material.[13]

The effort began the day after the earthquake when Lawson telegraphed Governor Pardee in neighboring Oakland: "The appointment of a scientific commission to investigate the earthquake in this state would have a beneficial effect upon the public mind." The commissioners would serve without pay, he said, but expenses would be paid by the state. Lawson put forward seven names, including his own. Those seven, plus an eighth, were included in Pardee's announcement of formation of a "Committee of Inquiry" two days later on April 21.

Four members were associated with the University of California. They were professors George Davidson, A. O. Leuschner of the Students' Observatory, Wallace W. Campbell of Lick Observatory, and Lawson. The remainder came from other institutions. They were Gilbert of the USGS, Professor Harry Fielding Reid of Johns Hopkins University, Charles Burkhalter of Oakland's Chabot Observatory, and Branner of Stanford University. Lawson was elected chairman at the commission's first meeting at the Berkeley faculty club on April 24. Leuschner was appointed secretary.[14]

Lawson leaned heavily on Gilbert and Reid for geologic input. He had a testy relationship with Branner. When Reid arrived from Baltimore, Lawson wrote Gilbert: "I am glad he is here, as I have been feeling geologically lonely on the commission."

The chairman's first concern was obtaining money for expenses. He didn't see much chance for raising funds locally because "of the great necessities of the people in their afflictions." He wired the Carnegie Institution in Washington, D.C., for a donation. Lawson also asked Wheeler and Jordan for $2,500 apiece from their respective universities.

All the money eventually came from out of state. True, Californians were going through hard times, but there was absolutely no desire to advertise the existence of earthquakes. The Carnegie Institution covered all the costs, $5,640.89, and donated an additional $7,500 for printing the first one thousand copies of the final report.[15]

Wanting to capitalize on public interest at the moment, the commission—it had changed its name to the State Earthquake Investigation Commission—issued the seventeen-page preliminary report, which connected for the first time the isolated observations along the fault line in a scientific document. The San Andreas Fault, it was then determined, extended from Mendocino County in the north to Riverside County in the south. Although the fault is actually longer, the overall description of the landscape was accurate:

> In general this line follows a system of long narrow valleys, or where it passes through wide valleys it lies close to the base of the confining hills, and these have a very straight trend; in some places, however, it passes over mountain ridges, usually at the divide separating the ends of two valleys; it even in some cases goes over a spur or shoulder of a mountain.

The movement along the 270 miles of the fault line had been mostly horizontal and had averaged ten feet and reached a maximum of twenty feet. "The great length of the rift upon which movement has occurred makes this earthquake unique," the preliminary report stated. The temblor was felt at Coos Bay, Oregon, to the north; Winnemucca, Nevada, to the east; and Los Angeles to the south. It registered on seismographs in Alaska, Japan, Germany, and other foreign countries.

In San Francisco the greatest damage was on made ground, which was not news. "This ground seems to have behaved during the earthquake very much in the same way as jelly in a bowl, or as semi-liquid material in a tank." There were many lessons to be learned, one of which was to carefully determine where large, costly public buildings accommodating many people should be located. Schools were also particularly vulnerable.[16]

The scientists and engineers, most of whom lugged cameras, scattered along the fault line as far north as Eureka and as far south as the Mexican border. Foremost among them was Gilbert, who headed toward western Marin County, just north of the Golden Gate, where it was first thought the epicenter was located at the end of Tomales Bay.[17]

To Lawson, who did not give praise lightly, Gilbert had "a worldwide reputation as probably the keenest mind in geology in our day." When one of Lawson's graduate students, Frederick L. Ransome, was named to fill the ailing Gilbert's position in the USGS in 1909, Ransome wrote his former professor: "But the broad philosophic outlook, the clear scientific insight, and the judicial quality of Mr. Gilbert at his best are so far beyond me that I have at times had almost a feeling of unworthiness in my promotion."[18]

Gilbert set off on April 26 for the first of a number of trips to Marin County with great excitement, having missed previous large earthquakes during his long career. He was ideally equipped for the task. He was not a specialist but believed in "the principle of scientific trespass." His biographer, Stephen J. Pyne, wrote: "Finally, the earthquake provided a living demonstration of earth tectonics just as the hydraulic-mining debacle gave him a natural laboratory for fluvial geomorphology."

Gilbert's work was both descriptive and interpretive, not theoretical, so it lacked the scientific jargon that came to dominate most later professional writing on the subject. What he observed and wrote was an excellent example of the quality and clarity of work that went into the commission's report.[19]

On his trips in April and May—he would return in May 1907 for a final look—Gilbert took the ferry to Sausalito and then took the train to various points of departure to the west. He then proceeded on foot or by carriage to the Bolinas Lagoon, the village of Bolinas, the Olema Valley, the shoreline of Tomales Bay, Inverness, the lighthouse on the tip of the Point Reyes Peninsula, and the commercial railroad hub of Point Reyes Station.

Travel was not easy in the remote countryside. It rained. Landslides and cracks caused by the earthquake forced detours on the dirt roads. Half the structures in the villages were knocked off their foundations. Chimneys and trees were toppled. Hotels were damaged, so Gilbert stayed overnight with ranch families. There was more damage on the west side of the fault line than on the east; more damage to villages than to farms. A stationary train had been flipped on its side at Point Reyes Station. Gilbert's excellent photographs documented fresh furrows in the earth, offset fences, fault line features, bent roads and piers, and collapsed structures.[20]

He crossed the fault zone that separated the two tectonic plates at the head of Tomales Bay and encountered a sharp jog in the dirt road, possibly the greatest offset. He described it thus:

> The road running southwest from Point Reyes Station and crossing the valley at the head of Papermill Creek delta was offset 20 feet. As the fault-trace at this point was between 50 and 60 feet wide, and as the embankment of the road for that distance was broken into several pieces, it was not possible to make certain that the dissevered remnants of the road had originally been in exact alignment. It is probable, however, that the road was approximately straight before the earthquake, and that the exceptionally great offset at this point is to be explained as the result of a horizontal shifting of the surface materials. The embankment of the road rested on marshy ground so soft that a portion of the embankment sank into it, and material of this character was in other localities demonstrably shifted.[21]

Just to the south, where the headquarters buildings of the Point Reyes National Seashore are now located, Gilbert found two fifteen-foot offsets in a fence and in the path leading to the front door of the W. D. Skinner residence.

Gilbert's work came to be appreciated later. Robert E. Wallace, wrote in a publication of the Geological Society of America in 1980: "Gilbert's records of the position and characteristics of surface faulting produced during the 1906 earthquake remain among the best records of such features ever recorded. Even in the 1960s and 70s they were much referred to in understanding the processes of faulting and for evaluating earthquake hazards for land use decisions in California."[22]

Gilbert and others sent their findings to Lawson. By January 1907, Lawson was back in Washington beginning to assess and organize the vast amount of material that was beginning to arrive from the field, clarifying inconsistencies and obscurities, and urging recalcitrant contributors, such as Stanford's Branner, to get busy and submit their work.

The post-quake investigation that was carried on under the intermittent direction of Branner differed markedly in quality from what Gilbert produced. Branner's graduate students, whom Lawson referred to as "your young men" in his nagging correspondence, did most of the work south of San Francisco.

Branner was a busy man who lacked Lawson's and Gilbert's single-mindedness of purpose. Although he had taken a look at what Lawson would name the San Andreas Fault in the 1890s (when Herbert Hoover, who went on to become a mining engineer, was one of his pupils), Branner was more interested in the geology of Brazil. He was also vice president of Stanford and was involved in the administration not only of the geology department but also of the entire university. Furthermore, his brand new geology building was in ruins.

As the contributions came in, the work Branner was responsible for was often incomplete, just plain wrong, or, in many cases, late or nonexistent. Other investigators, including a high school teacher and university professors, had to be dispatched by Lawson to fill the gaps left by Branner and his students.

The mistakes and incompleteness would plague scientists when they examined the 1989 Loma Prieta earthquake. Carol S. Prentice and Daniel Ponti of the USGS examined Lawson's and Branner's correspondence, the final 1908 report, and the evidence of faulting in 1989. They concluded: "As a result, we have identified major uncertainties regarding the extent and amount of 1906 surface faulting in the southern Santa Cruz Mountains. In fact, many of the specific questions that we have today were also raised by Lawson during preparation of the Report."[23]

Regarding a section of the fault west of Los Banos where there had been an account of high intensities, Lawson had to ask a Berkeley colleague to take a quick look. "Branner's men have been all around this territory," Lawson wrote from Washington, "but have not been through it, nor do they seem to have heard anything about it." Lawson found other problems with the students' work. He thought the location where the fault came ashore at Mussel Rock, the intensity of shaking, the faulting in a railroad tunnel beneath the Santa Cruz Mountains, and the precise locations of the fault line needed to be refined and described more accurately.

In March 1907, Lawson asked Branner for the description of the fault from south of Crystal Springs Reservoir to San Juan Bautista. "I think I have asked you for this before. You must pardon my insistence," wrote Lawson, "as I am really in need of it. I know you are fully occupied with other matters and have little time for getting this earthquake work out, but we have gotten to the stage now where I shall be hung up unless the balance of the data is forthcoming."

By April, Lawson had given up. The description from Humboldt County to the Colorado Desert was complete except for one gap, which Branner was supposed to have supplied. Lawson had to ask a University of California geologist to make the trip to Santa Cruz County. He had written Branner several times in the last few months, "but I have not succeeded in getting any satisfactory description." .

When Branner passed through Washington, D.C., on his way to Brazil "he seemed to take kindly" to all the changes in his work, said Lawson. Branner asked that he be credited for his work. Lawson said that he would credit both him and "your young men."[24]

Lawson ended his work in Washington, D.C., in the summer of 1907 and was back teaching in Berkeley that fall. Many details were still unresolved, including the inability of Harry Fielding Reid of Johns Hopkins University to complete his work on his elastic rebound theory. Reid's groundbreaking theoretical work, which would dominate thinking on the subject for the remainder of the century, was published in a second volume in 1910.

In the final product, with the help of Lawson's editing, the unevenness of contributions is barely noticeable. He successfully imposed his discipline of mind on the mass of material. Clear maps and relevant photos, whose locations can be ascertained today, served as useful illustrations. Lawson "was embarrassed by the great wealth of illustrative material" and regretted that he could use so little.[25]

Although he had accomplished a Herculean task in a short period, Lawson was not successful in all matters. When Jordan of Stanford was seeking contributors to a popular book, *The California Earthquake of 1906*, Lawson attempted unsuccessfully to stonewall the effort by forbidding contributions by persons working on the commission's report. The trustees of the Carnegie Institution would not print additional copies of the report for free distribution to participants, interested professionals, and relevant institutions beyond the 450 copies already allotted for that purpose, despite Lawson's pleadings. Of the 1,000 copies, only 550 were available for sale.[26]

The publication of the report was greeted with barely a public ripple. People did not want to be reminded of the unpleasant past and had other matters to deal with.

The question of who would continue to study earthquakes after the commission completed its work arose in early 1907. It did not appear that the University of California would assume the task, since Wheeler was refusing to fund the operation of the seismographs in the Students' Observatory.

Harry Reid wrote Lawson: "Is there not some rich man in California who could be interested in this subject and advance the necessary funds?" Reid added, "It seems very unfortunate that the most important seismological region of the United States should not be properly studied." There was, alas, no such patron of the art of earthquakes.[27]

While still in Washington, D.C., Lawson published a three-page "Plan for a Proposed Seismological Institute" in April 1907. One hundred and fifty-one scientists endorsed it. Pleas for support were sent to the Smithsonian Institution, the Carnegie Institution, John D. Rockefeller, and others. It seemed like a California problem to the remainder of the nation. The trouble was, Californians didn't want anything to do with it either.[28]

There was no course in the geology or the seismology of earthquakes in the nation, let alone the state. The first course in seismology, disguised as Geology 114, was taught in 1911 at the University of California. Perry Byerly, named the first professor of seismology in 1927, later said that some influential San Franciscans objected to the title, since it suggested that California experienced earthquakes.[29]

The birth of a professional group, the Seismological Society of America, was one of the few immediate by-products of the report. In June 1907, the society had 145 members. One year later, funds were being unsuccessfully sought for a publication. The first *Bulletin of the Seismological Society of America* appeared in March 1911. In the lead article, Lawson lamented the lack of interest:

> In the present state of public opinion in California for example it is practically impossible to secure state aid for the study of earthquakes. The commercial spirit of the people fears any discussion of earthquakes for the same reason as it taboos any mention of an occurrence of the plague in the city of San Francisco. It believes that such discussion will advertise California as an earthquake region and so hurt business.[30]

Nine years later, Stephen Taber, a special lecturer at Stanford University, decried the lack of support for earthquake publications and studies. Taber quoted the business leaders as stating: "Cut it out. Don't investigate it. Don't publish anything on it: don't publish any reports." As for the politicians, Taber said, "Like the rest of the people, they try to forget it, adopting the ostrich policy of burying their heads in the sand." As a result, such countries as Chile, Japan, Russia, and England were ahead of the United States in seismic studies.[31]

But the scientists were also to blame. Their objections to their closet status were confined to professional organizations and publications. "Until the 1930s," Arnold J. Meltsner noted, "Seismologists tried not to be misunderstood by the press and its public and not to precipitate hostility which might threaten scientific work in seismology." In his recent study of California earthquakes, Carl-Henry Geschwind wrote: "Thus, there simply was no concerted effort among California's scientists to counter boosters' disparaging of the state's earthquake hazards."[32]

The lurking menace was further obscured on maps. A 1978 publication of the state agency in charge of geologic mapmaking noted, in reference to the Geological Map of the State of California, prepared in 1916: "Another aspect of this map is somewhat puzzling—the absence of geologic faults. Although faults were by this time widely recognized and mapped—for example faults were shown in the atlas accompanying the 'State Earthquake Investigation Commission' report . . . not even the San Andreas fault is shown on the 1916 geologic map of California." The omission was not corrected on a statewide map until 1938.[33]

The Lawson report had an underground existence for sixty-one years until it was reprinted in 1969. It is still a primary reference tool for scientists.

"This treatise remains a model of an effective study of a great earthquake," wrote Berkeley's Bruce Bolt in 1985, "and it should be required reading for all those interested in what is likely to happen in the next great California earthquake." The next generation of scientists found the report equally valuable. A 1999 special paper written for the Geological Society of America by Carol Prentice stated that there was little, if anything, in modern earthquake science that did not owe its origin, or first clear expression, to what was contained in the two volumes and one atlas.[34]

In the last quarter of the twentieth century, earth scientists, using information gleaned from the Lawson report and other sources, focused their efforts on earthquake prediction. They failed, most noticeably in China and California. Now rather than predict, they offer probabilities. There is a 62 percent chance for a large earthquake in the Bay Area by 2033, they say. They estimate that there will be 10 million people living in the region by then; there were fewer than a half million in 1906.[35]

THE CULTURE OF DISASTER

MISINFORMATION

What were people thinking at the time? We really do not know what public opinion was, absent a massive sampling. But we do know what they were being told to think. Following the earthquake and fire a massive outpouring of printed words and photographic images was published. Much of the output serves as a lesson about what *not* to believe under such circumstances.

Newspapers at the time were the prevalent form of mass communication. They were combative, vastly competitive—and ultimately unreliable. Their owners were aligned with the oligarchy, if not actually members of that group.

The papers participated in what Arnold Meltsner labeled "the culture of suppression." He wrote: "The simplest way for a newspaper to deal with an earthquake was to refuse to acknowledge its occurrence. A good example of this was the reference to an earthquake in San Francisco in 1906 as 'fire' or as a 'conflagration.'"[1]

Less immediate because they were usually published on a weekly or monthly basis but equally competitive were the many magazines of the day. Most were published either on the East or West coasts.

A general rule of thumb can be applied to the magazines: the closer the magazines were to the epicenter, the more they participated in the campaign of cultural disinformation; the farther away they were, the more they gave credence and space to the views of the Progressive members of the oligarchy. In both cases the information they printed was incomplete.

The last to appear were the books. Many qualified as "instant" under the printing constraints of the time. They were by far the most maudlin and, in some cases, sensational.

Only the massive photographic record—compiled by professional photographers and, for the first time, by amateurs who owned the new cheaper cameras and roll film—came close to documenting the catastrophe in an accurate manner. The photographers, except for a few soft-focus pictorialists, had not yet learned how to manipulate images.

Because of the fast-moving nature of the event, the painted record was minimal. But thousands of three-dimensional photographs seen through stereopticons and two-dimensional commercial photos and tinted postcards filled the void and found their way into countless homes and personal scrapbooks.

NEWSPAPERS

The king of words and images at the time was William Randolph Hearst, who, besides owning the *Examiner* newspapers of Los Angeles and San Francisco, was the proprietor of two newspapers and *Cosmopolitan* magazine in New York City. A defeated candidate for mayor of New York and a congressional representative from that city, the San Francisco native in 1906 spent most of his time on the East Coast.

Hearst didn't trust what his own newspapers printed and thought the damage to the city had been exaggerated. Writing of his approach by boat to San Francisco on May 7, the man whose newspapers came close to running the country described the scene in the *Examiner* the next Sunday. "As the boat drew near the San Francisco side, however, the fearful havoc of the actual destroyer, the fire, began to appear. The destruction was awful, utter, complete."

Hearst then drew a comparison with New York, his adopted city:

Think of the water front districts of New York swept clean by fire. Think of Wall Street in ruins. Think of the East side and the West side destroyed. Think of all Broadway burned to the ground. Think of the wholesale districts destroyed. Think of all the big stores from Wanamaker to Macy's in heaps of ashes. Think of the beautiful residences on Fifth Avenue burned or blown up by dynamite. Think of the very trees in the parks bare and black and shriveled by the flames. Think of the streets littered with brick and iron and charred timbers two or even four and six feet deep, so that you can hardly walk on them or climb over them.

Think of men, women, and children huddled in Central Park and on Riverside Drive, living in tents or under shelter of sheets stretched upon posts. Think of men turning over the ruins of their homes and women weeping over them. Think of soldiers everywhere. Think of the temporary tracks of the New York Central laid from Forty-Second Street to the Battery, through the heart of the town, and wrecking trains carrying off the debris. Think of what all this would mean to you and you will have some idea of the great disaster in San Francisco.[2]

The *Examiner* was the brashest, most energetic, and innovative of San Francisco's major newspapers. It also had the largest circulation. The conservative *Chronicle,* whose owner, M. H. de Young, was a defender of business interests and a member of the oligarchy, was in second place. Closing fast on the *Chronicle* was the respectable *Call,* owned by John Spreckels, brother of Rudolph. In last place was the *Bulletin,* whose strident editorials were the work of Fremont Older.

The coverage of the San Francisco newspapers veered back and forth from the relatively sane to the hysterical. Some of the wilder rumors—such as looters lopping off the fingers of the dead to steal rings and the destruction of Los Angeles, San Diego, New York, Chicago, and the Hawaiian Islands—found their way into print, not only in San Francisco newspapers but also in newspapers published elsewhere. (In 1989, a London newspaper erroneously reported widespread looting in San Francisco, and a Paris paper said the moderate earthquake proved that the whole state could be swallowed up "like Atlantis.")

With the emphasis shifting from the disaster to the recovery effort, the influence of the working reporters diminished. An evenhanded 1940 Works Progress Administration (WPA) history of San Francisco journalism said: "The task of leading the way in the rehabilitation of the city would concern more directly the proprietors and editors who formed the policies of the papers."[3]

The San Francisco papers were read by a disheartened public that had to be roused by imaginative and premature stories with such headlines as the following:

SAN FRANCISCO WILL RISE FROM THE ASHES
A GREATER AND MORE BEAUTIFUL CITY THAN EVER
Vast Loan Is Offered
"Have $30,000,000

for Upbuilding
of Our City"
Business Firms Prepare to Adorn
The City with Stately Buildings
Realty Men Sanguine:
Great Future Assured
Future Is Bright for San Francisco
Great City Will Soon Rise:
San Francisco's Undaunted
Citizens Have Unfaltering
Hopes for Her Future
Twenty-five Structures Will Arise on Sites of
Landmarks in the Heart of Business District

According to another of Hearst's editorials, the rebuilt city had to be the "right kind of a new city." Recalling the previous fires, Hearst wrote: "Out of the ghastly tragedy which has laid San Francisco waste should arise a city as much more beautiful than the old San Francisco as the destroyed metropolis was to the straggling village that went up in smoke forty years ago."

Examiner editorials and the graphics that accompanied them hammered away at the theme of physical as well as emotional upbuilding. A snarling grizzly bear, the state's symbol, stood alive above a ruined city, pierced by arrows labeled "Earthquake," "Fire," "Famine." Above the wounded animal was the single word "UNDAUNTED!"[4]

The *Call,* a bit more restrained during normal times, was not to be outdone. The following story dominated page one on May 6:

QUAKE OPENS A BIG CHASM
FREAKISH WORK OF RECENT TEMBLOR NEAR BOLINAS
Parting of Earth Said to Be
300 Feet Wide
Ground Breaks under Cow
And She Meets Death

Although such a renowned scientist as Grove Karl Gilbert, as well as Stanford president David Starr Jordan, fell for the story without checking, it was not true. The bit of earthquake apocrypha that exists to this day was concocted by Payne Shafter, a rancher in Marin County.

Shafter, who lived near Olema, said later that he had a dead cow to bury.

"That night along came the earthquake which opened up a big crack in the ground; we simply dragged the carcass over to the crack and tipped it in with the feet sticking out. Then along came those newspaper reporters and when they got the idea that the cow had fallen in, we weren't about to spoil a good story."[5]

As well as being sensationalized, the effects of the earthquake were trivialized. Fremont Older of the *Bulletin* wrote an editorial titled "Common Sense Prevailing over Hysterical Terror." It began: "It is an element of mystery in an earthquake that terrifies. The direct loss of life from the earthquake last Wednesday was less than the loss of life caused every summer in any large Eastern city by sunstroke."

Then there was the staple of all disaster stories, the impressions of famous visitors, whether they be the president flying in for a one-hour visit clad in an *Air Force One* windbreaker today or, as in the case of San Francisco, the arrival of the celebrated actress Sarah Bernhardt in mid-May to perform Racine's *Phedre* at the Greek Theatre in Berkeley.

Distinguished drama and music critic Ashton Stevens of the *Examiner* and the photographer Arnold Genthe accompanied Bernhardt on a tour of the ruined city. Stevens's account was somewhat breathless, as he had a scoop and Bernhardt had an opportunity to promote her appearance.

"My God! My God!" Bernhardt sobbed, "It's too terrible. The world has never known such a cemetery. And this is what is left of San Francisco—sweet San Francisco!"

"I have seen actresses weep off the stage, as well as on," wrote Stevens. "I have quite impersonally admired the splendid plasticity of their emotions. But I have never seen an actress—and this includes Bernhardt herself—weep as Sarah Bernhardt wept yesterday afternoon when the wreck of San Francisco struck her fairly between the eyes."

The drive in a horse-drawn carriage continued. The actress felt her soul was dead. She remarked, "How small is the individual ego in such a theatre as this."

Would they rebuild San Francisco, she asked? "Assuredly Madame," answered Stevens. "See there, and there, and there—already they are rebuilding."[6]

The newspapers contained strong declarations about creating a new, more beautiful city and supporting the Burnham Plan until late May. Then they backed away from the City Beautiful concept and endorsed the city practical approach. "Let the business men alone," stated the *Call,* which had first attacked the *Chronicle*'s publisher for a similar attitude.

The San Francisco newspapers were criticized in the WPA history for following "unwise leadership in the actual rebuilding of the city." Writing in 1940, the anonymous author continued:

> Their editorials rang with stout-hearted words on the beauties that were to be in the new San Francisco, but in the final push that would have made these beauties realities they yielded to those influences which were intent on making quick profits. San Francisco is still ugly in some aspects of the city's lay-out. Its traffic arteries remain inadequate for the demands of the metropolis. Sections are overbuilt and overcrowded. The story is easily read in the editorial columns of today's newspapers.[7]

The newspapers of San Jose took an unusually upbeat attitude toward earthquakes that badly misled their readers. "Don't Be Despondent," "A Look on the Brighter Side," "All Danger Is Past," "Earthquakes Not Necessarily Dangerous," and "Tells Why There Will Be No More Shocks" read the headlines of news stories and editorials. No need to worry, a publisher assured his readers, because San Jose "is today safer from danger from earthquakes than ever before."

J. O. Hayes of the *San Jose Herald* based his argument on the historical record that showed damaging earthquakes occurring "seldom less than fifteen years and generally from twenty-five to two hundred years." Hayes then made a startling jump in reasoning:

> This carefully recorded history of these disturbances therefore gives us every assurance that San Jose, San Francisco and the region now visited by this temblor is within reasonable certainty exempt for all time from a recurrence of this experience. It is also reasonably certain that the entire State of California outside of the region now affected will be safe from any serious disturbances for 25 to 200 years, if any should ever occur again.[8]

Earthquakes were actually a blessing in disguise, Hayes argued, since without them the earth would either deflate or implode. The temblors relieved the earth of steam and gas during the process of cooling. Without this venting, he wrote, the planet "must either collapse from all sides at once like a crushed eggshell or simultaneously burst in all directions."[9]

The next day Hayes's newspaper carried a story about the extensive damage suffered in San Jose in the 1868 earthquake, thirty-eight years earlier.

The article seemed to contradict his "reasonable certainty" rule for future seismic activity in northern California.[10]

MAGAZINES

All the Bay Area's big literary names—Mary Austin, Gertrude Atherton, Jack London, James Hopper—and many lesser ones, too, contributed to the national magazines on this hot topic. Only Hopper's piece in *Everybody's Magazine* caught the drama and the power of the event. Even London, who was at the height of his career, acknowledged Hopper's mastery of the subject. "Hopper's article in *Everybody's* was great. Best story of the quake I've seen," London wrote a friend.[11] Henry Anderson Lafler, a local writer and one of the few critics of the army's performance, agreed publicly with London's assessment. He wrote in mid-June:

> Everybody, of course, wrote an account of the thing for some journal or other, and most of the accounts are amazingly bad. Mrs. Atherton's, Jack London's, Geraldine Bonner's, Mrs. Deering's, Herman Whitaker's are certainly not literature, and some are scarcely good journalism. Only James Hopper's, printed, I think, in *Everybody's,* has any style or merit as literature.[12]

Lafler wrote from personal experience. Unaware that a photograph was being taken of him amid the temporary graves and debris of Portsmouth Square, the homeless Lafler had sat at a makeshift desk surrounded by his books, a hat perched jauntily atop his head, and pounded away on his typewriter. The result was "My Sixty Sleepless Hours," an article for *McClure's Magazine* and perhaps the second-best journalistic effort.[13]

The disaster was the media event of its day. Single articles, entire issues, and multiple editions of magazines on both coasts were devoted to the subject. *Collier's, Harper's Weekly, McClure's, Cosmopolitan,* the *Literary Digest, Review of Reviews, Everybody's, Sunset, Overland Monthly,* the *Argonaut,* the *New San Francisco Magazine, Out West, Pacific Monthly,* and others in that age of print contributed to the outpouring of words and pictures.

Blind optimism prevailed. Much of the commentary was similar, noted the *Literary Digest,* a prominent New York magazine that published weekly summaries of press coverage in the United States and foreign countries. "The note of hope struck by the press of the entire country is the surest indication of that indomitable American spirit that will build a greater and more beautiful San Francisco on that magnificent bay of the Pacific," the *Digest* noted.[14]

Editors were desperate for copy. Hopper wrote a less-successful article for the May 12 issue of *Harper's Weekly,* an issue in which Gertrude Atherton's story "San Francisco's Tragic Dawn" also appeared. Mary Austin's story "The Temblor" was first published in the June issue of Charles Fletcher Lummis's *Out West.* The contributions were not limited to professional writers. Pardee, Phelan, and an ex-mayor of Seattle added to the torrent of words.

Jack London was the undisputed leader of the pack. London and his wife, Charmian, had spent the first night of the fire in the city, where he decided not to write about his experiences. "What use trying?" London said. "One could only string big words together, and curse the futility of them." When he arrived home in Glen Ellen he received a telegram from *Collier's* magazine asking for twenty-five hundred words on the earthquake.

London needed the money to repair his barn that had been ruined in the earthquake and for the construction of the *Snark,* the sailboat that was to take the couple around the world. The iron keel was to have been laid on April 18. The vessel wound up costing three times as much as originally estimated, mostly because of delays caused by the disaster.

He wrote the story for *Collier's* on April 24. "Hot from his hand I snatched the scribbled sheets," Charmian recalled, "and swiftly typed them." The manuscript was telegraphed on the same day, but the wired copy never arrived in New York. Another copy was sent by way of the postal service. It arrived in time for the May 5 edition of the national magazine. "Jack, it is only fair to record," said Charmian, "entertained the poorest opinion of his description."

The writer gave little personal thought to the earthquake and its tremendous consequences, focusing instead on haggling with the managing editor of *Collier's* over payment, worrying about the delivery of materials for his boat because of the priority given to relief trains, and contemplating a twelve-day horseback trip with Charmian north of San Francisco.

"Up late. Boxed with mate. Talked over lengthy horseback trip," wrote Charmian in her May 1 diary entry.

They set off two days later. Jack took photographs, and Charmian recorded impressions of natural beauty and the destruction of human artifacts in her diary.

There were two Californias that spring, and the Londons saw both. The land was alive, seasonal renewal was in the air, and the countryside was bursting with wildflowers after the winter rains. The air was clear and invigorating. The creeks, streams, and rivers fell in cascades down mountainsides and ran through valleys in Sonoma, Napa, Lake, and Mendocino counties where the Londons traveled.

When they came to a town, they saw death and destruction. Chimneys were down everywhere, gravestones and monuments were twisted or toppled as if jerked awry by a giant's hand, rock slides blocked roads, barns were canted, and, like missing teeth, there were gaps in the facades of the towns' streets.

The couple spent the first night in Calistoga at the head of the Napa Valley. Charmian was sore from the saddle. They rode the next day to The Geysers, where they were jolted that night by an aftershock. "Great trip. Country glorious. Happy," wrote Charmian.

On the third day they reached Lakeport on Clear Lake, where they went sailing. The ride on the fourth day to Ukiah was over mountains, through valleys, and across streams. Always there were flowers. A heavy aftershock hit Ukiah that night.

They found more beauty on the ride north to Willits, "which was pretty well shaken by the earthquake." In that remote town they found a copy of the *Collier's* that contained Jack's article.

On the way to Fort Bragg on the coast they stopped at a logging camp to watch the loggers, who were gearing up to supply San Francisco with lumber. They then rode "thro lilac-covered mountains and pink rhododendrons." At Fort Bragg they found near-total destruction. Jack wrote a correspondent:

Fort Bragg, on the coast, had every brick building but two shaken down on the ground, and these two were one-story brick buildings, and were badly damaged. A block and a half of Fort Bragg was burned and the whole town would have been burned, had not a steamer been lying in the harbor. This steamer pumped salt water on the flames. In Willits, in central Mendocino, we noted the same devastation—three story buildings tumbled into heaps. And so everywhere.

The observations of the Londons were seconded by the State Earthquake Investigation Commission. The report noted that "the destructive effects were as severe at Fort Bragg as at any other point within the zone of high intensities." Almost all the brick buildings in the largest town on the north coast collapsed. Of the fire, a local newspaper reported that the flames "spread rapidly, and as the water system in town was knocked out, the fire raged, and if the *National City* had not pumped water from the wharf, the whole town would have burned down beyond a doubt."

As the Londons continued their ride the scene turned grimmer. "Rode on down coast—saw crazy Navarro—deserted town at mouth of river shaken all away by quake." Three houses were left standing in Navarro, one of which was a fifty-year-old saloon. At Greenwood they stayed in a hotel whose two parts "were gaping apart." On the way to Boonville they saw the "severe results of the earthquake near coast—one crack in the hill some 5 ft. wide." They rode home through "wrecked Santa Rosa" in a rainstorm on the twelfth day.

London was tremendously proud of the stamina they displayed on the 350-mile trip. They rode hatless every day. The horses were tired, but the couple was in "great shape."[15]

Jack London and other leading western writers also wrote for *Sunset* magazine, which was then owned by the Southern Pacific Railroad. *Sunset* was the West's most prominent publication. When it came to disseminating information (or propaganda) regarding the earthquake and fire, the railroad, through *Sunset* and other in-house publications, reached the largest audience.

At the time Harriman's transportation empire was in no condition for him to loan the many millions of dollars to rebuild the city that San Francisco newspapers claimed he was capable of doing (as stated in the headline "Harriman to Lend 100 Millions"). It was Harriman's "year of discontent."[16]

Besides facing damages to its facilities, disruption of traffic, and the expense of supplying free freight and passenger service, the Southern Pacific Railroad was confronted with the huge task of closing off the Colorado River, which was pouring into the Imperial Valley to the south and creating the Salton Sea. Harriman also faced a stockholders' revolt at Wells Fargo & Co., and the looming financial panic of 1907 would further reduce his monetary resources. The trustbusters in government and Progressive-oriented publications were nipping at his heels.[17]

To offset these losses, Harriman and his minions immediately began a massive public relations campaign to restore West Coast revenues. The extent of the railroad's propaganda was described by Ted Steinberg in his book *Acts of God*:

> No organization was more dedicated to stoking the fire-oriented view of the disaster than the Southern Pacific Company, the dominant economic force in California at this time. Railroads were notorious in the West for their promotional activities, and when the 1906 calamity struck every effort was brought to bear in one of the great disinformation campaigns of turn-of-the-century America.[18]

Harriman fired the initial broadside in a statement that was disseminated widely: "Rapidly the city is becoming a beehive of activity, and ere long the imperishable spirit of San Francisco, clothed anew, will invite you within the gates of the new and greater metropolis of the Pacific."[19]

Harriman established the tone. His employees in various departments fell immediately into line. The General Passenger Department quickly picked up on Harriman's word *imperishable* and issued a pamphlet titled "San Francisco Imperishable." Like other messages that ignored California's known seismic history, the message was: "Earthquakes have never been in knowledge of man twice destructive in the same locality."

The railroad maintained that the earthquake in San Francisco amounted to less than 2 percent of the damage; the fire accounted for the remainder. Again, commerce was the yardstick. "Had there been no fire, the earthquake would have caused the same interruption to business that it did in Oakland across the bay—which was none at all."[20]

The Southern Pacific managed to put words into the mouth of Governor Pardee, with whom it traded small favors. The railroad prepared a draft for Pardee of a letter to be sent to the governors of all states and territories. It emphasized "the destruction of the commercial and residential portion of San Francisco was accomplished by fire, not by earthquake. . . . This could not occur again. . . . The lesson has been learned." The railroad's San Francisco passenger traffic manager scribbled at the bottom of the typed draft sent to the governor: "For the good of our common cause—the advancement of California." The letter was published in numerous newspapers and the railroad sent Pardee a large supply of the printed letter.[21]

The general passenger agent of the railroad, James Horsburgh Jr., sent a letter to the Stockton Chamber of Commerce and other chambers throughout the state. The purpose was "to keep California and San Francisco from being misrepresented by sensation mongers." Many people would be lecturing on the disaster, Horsburgh warned, advising the chambers to make sure that at least the last half of each talk was about "the clearing of a pathway to a greater San Francisco and the awakening to an even greater California." He added, "We do not believe in advertising the earthquake. The real calamity in San Francisco was undoubtedly the fire." The accommodating chambers of chamber passed resolutions to that effect.[22]

Sunset magazine—by way of paintings, drawings, maps, photographs, and many tens of thousands of words—spread the Southern Pacific's message even further and in a more palatable form. The magazine could afford to hire the best illustrators and writers. Its monthly circulation of four hundred thousand readers was the near equivalent of the prequake population of San Francisco and exceeded by one hundred thousand the combined circulation of the four major daily newspapers.

The original May issue had been destroyed as it lay on the presses waiting to be printed. The magazine called on the celebrated western artist Maynard Dixon to draw the covers of the first two postquake issues. Dixon hastily drew a black-and-white cover of the Spirit of the City, a nude, nippleless woman rising phoenixlike from the burning buildings. The "emergency edition" contained a few pages of text, including a message from Harriman that pledged: "The city will be rebuilt under requirements of the new laws which will prevent faulty construction and promote artistic and architectural effects."

The second issue, a combined June–July edition, had a painting by Dixon on the cover in the strong lines and bold hues of his Southwest work. The Coliseum-like dark ruins of the old city and its distressed masses at the bottom framed a new white city rising from an acropolis held in the passionless embrace of a now breastless nude woman rising cloudlike above the mere works of humans.

A poem by Joaquin Miller, flamboyant in his work as well as his life, introduced the text. Titled simply "San Francisco," it ended with the following:

And jealousies were burned away,
And burned were city rivalries,
Till all, white crescenting the bay,
Were one harmonious hive of bees.
Behold the bravest battle won!
The City Beautiful begun:

One solid San Francisco, one,
The fairest sight beneath the sun.

Harriman's message about "the imperishable spirit of San Francisco" was published for the second time, and the magazine contained a recapitulation of the disaster. The article, titled "San Francisco's Plight and Prospect," was preceded by an editor's note stating that San Franciscans were facing the future "bravely and almost gaily."

Nature, meaning the earthquake, was portrayed as the villain. Nature, with a capital N had toppled poorly constructed chimneys and severed water lines built hurriedly over suspect terrain. Of the start of the fires, the author wrote: "It was some time before the people awoke to a full realization of what was happening. It was then evident that Nature . . . was not playing entirely fair."

In another article, everyone was said to have performed flawlessly, as implied by the headline: "Handling a Crisis: How Affairs in San Francisco Were Controlled by Men Who Knew Just What to Do." All acted as one for the betterment of others: "Plebeians and aristocrats took off their coats and worked together, nabobs and native sons side by side with 'greasers' and Chinamen."

General Funston and Mayor Schmitz were praised as "men of the hour." The mayor was singled out for his "virile handling of the situation from the outset," his shoot-to-kill order that had a "salutary effect on the lawless element," and his appointment of the citizens' committee and especially James D. Phelan to head the finance committee.

The illustrations reinforced the impression of the perfect city only slightly damaged and ready to rebound quickly. They included prequake photos and drawings of tall structures, artfully arranged in montages; postquake photographs of bare steel-framed buildings that had been under construction, and thus looked unharmed; and hurried postquake architectural renderings of "paper buildings" scattered throughout the text.[23]

The emphasis after midsummer of 1906 was on reconstruction. That theme dominated Sunset's earthquake anniversary issue of April 1908.

Like other western cities, San Francisco looked to the East for validation. These cities were, and are, overly sensitive to criticism from that direction. There had been hard times in San Francisco during the intervening years, stemming not only from the almost superhuman recovery effort but also from labor and race riots, a city government seemingly steeped in graft, and a justice system run amok.

An editor's introduction took issue with the negative approach of eastern journalists:

> During its reconstruction period, and especially during the past year, San Francisco has been most viciously assaulted by certain anonymous correspondents of eastern journals. It is not enough for them to tell of the troubles due to the great fire or to the political corruption, but the average standard of ethics and of general conduct were denounced and citizens held up to harsh criticism and ridicule.

The magazine called upon the two most prominent men in the Bay Area who had not been sullied by recent events to defend San Francisco. Wheeler and Jordan obliged in separate statements jointly titled "Two University Presidents Speak for the City: Vigorous Defense and Protest in Reply to Eastern Critics." Wheeler offered this portrait of life in the East versus life in the West, taken from the western version of the Progressive credo:

> The green-blinded, white-painted civilization of the East with maiden aunts looking out of the windows, and determining at the tea-table how men ought to behave, is not potent in California. For this reason, a weak backbone in California means an evil life, and the men who do well are those who stand on their feet, with their own head under their own hat, and their course of life determined by their own ideas of what constitutes righteousness.

The articles and photographs in the anniversary issue celebrated "the greatest work of reconstruction ever accomplished by any city of the world."[24]

BOOKS

No lasting literature was generated by the earthquake and fire. In fact, the only fictional account of any type that has withstood the test of time is the 1936 movie *San Francisco,* now considered a classic for some reason. It can still be rented as a videocassette or seen on late-night television.

In novels and other fictional portrayals, the 1906 disaster, and earthquakes in general, have mostly been employed as a plot device. The San Francisco temblor was used, for example, to bring Clark Gable and Jeanette MacDonald together in the movie. The screenwriter Anita Loos said: "As an added feature we included the Great Earthquake, which, with true Frisco loyalty, Hoppy [Robert E. Hopkins, Loos's collaborator on the script] and I termed a 'fire.'"[25]

Countless pamphlets and books were published after the calamity. One search turned up 82 popular accounts, many of them illustrated, and all published in 1906. Another recent search of libraries in the United States turned up 572 citations—a record for a single disaster.[26]

Besides the sentimental works, quickie books were published that concentrated on the horrific aspects. These were generally imagined from afar, badly overwritten, and designed to sell many copies. Promising to tell the story of "the annihilation of San Francisco" and to depict "scenes of death and terror," they bore such titles as *The Doomed City: A Thrilling Tale* and *San Francisco's Horror of Earthquake and Fire.* The latter began:

> Shivering, but sure in its rock-ribbed grasp, the hand of Destruction has reached up through the thin crust of the world and, waving a giant torch of quenchless flame, swept from her proud seat at the edge of the sunset sea the splendid city of the Golden Gate.

Urban legends and racial and ethnic stereotypes predominated in these accounts. Robbers ran rampant through city streets, and white girls were accosted by drunkards. All such lawbreakers were summarily shot. "Life was cheap for those who did not respect military rule on the edges of the burning hell," wrote James Russel Wilson, whose promotional blurb describes him as a "well-known author," the description making the claim somewhat dubious.

In Wilson's book, a ghoul was caught robbing corpses and hung from a beam at the entrance to the Palace Hotel. Another lopped off "the stiffened fingers" of a dead woman to steal her rings. Eleven bullets were pumped into his body by soldiers, who dumped the corpse in an alley. Photographs were faked, and drawings showed wide-eyed, frenzied Chinese men trampling whites in their rush to flee Chinatown.[27]

The culture of delusion culminated in the publication of two popular books, both of which were more booklets than books. While they initially sprang from more ephemeral formats, their instant popularity gave them heft, and eventually they took the form of short books. Neither author had been in San Francisco at the time, nor did they have to be in order to produce the type of essays that they wrote. Both employed nostalgia as a device, which was one way to avoid the unpleasantness of the present.

Will Irwin was a Stanford graduate who had gone to work for the *Chronicle* in 1900 and then left for a job on the *New York Sun* in 1904. His knowledge of San Francisco was thus derived from his Gilded Age college days. The ambitious Irwin, tiring of newspaper reporting, had begun working part-time for *McClure's*. He was at the magazine on April 18 when he saw an early edition of an evening newspaper that carried news of the earthquake.

Irwin rushed to the *Sun*. For the next forty-eight hours, with little sleep, he wrote a running account of the catastrophe, calling on all the sources and skills of a talented rewrite man given the opportunity to write the story of a lifetime. He smoked, drank coffee, ate at his desk, slept in his clothes on an office couch, and avoided alcohol. At the end of eight consecutive days, Irwin had produced seventy-five columns of type.

When the story slowed on the third day, his editor suggested that he put the disaster in perspective. From Irwin's typewriter flowed an essay that was given the headline "The City That Was." Published on April 21, the story began:

> The old San Francisco is dead. The gayest, lightest hearted, most pleasure loving city of the western continent, and in many ways the most interesting and romantic, is a horde of huddled refugees living among ruins. It may rebuilt; it probably will; but those who have known that peculiar city by the Golden Gate and have caught its flavor of the Arabian Nights feel that it can never be the same.

After the brief introduction, the essay settled into the form of a romantic love letter written by a privileged young man to his immediate past. Passages described selected aspects of the place ("a city of romance and a gateway to adventure"); the people ("above all there is an art sense all through the populace"); food ("San Francisco was famous for its restaurants and cafes"); nightlife ("the city never went to bed"); generosity ("hospitality was nearly a vice"); and foreign quarters ("that feeling of huddled irregularity which makes all Chinese built dwellings fall naturally into pictures").

The essay ended: "The bonny, merry city—the good, gray city—O that one who has mingled the wine of her bounding life with the wine of his youth should live to write the obituary of Old San Francisco!"[28]

A few weeks after the article appeared in the *Sun* a slightly expanded version with the same title was published as a small book. It went through at least four printings.

It is hard to imagine San Franciscans objecting to this rather maudlin effort, but object they did. It was the title and the first few paragraphs and ending that provoked them. Their imagined San Francisco was *not* dead.

Sunset commissioned Rufus Steele to write a rebuttal. "The City That Is" appeared in the April 1909 issue and was then rushed into print as a small book in October of that same year. Steele was a member of the Bohemian Club and the author of one of the plays, *The Fall of Ug,* performed at the summer encampment. "Will Irwin may dry his tears," Steele wrote. "Of a truth, the things which he meant by 'the old San Francisco' did not die and are not dead."[29] (Whether Irwin or Steel was aware what the Englishman John Evelyn had written after the fire of 1666 is not known: "O the miserable & calamitous spectacle. . . . London was, but is no more!")[30]

The stigma of Irwin's first words persisted into the early 1970s, when Oscar Lewis, a well-known San Francisco writer of the mid–twentieth century, edited a book of four stories about the disaster. "These four were chosen because all were authors of the first rank who succeeded in conveying not only the dramatic impact of the earthquake and its aftermath," said Lewis, "but also something of the character and flavor of the city then being shaken and consumed."

Irwin's story was the first. Curiously—and unpardonably—an ellipsis marks the start of "The City That Was." Lewis skipped over Irwin's downbeat beginning and started the selection with a harmless descriptive passage. London's and Atherton's articles were included. Hopper's realistic account was absent from the anthology.[31]

The fourth author whom Lewis selected for inclusion had never visited San Francisco. William Marion Reedy edited *Reedy's Mirror,* a weekly political and literary review published in St. Louis. "The City That Has Fallen" was reissued several times after first appearing on April 26, 1906, in Reedy's publication. It was published in 1933 as a small book by the Book Club of California. Again, it was another paean to the past. But the overly flowery prose shifted momentarily, like gently drifting fog, to hint at darker shadows:

A strong sense of beauty somehow clung to the mental image of the town, even to one who, as I, had never seen the place, its glamour always had a sort of hidden foreboding in it. There was ever the same suggestion of lethal malefic genius behind all the story that was told of its curiously *morbidezza,* amorousness of the day, and its childlike desire to forget the night. It was too far, as it sometimes seemed, and in the glory in which it lay and in which it lingered in thought, there seemed something of a light that held a pale tone of bale back of all its bliss. Its people loved it with that intensity with which we love what we are likely to lose.[32]

Reedy visited San Francisco for the first time to attend the 1920 Democratic National Convention. He unexpectedly died in the city on July 28 of that year.

Gertrude Atherton, the most celebrated California woman writer of her time, incorporated accounts of the earthquake and fire, which she had experienced firsthand, in a novel, *Ancestors,* and her autobiography, *Adventures of a Novelist.* Similar portions of the fictionalized and nonfiction accounts bear comparison.

From the novel (1907): "And then, while her eyes were still staring, and something in her brain moving towards expression, she heard a noise that sounded like the roar of artillery charging across the world."

From the autobiography (1932): "In the dawn of the eighteenth I was awakened by a noise like that of a regiment of cavalry charging across the world. I had a fancy that it roared straight through the Golden Gate and a quarter of a second later precipitated itself against the Berkeley Inn with a shock that nearly disrupted the foundations."

Atherton rushed to San Francisco to save the *Ancestors* manuscript and other personal items stored in a hotel. Her biographer, Emily Wortis Leider, wrote: "Gertrude prided herself on her fearlessness, the mark of a California thoroughbred."[33]

Some valuable books were published at the time that commanded smaller audiences. Besides the magisterial two-volume *Report of the State Earthquake Investigation Commission,* two other books have lasting value. *After Earthquake and Fire* was a reprint of articles that initially appeared in the *Mining and Scientific Press. The California Earthquake of 1906,* edited by David Starr Jordan, included Mary Austin's magazine article as well as a number of readable scientific accounts. It was Jordan's and Stanford's answer to the University of California–dominated state commission report.

PHOTOGRAPHY

Where words failed, photographs succeeded. "In the modern way of knowing," as Susan Sontag has written of wars and natural disasters, "there have to be images for something to become 'real.' Photographs identify events. Photographs confer importance on events and make them memorable." No previous event had gained such widespread importance by means of photographs.[34]

While there were hundreds of written accounts, there were many thousands of photos. Most of the photographs were not well composed and some were out of focus. Still there was more than enough excellence among the pictures of amateurs and professionals alike to convey the crackling drama of the moment, the vast immensity of the ruins, and the transient lives of the refugees.

Mass photography—made possible by cheaper, easy to handle cameras, roll film, and painless processing—had come into its own on the eve of the earthquake. The disaster attracted the single greatest use of cameras and film since their invention. *Camera Craft*, the monthly publication of the California Camera Club, stated:

> The probabilities are that never since cameras were first invented has there been such a large number in use at any one place as there has been in San Francisco since the 18th of last April. Everyone who either possessed, could buy, or borrow one, and was then fortunate enough to secure supplies for it, made more or less good use of his knowledge of photography.[35]

By the end of the nineteenth century, cameras small enough to be handheld were commercially available. No longer did a photographer have to lug a heavy camera and a bulky tripod, although there were still advantages to large-format cameras. In his book *The History of Photography*, Beaumont Newhall wrote: "Convenient, ready-sensitized dry plates and film of unprecedented speed, ease of processing and printing, fast lenses, quick-working shutters, hand cameras—all these technical advances led to a casual use of photography by untrained amateurs." The amateurs took "snapshots," a word derived from the hunter's lexicon.

Kodak led the way in developing the new cameras, roll film, and commercial processing. A package deal consisting of all of the above, plus a leather case, cost $25. "You press the button, we do the rest," was the firm's motto.

Camera clubs, to which professionals and serious amateurs belonged, proliferated; there were four in the United States in 1880 and one hundred by 1900. The California Camera Club in San Francisco was one of the largest in the world.

The club's monthly publication, *Camera Craft*, was the forerunner of today's photography magazines. It specialized in how-to articles. The author of a March 1906 article, "A Tale of a Kodak," swore by his 3-A model: "The Kodak's popularity is demonstrated by the frequency with which we see it used. Its compact and inconspicuous form, the ease with which it can be carried and operated, coupled with the almost certain degree of success which is assured in the improved form, render it well nigh impossible for one to resist its allurements."

The rank amateur consumed film with indifferent results. More serious amateurs and professionals were concerned with the accurate representation of fact. Their photos were crisply focused, and generally a large scene was carefully composed. A few amateurs and some professionals were interested in developing an art form. They experimented with various painterly effects, frequently producing impressionistic results of small scenes with softened edges and classical allusions. Such photographers became known as "pictorialists," and their genre, as "pictorial photography" or "pictorialism."

At the same time this explosion in equipment and techniques was revolutionizing photography in the 1890s, the halftone process was developed, making it possible for newspapers, magazines, and books to carry photographs on the same pages as text. Photojournalism was born, and the national magazines led the way. Hearst, who owned a national magazine and was an innovator, pressed for greater use of photos in his newspapers. After the disaster, he added special sections featuring panoramic photographs taken from the air.

All these different facets of photography coalesced on April 18 and during succeeding days and weeks, not only in San Francisco but also in nearby cities and in places along the fault line. The result was not only the first massive photographic documentation of a single event but also the first baseline documentation of a sizable cross-section of California.[36]

When the fires and smoke rose into the sky and it became obvious that much of the city was threatened with destruction, photographers were faced with the same basic decisions as everyone else: what to do, what to save, and where to go. They also had to decide whether to take their cameras into the streets and record this incredible disaster for immediate commercial gain, family photo albums, or posterity. As might be expected, different people made different choices.

After breakfast, Fayette J. Clute walked to the California Academy of Science building on Market Street, where the *Camera Craft* office was located on the fifth floor. He took a small camera with him and took two snaps of the fire approaching from the south. Only one was printable. There was no further mention of photography in Clute's recollection of events in the May issue of the magazine. Clute moved his personal belongings to a friend's home to the west and watched the fire from Lone Mountain.

Dr. H. D'Arcy Powers cited the photographer's frustration with capturing an actual earthquake on film, still a near impossibility given its unexpected and momentary nature. (Continuously running video surveillance cameras have captured recent earthquakes.) The City Hall was the ultimate symbol of ruin to Powers, as it was to other photographers. "I had no camera to record that first terrible impression, and it is doubtful whether any record was made," said the doctor. "But few subjects would offer a more dramatic field for a great artist than the wreck of that mighty building standing in its yellow cloud of dust against the tender blue of the spring day. Such was the great earthquake!"

The doctor, who lost more than two thousand negatives in the fire, thought the subject matter was too vast to capture on film. It did, however, offer some opportunities for "the clever snapshotter."

He visualized the scenes not through the black and white of ground glass but with a painter's eye for color, like the violent reds of the fire and the sun, the latter visible as a glowing disc as if seen through smoked glass. At night the scene became even more dramatic: the sky turned bluish green in vivid contrast to the blazing fire, and the houses were "bathed in brilliant sunshine against the dark water behind them." Color photography was in its infancy at the time.[37]

The photographers who flocked to San Francisco from Oakland, elsewhere in California, and even from out of state faced difficult technical problems. "A pall of smoke hung over the burnt and burning district for several days," one noted. "Therefore it was both smoky and cloudy, and when the sun appeared it was accompanied with high winds" that knocked over cameras mounted on tripods.

Another problem was the intense heat. While photographing a burning school, a photographer looked down and saw that the wooden legs of his tripod were on fire. And with streams of people moving by, time exposures were not practical "and snaps were a necessity."

There were the difficult choices to be made that arise in any emergency situation for the writer and photographer. Some photographers "were rushing around trying to cover as much territory as possible, apparently afraid the fire would be subdued before they secured all the pictures they wanted." Others helped family and friends. A few felt it was indecent to make money off the misfortune of others.

A lot of money changed hands. The photos that were in most demand were those that spouted smoke and fire. Also, anything showing ruins went, said one photographer. Writing in *Camera Craft,* a photographer noted: "One professional told me he had made more than two hundred and fifty exposures in ten days, and . . . he had sold several thousand prints from them in states on the other side of the Sierras."

Some photographers copied the superior prints of their colleagues and sold them as their own. "One gentleman who has some very fine fire effects had to send a lawyer to a prominent gallery to compel them to stop selling copies of his pictures," the magazine noted.

The aesthetically inclined had to contend with dangling electric wires, newly plastered advertising signs on walls, the lack of trees and grass, the boring regularity of the army's tent cities, and grotesque piles of rubbish and debris. On the other hand, the fallen Corinthian columns of City Hall, the small thatch of homes atop a barren Russian Hill, classically columned doorways with nothing behind them, and details of ruined churches formed pleasing compositions.

How long would the photographic bonanza last? "I shall expect to make it a profitable hunting ground for many a day to come," wrote one photographer. Another thought the window of opportunity was quickly closing: "The hammer of the workman is sounding the death knell of the artistic photograph, which, if it is to be made at all, must be made quickly. . . . Instead of beholding one of the mighty tragedies of history, we shall soon be spectators at a common-place, every-day drama."

The smoke, poor lighting, overused developing chemicals, and careless printing combined, the club photographers thought, to produce mediocre results. But there was some excellence amid the dross.[38]

Arnold Genthe, the socially connected portrait photographer, was one of those who chose to take pictures. As a result he lost his work and personal possessions in the fire. Genthe tended toward the pictorialist end of the fine arts spectrum and was the best-known photographer in the city. He was a member of the California Camera Club. It was Genthe who spotted Enrico

Caruso in Union Square and quoted him as stating that he would never return to the city.

When Genthe returned to his studio-apartment at 790 Sutter Street Wednesday morning to grab a camera, he found that all his smaller cameras had been damaged from falling plaster. He walked to George Kahn's photo shop on Montgomery Street and asked the proprietor for the loan of a camera. "Take anything you want. This place is going to burn up anyway," said Kahn.

Genthe selected a 3-A Kodak—"the best small camera," he thought. He stuffed his pockets with roll film and departed. Only then did Genthe realize the extent of the disaster. In words that are suggestive of a modern-day war correspondent or photographer, Genthe later wrote: "I have often wondered, thinking back, what it is in the mind of the individual that so often makes him feel himself immune to the disaster that may be going on all around him."

Through midday Genthe wandered the city taking photographs "without a thought that my studio was in danger." He had a drink, punctuated by dynamite blasts, with friends. The European-educated photographer quoted a line from the Roman poet Horace about standing fast as the whole world collapses around one. While on his way to the Bohemian Club, he was told that his studio-apartment was about to be dynamited.

He rushed to Sutter Street, where a soldier barred entry. Genthe momentarily bribed him with a bottle of whiskey and then was told unceremoniously to depart. He escaped to Golden Gate Park. The second day Genthe took more pictures and was commanded several times by soldiers to pile bricks. On succeeding nights he found refuge in friends' homes. Sacramento Street and Nob Hill provided particularly rich photographic opportunities.

Genthe felt numb for weeks afterward. His photographic plates of Chinatown, at the insistence of a friend, the writer Will Irwin, who thought San Francisco was ripe for fire, had been stored in Carmel before the earthquake. All else was lost. The thousands of plates that represented a life's work "were now but chunks of molten, iridescent glass, fused together in fantastic forms."[39]

⸻

Although he was the best-known and the best-remembered photographer from that era in San Francisco, Genthe's work was equaled or excelled by lesser-known or anonymous photographers. Such names as Louis J. Stellman, the Bear Photo Company, Stewart & Rogers, W. E. Worden, and the Padilla brothers deserve special mention, as does Harry J. Coleman of the *Examiner,* perhaps the most courageous (or foolhardy) of all the photographers.

Coleman climbed to the top of the wrecked City Hall dome with twenty pounds of camera equipment in order to take a panoramic photograph. He and a reporter had to sign a release agreement before the police chief would allow their dangerous ascent. Coleman described the final push to the summit:

> From that point, we smashed the glass and climbed the interlaced iron work of the inner dome to the apex. There a small, spiral stairway leading to the top of the dome had been broken in many places and was scarcely secure enough to hold us, but we kept on going until we reached a small platform, 300 feet above the earth, upon which rested a tottering ball surmounting the dome. We could go no higher. Cooped deep in the ball and crouched at the very feet of the Goddess of Liberty [the crowning statue], I held my camera and photographed the ruined city.[40]

The single largest and most meaningful body of work was produced for the State Earthquake Investigation Commission by scientists and engineers who lugged cameras into the field. The scientists and engineers ranged from the dense forests of Humboldt County to the open deserts of San Bernardino County and produced hundreds of negatives.

These men, who had mastered the newest scientific tool, not only documented the fault line and damage to natural and manmade objects but they also inadvertently provided a visual baseline for five hundred miles of the California landscape that can be compared to what exists a century later.

The photos show a vastly different California. Hillsides were bare and uninhabited. Other than grasslands, little vegetation existed except along infrequent watercourses, because heavy grazing and logging had denuded the landscape. Water used to grow trees, plants, and flowers would be applied later when dense suburban developments transformed the coastal hills.

Crisp, clear photos of the damage to San Francisco, Berkeley, Oakland, Stanford, San Jose, and Santa Rosa as well as to less-populated areas in Santa Cruz, Monterey, Marin, Sonoma, and Mendocino counties are also represented in this collection of outstanding historic value. A few of the photos have been used to illustrate the commission's report and more recent scientific articles in technical journals. But most have been preserved in relative obscurity in the archives of the Bancroft Library.

The military and commercial photographers who hoisted cameras on balloons and kites above San Francisco to obtain panoramic aerial photographs of the ruined city produced the most effective and powerful overall images. They displayed inventiveness, technical skills, and a certain amount of creativity. The techniques they developed in 1906 were used for reconnaissance purposes during World War I.[41]

Balloons and kites with attached cameras were sent aloft by the Army Signal Corps in early May 1906 under the direction of Captain Leo D. Wildman. The captain was the army's technology whiz. He had been in charge of balloons during the Spanish-American War in Cuba (where at least one was shot down with rifles wielded by Spanish soldiers), had worked with balloons attached to cables in the Philippines, and had helped develop wireless telegraphy.

The *Examiner*'s first attempt to photograph the city from aloft ended ingloriously. The newspaper ran a "balloons wanted" ad, and a Petaluma showman responded with an ancient device. Harry Coleman, the intrepid photographer who had hiked to the top of the ruined City Hall dome, climbed aboard with many misgivings. The balloon slowly rose to 150 feet above Twin Peaks, the basket swung wildly, and then the leaking orb sank slowly to the ground without Coleman snapping a picture.

The George R. Lawrence Company of Chicago had much better results with the Lawrence Captive Airship, from which panoramic photos were taken at heights between six hundred and two thousand feet above the city and the bay. Lawrence launched his custom-made wood and aluminum camera that weighed forty-nine pounds into the air on as many as seventeen kites in a linked train. The shutter was tripped by an electrical current that ran through an insulated line from the ground to the camera.

What Lawrence produced was astonishing. Contact prints were made from the forty-eight-by-twenty-inch negatives that took in an incredibly detailed 130 degree panorama. Hardly anyone except a few balloonists had seen the city from this perspective before and no one had seen it in ruins.

Lawrence's dramatic photographs ran in special sections and in the regular news columns of the *Examiner* through August. They were also printed and sold separately as souvenirs for $125 apiece. The photographer earned a total of $15,000 by selling his prints.

It was a marvel that San Franciscans, after viewing them, did not just give up and go away. They were the equivalent of later images of Dresden, Hiroshima, and the leveled World Trade Center.[42]

DISASTER AND RACE

THE CHINESE

It was as if the earthquake had released the Furies of race. News filtered out of San Francisco, but the situation was unclear: what was happening to the Chinese, who numbered somewhere between fourteen thousand and twenty-five thousand?[1]

They had fled in disarray during the first two days of the fire after the combined forces of the earthquake, explosives, and firestorms razed the dozen or so blocks of Chinatown and left a dead zone. The *Oakland Tribune* reported, "A heap of smoking ruins marks the site of the wooden warrens where the slant-eyed men of the Orient dwelt in thousands."

"In Chinatown," a contemporary observer noted, "everything is an indescribable mass of ruins. Most of the streets are so filled with debris that one could not pass through them, but had to pick one's way with great care slowly. Not a soul visible, but a stench in many places indicating that mangled human remains would be found in numbers when the ruins can be cleared up."[2] If true, then those dead were never found and counted.

The vast majority of Chinese refugees found their way to Oakland. Others took refuge in Berkeley, Richmond, and Hayward in the East Bay; in Central Valley communities; and in Los Angeles. A few hundred made the unwise choice of remaining in San Francisco. Some fifteen hundred returned almost immediately to China.[3]

A few days after the earthquake President Roosevelt became concerned about the treatment of the Chinese and dispatched Secretary of Commerce Victor H. Metcalf westward to report on any discrimination and the overall condition of the city. After briefly huddling with members of the oligarchy, Metcalf telegraphed the president: "It is reported to me that no discrimination of any kind has been shown against anyone on account of race or color. The spirit has been and is to assist the suffering whoever and wherever they may be. Cases of violence and crime have been exceedingly rare."[4]

The Chinese outside of the city were worried. The first secretary of the Chinese Legation in Washington, D.C., Chow Tszchi, arrived in San Francisco on April 26 to reinforce the efforts of the consul-general in San Francisco.

From Victoria, British Columbia, came the following telegraphed enquiry from the Chinese Consolidated Benevolent Association to the governor of California: "Are our Chinese being cared for? Where are they now? We have subscribed over twenty five hundred dollars here. What shall we do with it? Answer." Other Chinese benevolent organizations in this country and the government of China had similar concerns.[5]

Governor Pardee replied: "Chinese largely departed to nearby towns, where are being assisted. Money sent to James D. Phelan, chairman committee will be expended according to your direction."

The Chinese in San Francisco and Oakland were, indeed, being assisted— assisted in being moved to remote camps far from any whites.

Racial fear and hatred were ingrained in the history of California. One piece of restrictive legislation after another had been passed at the local and state levels. As a result, the Chinese population was declining. Pardee, the Republican governor and a Progressive; Phelan, an antilabor Irish-Catholic Democrat and Progressive; and Ruef, a prolabor Jewish Republican were united on ridding the city of the Chinese.

The governor of the state had voiced his opinion on the immigration of the Chinese and Europeans in a letter to a correspondent that spring.

> You must keep in mind, with inconsiderable exceptions, the Chinese who have immigrated to this country have represented the lowest class of the Chinese population. The immigration of a corresponding class of Europeans is not regarded as desirable, and much more of the incoming of the Chinese of this class is likely to be a detriment to the country.[6]

For the relatively few Chinese who remained in San Francisco, the first designated refuge to which they were herded from scattered camping spots was a small park between Chestnut Street and Black Point, where other refugees were camped. White women objected to the Asians' presence and asked that they be removed.

The soldiers honored the request. They came through the camp on a daily basis shouting for everyone to move. These demonstrations, one woman recalled, were not for the white campers. They "were really intended to frighten the Chinese and Japanese into moving. . . . It is true that after each season of such vociferations a few more Orientals abandoned their stopping places and crept away and in the end those that remained were made to move to the neighborhood of the Fontana Building at the foot of Van Ness Avenue."[7]

This new camp lasted one day.

At the meeting of the citizens' committee on April 26, the situation was fully explored. James Phelan, the author of an article titled "Why the Chinese Should Be Excluded" in a national publication, "objected strenuously" to the Van Ness Avenue location. He thought it would be "extremely difficult" to dislodge the Chinese, should the property owners find it profitable to house them in that location. Phelan favored moving them to remote Hunter's Point on San Francisco Bay.

Gavin McNab, a Democratic boss, pointed out that Hunter's Point was just across the line in San Mateo County. San Francisco, he said, needed the Chinese property taxes and poll taxes. The politically connected lawyer Garret McEnerney thought it would "prove difficult" for the Chinese to obtain the needed building permits from the mayor and the Board of Public Works to erect anything permanent at the foot of Van Ness. "I would like to buy a long pool on that," said McEnerney.

Abe Ruef explained that the purpose of the Van Ness encampment was to keep the Chinese in one place "so that they might be moved more advantageously to permanent quarters when secured." Ruef was appointed chairman of a committee to find such a place, and Phelan was named to the committee.

Secretary Metcalf reported to President Roosevelt after the meeting:

At the meeting of the Citizens' Committee this morning at which were present Governor Pardee, Mayor Schmitz, Doctor Devine, Generals Greely and Funston and other officers of the army, it was determined to move the Chinese to the military reservation at the Presidio where they will be under the direct control and supervision of the army and where especial attention can be paid to matters of sanitation. The Chinese consul called on me today and when informed of this arrangement, expressed his gratification. I shall visit the Chinese camps this afternoon for the purpose of ascertaining their exact condition from personal inspection and examination.

The Chinese were settled on the military golf course at the Presidio. They remained there one day. The neighbors "objected to the establishment of the Oriental quarter so close to their homes, where the summer zephyrs would blow the odors of Chinatown into their front doors," according to the *Chronicle*. The military then moved them to the most remote, fog-shrouded, wind-lashed, rain-swept location on the post, if not in all of San Francisco, that being the parade ground just above Fort Point.

The number of Chinese in San Francisco had been steadily decreasing. In her book on the earthquake and the Chinese, Erica Pan wrote: "Their constant odysseys showed that once the crisis was over, discrimination revived. This phenomenon was repeated in Oakland where the majority of Chinese camped."[8]

———————

With the Chinese outside the city prohibited from returning and those inside being held virtual prisoners in their camps, the wholesale looting of what had been Chinatown by "respectable" citizens and National Guardsmen took place without anyone being shot under the illegal "shoot to kill" order.

The looting began as soon as the fires died out. On April 21 the Chinese consul general in San Francisco, Chung Pao-hsi, complained to Governor Pardee that "the National Guard was stripping everything of value." Pardee was protective of the guard and not sympathetic toward the Chinese.

The looting became a feeding frenzy on April 27, when civilians were allowed unrestricted access to the city for the first time in nine days. The *Chronicle* reported: "Chinatown was looted yesterday—looted by hundreds of relic hunters, people who three days ago would have shot down a man had he so much as touched his hand to a piece of valuable property."

The newspaper put the number of looters at a thousand or thousands. "A tinge of respectability was given to the action of the looters by the presence of a lot of men in uniform," the newspaper noted. "They seemed to encourage the workers to go deeper into the ruins. Men and women joined the ranks and huge sacks of melted bronzes were carried away. It was the chinaware that attracted most."

The rumor spread that burned pieces of china were the most valuable. "It was the soldiers that got this cue first—that is the men who wore the khaki uniform and had done duty as national guardsmen. Everybody grabbed for the valuable china."

A crowd returned in the late afternoon to the East Bay on ferry boats. The stolen china was offered for sale on the ferries: $2 for teacups, $3 for plates, and $2 to $15 for pitchers and teapots. One man's loot, carried in two wicker baskets, was broken by passengers who were angered by where and how he had obtained "the best the Chinese Empire ever sent out in the way of ware."

Finally, a detail of regular army soldiers, led by two police detective sergeants, descended on the few remaining looters. After a brief standoff, more than a dozen National Guardsmen were led under guard to their camps. A special guard was to be mounted on the ruins of Chinatown the next day, and, it was warned, looters would be shot.[9]

The looting did not halt, nor were any extreme measures taken to prevent it. Soldiers were not the only looters. "Respectably dressed women" dug in the ruins, claiming they had been encouraged to do so by the soldiers. "It would astonish you if I mentioned the names of high railroad officials, of society people in Oakland and San Francisco, and reputable business men" who were combing the ruins for valuables, wrote a *Chronicle* reporter. The governor's wife acquired two statuettes in this manner.[10]

Three days later, after the ruins had been picked over, the Chinese were allowed back to reclaim what property remained. A young National Guard lieutenant was given the job of investigating all incidents involving the militia that were reported in the newspapers. Of the fifteen to twenty suspected looters, the lieutenant reported to the adjutant general: "The men turned over to General Koster accused of looting were found guiltless. In the case of the two men [arrested and charged] with looting: Charges were without foundation, and the men were released from arrest. They were merely sightseeing."[11]

Women looters were warned that they would be put to work if caught again. Males performed menial tasks such as clearing the streets. Two weeks later the *Examiner* noted: "Despite the many warnings the police say the number of looters shows no sign of diminishing and in a few weeks at the present rate most of the streets in the Chinatown and North Beach districts will be cleared of debris, without cost to anyone."[12]

Meanwhile, the movement to establish a new Chinatown at Hunter's Point had been gathering momentum, not only in San Francisco but also in editorial columns across the country. The old Chinatown had a dual effect on tourists and the imaginations of readers. It both attracted and repulsed whites.

The newspapers and magazines outside of San Francisco puffed up their collective editorial chests. Considering a possible move of its own Chinatown, the *New York Times* commented self-righteously:

> The old Franciscan Chinatown was a much greater blemish and absurdity than that of New York. For it occupied the slope of the hill at the base of which is the chief commercial quarter, and at the top of which is the chief residential quarter. No Franciscan of those parts could pass from his business to his home or back again without passing through it. What is more, his womankind could not "go shopping" without traversing it. Our little Chinatown, on the other hand, modestly withdraws itself where nobody need ever enter it who does not betake himself to it for that express purpose.[13]

The *Cleveland Plain Dealer,* whose city had no such ghetto and thus could afford to be critical of both cities, drew parallels between the Chinatowns in New York City and San Francisco: "A shame of this kind has long been tolerated in each of the two great cities at either extremity of the continent, for New York has a Chinatown only less offensive and demoralizing than that wiped out in San Francisco, and even now a movement is on foot to turn its site into a public park."

The *Washington Star* was blunt: "About the only gratifying feature of the San Francisco horror is the fact that Chinatown has been destroyed. That pestilential community is no more." The *Toledo Blade* shook its finger at San Francisco: "When a city seeks notoriety rather than fame, it is on the wrong track, and Chinatown made the California metropolis notorious." *Collier's* magazine said it favored "the ordered homes of commerce" in that location, a position that agreed with those who belonged to the San Francisco oligarchy.[14]

The core of the old city built by the forty-niners became Chinatown, an area with many of its gold rush architectural embellishments still intact. Chinatown had been coveted for a number of years by white real estate interests. "They base their opinion on the fact that the land is sheltered from the winds, is on high land, is accessible to car lines and in many other ways is most desirable," stated the *Examiner.* An additional benefit was that the fire had vaporized "all germs."

The editor of the weekly *Argonaut* argued that the Chinese should be moved because Chinatown was in "one of the best parts of the city" and "in the fifties and sixties it was occupied by the best families." Ruef said the move "would be for the Chinese [people's] own protection and safety and happiness to live together as they had in the past."[15]

At the beginning of May, the usually docile Chinese mounted an effective counterattack that took the whites by surprise. "What has been done to ruffle the temper of the Chinese?" a puzzled Boss McNab asked.[16]

The Chinese launched their offensive at a closed-door meeting of the Sub-committee for Permanent Location of Chinatown. Ruef and the others listened while the consul-general and representatives from the Washington legation and the Chinese Six Companies, who represented local Chinese interests, presented a united front. The consul-general led the attack in "emphatic but courteous terms."

He pointed out that the consulate within Chinatown was on grounds that belonged to the Chinese government and was not subject to local whims. Furthermore, the government was considering moving the consulate to Oakland, he said. There might or might not be a branch office in San Francisco.

The stakes were raised a few days later at the daily meeting of displaced Chinese in Oakland when a leading San Francisco merchant, Chuen Hung, said the Chinese would rather leave the city than live next to the mud flats and slaughterhouses at Hunter's Point. "What is there for us at Hunter's Point?" he asked. There were better places for the Chinese to live elsewhere on the West Coast, he said.

"We are not overlooking the fact," Hung said, "that Portland, Tacoma or Seattle, which already have large Chinese colonies, desire the investment of many millions of money." Delegations from those cities had been sent south to woo the San Francisco Chinese, who sent their own delegations north to investigate conditions and put pressure on the San Francisco citizens' committee. Perhaps, it was also delicately hinted, trade would not be permitted with China.

Then there was the matter of property rights, for Chinese and white landowners alike. The Chinese owned thirty-five lots in Chinatown. White landlords, who derived substantial amounts of income from the Chinese, organized to fight the move.

The *Call* resisted:

Strike while the iron is hot. Preserve this fine hill for the architecture and occupancy of the clean and moderate Caucasian. We now hold the situation in the hollow of our hand. We have but to say the word and fine edifices will in the future grace that commanding slope, filched from us by the insidious, gradual occupation of the Mongol.

But it was not to be. The Chinese, it developed, held all the cards and played them masterfully. The cards were marked with dollar signs that the whites easily recognized. Chinatown would remain an anomaly within the heart of the city. It would be even more exotic than before because of the Oriental flourishes applied by white architects. Nearly two years after the disaster, the *New York Times* could report that fifteen thousand Chinese had returned to a Chinatown that contained "new buildings, as picturesque as those destroyed by the fire and earthquake, but more convenient and sanitary."[17]

An unexpected benefit of the disaster for the Chinese in San Francisco was a temporary upsurge in immigration due to "paper sons." The municipal records were destroyed. When the Chinese went to fill out new certificates of residence, they could claim they were American citizens, thus permitting their wives to join them. They could also fabricate new sons, known as "paper sons" (and a few paper daughters) to allow more distant relatives or even strangers, for a price, to immigrate.

When immigration officials caught on to the ruses, they quarantined arriving Chinese at Angel Island, where they were subjected to rigorous questioning. Angel Island, just north of Alcatraz Island, had been one of the locations considered for the establishment of a Chinese relief camp immediately after the earthquake.

The earthquake and fire in San Francisco and disastrous floods in China that same year brought change. In San Francisco there was a convulsion in the municipal government. In China the death of the empress dowager and prince signaled the demise of the Ch'ing Dynasty. Erica Pan wrote: "In their belief system a major natural disaster always signaled an upheaval or break in the dynastic order of the country."[18]

THE JAPANESE

In resisting the move to Hunter's Point, the Chinese accomplished one of the greatest social victories achieved by a minority in California outside of the courts of law and the ballot box. The postquake experience of the Japanese, hated even more virulently than the Chinese, was uglier.[19]

The earthquake and fire constituted "a catastrophe which had much to do with the later treatment of the Orientals in San Francisco," wrote

Stanford University historian Thomas A. Bailey. The racial violence escalated to the point where war with Japan was openly discussed in both countries. An urban tragedy of national proportions was elevated to one with international consequences.[20]

The Japanese burst suddenly upon the consciousness of many Americans at the turn of the century. The military competence they displayed in the 1905 war with Russia gained them attention from Americans and respect from President Roosevelt. The rising number of Japanese immigrants to the West Coast kindled fears of economic displacement, worries about the possibility of miscegenation, and tribal loathing for the other, who was slow to adapt to the white man's culture.

Most of the new wave of immigrants, who came by way of Hawaii after 1900, scattered to rural areas to farm successfully, despite being constrained by land laws pushed by the Progressives that did not allow them to own farms, and by policies that placed other hindrances in their way. A few, mostly merchants and service employees, remained in San Francisco. It was in the postquake city, riddled with fears, where the first incidents of violence occurred.

Into this race-charged atmosphere a delegation of Japanese scientists, the most knowledgeable in the world about earthquakes, descended from the gangplank of the steamship *Tango-Maru* on May 18. They were to study the earthquake for almost three months and share their findings with their American counterparts.

The leader and most distinguished member of the delegation, Fusakichi Omori, was professor of seismology at the Imperial University of Tokyo. Omori brought with him one of the seismographs that he had designed and gave it to the University of California. The new seismograph, which replaced an older one at the Students' Observatory, recorded its first earthquake on June 15. He told the San Francisco press what it wanted to hear, namely, that the danger from more destructive earthquakes had vanished "for a long time to come, and perhaps for ages."[21]

Omori was thanked for his generosity and expertise by being stoned and beaten, and his colleagues were similarly attacked. They made no official complaints.

The first incident was brought to the attention of the press and government officials by Professor George Davidson of the University of California, who wrote a letter to newspapers on June 11. While Omori was taking pictures of earthquake damage on Mission Street near the post office in early June, he "was attacked by a gang of boys and young men. Some of them

[were] wearing the livery of the postal service, and his hat was crushed by a stone as big as an egg."

Omori's colleague, F. Nakamura, professor of architecture at the Imperial University, was stoned, and sand and dust were thrown at him and his assistants. The Japanese delegation had been subjected to "insults of similar. kind, but varying in degree . . . not less than a dozen times since they began their work in this city," said Davidson.

The postmaster, mayor, and governor wrote letters of apology. Omori replied to Governor Pardee: "I appreciate highly your courtesy in writing to me in connection with a boy who threw a stone at me."

Omori arrived in Eureka in northern California to investigate earthquake damage in early July. He had traveled on a steamship that had an Asian crew. On taking a walk, he was accosted by a white man who asked if he was a member of the crew on board the steamship. Omori replied jokingly that, yes, he was. He pulled ropes and scrubbed the decks, he said, whereupon the man knocked Omori down and kicked him.

The mayor of Eureka blamed the incident on "labor troubles now prevailing on this coast." (A salmon cannery had hired twenty-three Chinese and four Japanese laborers earlier that year. The local newspaper declared in a blazing headline "THE CHINESE MUST GO!" And go they did.) The mayor also apologized to Omori.[22]

Safely back in Japan, Omori wrote that great earthquakes never occur twice in the same place. He added that "a slight amount of precaution taken in building houses would ensure an almost perfect immunity from earthquake shocks." Omori's comments and writings on the earthquake, at least those that appeared in this country, seemed overly cautious. Perhaps he did not want to offend, or perhaps he wanted nothing more to do with the Americans.[23]

The Japanese contributed more than $100,000 toward the San Francisco relief effort. "Such exhibitions as these, which undoubtedly were the results of race prejudice, would have been resented by the Japanese in any circumstances," historian Bailey wrote, "but they seemed all the more inexcusable in view of the distinguished character of the visitors and the recent generosity of Japan toward the unfortunate city."

Less-prominent Japanese in San Francisco were being attacked at the same time. While Commerce Secretary Victor Metcalf, an Oakland resident, had reported "no discrimination" in his cursory look at postquake conditions in May, he hurried back to San Francisco later in the year, and this time wrote a more thorough report for Roosevelt.

The document said that although there were no reported cases of assault against the Japanese before the earthquake, nineteen cases were reported afterward. Minor attacks such as stonings were not counted. The San Francisco newspapers, led by the *Chronicle,* maintained that there were no more assaults committed against Japanese victims than against white victims. "The assaults upon the Japanese," Metcalf countered, "were not made in my judgment with a view to robbery, but rather from a feeling of racial hostility, stirred up possibly by newspaper accounts of meetings that have been held at different times relative to the exclusion of Japanese from the United States."

Metcalf took depositions of beatings and vandalism from Japanese students, storekeepers, laundry owners, a shoemaker, a clerk, a doctor, and the secretary of the Japanese Association of San Francisco. The complaint of a laundry owner was typical:

G. N. Tsukamoto, 3500 Twenty-third street. I am proprietor of the Sunset City Laundry. Soon after the earthquake the persecutions became intolerable. My drivers were constantly attacked on the highway, my place of business defiled by rotten eggs and fruit; windows were smashed several times. I was forced to hire, on September 6, two special policemen at great expense, and for fully two weeks was obliged to maintain the service. The miscreants are generally young men, 17 or 18 years old. Whenever newspapers attack the Japanese these roughs renew their misdeeds with redoubled energy.

Much of the violence centered around the boycott of Japanese-owned restaurants by white unions. The boycott was encouraged by the newly formed Japanese and Korean Exclusion League, which claimed a membership of 78,500, three-fourths of whom lived in San Francisco. Many were members of labor unions. The Cooks and Waiters Union printed up matchboxes stating: "White men and women, patronize your own race." Japanese restaurant owners raised $350, of which $100 was handed over to the union. The boycott ended forthwith.[24]

The troubles then shifted to the schools. One thousand new Japanese immigrants were arriving in California every month. Japanese students in their twenties, eager to learn English, sat next to grade school children in San Francisco—not a good mix, thought white parents.

Informally, there had been separate schools for African Americans and Chinese Americans dating back to the 1850s in California. An "Oriental School" was built with state funds in the city for the Chinese in 1885. With the number of Japanese increasing, the board of education, pushed by the exclusion league, sought construction funds in 1905 for additions to the Oriental School so that it could also accommodate Japanese students.

The reason given by the board of education for this further segregation of the races was that "our children should not be placed in any position where their youthful impressions may be affected by association with pupils of the Mongolian race." No money was made available for the addition to the school.

Additional controversy arose around the issue of Japanese laborers taking the jobs of white laborers. A resolution unanimously passed the state legislature urging drastic limitations on the immigration of "immoral, intemperate, quarrelsome men bound to labor for a pittance."

The racial turmoil in California caught the attention of Roosevelt. The president admired the Japanese. He was also sensitive to their military prowess and the potential threat they posed to the United States if provoked by such actions as were being taken in California. Roosevelt called these measures "as foolish as if conceived by the mind of a Hottentot."

The extensive damage wrought by the earthquake and fire thrust the races together in schools. The exclusion league got busy again and lobbied the school board, which passed a resolution on October 11, 1906, segregating all Asian students from white students. Chinese, Korean, and Japanese students were given four days to enroll in the rebuilt Oriental Public School on the south side of Clay Street, between Powell and Mason streets, the old school having been destroyed by the fire. Room was available in the school because of the flight of the Chinese. The order affected ninety-three Japanese, twenty-three Chinese, three Koreans, and one Alaskan native who were attending other San Francisco schools.[25]

The resolution produced the most serious crisis to date in Japanese-American relations, resulting in an immediate threat of war and one of the many insults originating on the West Coast that lodged in the collective national consciousness of the Japanese prior to World War II. The American ambassador telegraphed the Department of State that the issue of school segregation provoked "the deepest offense" in Japan. Some Japanese newspapers advocated war.

President Roosevelt sent a back-channel message to the Japanese government. To his Harvard classmate and friend, Baron Kentaro Kaneko, Roosevelt confided that the action of the school board was "so purely local" that Washington had not heard about it until receiving word of the Japanese reaction.

The president said that it caused him "the gravest concern," and "I shall exert all the power I have under the Constitution to protect the rights of the Japanese who are here." Kaneko was to treat the letter as confidential, with the exception that "you are entirely welcome to show it to any responsible official of your Government."

For a moment, war seemed imminent. The rest of the country blamed San Francisco. The *Cleveland Plain Dealer* regretted that "California is beyond reach of the paternal slipper of the national administration." Roosevelt—known more for his big stick than for the paternal slipper—was incensed. "I am being horribly bothered about the Japanese business," he wrote his son Kermit. "The infernal fools in California, and especially San Francisco, insult the Japanese recklessly and in the event of war it will be the Nation as a whole which will pay the consequences."

Indeed, the president had a great deal of xenophobia to deal with in California. One of the "infernal fools" was James Phelan. To the *Chicago Tribune,* which asked his opinion on the Japanese question in early December, however, Phelan was San Francisco's "foremost citizen." The former mayor telegraphed the newspaper:

Japanese naturalization out of the question. They will not assimilate, remain foreign, and are loyal to their home government. Their competition will undermine the standards of American civilization and destroy the native population. Weakened by the infusion of Japanese and harboring an enemy within our gates, this Coast would be an easy prey in case of an attack. Not less dangerous, however, is the silent invasion which is now going on. Japanese coolies should, like Chinese coolies, be excluded. It is simply a question in the long run of the preservation of the Republic.

San Francisco newspapers were Phelan's chorus. The audience was the great majority of white citizens in the city.

Stating that "for all practical purposes" Hawaii was a Japanese colony, the *Chronicle* warned: "What we are fighting for on this coast is that California and Oregon and Washington shall not become what the Territory of Hawaii now is. If the Japanese are permitted to come here freely nothing can prevent that except revolution and massacre, which would be certain." It was this type of rhetoric that incited local youths to attack Japanese on the streets.

The president's solution to the immediate problem was to press, through "comity" rather than a lawsuit, the reinstatement of Japanese school children in public schools scattered throughout the city but to restrict Japanese primary school students in their teens to the new Oriental School.

The real issue was not so much about schools, however, as it was about halting immigration, preventing "race suicide," and protecting white workers. A labor newspaper stated that "the school question is a mere incident in our campaign for Japanese Exclusion."

A solution to the crisis began to emerge in Roosevelt's mind that took into account—in fact, granted—Californians' wishes. Roosevelt wrote General Harrison Gray Otis, the bellicose publisher of the *Los Angeles Times,* a letter in January.

> In strict confidence, I am now endeavoring to secure what I am sure we must in the end have; that is, preferably by mutual agreement, the exclusion of Japanese laborers from the United States. . . . I entirely agree with you as to the great undesirability of the influx of Japanese to the United States.

A delegation from San Francisco, headed by Mayor Schmitz, arrived in Washington on February 8 to meet with Roosevelt. A compromise emerged from the meeting. Chinese and Korean students would be segregated, but not Japanese students, in return for which Roosevelt would issue an executive order prohibiting the immigration of Japanese from the Territory of Hawaii to the mainland. Legislation and a "gentlemen's agreement" cemented the deal.

Roosevelt had come to understand and agree with the racial antipathy of the Californians. "But President Roosevelt's concern for the Japanese in San Francisco was merely strategic," the scholar Ronald Takaki wrote, "shrouding for the moment his personal racial attitudes." The president was also very mindful of the Japanese military threat.[26]

A fragile peace prevailed on the broken streets of San Francisco until May 20, 1907, when it was violently shattered.

A mob of fifty ran amok that night, destroying a Japanese restaurant and driving off the patrons. Then they crossed the street and damaged a Japanese bathhouse. The police took their time responding, despite repeated calls for help. Mobs gathered on the streets, threatening Japanese business establishments for more than a week. The police held them in check.

The exact cause of the renewed violence in the city was impossible to determine with any accuracy. An analysis would have to take into account a city fractured by an earthquake, blackened by fire, overrun by the homeless, afflicted by deadly diseases, split by racial hatreds, beset by a crippling streetcar strike that bred its own type of labor violence, and torn asunder along social, religious, and political affiliations by a municipal vendetta.

Truly, few American cities have worn so many hair shirts at one time. Under the headline "Social Order at Stake in Unhappy San Francisco," the *New York Times* declared: "In San Francisco, the ninth city in size in the Union, there is presented today the amazing spectacle of a condition of social disorder which amounts practically to municipal outlawism. Anarchy is a harsh word; it has an ugly sound, and it is not well to use it recklessly, but the conditions existing in San Francisco would almost excuse the application of the word."

Recalling the earthquake and fire, the leading business interests opposed the declaration of martial law and the troops on the streets. They feared, once again, "the effect it [would] have on Eastern capital" needed to rebuild the city. Quietly, Roosevelt arranged to have troops in the immediate area. They would not appear on the streets until he was "very certain" they were needed.

In Japan there was far greater concern, and it soon escalated into "the second San Francisco incident, the first being the school issue." War was mentioned again. It seemed more of a possibility in the summer of 1907 than it had in the fall of 1906.

Roosevelt received word that the Japanese believed that the United States was beatable and had stepped up their armament purchases. The president approved shifting the Atlantic fleet to the Pacific Ocean, a grand gesture that would speed the Great White Fleet of sixteen vessels to San Francisco, its farthest publicly announced port of call. That would placate the

California alarmists, he thought. Privately, Roosevelt planned to send the fleet around the world.

To Baron Kaneko, Roosevelt wrote of his frustrations over the events in San Francisco: "Nothing during my Presidency has given me more concern than these troubles."

When the fleet arrived in San Francisco on May 6, 1908, it was given an enthusiastic public welcome, tinged somewhat by the bitterness of the politics of disaster. The successful completion of the fleet's cruise around the world signaled the emergence of the United States as a world power.[27]

THE POLITICS OF DISASTER

ABE RUEF

San Francisco split apart one last time during this period of intense seismic activity and accompanying aftershocks. One man became the ultimate scapegoat for the city's collective ills. In his defense, there were three things that could be said about Abe Ruef.

First, he was not a boss in the conventional sense of the word. A loner, Ruef controlled no machine. His power derived from the mayor, who depended on the knowledgeable attorney for advice. He was a technocrat and was a boss only in the sense that he could make things happen at a time when local government was inefficient. According to a veteran of Boston's political wars, he was an "operator" in terms of twentieth-century Chicago and Boston politics and was comparable to a competent lobbyist at the Washington, D.C., level.[1]

Second, there is no question that Ruef took money and dispersed it to others. What he received, Ruef insisted, was attorney's fees. With part of the money, he rewarded the mayor and purchased the votes of San Francisco supervisors. Graft of this type was not unusual at the time. In a widely used textbook on California history, Walton Bean, who was also the author of the major book on Ruef, wrote: "Such instances of corruption were by no means unprecedented, either in San Francisco or in other large American cities of the time." Yet Ruef was singled out and severely punished.

Bean later wrote one of Ruef's relatives that the attorney was a victim of "the circumstances of his time." Bean thought that he had not stressed the "religious-ethnic factor" enough in his book, titled *Boss Ruef's San Francisco*. In writing the book he had relied to a great extent—as did others—on

Franklin Hichborn's *The System,* which was financed by Spreckels and Phelan.[2]

Third, Rudolph Spreckels, who furnished the money for the prosecution, and Fremont Older, who wrote the *Bulletin's* editorials and directed the news coverage, later regretted their actions. They deemed the extensive legal proceedings unfair and overzealous. James Phelan, the other member of the prosecution's inner circle, had no such regrets. All three viewed the campaign as a moralistic crusade, which Phelan described thus:

> You may safely say that Mr. Spreckels, Mr. Fremont Older and Mr. Francis J. Heney [the chief prosecutor] were inspired by holy zeal to uproot corruption when they began this campaign. Conferences were held in my office and I was a party to it all and speak with authority. So, you can put down the Graft Prosecution as a sincere effort of an awakened public conscience to purify political life.[3]

ONE LEGACY OF THE CALIFORNIA PROGRESSIVES

The California Progressives, with President Roosevelt quietly cheering them on from the sidelines, were guilty of unleashing a violent, divisive drama in a city that badly needed an intermission from chaos in order to heal. They thought they were purifying a city, but what was clean and what was dirt was in the eye of the beholder. What they also achieved, under the guise of a moral crusade, was the seizure of political power and all the advantages that came with it.

The traumatic disaster of the earthquake and fire, the evangelical crusade, the grab for power, and anti-Semitism were all part of the mix that accounted for Ruef's downfall. Seen in retrospect, the basic plot was beyond belief. San Francisco was truly gripped by madness.

Ruef, the mayor, and many of the city's leading corporate executives were indicted by grand juries on graft and bribery charges. As a result, a key witness's house was damaged in a dynamite blast. Older was "kidnapped." Heney was shot in the courtroom. Heney's assailant committed suicide, or was murdered, in jail. The police chief drowned in the bay. Friends became bitter enemies. The legal process was corrupted. Mayor Schmitz and the supervisors were dethroned, and others—more pliable to the wishes of the Progressives—were installed in their places.

For some Progressives like Hiram Johnson and James Phelan, future political careers at the national level were assured by these events. Other careers were ruined. Of the 383 indictments obtained by prosecutors from grand juries, only one man, Abe Ruef, was convicted and had the conviction upheld—just barely—on appeal. Only Ruef went to prison.

The "microscopic results"—the term of a Progressive historian—came after an intensive five-year prosecutorial effort financed and directed by private citizens.[4] The prosecution was funded mainly by Rudolph Spreckels; Phelan was the driving force behind it. The prosecution depended on the questionable investigative techniques of William J. Burns, a private detective. Prospective jurors were interviewed by Burns and his operatives before they appeared in court, impaneled jurors were intimidated, and the judges who tried the major cases were prejudiced toward the prosecution.

Ruef, a Jew, was singled out for special treatment. He was given the third degree, coerced by Burns and others into signing a porous immunity agreement, was tried once, acquitted, and then tried again. Ruef was convicted by a jury that was threatened by Hiram Johnson, who took over after Heney was shot, and intimidated by rowdies recruited by Fremont Older. Ruef was given the maximum sentence of fourteen years in San Quentin.

"To Abraham Ruef," wrote Bean, who was not one of Ruef's admirers, "of all the figures in the history of the graft prosecution, fortune was most unkind." The word "fortune," however, indicates blind fate. That was not the case. Ruef was San Francisco's equivalent to France's Alfred Dreyfus, another French Jew, who was persecuted at about the same time in France.[5]

The graft prosecution, as it came to be known and celebrated by various historians, ranks as one of the darkest hours in American jurisprudence. It was no accident that it came after the earthquake and firestorms.

ANTI-SEMITISM RAISES ITS UGLY HEAD

The attacks on Ruef greatly intensified after the disaster. The *Overland Monthly,* a San Francisco–based publication with a long history of serving the West, published the most vicious diatribe. The *Overland Monthly* was founded in 1868 with Bret Harte as its first editor. Over the years Mark Twain, Jack London, Frank Norris, Gertrude Atherton, Joaquin Miller, and others contributed to the magazine.

A new publisher and editor took over with the November 1907 issue. In that issue, a "Publisher's Announcement" promised "not only to maintain the present high literary prestige of the magazine, but to inaugurate improvements in the policy, vigor, tone and quality of *Overland Monthly*."

Among the offerings for that November issue was an article by "Q," entitled "Ruef—A Jew under Torture." An editor's note explained that the information contained in the "psychological study" was trustworthy, but "it is obviously impracticable to reveal the name of the author or the sources of his information." Why it was impracticable was not explained.

From clues within the text, a good case can be made that the author was probably Fremont Older—a Progressive, an admirer of Phelan, and the "crusading editor" (his most frequent designation) of the *San Francisco Bulletin.* Q said he had been "the first to begin a campaign of publicity" against Ruef, which, along with other hints, fits Older.

Q, or Older, began the article by establishing that Jews were of "Asiatic descent," thus lumping them with the hated Chinese and Japanese. He continued:

> The Jew is a problem of centuries, and there must be somewhere in his make-up an element so terribly at variance with the rest of mankind that throughout countless ages he has been accounted an offending enigma.
>
> Abraham Ruef represents this enigma in a marked degree. He has been banker of thousands, and his usury has been wrung from an entire community who have paid unconscious and unwilling tribute. He is the very quintessence of self-conceit. He is an abnormally intelligent man, who has solved the problem of indirect accomplishment. Early in life he made a study of making his fellowman do his drudgery, willingly, cheerfully and unconsciously. He used the system in school and in college, and graduated as an "honor" man, but not as a man of honor.
>
> He is a strong man mentally, but ever and anon the persecution of the ages oozes out of him, and he cries in fear and shifts. It is the tortured adopting Christianity to escape the lash. It is the cunning of the Asiatic asserting itself by fawning and smiling, by the witty retort and the eloquent speech currying favor to parry the blow. Ruef is sensitive to a degree. Ruef is vain to a degree. Ruef owes his downfall to his over-weaning appetite for power and pelf.[6]

Lincoln Steffens, the New York City–based muckraker and native Californian, came to town after the earthquake and conferred extensively with Older, Phelan, and Spreckels. Steffens was at the height of his journalistic career. He identified closely with those sources for his stories, including the two San Francisco business leaders, who were socially prominent and espoused similar causes. The result was a series of four articles in the *American Magazine,* a Progressive publication founded by Steffens and his associates, about graft in San Francisco. Steffens described Phelan as "a rich Irish gentleman." Of Ruef, he wrote: "A Latin Jew, Ruef has a cunning mind, but at heart he is an artist, a histrionic artist."

Referring to Older, Phelan, Spreckels, and others on the team that prosecuted Ruef, Steffens wrote in his autobiography: "They were after Abe Ruef, the arch bribe-giver." They and "most everybody was for that, too," he said. When the prosecution wasn't going well, Steffens privately consoled Older: "Well, never mind; I see by the papers that immigration is breaking all records. Maybe the scum of Europe will improve our breed."[7]

While some of the Irish, as typified by the Phelan family, had, through hard work and persistence achieved financial success and been assimilated into the mainstream of San Francisco society, members of the smaller Jewish population had yet to be fully accepted, as the following story illustrates.

Harry J. Cooper had a temporary job with Lester, Herrick & Herrick, a firm of public accountants. The firm kept the books of the finance committee, headed by Phelan. Cooper's boss, William Dolge, wanted to hire Cooper permanently. Years later, Cooper, who by then had been president of the California Society of Public Accountants, recalled: "One day Mr. Dolge came to me and said: 'Harry, I like you and I like the work you've been doing, but you needn't figure on going on the staff of Herrick and Herrick because the members of the staff refuse to work with a Jew.' And I said, 'Thanks Bill, I think I better get out now.'"[8]

The Jewish community was divided on Ruef's character and culpability. Rabbi Jacob Nieto of Temple Sherith Israel, a friend of the Ruef family, thought Ruef was being made a scapegoat for higher-ups and that the well-funded, aggressive prosecution that focused on Ruef was driven by anti-Semitic motives. A local Jewish newspaper talked of "the would-be reformers who turned out to be persecutors rather than prosecutors."

Many Jews remained silent or distanced themselves from Ruef, who was an embarrassment to them. A Los Angeles attorney wrote Rabbi Nieto: "We have no cause at all to feel a bit proud of Mr. Ruef and would like people to forget that he is one of us." Rabbi Stephen S. Wise of New York said: "Israel is not responsible for Ruef's crimes. . . . Israel is unutterably pained by this blot upon its record of good citizenship in America." Rabbi Wise added that Ruef was "a cancerous sore on the body of the city."

Today Ruef is considered an aberration by the San Francisco Jewish community. Irena Narell wrote in *Our City: The Jews of San Francisco:* "Like all the major Jewish characters in the early history of San Francisco, Ruef came from a pioneer family. There the resemblance ended. In contrast to the middle-class virtues and solid citizenship they displayed, Ruef, a man without scruples, was a flamboyant and consummate scoundrel."

A less harsh and, in my opinion, more accurate assessment is contained in a docent training manual for the Judah L. Magnes Museum in Berkeley: "Later, some felt that Ruef alone was convicted because he was a Jew. Others argued he was a political boss, fifteen years too late, caught in the middle of a fervent, national zest for progressivism. And others felt he got what he deserved."[9]

REGENERATION

Like the concept of "upbuilding," purging city hall after the disaster had its own special designation. It was called "regeneration."

Change was in the air, and a correspondent of the *New York Times* sniffed it out. "The earthquake and fire of April 18, 1906 were psychological events which made possible the realization of certain plans—political and commercial—which might never have been realized had not Providence intervened." The chief agents of political and economic change were Rudolph Spreckels, James Phelan, Fremont Older, and "other men of wealth and energy."[10]

The Progressive movement gathered headway in California in 1906. The three targets of the reformers were the Southern Pacific Railroad, organized labor, and the labor-oriented municipal government headed by Mayor Eugene Schmitz and Abe Ruef.[11]

The railroad, or "the Octopus," as it was called after publication of Frank Norris's novel of the same name, was the principal public target of the Progressives. (Two modern-day California historians, William Deverell and Tom Sitton, have identified "the Octopus School" of history, meaning those novelists and historians who have given too prominent a role to the Southern Pacific. They were guilty of the "wholesale acceptance of the narrow offerings of progressive historians," wrote Deverell and Sitton. Franklin Hichborn was one of those progressive historians.)[12]

"I know this," said Phelan in a fiery speech that implied the railroad was responsible for the assassination attempt on Heney, "that there is organized in this city a combination of interests, headed by the Southern Pacific Railway . . . who are bent not only upon arresting the orderly process of law and giving acquittance to the men who have violated the law, but they are organized in society and in the clubs and in financial circles, to destroy every man who has taken part in this struggle or who sympathizes in this struggle."[13]

The Progressives railed against the Southern Pacific continuously, but meanwhile Phelan was dabbling in its stock, and Older's newspaper was accepting secret subsidies, perhaps more accurately termed bribes, from the railroad, which resulted in certain stories being killed. Curiously, none of the hundreds of indictments handed down by grand juries naming San Francisco's leading capitalists were for employees of the railroad, although almost all the other utilities were represented.[14]

In an unusual arrangement—one that again bypassed the democratic process and trampled on civil liberties—Spreckels (with some help from his father, the sugar baron Claus Spreckels, and Phelan) financed the district attorney's prosecution efforts. The *New York Times,* in a long article that possessed the detachment that San Francisco papers lacked, characterized the prosecution as "a 'closed corporation,' although nominally representing the citizens of San Francisco and using the legal machinery of the city, paid for by the taxpayers, to carry out their private ends."

The dominance of "trade unionism"—symbolized by the labor-oriented government of Schmitz and Ruef, which in the eyes of the Progressives had become "a vast conspiracy to thwart the ends of justice"—was what the Progressives were really out to change by fair or foul means. Economic advantage and political power were the ultimate goals. The *Times* said that by bashing the Southern Pacific, "a 'machine' dominated by the Spreckels-Phelan combination can be built up in its place." This journalistic assessment proved to be remarkably prescient.[15]

When Schmitz stepped down after being indicted, Edward R. Taylor was elected mayor along with a new slate of supervisors. The election was redolent of irony. The success of the Progressives' handpicked candidates allowed Phelan to assume Ruef's role as the principal expediter in civic affairs. In other words, Phelan became "the boss."

Phelan boasted in a letter to his cousin in New York City: "Our election was most satisfactory. My friend, Dr. Taylor was elected Mayor and practically the whole ticket . . . was nominated in my office, where the leaders met." In another letter four months later, Phelan said he did not want it known that "the Supervisors are new at the work, and they frequently come to me for advice and assistance."[16]

In an article titled "Abe Ruef Was No Boss," James P. Walsh wrote in the *California Historical Quarterly:* "By placing Taylor in the mayor's office, the triumvirate chose a man as unrepresentative of San Francisco as he was respectable and acceptable—to those who chose him." Walsh, who would later coauthor a biography of Phelan, added: "More significant is that through the graft prosecution San Francisco became governed extra-legally and undemocratically by a private and narrowly-based clique."[17]

The question of what types of people constituted the narrowly based clique can best be answered by examining who the California Progressives were. The California Progressives, explained George E. Mowry—one of their laudatory historians—consisted of "an extremely small group of men." With a few exceptions, they had northern European last names, came from "old American stock," possessed "the long religious hand of New England," were well educated, tended to be attorneys or journalists or independent business leaders, were "well fixed" financially or members of the upper middle class, tended to be Masons and members of chambers of commerce, and were admirers of Teddy Roosevelt. "The progressive's bias against labor was always greater than against large corporations," said Mowry.

They were clannish and spoke and wrote of "our crowd" and "the better element." They tended to view matters in the stark colors of black and white. They made much of their manliness and claimed the moral high ground. Kevin Starr referred to the graft trials as "the deeply divisive effort to pursue virtue."[18]

George Kennan, acting as both cheerleader and coach, described the daunting task facing the group in the progressive magazine *McClure's:*

> If the business men of San Francisco showed such energy and determination in coping with the tremendous catastrophe of April 18th,— if they were able to reconstruct their wrecked and burned city at the rate of a new building every forty-five minutes,—why could they not overthrow a notoriously dishonest administration headed by a comparatively insignificant Jewish lawyer and a fiddler from the orchestra of the Columbia Theater?
>
> The answer to these questions is to be found in the domination of San Francisco by labor-unions, and in the unwillingness of the labor-union men to give up power for the sake of principle.[19]

THE PERSECUTION BEGINS

It was against this background that events began unfolding in 1905 that led to the extensive persecution of Ruef. Fremont Older fired the first salvos from his aerie as editor of the *Bulletin*. It was not an exalted or a very principled perch, as Older would later recall.

The lanky, walrus-mustached, bald, cigar-smoking editor had risen from the ranks of printers' devils to the position of managing editor of the struggling *Bulletin* in 1895 without the benefit of formal education. But he had a great deal of on-the-job training.

Older's immediate task was to raise circulation. "So I decided it was not a time to concern myself too much with the ethics of journalism," he said. "They could be considered later when the paper was on a paying basis." Looking backward, Older could see that he had "no ideals whatever about life, and no enthusiasm beyond newspaper success."

> Circulation. Circulation. There was no room in my mind for any other thought. I couldn't help knowing, however, that the business office was soliciting and securing subsidies from the railroad and other corporations. I protested feebly, but was told by the business manager that without this aid we would go under.[20]

The Southern Pacific's subsidy of the *Bulletin* increased from $125 a month—paid for "friendliness"—to $375 during the administration of Phelan, whom Older backed for mayor. Phelan believed Older was honest, an illusion Older strove to maintain. The editor blamed the newspaper's publisher for any dishonesty, while continuing to draw his salary. Older did not disclose the conflicts and illegal deals until many years later. "Worldly success was my only ideal," repeated the editor.

Older killed several articles the railroad didn't like, solicited contributions from politicians for the paper's support, and conspired, along with the publisher of the *Bulletin* and the publisher of a Southern Pacific–owned newspaper, in a "felonious agreement" to obtain the city's printing contract.

The "crusading editor," whose newspaper increased circulation and made a profit during the graft trials, was well aware of the parallels with Ruef's career.

> I was fully awake by this time to the grafting idea and saw the inconsistency of my hammering at Ruef and Schmitz for doing the same thing that we were doing. I wanted to be clean, and I wanted the paper to be clean. I was dimly conscious that I was as bad as Ruef as long as I was taking part of my salary from the same source, and I felt it keenly.[21]

However, another more dangerous aspect to Older's character—namely, the same zealotry that possessed the others on the prosecution team—took over. Cora Older, Fremont's wife and a writer herself, later explained to Walton Bean: "We had the feeling of being crusaders, the only people in the world always right."[22]

The *Bulletin* joined the Southern Pacific in backing the mayoral candidate that ran against Schmitz in 1905. The newspaper was interested in reform; the railroad feared Ruef's growing power. They formed an unholy alliance. "I plunged immediately into a most vicious campaign against Schmitz," said Older. "The *Bulletin* was filled with cartoons showing Schmitz and Ruef in stripes. Our editorials declared that these men should be in the penitentiary and would be put there eventually. I spared no effort in running down and printing news stories to their discredit."[23]

The crusade was launched on a number of fronts. A fiery San Francisco attorney, Francis J. Heney, who was working as a special prosecutor for the federal government on land fraud cases in California and Oregon, spoke for a few moments at a political rally in the Mechanics' Pavilion shortly before the election. "If Schmitz is re-elected and this graft continues," Heney pledged to the twelve thousand spectators, "I will devote my best energies to sending Abe Ruef to the penitentiary. I personally know that Abraham Ruef is corrupt, and I say to you that whenever he wants me to prove it, I will." Before a grand jury a few days later, Heney admitted that he had no proof.[24]

An ambitious and promising Secret Service agent, William J. Burns, had been detached from his routine work on counterfeiting in Washington, D.C., and sent westward to work with Heney on the land fraud cases. The portly, derby-hatted Burns and the tough Heney, who was used to fighting with his fists as well as his words, operated together as a team with great success. The resulting publicity brought them national attention.

Having returned to his hometown, Heney had political ambitions. Burns, who was eyeing a career as a private detective, would become known for his "excessive zeal" in getting the "right kind" of juror, his "heavy third degree measures," and his "dirty tricks." Burns's biographer wrote of this time in the detective's career: "Unfortunately, even when he was a champion of the people acting for the Secret Service, Burns crossed the line in using the third degree, break-ins, and other commonly employed unscrupulous practices." Slaying the jackals in San Francisco was the perfect career move for both Heney and Burns.[25]

The Southern Pacific, the *Bulletin,* and the Republican-Democratic-backed fusion effort was overwhelmingly defeated by the incumbent Union Labor Party in the mayoral election of 1905. Even the better residential districts in the Western Addition voted for labor's Schmitz and his slate of city officials, supervisors, and, behind them all, the presence of Ruef. The attorney was surprised by the immensity of the victory. The emotional Older was greatly depressed.[26]

If labor could not be defeated at the polls, well then, the Progressives thought, let's try the courts. Older met Heney in Washington on December 2. The attorney said an investigation of Schmitz and Ruef would be possible on three conditions: it would have to be conducted through the office of the district attorney, there needed to be a special fund of at least $100,000, and Burns must be the chief investigator. Older met with President Roosevelt the next day. Roosevelt was sympathetic to the cause of getting rid of urban corruption, which had a high priority on the Progressives' agenda.

On returning to San Francisco, Older met first with Phelan and then Rudolph Spreckels. The latter, educated by private tutors, had gone to work at an early age in one of his father's sugar refineries and had shown an aptitude for business. He had accumulated a fortune of his own through shrewd real estate deals and speculation in corporate securities. Ruef had once offered Spreckels a shady business deal, which greatly offended him. Spreckels and Phelan, the two richest men in San Francisco, were partners in various business ventures.

Spreckels entered the fray and emerged as the darling of the Progressives. Lincoln Steffens referred to him as "the political ideal of the business world." Steffens continued:

> There is no doubt about Rudolph Spreckels. He is only thirty-five years old, but he went into business, big business, when he was seventeen, and his character is as mature as his splendid physique. He has his faults, and they are great faults, but plain; and he has his virtues, and they are also great and plain. Big, handsome, blue-eyed, sure of himself, this young man is as open as his own countenance.

Spreckels thought at first that he could form a like-minded committee of fifteen businessmen and raise the $100,000 from his fellow capitalists. But there was little enthusiasm for such a venture into uncharted waters when the known waters had been fished so profitably. Claus Spreckels and Phelan contributed $10,000 apiece, and Rudolph Spreckels came up with the remainder, which would eventually surpass $100,000. Taxpayers' funds were also expended in the prosecutions. With Roosevelt's blessing, Heney and Burns came on board.[27]

Burns set up his office in the district attorney's quarters in February 1906. Heney, who had offered his services at no charge, needed to complete his work in Oregon. He did not return to San Francisco until the fall.

In the meantime, earthquake, fire, homelessness, relief, and reconstruction preoccupied San Francisco. Older needed to resurrect the *Bulletin*. "But my mind was so filled with one idea," he said, "that even in the midst of the ruin I thought only of getting Ruef and Schmitz, and lamented the delay that I feared that the fire would bring about."[28]

———————

Given the extensive ruins that lay all around them, the loss of their businesses, and their preoccupation with recovery, it was remarkable that Phelan, Spreckels, and Older persisted. But persist they did, and with a vengeance that seemed to suck sustenance from the very bitterness and devastation that surrounded them. The city needed a scapegoat—an identifiable person or persons on whom residents could pin their collective ills.

District Attorney William H. Langdon, who had been elected to office in 1905 as part of the Schmitz-Ruef slate of candidates, acted independently of his nominal bosses and cooperated with the "regenerators." He appointed Heney as a special prosecutor in late October and impaneled a new grand jury to look into the charges of graft.

Like everyone else involved in these convoluted matters, Langdon was not a disinterested party. At the time, he was running for governor on a reform ticket backed by Hearst, whose *Examiner* was gunning for Ruef. The newspaper tycoon was running for governor of New York State that fall. Both Langdon and Hearst lost their respective races.[29]

When Heney arrived in the fall, there was no question to whom he was primarily beholden, and it wasn't the district attorney. He was a pro forma public servant who was endowed with special powers. The special prosecutor was attached to the district attorney's office, had police and subpoena powers, dealt directly with grand juries, and prosecuted cases in court in the name of the people. Heney reported to Spreckels and Phelan.

(The investigative team looked into a number of matters, not all of them related to the issues directly at hand. Phelan, who had long favored a municipal water company and the procurement of a source of water in Yosemite's Hetch Hetchy Valley, pointed the prosecutor in that direction and requested "a Water Investigation as soon as possible in order to report upon the conduct of the Board of Supervisors and for the enlightenment of the public, even if no indictments are likely to follow." The investigation was motivated to influence an election that was never held. Heney did as he was told.)[30]

With these unfriendly forces allied against him, a changed political and ethical climate in the offing, and with disclosure threatened, Ruef panicked and made the worst tactical mistake of his political career. Mayor Schmitz was in Europe and the acting mayor was Supervisor James L. Gallagher. The charter of the City and County of San Francisco provided for the suspension of "any elected officer" by the mayor and removal "for cause" by the supervisors, all of whom were controlled by Ruef. Gallagher suspended District Attorney Langdon, and the supervisors fired him. Ruef was appointed as the acting district attorney.

Older flooded the streets with free newspapers, there was a great public outcry, and, according to Cora Older's account, all the available police and deputy sheriffs were called out "to keep in order five thousand of the most prominent men in San Francisco who responded to the call" to influence the judicial decision. "Armed, ropes in pockets, the citizens glared at Judge Graham when he entered his court-room. They peered at him through the windows. They decided it. It was Ruef's Black Friday." The judge ruled that Langdon, not Ruef, was the district attorney.

The carefully chosen new grand jury listened as Heney questioned witnesses. It issued five joint indictments against Schmitz and Ruef for extorting money from "French restaurants" in exchange for liquor licenses. (On the ground floor such restaurants served families, while upstairs there were more discreet facilities for eating, drinking, assignations, and whoring.) Schmitz was on his way back from Europe. Ruef was freed on bail.[31]

THE SYSTEM OF CRIMINAL INJUSTICE

The criminal justice system that Schmitz and Ruef faced had been badly askew for years. It could more accurately have been called the criminal injustice system.

The presumption of innocence was absent. First, extremely prejudicial press coverage was the rule. A newspaper story presumed—if it did not state outright—that the named party was guilty. Potential jurors were carefully screened by the prosecution before they were called for selection. Judges took sides, as will become evident.

The appeals courts tended to overrule the trial courts. It was a miracle—

or a testimony to the prosecution's overzealousness and ineptness—that a number of hung juries or outright acquittals actually occurred at the trial court level. Theodore Bonnet, a San Francisco journalist who was no admirer of Ruef, wrote the following in his study of the graft prosecution:

> Obviously if justice was "broken down" in San Francisco, as the regenerators have frequently asserted, the catastrophe occurred in the jury box, over which the prosecution exercised a supervision never surpassed in the history of the criminal courts of this country. To the recalcitrance of jurors, if not to the inherent weakness of the evidence, must be attributed the failure of Heney and his associates to procure the conviction of the higher-ups.[32]

Both sides were guilty of jury tampering, but the prosecution, led by Burns and his investigators, had the distinct advantage of far more money and manpower.

The Citizens' League of Justice, to which Phelan and his sister contributed $50 a month, was formed to back the prosecution. Its executive director, George H. Boke, chairman of the University of California's Department of Jurisprudence, assured Phelan: "We plan to start a campaign for justice that shall not stop until the City finds itself in its right mind."[33]

The names and addresses of prospective jurors were obtained from the jury pool lists for grand jurors and trial jurors. Members of the league were asked for any information that would "be of distinct value to our cause" and "assist us in securing an unbiased jury."[34]

Meanwhile, Burns and his operatives checked out names from a list of "several hundred" potential jurors that just happened to be dropped off at their office. Burns's assistants were given between twenty-five and thirty names and addresses apiece. They knocked on doors.

Potential jurors were told that the investigators represented a citizens' committee that was circulating a petition requesting that the prosecution be halted. If signed, the citizen would become a member of the San Francisco Improvement Club. There was no such club.

The petition was the bait that the prosecution used to troll for the right kind of fish. The cleverly worded petition read in part: "And we do protest against the prosecution in general as not being conducive to the city's best interests, and decidedly inimical to its welfare; and we believe that the ends of justice would best be served by the dismissal of the indictments. . . ."

If prospective jurors signed the petition, it gave a clear indication where they stood. They would then be challenged by the prosecution if they showed up in the jury box. Many citizens signed the petitions and added pungent oral comments about their unhappiness with the prosecution. One said, "Mr. Heney and some of the others should be tried instead of Ruef." Heney read the reports on the jurors. Spreckels was aware of what was being done with his money.

At times the sad affair almost resembled a dated comedy, at least in retrospect. Burns's investigators also trailed—"shadowed" in the parlance of the time—potential jurors to see with whom they consorted.

One of Burns's detectives saw an Armenian-looking person "shadowing" one of their investigators and determined that it was the opposition. The "Armenian" was a law student, who questioned a dozen potential jurors posing as a newspaper reporter. He was paid no salary but was given lunch money and a streetcar pass by the defense.[35]

The prosecution feared toughs such as the Banjo-Eyed Kid, and the defendants saw Burns's people everywhere. Ruef's lawyer, Henry Ach, invited one to have a seat in his office. On the streets people were "shadowing" people who were following other people. The city was crawling with real, amateur, and imagined detectives.

―――――――

The prosecution's advantage extended to at least two judges. Steffens wrote about their loyalties quite clearly and openly: "The law is on trial in San Francisco and it should have its day in court, which Spreckels and Heney are giving it, and some of the judges, notably Dunne and Lawlor, are standing bravely for it." He was referring to Judge Frank H. Dunne, the judge in the French restaurant trial, and Judge William P. Lawlor, who would preside over Ruef's bribery trial.

In the extortion trial as well as the bribery trial, a reading of the transcripts reveals that both judges repeatedly sustained the objections of the prosecution and overruled those of the defense. There were bitter exchanges between the judges and the defense attorneys, who accused the judges of extreme bias.

In the appeal of Ruef's conviction in the bribery trial, attorney Ach made an unusually blunt statement in the 541-page brief, titled "Misconduct of Judge." Ach, who was not aware of the full extent of Judge Lawlor's transgressions at the time, stated: "It seems that a grosser abuse of the defendant's rights by a presiding judge over a trial could not be imagined."[36]

There was no mistaking whose side Dunne and Lawlor favored. At the League of Justice rally following Heney's shooting, one of the speakers openly declared: "Thank God for Judge Dunne's election." The transcript then noted prolonged applause. This speaker was followed by Phelan, who praised the two judges: "But our civilization and our institutions are safe. That vote the other day, and the election of Judge Dunne (applause), the election two years ago of Judge Coffey and Judge Lawlor (applause) give us courage and confidence to believe that, under the constitution and the laws, we can win our battle if you only give us time."[37]

Although not specifying which judges were offered the money (which I assume was campaign contributions or was tendered as such) or if it was received, Older expressed at least the intent "to help the judges" privately. Older wrote Phelan on November 1, 1907:

> Rudolph Spreckels was opposed to using my money from the fund to help the Judges, but signified his willingness to contribute—privately and separately. Heney and Cobb [Charles Cobb, Heney's partner] will give something. It will only require $1,000 instead of $2,000. It ought to be done. Will you take the matter in hand?[38]

Fremont Older believed that the two superior court judges were "fired with the crusading spirit." But the mercurial Older's relations with Judge Lawlor ended badly after a heated discussion in his newspaper office following the editor's mea culpa.

The conversation got off to a poor start when Lawlor said, as quoted by Older in his autobiography: "He was sorry that I had been unfaithful to the graft prosecution." Older exploded. The judge then made the further mistake of questioning the veracity of the editor's account about the prosecution bribing a witness. To Older, it was a "felonious bargain" of which the judge was aware.

Lawlor differed with Older. "'We presented the case honestly,' said Lawlor with considerable heat. He continued, 'If that was done did that—'" Older interrupted, according to his account.

> He got no further. In a frenzy I shouted at him:
> "How dare you say 'If that was done!' How dare you question what I am telling you occurred in this room? Further than this, you committed perjury yourself when you made an affidavit that you were impartial and could give Ruef a fair trial. Only a short time

before you made the affidavit you told me in your room at the Family Club that the dirty blankety-blank should be made to crawl on his hands and knees from the county jail and be tried on one of the big indictments. I think I agreed with you at the time and rejoiced in your attitude, but I see it differently now that I have had time to reflect."

It is humiliating to relate—but my voice carried far out into the local room and alarmed the reporters. Of course, I was sorry for what I had said.

Lawlor left my room with foam on his lips. He never forgave me.[39]

Judge Lawlor admired Phelan, whom he had known for a long time. In thanking Phelan for his financial support in his 1912 reelection campaign, the judge wrote that "your attitude toward the government from your earliest manhood has been an inspiration to me."

When Lawlor was elevated to the California Supreme Court, he wrote Phelan in 1915: "I am appreciative not alone for what you did in the late contest, but also for the generous interest you have always taken in my public career."

Of Phelan's election to the U.S. Senate, Lawlor said, "It was a glorious victory, for it placed the seal of approval on your virtues and capacities as one of its best citizens."[40]

THE THIRD DEGREE

Schmitz and Ruef were arraigned on December 6, 1906, in Judge Dunne's courtroom, located in Temple Sherith Israel. "By a curiously dramatic fate," Cora Older noted, "Ruef appeared in the house of worship of his fathers to be judged." The newly built stone temple, on California Street in the Western Addition, was outside the burned district. It had sustained light earthquake damage. Because of the destruction of the court building, the superior court rented rooms in the temple.[41]

The defendants were represented by different lawyers and requested separate trials. Various motions and delays followed. The mayor traveled to Washington, D.C., on the Japanese school matter in February. In early March Ruef either went into hiding or took a brief vacation; explanations differed, depending on who offered them. In any case, detective Burns knew where to find him, near the beach. Bail was denied by Judge Dunne.

Ruef's long incarceration, with two brief periods when he was out on bail, began even before the first trial. Not trusting the sheriff or the police, who might be swayed by whatever residual clout Ruef possessed, the defendant was placed in the custody of an elisor, a special officer appointed by the court. His first place of confinement was the newly built wooden structure that served as the temporary St. Francis Hotel.

The elisor, William J. Biggy, appointed Burns as his deputy. Burns arranged a less expensive and more appropriate accommodation: the mayor's old home at 2849 Fillmore Street. This unusual arrangement allowed Burns unrestricted access to Ruef. Sharing the house with Ruef were Burns, Biggy, and eight guards.

From then on, Burns and the prosecution, not Biggy and the court, had physical control over Ruef. Burns went to work on Ruef. He supplied the multilingual Ruef with such books as *Half a Rogue, The Malefactor,* and *The Fighting Chance.* At the other end of the scale he subjected the prisoner to various forms of maltreatment that bordered on physical torture.[42]

Older went to see Ruef and found him confined in Schmitz's former bedroom. He was sitting in a rocking chair, a grim Biggy beside him. Ruef obligingly held a copy of *Half a Rogue* in his hand as a photograph was taken. Older, writing as Q, offered this description of Ruef's captivity: "He is not the impassive Ruef of other days. He is the apprehensive, beaten Asiatic, ready to place his hand on the Christian bible or the Moslem Koran, to embrace Christ or Islam to escape the rack—Burns."

Not for Burns were the electric shock, thumb-screw, and other "brutal devices" of torture. "He has developed a system which is slower and surer." Older described the detective's system: "They have not given Ruef 'the cold water hose, the flash of blinding light or the secret blow,' but they certainly have given him in a refined way brutal shocks to terrify his imagination."

Like a goose, Ruef was stuffed with food and induced to sleep, a sleep that was carefully monitored, according to Q.

> Ruef loves his table comforts. Ruef likes books and conversation. He is therefore indulged. He is fed to such an extent that the gorging and the lack of exercise induce him to talk in his sleep. Every word is jotted down. Every time a word recurs, it is noted. A name is mentioned, and the patient watcher records the dreamland whisper. The next night Burns enters the room to hold communion with his prisoner, to urge him to confess, to answer questions suggested by the words of his dream babblings. Then he is told that he talked in his sleep. The next night he does not sleep, but watches the eyes of his guard and

suffers tortures before tired nature asserts itself and he is folded to the arms of Morpheus.

The questioning was constant. "Or you may imagine insistent questioning, persistent probings, based on isolated facts, until the brain can struggle no longer, and gives up its secrets. Ruef has fought valiantly against all these artifices to probe the dark depths of this duplicity."

Burns played the roles of both the good cop and the bad cop in this melodrama.

One day he is allowed all kinds of privileges, a ride to the Park in an automobile, a visit from his father and sister and friends. Books, flowers and food to his liking, a guard of his acquaintance who is pleasant. Burns himself is cheerful; he seems less the Nemesis whose nightly visits the fallen boss has come to dread. Burns laughs and jokes. The laugh does not ring exactly true, and the jokes are heavy, but the change is welcome. This demeanor toward the prisoner continues for a day or two, when suddenly all visitors are denied, flowers are thrown out the window, the guard is changed, there are guards at the doors and windows, all of them are strangers, and all are mute and wear threatening looks. The guards remain in the room all through the night. Every few minutes a face appears against the pane from the outside. There are whisperings and strange noises, and vigilant, never-closing eyes watch the nervous prisoner, who does not sleep. The next day, imagine the entrance of William J. Burns, his brow darkened by a frown. He looks on the prisoner as one would look at a venomous snake just before crushing it with the heel. Then the room is filled with invective, with threat, with charge of treachery and with curses! The prisoner cringes, but finally, after two or three days of this kind of torture, of food he does not like, of utter silence and thunder-voiced contempt, he is ready to confess; and does confess.[43]

In real life rather than the pages of the *Overland Monthly*, Ruef did not confess because of these heavy-handed techniques, which seem almost comic now. But they must have exhausted him and weakened his resistance in the long run.

Older's account of Ruef's confinement was substantiated by William R. Hunt in his 1990 biography of Burns that drew upon different sources, including Burns himself, to describe the same activities. It was a story, Hunt said, that Burns told frequently, "as a self-serving tribute. He glowed like a boy describing the catch of his first salmon when he launched into his account."[44]

A *New York Times* reporter who also visited Ruef wrote an account similar to Older's. Referring to Ruef as "the shrewd little boss," the anonymous reporter called his ordeal "an extraordinary tale of mental crucifixion" and "a system of 'sweating' that has never been surpassed for ingenious cruelty."[45]

Over the first sixty days of his captivity, Ruef testified in court that Burns visited him approximately 150 times. (This works out to an average of more than twice daily, although some days Burns did not visit his prisoner.) The previous night, Ruef testified, Burns had been in his room from 5:30 to 7:30 and from 8:30 to 11 P.M. Sometimes when Burns visited him "testimony which should be given in this court was discussed." Ruef added, "It would seem that Mr. Burns has access to me whenever he so desires. Mr. Burns has come whenever he wanted to come."[46]

Ruef and his attorney petitioned the superior court and California Supreme Court for relief from the custody of the elisor. Ruef thought it might establish the dangerous precedent of private jails in California. "Private funds, as in my case, and private friends [Burns and Biggy], make any kind of persecution possible under these circumstances," Ruef argued. The petitions were denied.

The result of all these legal moves and out-of-court machinations was to force "the strongest elements of honest Jewry to come to his help" so that disgrace "may not fall on the elect, on others who are high in the temple, the counting house and the market place," said Older. He was referring to Rabbi Nieto.[47]

The rabbi approached Burns on April 2 and suggested that he speak to Ruef and urge him to tell his side of the story. Burns, seeing the advantage of such a meeting, consented. Ruef told Nieto that he would not confess. A few days later Nieto asked Burns's permission to take Ruef to see his parents. Burns, suspecting the outcome of such a visit, quickly consented. The visit broke Ruef.[48]

> When I entered the room my mother was lying in bed. She was pale and very much changed. My old father was standing beside her. She

stretched out her arms, with tears pouring down her cheeks, and said, "Oh, Abraham, Abraham!"

The rabbi said: "You see what you have done to your mother and to your gray-haired father. It is because of what you have done that your mother lies here, as you see her now. Will you not try to spare them further shame and disgrace?"

My mother said, "Listen to our friend, my son. Do as he tells you, for my sake."

Then for the first time I broke down. I wept, and I said that I would do anything they wanted me to do.[49]

Meanwhile, the entire board of supervisors, after being entrapped by Burns, confessed to being bribed and were given immunity in exchange for their testimony. They were allowed to remain in office but were held on a very short leash by Heney's team. The eighteen supervisors were no longer beholden to Schmitz and Ruef but rather to the prosecution, who could revoke their immunity if they did not do its bidding.

For Ruef's part in what the supervisors disclosed, the grand jury on March 20, 1907, returned sixty-five indictments against the attorney for bribery in four separate incidents.

Burns intensified his efforts to obtain a confession from Ruef. The prisoner told Burns that he was willing to confess in return for full immunity. Prolonged negotiations followed. Heney refused to grant full immunity and held out for a short prison sentence to placate his constituents. Rabbi Nieto and a second rabbi took part in the talks. At the end, the two judges participated in clandestine midnight conversations with the rabbis.

The oral agreement, which was later bitterly contested, provided for Ruef to plead guilty to one charge of extortion in the restaurant case. Sentencing would be delayed. Ruef would then testify in the other cases. Heney would decide the degree of immunity he would recommend to the judges, who said they would listen carefully to what the prosecutor said. The rabbis believed full immunity was a distinct possibility.

Heney, District Attorney Langdon, and Ruef signed an immunity contract on May 8. Ruef would make "full and fair disclosure" of "the truth, the whole truth, and nothing but the truth" in return for which the prosecution would "grant and obtain for said A. Ruef full and complete immunity." Ruef's understanding of the loosely worded agreement—after numerous discussions with Burns, Heney, and Langdon—was best expressed in his testimony: "If I testify fully and fairly to the truth in these matters I expect these gentlemen connected with the prosecution in this case to use what influence they have in my behalf and secure for me leniency upon certain criminal charges now pending against me. I shall insist that I am to be the judge as to whether or not my testimony is true." Ruef changed his plea from not guilty to guilty. Judge Dunne postponed sentencing.[50]

A FEEDING FRENZY

Other than Older's *Bulletin,* the press had been somewhat diffident in its coverage of the graft proceedings up to the promise of dramatic disclosures inherent in the guilty plea. The papers began smelling blood, and a feeding frenzy ensued. They displayed near-unanimous approval for the prosecution. Who would be indicted next was the question that was asked most frequently. The speculation rose to the heights of Harriman and Herrin of the Southern Pacific, but that was not to be.

Indictments on bribery charges were issued by the grand jury naming business leaders who dealt with prizefights, water, gas, telephones, and railroad and trolley franchises. The business leaders had allegedly sought, by way of Ruef, favors from the mayor and supervisors. It seemed as if few persons of consequence were immune from graft in the postquake city.[51]

During this time, Schmitz and Ruef exchanged messages and met once face-to-face in the mayor's former bedroom. They decided to go their separate ways. Schmitz's trial began. Rather than extorting money from the French restaurants for liquor licenses, Ruef testified that he received $8,000 in attorney's fees and gave Schmitz half.

It was essentially the same testimony Ruef would give in the bribery cases. He was paid for his services as a lawyer. When Ruef handed money to elected officials, he maintained that nothing explicit was said.[52]

Walton Bean believed that there was some merit to Ruef's defense. "There is much to be said for the theory that these statements were true," he wrote. Ruef was a lawyer dealing mainly with corporate lawyers. It would be difficult to convict "the higher-ups" on such arrangements. Heney refused to believe Ruef's constant assertions, Bean said, because of his "intense and stubborn determination" to send all the defendants to the penitentiary.

The jury convicted Mayor Schmitz on the first ballot. Judge Dunne sentenced him to the maximum five years in San Quentin Prison, stating that he regretted that the law did not allow a longer term. Schmitz shouted that the higher courts would reverse the conviction, and they did. Still, twenty-seven additional indictments remained against Schmitz. Ruef, who had pleaded guilty in return for immunity, awaited further judicial proceedings while being kept under guard.

======

Events became even more bizarre after the trolley franchise trial got under way in late August 1908. In fact, the city had begun to unravel earlier.

In 1904 United Railroads had begun a campaign to convert the remaining half of San Francisco's streetcar system from horse- and cable-drawn cars to electric cars drawing their power from overhead lines. United Railroads was owned by Patrick Calhoun, a southerner and a grandson of John C. Calhoun, who had been an outspoken champion of slavery and Southern causes in the U.S. Senate. San Francisco was a Union town, and Patrick Calhoun was a rich, aggressive, and tough-minded outsider. He acquired the privately owned San Francisco streetcar system in 1902 and promptly put Ruef on his payroll as a "consulting attorney."

Calhoun first suggested electrifying the Sutter Street line in 1905. Phelan and Spreckels owned property on Sutter Street, and Spreckels's home was located on one of the branches of the proposed line. They were also leaders in the City Beautiful movement. Overhead trolley lines were regarded as unsightly, although they were the cheapest and most popular source of power for public transportation in the country. To counter Calhoun, Phelan and Spreckels developed plans for a less-obtrusive Sutter Street line and filed articles of incorporation in California on April 17, 1906.

After the earthquake and fire everyone sought a rapid return to normalcy. It was clear that trolleys with overhead lines were the fastest way to restore the transportation system. As a symbol of recovery, a United Railroads streetcar with the mayor and various dignitaries on board made the first sustained run on April 27, to the accompaniment of loud cheers.

An ordinance allowing United Railroads to operate electrical trolleys on the entire system was passed by the board of supervisors with little dissent on May 21. No one outside a very small circle knew until nearly one year later that Ruef had received a payment of $200,000 for his services, the largest fee paid in all the cases brought to trial. Ruef gave $85,000 to the supervisors, most of whom would have voted for the ordinance in any case. Mayor Schmitz received $50,000.[53]

Spreckels' and Phelan's role in the prolonged prosecution of Ruef and Calhoun (the latter of whom the prosecution could not convict and against whom all remaining indictments were finally dismissed in 1911) was related to the competition for the streetcar franchise. The *New York Times* thought that the grants of immunity and retention of the indicted supervisors in office "was the first outward indication of the beginning of the formation of a political machine to be used by Spreckels, Phelan, and others, to carry out their plans of revenge and the ruination of certain corporations which stood in the way of their plans."

Referring to a bloody streetcar strike and the use of strikebreakers in the summer of 1907, which resulted in scores of deaths and hundreds of injuries, the *Times* noted:

> When Rudolph Spreckels saw that Calhoun was in a situation where he could be greatly hurt by aid and comfort being given to his opponents, the strikers, he turned upon him with an exultant and remorseless energy, and on the very day that the strike was declared caused him to be summoned before the Grand Jury, and a few days later, in spite of the assurance made some time previously by Heney (and before he had consulted with Spreckels) that Mr. Calhoun would not be indicted, he was indicted upon a number of counts. From that time forth Calhoun has been harassed, fought and attacked by Spreckels, privately, publicly, and in every way which might tend to embarrass him in his fight with the strikers and weaken his powers of resistance and courage.[54]

The formidable corporate forces retaliated on the social and economic fronts after the wide-ranging indictments were handed down. As if the city were not troubled enough with the aftermath of earthquake and fire and bloody race and labor riots, members of the elite used their tongues and silence to lash one another. Friends, fellow clubmen, longtime associates, and their wives turned against one another.

Phelan, Spreckels, and Older were given the cold shoulder and isolated. The latter, being more vulnerable, resigned from the Bohemian Club, where he had spent many happy hours. "Women reserved their sweetest smiles for the candidates for State's prison," wrote a bitter Cora Older. Lincoln Steffens was no longer welcome at the Pacific Union Club. The *Bulletin* suffered a drop in advertising. Money was withdrawn from Spreckels's bank.[55]

The hurt and pettiness on both sides extended to the way the officers and enlisted men of the Great White Fleet were entertained when they visited San Francisco on the orders of President Roosevelt. Phelan was chairman of the reception committee. William C. Ralston, a member of the finance committee for the festivities, said that many large corporations such as the Southern Pacific and the banks had refused to contribute to the festivities because "they disliked Phelan." Ralston was the subtreasurer of the San Francisco Mint.

Phelan wrote Ralston's boss, the secretary of the treasury, saying that President Roosevelt supported the prosecution. Therefore, he continued, Ralston was "an apologist for grafting, being in sympathy with the men under indictment for bribery." Phelan asked that Ralston be censured.[56]

The Progressive coterie kept in close touch with one another during this time. President Roosevelt told Phelan: "Naturally, I am interested in the recent developments in San Francisco." From the tranquil campus of the University of California on the other side of the bay, a puzzled Benjamin Ide Wheeler wrote Roosevelt: "I find matters in San Francisco in a very confused condition. What I consider the stable elements of society have switched over into opposition to Rudolph Spreckels, Phelan and Heney. It is hard to see why this is taking place." Franklin Lane, who served in Washington as the informal link between the president and the California Progressives, wrote Older that Heney would have the president's support in a run for public office.[57]

The city's newspapers and magazines had almost unanimously supported the prosecution while it had been indicting politicians—the easy, traditional targets of the press. Wealthy businessmen who advertised in newspapers and socialized with publishers were another matter. Besides, the story had run long enough. It was time to move on to other matters, ones that would contribute to the betterment of the city.

The shift in the press worried the prosecution. Newspapers influenced public opinion, the public voted, and the public could vote into office a district attorney who might want to end the prosecution. A countercampaign was launched to influence the press. The League of Justice sent its members a list of newspapers that were the enemy. Among the papers were the *Examiner, Chronicle, Oakland Tribune, Argonaut, Wasp, Town Talk,* and *San Francisco Evening Globe.* The Spreckels-owned *Call* and the *Bulletin* were not on the list of papers that "have done everything in their power . . . to defeat the ends of justice." A litany of newspaper abuses was described. A sample letter was offered to those who wanted to discontinue their subscriptions.[58]

Phelan publicly advocated a boycott at a mass meeting called by the league: "And if every man within the sound of my voice simply resolves with himself neither to read nor to advertise in those papers, all or any of them, and I have mentioned them, or to even patronize the firms that advertise in them (great applause), and if they do not go out of existence, they will make the sharpest about-face you ever saw."[59]

Phelan attempted to muster support for the prosecution in churches. He organized "a general expression in the pulpit concerning the lawlessness" and arranged for the Catholic archbishop to be interviewed by a friendly newspaper. It was a matter not only for God but also for country. Phelan was quoted as stating: "I do not hesitate to say that anyone who does not give his moral support to the work is a traitor to his country."[60]

<hr />

A startling series of violent events coincided with the highly charged atmosphere that permeated the city. The incidents were attributed to Ruef and his associates by way of innuendo and unproven statements.

As the trial of the attorney for United Railroads (who allegedly gave Ruef the bribe money for the supervisors) got under way, a news story in the *Bulletin* confused two men by the name of Brown who were employed by the streetcar company. The wrong Brown, who was the head of the company's detective bureau and a family man, was accused of carousing with loose women. He filed a suit.

Seeking to have Older tried on a criminal libel charge in a less-prejudiced venue, a United Railroads attorney obtained a warrant in Los Angeles. Two constables traveled to San Francisco to serve the warrant, which was signed by a superior court judge in San Francisco who did not have strong ties to the prosecution.

Older was picked up on the street, and the badly frightened editor was put on a train to Los Angeles with the constables. Friends and coworkers of Older were alerted, and Older was taken off the train in Santa Barbara and returned to San Francisco. One of the "kidnappers," a United Railroads employee, was tried and acquitted by a visiting judge.

The incident made headlines around the world. Older and his wife, in separate accounts, said they thought the intent had been to kill the crusading editor. The "kidnapping," said one writer, enabled Older "to pose as a martyr to the cause."[61]

On the night of April 22, 1908, the Oakland home of a key witness, former supervisor James Gallagher, who had served as Ruef's go-between with the other supervisors, was dynamited. Three residences that Gallagher and a partner had built were also destroyed by explosives.

Suspicion fell immediately on Ruef and his henchmen, whoever they might be. Phelan charged that the allies of the defense "do not hesitate at assassination in order to remove the pivotal witness of the people against public crimes."[62]

But it was more likely that the explosions were the work of the prosecution—one of Burns's dirty tricks to make Ruef appear culpable. None of the eight members of the Gallagher family were injured. They were not in the house, which was extensively damaged. The family had obviously been forewarned.

Older asked Burns what he could do to keep Gallagher in town as a witness and was told "that Gallagher should at least be reimbursed for the destruction of his flats." They agreed that no one officially connected with the prosecution should offer Gallagher the money. So Older promised him $4,500, stating that "we had to fight fire with fire, and meet crookedness with devious methods, [and] we did that." Two Greek brothers confessed, and a third member of their family, who ostensibly knew who had commissioned the crime, fled to Europe.[63]

The dynamiting occurred during jury selection for Ruef's trial on a charge of bribing a supervisor to vote favorably on a railway franchise agreement. Heney had decided to try Ruef for this charge because an appeals court had struck down the extortion indictment to which Ruef had pleaded guilty in return for immunity. The prosecutor was also unhappy with Ruef's testimony. So Heney unilaterally revoked the immunity agreement "for good and sufficient reasons," setting off a firestorm of criticism. The two rabbis thought they had been used by the prosecution and that Ruef had been double-crossed. The *Jewish Times* said Heney's action was "in direct line of the whole course of the prosecution, begotten of hatred and personal vituperation and revenge."

Rabbi Jacob Voorsanger was the most universally respected Jewish leader in San Francisco. The rabbi had served on the citizens' committees. His newspaper, *Emanu-El,* cited the "improper and sinister control of a public office" and added: "These startling and disgraceful revelations put to shame every man connected with them. They open a chapter of disgrace unequaled in the history of San Francisco. The crimes of the supervisors, heinous as they were, can not equal in shame the degradation of judicial office."

Heney was optimistic about obtaining a guilty verdict, for he had granted immunity to both the businessmen who sought the railway franchise and the supervisors who granted it. The jury split six-six, and Heney was unable to obtain a conviction.[64]

"THE LITTLE JEW DID IT"

Ruef's last trial, which involved the charge of bribing one supervisor in the matter of the trolley ordinance, began on August 27 and lasted seventy-two days. Not until November 6 was a full jury of twelve men seated, and then only after a pool of 1,450 potential jurors had been exhausted.

Henry Ach, Ruef's lawyer, began cross-examining Gallagher, also a key witness in this trial, at 3 P.M. on Friday, November 13. A five-minute recess was called at 4:20 P.M. About half the spectators began filing out of the crowded courtroom. The jury went to their adjacent room, some thirty feet from where Heney sat at the table for the prosecution attorneys. The door to the jury room was left open.

A short, nervous man made his way into the courtroom against the outward flow of spectators, drew a pistol from the pocket of his overcoat, and shot Heney in front of his right ear. A single bullet pierced his jaw. The assailant was immediately apprehended.

The jury heard the shot. Some saw the shooting. Others peeked into the courtroom and spied a bleeding Heney prostrate on the floor, as if dead.

Shouts were heard: "The little Jew did it." Rudolph Spreckels rose from his seat in the spectator's gallery and declaimed: "Are there no American citizens left to resent this outrage?"

Judge Lawlor convened the court in the hallway. The shaken defendant, his lawyers, and the remaining prosecutors stood about. The judge dismissed the jury.

Lawlor revoked Ruef's bail, the defendant having been free since July. Ruef was quickly dispatched to the county jail. By Lawlor's action, which soon became widely known, Ruef was presumed to have had a hand in the assassination attempt.

Older wrote of the tumultuous events and a suggestion by Hiram Johnson that Ruef be lynched:

> I was, of course, pretty nearly insane. I followed the ambulance to the hospital and got such news as I could of Heney's condition. The sur-

geons could not say whether or not he would live. [He recovered quickly.] I rushed back to the hall that was being used by Judge Lawlor as a courtroom, crying out for Ruef, trying in my half-mad condition to further infuriate the already infuriated crowd there into taking some violent action.

The streets were flooded with [newspaper] extras, and the city was for once thoroughly aroused. Crowds gathered on the streets and in the hotels, the air was electric. Phelan hurried up from San Jose, found me in my office, and wanted to know what should be done. Hiram Johnson appeared, pale, trembling, earnest, and said: "I'm ready for anything we decide is the thing to do. If it's the rope, I'm for that."

The defendant's lawyers received numerous death threats. They were given police protection. More than fifty mounted police officers guarded the county jail where Ruef was incarcerated.

Cooler heads prevailed. Immediate action was channeled to the mass meeting called at the Dreamland Skating Pavilion by the Citizens' League for Justice the next evening. Mayor Taylor was the first to speak. He urged the crowd to restrain itself: "Let us not add to the afflictions that are upon us the affliction of mob law." There were many speeches that night.

That same evening in the county jail the tragedy was compounded. While lying under a blanket on his cot, and with the eye of the guard supposedly fixed upon him, the would-be assassin, identified as Morris Haas, fatally shot himself in the head with a derringer.

The police swore that he had been searched thoroughly before being put in his cell. Who gave him the weapon, or was it well concealed? No one knows to this day.

A frustrated William Burns, who believed Haas was a hired assassin and who had badly wanted to question him, blamed the police, whose chief was then the former elisor, William Biggy.

If anyone was to be blamed for the shooting of Heney, that person was Heney himself. The police chief believed that Haas had been unhinged by Heney.

Seven months earlier, during jury selection for Ruef's first trial, Haas had been provisionally accepted as a juror after being questioned by Heney and then asked by the judge if there was any reason he should not be a juror. Haas said there was none.

Heney then learned that Haas had served a term in San Quentin for embezzlement. The prosecutor, who did not want to waste a preemptory challenge, angrily confronted Haas with his prison photo. The shaken man was publicly shamed and voluntarily stepped down. At the time, some thought this treatment was needlessly cruel.[65]

One sudden death begat another. Chief Biggy was criticized by Burns and Spreckels for siding with the defense. The Spreckels-owned *Call* said Biggy had been negligent. The newspaper even went so far as to suggest that Biggy had assisted Haas's murder or suicide, the object being to conceal the assassin's bosses. Older's *Bulletin* hounded the chief. Burns had Biggy shadowed. The League of Justice called for his resignation.

The chief was depressed. He traveled across the bay to Belvedere in the police launch to confer with one of the police commissioners. On the return trip he disappeared over the side of the launch. The pilot, who was facing forward, did not know what happened and kept declaring his innocence up to the time he was committed to a mental institution two years later.[66]

Meanwhile, Ruef's trial continued. Hiram Johnson had become the chief prosecutor. Ruef was transported back and forth in a closed van surrounded by mounted police officers, which did not improve his public image. A score of uniformed and plainclothes officers circulated throughout the courtroom.

Ach, who was accused by the *Bulletin* of "clogging the wheels of justice," was insulted when he entered the courtroom. Ruef's friends were denied access. There were more mass meetings.

The jury saw or read about many of these events. The defense filed for a change of venue, stating that the jury had inferred that Ruef was implicated in the shooting. Judge Lawlor denied the motion.

Ruef asked that the twelve jurors be dismissed, stating that the door to the jury room was open, that the jurors saw Heney shot, and that "the jury had been told that the defendant was in some means responsible for the shooting of Heney." Motion denied.

The trial resumed on November 18 with Judge Lawlor instructing the jury: "The Court realizes that the jurors may have heard or seen a part of that transaction [the shooting], or that phases of that transaction may have been communicated to the jury," but what had happened "is to stand as though it had not occurred."[67]

The time came for final arguments. Burns gave Johnson the names of four jurors who he believed were fixed. Johnson called each by name; and pointing at each in turn, declared in a loud, emphatic voice: "YOU, you DARE not acquit this man!"

Intimidating the jury, said Ach.

No, said Judge Lawlor.

The prosecution hoped for a quick verdict. The day wore on. At 2 P.M. Older telephoned the league's office. The organization had a number of "minutemen," who could be called upon for quick action. The editor continued the account:

> Fifty, or perhaps a hundred, came immediately, and I told them to jam the courtroom, which was immediately under the jury room, remain there until I arrived with Heney, and as we appeared in the hall to shout as loudly as they could.
>
> I reasoned that while the shout could be considered merely a welcome to Heney, it would have the effect of so thoroughly scaring the jury that it would bring in a verdict.
>
> Heney came. I walked in with him, and I have never heard such a roar as went up. It lasted for five minutes. Twenty minutes later the jury came in, some of them white, shaking and with tears on their cheeks, and returned a verdict of guilty.[68]

It was the prosecution's biggest and only lasting victory, and it launched Hiram Johnson's political career. "Johnson's participation in the San Francisco graft prosecution," said his biographer, "was the bridge that brought him into the inner circle of California's reformers." He went on to serve two terms as governor of California and five terms as a U.S. senator. Heney also sought political office but failed twice.[69]

Judge Lawlor sentenced Ruef to fourteen years in San Quentin Prison, the maximum sentence. Ruef was held in jail for one year, then released on $600,000 bail, pending the outcome of his appeal.

A thick multivolume appeal brief, containing such individual tomes as "Misconduct of Judge" and "Misconduct of District Attorney," was filed. The district court of appeals unanimously upheld the conviction. The California Supreme Court seemingly sent the appeal back for a rehearing, but after a lot of bumbling, it was determined that the signature of one justice was invalid. The conviction stood.

On March 7, 1911, Ruef entered San Quentin, where he worked in the jute mill, wrote a play for the prisoners, advocated for prison reform, and received constant visits from Fremont Older, who became his friend and campaigned for his early release.

To jail Ruef, Older admitted the next year, had taken immoral and illegal means. The conscience-stricken editor, who suffered from mood swings but had a strong sense of personal honesty, wrote a critic about his reversal of position: "I learned that the acute disease which Ruef was suffering from was noticeable in all of us in variloid form." To shoot one animal when the whole herd was diseased made no sense, said Older.[70]

In the late spring of 1912 charges against Schmitz were dropped, thus ending his ordeal—and bringing to a close the graft trials that had unearthed so little criminal activity. There is no record how Ruef felt about being the only defendant among so many to have gone to prison. His lips remained sealed.

The termination of the seven-year effort, which yielded political dividends but was legally unproductive, was announced in a four-paragraph item in the May 25 issue of the *Bulletin*. The headline declared: "SCHMITZ INDICTMENTS DISMISSED: Calendar Almost Cleared of Graft Cases; Ruef Only Defendant in Prison." Schmitz had not been brought to trial speedily enough, the California Supreme Court had ruled, and there was insufficient evidence against him. The brevity of the news item contrasted with the great length of prior stories.[71]

Schmitz ran for mayor again in 1915 but lost to the popular incumbent, Sunny Jim Rolph. Two years later Schmitz ran successfully for supervisor and was reelected for a number of successive two-year terms. Upon his death in 1926, he was accorded full civic honors.

Ruef left two oblique paper trails, one public and the other private. The public one began on May 20, 1912, when a series supposedly written by Ruef from his six-by-ten-foot prison cell began to run in the *Bulletin*. "The Road I Traveled" promised much but delivered little.

The series was intended to influence the State Board of Prison Directors to parole Ruef, and coupons petitioning for his parole were printed in the newspaper. How much Ruef wrote and Older edited is debatable. There are indications in headlines and promotional copy that Ruef was hesitant, while Older pushed for dramatic revelations. The series petered out in September.[72]

Ruef's private correspondence was more revealing. He did not want his family to see him in prison stripes. Ruef wrote charming, illustrated letters to his niece, who remembered him in later years with great affection. Three of the letters survive.

Ruef took great care with the illustrations that were drawn or pasted on the envelopes, which had no revealing postmark, and the many sheets of paper sent to his niece, Bertha Altmann. She was repeatedly instructed to pass Ruef's love on to his family. Uncle Abe gently and imaginatively coached his niece in art and arithmetic and spun long fairy tales. There were hints that he wasn't free: his supply of materials was limited, and he hadn't yet seen the Panama-Pacific International Exposition. He relied instead on a fairy to guide him through an imagined visit to the fair until his niece could do the same.[73]

A friend visited Ruef frequently and brought his small daughter with him. The daughter, Frannie Heppner, recalled that Ruef loved chocolate. Her father wore a large overcoat whose pockets contained chocolate bars whenever they visited the prison. Years later Frannie Heppner recalled: "But you see, people don't realize what happened here at the time of the earthquake. It's sixty-eight years ago. Everybody wanted something to rebuild."[74]

Ruef was paroled after serving four years and seven months of his sentence. He was disbarred, but he prospered for a time as a real estate developer. Ruef was pardoned by the governor in 1920. He died in 1936.[75]

───────

Rudolph Spreckels and Fremont Older came to deeply regret their roles in the persecution of Abraham Ruef. Senator James Phelan had no such reservations.

Spreckels told Walton Bean in 1946 that the prosecution effort was "an utterly useless undertaking. It did not overcome the evils of corruption." Looking back from the immediate post–World War II period, Spreckels said that "human greed and lust for power on the part of men in all walks of life" were responsible for evil in the world.[76]

Older thought in hindsight that morality was not involved in the crusade; rather it was a matter of financial gain. He had pandered to sell newspapers. The newspaper editor rued the self-righteousness of the Progressives. "If our intensive activities through the years accomplished any permanent good, I have not been able to discover it," he said.[77]

To the consternation and anger of his former compatriots, Older had fought continuously—and with many words—for Ruef's early parole. In that capacity he became the "French Jew's" Émile Zola. The immediate outcome of the Dreyfus Affair was to bring the French left to power. In the United States, the Progressives ascended briefly.[78]

THE FAT LADY SINGS

An Italian opera singer sang on opening night of this extended disaster. Although events of such massive proportions never really cease to reverberate in people's individual psyches, the years of physical and emotional upheaval were seemingly brought to an end by another.

This time the singer was not Caruso, who stuck to his vow never to return to San Francisco. Instead, in December 1910 the press anointed Luisa Tetrazzini, a stout Florentine soprano, as the vehicle for closure.

Once again the trials and jubilations of a celebrated opera singer bound for San Francisco were documented by the city's newspapers with all the fervor of fan magazines. Madame Tetrazzini's departure from New York City might be held up by a court suit filed by her former impresario, it was reported. But no, the judge provided a reprieve for the heroine and the stricken city at the last moment. The opera star boarded the train with her retinue, clutching a tiny Chihuahua in her arms.

Reporters met the train in Sacramento and accompanied the diva to San Francisco, where she was greeted by cheering crowds on Market Street and the headline: "SONGBIRD TRILLS IN PULLMAN CAR AND BUBBLES WITH GLADNESS WHEN TRAIN NEARS HER FIRST LOVE—'MY SAN FRANCISCO.'"[1]

In the year before the earthquake, seemingly so long ago, San Francisco had accorded Tetrazzini her first operatic triumph in this country. At the time she was being compared to Melba and other luminous sopranos. Tetrazzini had, an opera historian said, "technical gifts of the highest order, a dazzling ease and agility in virtuoso passages, and a tone of warm, clarinet-like beauty."[2]

That December the long sad saga was seemingly drawing to an end. Ruef was sentenced to prison, the rebuilding of the city was declared virtually complete, and San Francisco's bid for the 1915 Panama-Pacific International Exposition was being debated in Congress.

Tetrazzini gave her first paid concert at the Dreamland Pavilion, because an auditorium for concerts and operas had not been constructed yet. A newspaper said of the audience of five thousand: "San Francisco has seen no other throng of this kind on any other night since the conflagration of 1906, and the Tetrazzini concert establishes a new standard on which to base our later-day comparisons."

The soprano was beseeched by city officials to supply a public coda to the desolate years in the form of a free outdoor Christmas Eve concert. Tetrazzini had a warm heart and keen promotional instincts. She readily assented.[3]

A platform, complete with bunting more appropriate for the Fourth of July, was constructed in the large triangular space where Market, Kearny, Geary, and Third streets converge at Lotta's Fountain, which was a gift to the city from another singer and had survived the cataclysm. The fountain has been the gathering place for anniversaries of the earthquake.

The diva ascended the steps accompanied by a loud roar from a vast crowd, variously estimated by an exaggeration-prone press to number between 90,000 and 250,000 people. Years later, Tetrazzini, who sang in all the great opera houses of the world, remarked: "Never in my life have I seen such a vast congregation."

Lighted by spotlights and suffused in a surreal green glow cast by special fires lit atop nearby buildings, the robust opera star shimmered in a luminous rhinestone-encrusted gown; a wide-brimmed, ostrich-plume hat; and a rose-pink cloak that kept slipping off her shoulders. Various gentlemen leaped to accord her the honor of replacing it.

An army officer, charged with keeping order, approached.

"Madame Tetrazzini," he said, "I do not know your language, but I will speak to you in the language that all the world understands." He kissed her hand. His name was Pershing, and he would become commander in chief of the American Expeditionary Force in Europe during World War I.

After a fanfare of trumpets, Tetrazzini sang two songs, both strange choices for Christmas Eve. But, then, this concert was much less about a holiday and more about finality. The songs were "The Last Rose of Summer" and the waltz song from Gounod's opera *Romeo and Juliet.*

One reporter had the poor taste to note that there was "some restlessness" in the vast throng during the second song. But generally the newspapers pulled out all the stops on their front pages and multiple inside pages, as they had done in those fire-singed editions after Caruso sang.

The front-page story in the *Examiner* emphasized the difference that four years made.

> Where but a few years ago the heaped up debris of the ruined city smoked, Tetrazzini stood. Around her in a breath-caught hush almost the entire population thronged. Giant buildings reared in defiance of disaster flung back and forth the echoes of her voice. . . . It was the most distinctive Christmas Eve celebration held in blithe San Francisco either before or after the big fire that cindered the streets four years ago.

The *Chronicle* thought that if Madame could sing for Congress, she could get San Francisco the world's fair on the first ballot.[4]

After a pleasant stay in the rebuilt Palace Hotel, where the chef created a dish in her honor called Chicken Tetrazzini, Madame gave her last concert two days later to another capacity audience and then departed San Francisco.[5]

1915

An international exposition had become a glimmer in the eyes of San Francisco merchants in 1904. They were looking for a way to make a prosperous city appear more prosperous. The idea lay dormant until 1909 when, according to a history of world's fairs, it became "part of a program of economic recovery, reflecting anxieties produced by the earthquake, fire, and graft trials of the intervening years." The opening of the Panama Canal was the excuse.

The success of the Portola Festival in October 1909 (ostensibly marking the Spanish discovery of San Francisco) demonstrated that a public spectacle on a large scale could divert the attention of local citizens from the woeful events of the immediate past and promote San Francisco and California business enterprises to the world. Besides, San Franciscans believed they were owed an extravaganza.

At a December 7 mass meeting in the cavernous hall of the Merchant's Exchange, Gavin McNab, who was known for his eloquence, cited a number of reasons for staging the fair:

But more than this, are reasons stronger than geographical or commercial conditions: We claim it is a right. The greatest physical work of any nation is the cutting of the Panama Canal; but the greatest physical achievement of any City in History has been the rehabilitation of San Francisco. In three years we have swept away the vestiges of a calamity greater than befell Rome under Nero, or London under Charles. Since Adam stood alone on the morning of the sixth day, confronted with the destinies of his race, there has been no grander spectacle than the San Franciscan the day after the great fire; and we now ask recognition for our services to American fame and name in rebuilding this City with our own hands.[6]

James Phelan also took an active role in the campaign for the fair, not only because of its obvious commercial value but also because of the racial advantages of the Panama Canal. The canal would, he said, bring "the men of Europe" to the West Coast and be "a great factor in preserving Western civilization" from "the Chinese, Japanese, and other non-assimilable people [who] will neither be needed nor tolerated: a great race struggle will be averted, and American institutions will grow and develop."[7]

The commercial forces organized. The drumbeats of civic enthusiasm reached a crescendo in December 1910 when Congress took up the matter. So many promotional postcards were printed that the West Coast ran out of cardboard. Meanwhile, New Orleans emerged as a contender for the fair.

The Southern Pacific's *Sunset* magazine was one of the principal institutional backers of the San Francisco cause. The December issue was devoted to the exposition. On the front cover a Greek warrior straddled the bridgeless Golden Gate with a sword in one hand and a shield emblazoned with "San Francisco, 1915" in the other. In the background, once again, was a shimmering white city. An ad for the Palace Hotel on an inside page declared: "Entirely rebuilt since the fire on the original Market Street site."

The "Worth-While Shop Talk" column that introduced the contents of the magazine and set the tone for the articles and photographs that followed had this to say about the passage of time: "It seems only yesterday that Bill Irwin, beloved vagabond from California, wrote a tearful threnody, 'The City That Was.' Then a doughty writer rose and wrote, 'The City That Is,' and the chorus sang. It all happened in four years—the city rebuilt, palatial hotels and shops, people waiting for something new."

The magazine published fifteen pages of carefully composed and partially retouched photographs of the business district that gave the impression that the entire city was rebuilt. A visiting eastern architect noted two years later in an architectural publication that the streets outside the center of the new city were "occupied still only by the ruins of the old city." A. C. David went on to state that San Francisco had become ordinary, like Cleveland or Seattle.

To celebrate the newfound harmony, Steele (the writer of "The City That Is") contributed the lead article and Irwin (of "The City That Was" fame), a poem that began "We have tunneled the heart of darkness." Puff pieces were contributed by the governor, the president of the exposition, and the fair's publicity chief. One article promised "a fireless fair," since electricity would be generated by hydro power, not coal-burning power plants.[8]

San Francisco was awarded the prize by Congress and President William Howard Taft in February 1911.

The Panama-Pacific International Exposition was constructed on 635 acres of what was then called Harbor View and what is now known as the Marina District. Debris from the 1906 earthquake and fire had been dumped in the marshy area. As they rose from the "made land," the fair buildings far exceeded in opulence and size those structures that now symbolize arriviste cities, meaning new baseball and football stadiums.

The structures were the ostentatious equivalent of the display of jewels at the opera nine years previously. The apex of the exposition was the 432-foot Tower of Jewels, whose 102,000 "Novagems," faceted glass backed by mirrors, symbolized the burning of San Francisco when moved by the wind and bathed in the glare of concealed ruby lights.

Despite the exuberance and expansive mood of the architecture, the exhibits, and the fairgoers themselves, darkness—like the ever-present fog—dimmed the edges of the glowing exposition. The pastel-tinged world's fair was the last collective expression of the naïve optimism of nineteenth-century America. The early stages of World War I were being fought in Europe. For one flickering moment sandwiched between a domestic tragedy and a world war there was brightness.

Following a successful ten-month run, the ornate structures were immediately dismantled by axe, steam shovel, and dynamite. The grounds became a city dump. A suction dredge worked for four months to fill the area to the level specified in the leases, thus creating the vulnerable foundation on which the current Marina District was constructed.[9]

When the next sizable earthquake struck in 1989, once again susceptible structures on suspect terrain toppled to the ground and water lines burst. Fires flashed across the Marina District. Debris from 1906 and the exposition gushed to the surface, bearing either burn marks or the telltale faux travertine that had covered fair buildings.

Hoses extending from a fireboat in the bay and from the lagoon of the Palace of Fine Arts, the one structure that had survived the exposition, provided the water to extinguish the fires that would have spread, had there been the customary strong wind.

The weakening of building code standards after 1906, construction of row houses and high-rises, interior use of combustible synthetic materials, installation of a more flammable high-pressure natural gas system, and the same vulnerability of the water distribution lines made San Francisco more prone to major conflagrations and firestorms than ever.

"Fire remains the big threat," wrote a former fire chief of the 1989 earthquake. Given the off-hour of the 1906 and 1989 earthquakes, San Francisco had once again been extremely fortunate. It is not likely that the city's luck will hold out forever.[10]

A view from Nob Hill to the north. With the exception of the small group of houses and vegetation on Russian Hill seen here, the 360 degree view from Nob Hill resembled the ruins of Dresden or Hiroshima in World War II.

A view from Nob Hill toward the south and the City Hall.
Arnold Genthe, Fine Arts Museums of San Francisco.

A young girl on a swing attached to the leafless branches of a dead tree,
the only sign of life in a scene of utter desolation.
The Bancroft Library, University of California, Berkeley.

A ruined Dupont Street, now Grant Avenue.
The Chinese were almost evicted from Chinatown.

The Bancroft Library, University of California, Berkeley.

The ruins of a steel-framed building. Temperatures in excess of
2000 degrees Fahrenheit transformed rigid steel into limp pastalike forms.
The Bancroft Library, University of California, Berkeley.

Refugees lined up for food at one of the tent camps.
The Bancroft Library, University of California, Berkeley.

Refugees stand among the partially enclosed stoves
where families in some of the tent camps cooked their own food.
The Bancroft Library, University of California, Berkeley.

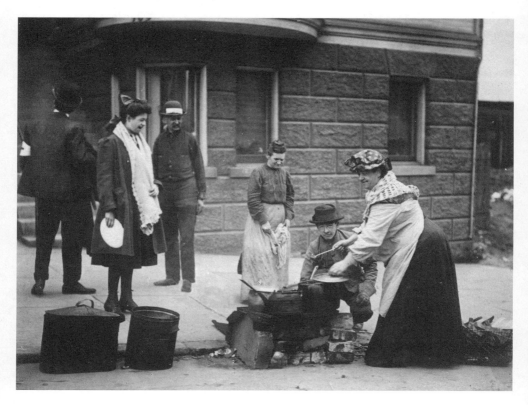

Where houses still stood but chimneys were damaged,
cooking on the street was often a communal affair.
The Bancroft Library, University of California, Berkeley.

A family dining alfresco in sight of the ruined City Hall
with belongings rescued from their home.
The Bancroft Library, University of California, Berkeley.

A group of scavengers or looters? It was often difficult to distinguish.

Andrew C. Lawson of the University of California was the first to identify a portion of the San Andreas Fault and was primarily responsible for compiling the monumental State Earthquake Investigation Commission report.

The Bancroft Library, University of California, Berkeley.

The prosecution team, from left to right: Francis Heney, William Burns,
Fremont Older, and Rudolph Spreckels. They secured only one graft conviction
that was not overturned. Hiram Johnson replaced Heney after he was shot.

The Call Building rises again as San Francisco hastily rebuilds.
The Bancroft Library, University of California, Berkeley.

The Tower of Jewels illuminated at night to simulate a fire
at the 1915 Panama-Pacific International Exposition.
California Historical Society, San Francisco.

AUTHOR'S NOTE

The reader should know that all histories are incomplete, and this history is lacking in five ways.

First, the story has been told mainly from the perspectives of middle- to higher-income whites of Anglo or northern European descent. Despite making an extensive search and asking others for help, I was able to locate only a few accounts by low-income Anglos, Asians, and southern Europeans. Native Americans and Afro-Americans were minorities within a minority of color at the time. It was as if they hadn't existed.

That loss represents a huge hole in the narrative. These groups suffered most, they and their interests were not represented by the de facto municipal government, and relief efforts were driven by upper-middle-class values that did not fit their needs. I have attempted to make up for the loss of individual accounts by weighting the narrative in other ways. I quote the references to foreign populations by nativists, thus giving an idea of how the people were viewed and subsequently treated. I deal with the poor and Asians as communities, for which there is a smattering of accounts.

These voices are absent for a number of reasons. Such persons may not have been literate, or literate in English; they may have lacked a tradition of documenting personal experiences; they may have sent their accounts overseas to friends and relatives; they certainly did not have easy access to publication, the usual way such stories survive; and archivists and librarians did not seek out such accounts or, perhaps, were not offered them.

Second, the single largest collection of written materials on the earthquake and fire—in effect, the Rosetta stone of the disaster—has been lost for eighty years. It consisted of some three thousand personal interviews; eight hundred newspapers from across the country, from which thirty-six thousand articles had been extracted; and numerous documents and reports stored in forty cartons, two full filing cabinets, and assorted trays and bundles. The full story of that irreparable loss is told here for the first time.

Third, the death count, given the chaos of events, will never be known with any precision. To cite the number of deaths as being below one thousand, as some government agencies and authors continue to insist upon doing while adhering obstinately to official numbers issued at the time, is demeaning to the victims and to the goal of accuracy. To cite a number over five thousand, I believe, is an exaggeration. The truth, as usual, lies somewhere in between.

The fourth void has to do with money. One-hundred-year-old dollar amounts do not reflect current monetary values and skew perceptions by vastly undervaluing relative costs. An inflation calculator can be found on the Internet at http://www.westegg.com/inflation/, but the inflation of the dollar is only a small part of the problem of equivalency.

Costs have risen far beyond the rate of inflation. For instance, fifty cents was considered extortionary for a loaf of bread after the earthquake; five cents was a fairer price. A nickel in 1906 has inflated to a dollar now. I just bought a loaf of sliced bread for $3.09. Thus, $2.09 of the increase was due to factors other than inflation.

To state, as is currently done, that Hurricane Andrew was the costliest natural disaster in this nation's history—even if an accurate total cost could be determined for that disaster, which it cannot—is to compare 1992 Florida oranges to 1906 California grapes. There are too many variables to permit an easy way to calculate an equivalent cost beyond the inflation factor. The easiest solution for the reader is to imagine a much higher approximate value.[1]

Fifth, it is a writer's job to make sense out of a confusion of events. But to bring absolute order to the chaotic three days and the aftermath would be a disservice to reality and would rob the account of authenticity. So I have imposed some order—mainly by organizing through chronological time, geographical location, and subject matter. However, a hint of disconnectedness pervades the account, as it should.

ACKNOWLEDGMENTS

One individual was responsible for advancing this project more than anyone else. Without the help of former state librarian Kevin Starr, to whom this book is dedicated, I could not have written it and survived financially.

The arrangement that benefited everyone evolved in the following manner. Starr, who was enthusiastic about my proposal, encouraged Charles B. Faulhaber, director of the Bancroft Library, to apply for a federal Library Services and Technology Act grant administered by the California State Library.

The Bancroft received the grant, and I became the consultant who selected the voluminous amount of materials on the earthquake and fire that would make up a huge online archive that would be accessible to the public. The materials came not only from the Bancroft but also from other major depositories of information on this nation's greatest urban disaster.

Along with a small advance from the University of California Press, this meant that I could earn a living wage while writing the book and accomplish two complementary tasks at the same time. Because one person performed the two jobs and because of the vastness of the material, this may be the first book whose raw documentation and photographs—both far in excess of what is in print—are available on one Web site that houses a huge online archive. Approximately ten thousand digital images and thirty-five thousand pages of electronic text are available on the site, which can be accessed through a link at http://bancroft.berkeley.edu/collections.

Kevin Starr has done for California what Wallace Stegner did for the West: he has helped put the state on the literary map. Through his encouragement of young scholars and older writers like myself, his many articles and books, his administration of the state library and his dealings with governors and legislators, his teaching at the university level, and his vast stores of energy and enthusiasm, Starr has given Californians their past. Unfortunately, history is not a commodity that is valued greatly in this state. It may be someday, and it is for that time that we toil.

My work for the Bancroft allowed me to prowl the congested corridors of the library and work with the most congenial and helpful group of librarians, curators, staff, and pages that I have ever had the pleasure of meeting. I would especially like to thank Theresa Salazar, Susan Snyder, James Eason, Chris McDonald, Emily Balmadge, and Joyce Mao.

At the University of California Press I have worked with pleasant and knowledgeable people on three paperback reprints of hardcover editions of my books and two original manuscripts. Charlene Woodcock, the former paperback editor, referred me to Monica McCormick, who acquires history titles. Jim Clark, then the director, Monica, and I had lunch in May 1999. It was a done deal, with details to be worked out later not only for this book but also for its predecessor in the earthquake trilogy, *Wildest Alaska*. When Monica left the press, Sheila Levine took over this project. Victoria Kuskowsi devised a stunning design scheme and Marilyn Schwartz helped me smooth the first forty pages of text.

I have been involved in another book about 1906, also to be published by the same press that has the first two books of my earthquake trilogy in print. As this project wound down, I thought there should be some innovative way to use the earthquake and fire photos that I had seen in various archives. I contacted photographer Mark Klett, whose specialty is the re-photography of the American West. Klett is an expert at finding the exact spot from where an historic photo was taken and producing both a document and a work of art by juxtaposing the original against his contemporary photograph of the same scene. His book of earthquake photos, with essays by Rebecca Solnit and myself, will be published by the University of California Press in early 2006. There will be a major exhibition of this work in the spring of the centennial year at the California Palace of the Legion of Honor in San Francisco.

There were others who helped during the six years it took to move this book from vague concept to publication. The librarians and curators of special collections who aided my searches along the way were Mary Morganti of the California Historical Society Library, Patricia Keats of the Society of California Pioneers Library, Susan Goldstein of the San Francisco Public Library, Sue Hodson of the Huntington Library, Margaret Kimball of the Stanford University Library, Daryl Morrison of the University of Pacific Library, and Gary Kurutz of the California State Library. Their staffs were unfailingly helpful. In addition, I was helped by the reference librarians who happened to be on duty when I arrived looking for guidance at the public libraries in Fort Bragg, Santa Rosa, Oakland, San Jose, and Santa Cruz.

I asked five people whose judgments I respect to read and comment on the entire manuscript. They were Doris Ober, a freelance editor, who has spotted redundancies and other infelicities in my manuscripts and commented on their value for the last fifteen years; Connie and Michael Mery and my wife, Dianne, whom I regard as the type of readers I would like to reach; and James P. Walsh. Jim, who taught California history and was a dean at San Jose State University, wrote a biography of James D. Phelan and an article for the *California Historical Society Quarterly* on Abraham Ruef. Since I was breaking new ground in my interpretations of their actions, I asked him to review the manuscript.

I have striven for accuracy, fairness, and readability—in that order—in all my books. I have been helped by specialists, who have reviewed portions of my manuscripts for accuracy of facts and fairness of interpretations. The following experts read sections of this work: fire historian Stephen Pyne on fire, Mary Lou Zobeck and Carol Prentice of the USGS on seismic matters, Gladys Hansen on the death toll, Charles Faulhaber on the missing history collection, and James Eason on photography.

In the end, of course, I am solely responsible for the accuracy of facts and the fairness of interpretations.

I was in need of lodging at times. My friend Gary Ireland loaned me his San Francisco apartment so that I didn't have to drive the forty miles to my home on the edge of the San Andreas Fault every night when working in San Francisco. My son, Alex Fradkin, and his close friend, Heather Mahaney, let me use a bed in their Berkeley apartment when I needed to return to the Bancroft Library the next day.

NOTES

The abbreviations for libraries most often cited are: Banc, Bancroft Library, University of California; CHS, California Historical Society Library; CSL, California State Library; CSP, California Society of Pioneers Library; Stan, Stanford University Libraries, Special Collections and University Archives; and HL, the Huntington Library. The James D. Phelan Collection at the Bancroft Library and the series of sixty-nine articles that ran in the weekly *Argonaut* newspaper from May of 1926 to August of 1927 are the two best sources of information. Many of the following sources, along with photographs, can be found on the Bancroft Library's 1906 earthquake and fire Web site, which is available through a link at http://bancroft.berkeley.edu/collections.

UNTITLED PROLOGUE

1. Commander John E. Pond, "The United States Navy and the San Francisco Fire," *U.S. Naval Institute Proceedings,* September 1952, p. 992.

2. The document, contained in box 2 of the Hooker family papers in the Bancroft Library, has a handwritten "Eleanor?" on its cover page.

3. The students' papers are located in the George Malcolm Stratton Collection, Banc. Edward C. Tolman, "George Malcolm Stratton," in *Biographical Memoirs,* vol. 35, Washington, D.C.: National Academy of Sciences, 1961, pp. 291–306.

BEGINNINGS

1. Rutherford H. Platt, "Natural Hazards of the San Francisco Mega-City," in *Crucibles of Hazard: Mega-Cities and Disasters in Transition,* New York: United Nations University Press, 1999, pp. 343–344. Ted Steinberg, *Acts of God: The Unnatural History of Natural Disaster in America,* New York: Oxford University Press, 2000, pp. 25–26. Rutherford H. Platt, *Disasters and Democracy: The Politics of Extreme Natural Events,* Washington, D.C.: Island Press, 1999, p. 1.

2. William Langewiesche, *American Ground: Unbuilding the World Trade Center,* New York: North Point Press, 2002. "Rebutting an Account of Tarnished Valor," *New York Times,* March 23, 2003. "The Return of New York," *New York Times Magazine,* November 11, 2001. "Leaping from One Void into Others,"

New York Times, December 23, 2001. "After September 11, a Legal Battle on the Limits of Civil Liberty," *New York Times,* August 4, 2002. Simon Schama, "A Whiff of Dread for the Land of Hope," *New York Times,* September 15, 2002. "No Catastrophe Is Off Limits to Fraud," *New York Times,* January 5, 2003. "Ground Zero Or Bust," *New York Times,* July 13, 2003.

3. Charles G. Muller, *The Darkest Day: 1814: The Washington-Baltimore Campaign,* Philadelphia: J. B. Lippincott, 1963, pp. 133–154. Joseph A. Whitehorne, *The Battle for Baltimore, 1814,* Baltimore: The Nautical & Aviation Publishing Company of America, 1997, pp. 138–139. William Key, *The Battle of Atlanta and the Georgia Campaign,* New York: Twayne Publishers, 1958, pp. 82–83. Albert E. Castel, *Decision in the West: The Atlanta Campaign of 1864,* Lawrence, Kans.: University Press of Kansas, 1992, pp. 522–534, 548–549, 555. Richard M. McMurry, *Atlanta 1864: Last Chance for the Confederacy,* Lincoln: University of Nebraska Press, 2000, p. 164. Winston Groom, *Shrouds of Glory: From Atlanta to Nashville: The Last Great Campaign of the Civil War,* New York: Atlantic Monthly Press, 1995, p. 113.

4. Elting E. Morison, ed., *The Letters of Theodore Roosevelt,* vol. 5, Cambridge, Mass.: Harvard University Press, 1952, pp. 475, 671. Edmund Morris, *Theodore Rex,* New York: Random House, 2001, pp. 484–485, 493–495. Thomas A. Bailey, *Theodore Roosevelt and the Japanese-American Crisis,* Stanford, Calif.: Stanford University Press, 1934, p. 298.

5. James F. Simon, "Making a Federal Case," *New York Times Book Review,* April 21, 2002, p. 22. "Justice Rehnquist's Ominous History of Wartime Freedom," *New York Times,* September 22, 2002.

6. Henry Winthrop Ballantine, "Military Dictatorships in California and West Virginia," *California Law Review,* July 1913, pp. 413–426.

7. Mary Austin, "The Temblor," in *The California Earthquake of 1906,* David Starr Jordan, ed., San Francisco: A. M. Robertson, 1907, p. 346.

8. U.S. Geological Survey (USGS), "Earthquakes in History," http://pubs .usgs.gov/gip/earthq1/history.html. USGS, "1906 San Francisco Quake," http:// quake.usgs.gov/info/1906/magnitude.html.

9. John F. Davis, "The History of California," in *The Pacific Ocean in History: Papers and Addresses Presented at the Panama-Pacific Historical Congress Held at San Francisco, Berkeley and Palo Alto, California, July 19–23, 1915,* New York: Macmillan, 1917, pp. 93–94.

10. Alan R. Nelson et al., "Radiocarbon Evidence for Extensive Plate-Boundary Rupture about 300 Years Ago at the Cascadia Subduction Zone," *Nature,* November 23, 1995. Tina Marie Niemi, "Late Holocene Slip Rate, Prehistoric Earthquakes, and Quaternary Neotectonics of the Northern San Andreas Fault, Marin County, California," PhD. dissertation, Department of Geology, Stanford University, 1992, p. 55. "Evidence of Giant Quake in 1700s," *San Francisco Chronicle,* November 28, 1995.

11. A. L. Kroeber, "Notes on California Folk-lore," *Journal of American Folk-lore,* vol. 21 (1906), pp. 322–323. A. L. Kroeber, *Yurok Myths,* Berkeley: University of California Press, 1976, pp. 174–177, 417–418, 460, 464.

12. Herbert W. Luthan, ed., *Surviving through the Days: A California Indian Reader,* Berkeley: University of California Press, 2002, pp. 67–76.

13. Martha H. Lowman, "California's Mission San Juan Bautista," Mission San Juan Bautista, n.d., pp. 2–6. Hubert Howe Bancroft, *History of California,* vol. 2, San Francisco: The History Company, 1886, p. 200. John B. Trask, *A Register of Earthquakes in California: From 1800 to 1863,* Towne & Bacon, 1864, pp. 5, 7. Henry L. Oak, *A Visit to the Missions of Southern California in February and March, 1874,* Southwest Museum, 1981, p. 46. California Division of Mines and Geology, T. R. Toppozada et al., *Preparation of Isoseismal Maps and Summaries of Reported Effects for Pre-1900 California Earthquakes,* Sacramento, 1981, pp. 134–140.

14. George D. Louderback, "Central California Earthquakes of the 1830s," *Bulletin of the Seismological Society of America,* vol. 37 (1947), p. 73. Tousson R. Toppozada and Glenn Borchardt, "Re-evaluation of the 1836 'Hayward' and the 1838 San Andreas Earthquakes," unpublished manuscript, California Division of Mines and Geology, Sacramento, Calif., 1997. Carl W. Stover and Jerry L. Coffman, *Seismicity in the United States, 1569–1989* (Revised), USGS Professional Paper 1527, 1993, pp. 99–100.

15. John S. Hittell, *A History of the City of San Francisco and Incidentally of the State of California,* San Francisco: A. L. Bancroft, 1878, pp. 133, 156–157, 168–169, 170–172. Samuel Richards, "My Early Experiences and Recollections of the Great Fires and the First Fire Department in San Francisco," address to the Pacific Coast Underwriters' Association, January 14, 1908, HL. Ira B. Cross, *Financing an Empire: History of Banking in California,* vol. 1, San Francisco: S. J. Clarke Publishing, 1927, p. 55. Battalion Chief Frederick J. Bowlen of the San Francisco Fire Department, "Fires We Have Fought," 1944, Banc.

16. California Division of Mines and Geology, *The Loma Prieta (Santa Cruz Mountains), California, Earthquake of 17 October 1989,* Special Publication 104, Sacramento, Calif.: California Division of Mines and Geology, 1990, p. 21. B. E. Lloyd, *Lights and Shades in San Francisco,* San Francisco: A. L. Bancroft, 1876, p. 320. Edgar Marquess Branch and Robert H. Hirst, eds., *The Works of Mark Twain: Early Tales & Sketches,* Berkeley: University of California Press, 1981, pp. 304, 307–308. Stover and Coffman, *Seismicity in the United States,* p. 104.

17. William Henry Knight to his mother, October 23, 1868, Banc.

18. Lloyd, *Lights and Shades,* p. 322. State Earthquake Investigation Commission, *The California Earthquake of April 18, 1906,* ed. Andrew C. Lawson, vol. 1, part 2, Washington, D.C.: Carnegie Institution, 1908, pp. 434–449. Charles Wollenberg, "Life on the Seismic Frontier: The Great San Francisco Earthquake (of 1868)," *California History,* Winter 1992/1993, pp. 495–509. Philip L. Fradkin,

Magnitude 8: Earthquakes and Life along the San Andreas Fault, Berkeley: University of California Press, 1999, pp. 76–80.

19. USGS, *The San Francisco Earthquake and Fire of April 18, 1906,* USGS Bulletin No. 324, 1907, p. 16.

20. USGS, *The San Francisco Earthquake and Fire of April 18, 1906,* USGS Bulletin No. 324, 1907, p. 16.

THE TALE OF TWO CITIES

1. Donald R. Miller, *City of the Century: The Epic of Chicago and the Making of America,* New York: Simon & Schuster, 1997, pp. 15–17, 26–27, 33–37, 42–49, 141–142, 158–159. Karen Sawislak, *Smoldering City: Chicagoans and the Great Fire, 1871–1874,* Chicago: University of Chicago Press, 1995, pp. 1–17, 74, 80, 83, 262–264.

2. Paul N. Angle, ed., *The Great Chicago Fire,* Chicago: Chicago Historical Society, 1946, p. 22.

3. Jan Harold Brunvand, *The Big Book of Urban Legends,* New York: Paradox Press, 1994, p. 152. Jan Harold Brunvand, *The Truth Never Stands in the Way of a Good Story,* Urbana: University of Illinois Press, 2000, p. 6.

4. Sawislak, *Smoldering City,* pp. 49–67. Carl Smith, *Urban Disorder and the Shape of Belief: The Great Chicago Fire, the Haymarket Bomb, and the Model Town of Pullman,* Chicago: University of Chicago Press, 1995, p. 55. Robert Cromie, *The Great Chicago Fire,* New York: McGraw-Hill, 1958, pp. 260, 265, 270–276. Miller, *City of the Century,* pp. 149–150, 161, 164.

5. Denise Gess and William Lutz, *Firestorm at Peshtigo: A Town, Its People, and the Deadliest Fire in American History,* New York: Henry Holt, 2002. Sawislak, *Smoldering City,* pp. 21–23. Miller, *City of the Century,* pp. 161–162.

6. Stephen J. Pyne, *Fire in America: A Cultural History of Wildland and Rural Fire,* Seattle: University of Washington Press, 1997, pp. 23–24, 26, 33, 204, 206, 246. Stephen J. Pyne et al., *Introduction to Wildland Fire,* New York: John Wiley & Sons, 1996, pp. 257–260. Stephen Pyne, personal communication, June 19, 2003. Neil Hanson, *The Dreadful Judgment: The True Story of the Great Fire of London 1666,* New York: Doubleday, 2001, pp. 93–105.

7. W. G. Sebald, *On the Natural History of Destruction,* New York: Random House, 2003, pp. 3–5, 10–13, 24–25, 27, 70, 89.

8. Horatio Bond, ed., *Fire and the Air War,* Boston, Mass.: National Fire Protection Association, 1952, pp. 5, 7, 82, 85, 94, 96–97, 100, 112, 168, 191.

9. Sawislak, *Smoldering City,* pp. 76–80, 124–136, 163–169, 282. Miller, *City of the Century,* pp. 147, 149–150, 159, 167–168. Ross Miller, *The Great Chicago Fire,* Urbana: University of Illinois Press, 2000, pp. 64, 86 192–208, 240–241, 244. William Cronon, *Nature's Metropolis: Chicago and the Great West,* New York: W. W. Norton, 1991, pp. 345–350. Christine Meisner Rosen,

The Limits of Power: Great Fires and the Process of City Growth in America, New York: Cambridge University Press, 1986, pp. 3–4, 96–104, 107, 113–114, 176, 326, 331–334.

10. David G. McComb, *Galveston: A History,* Austin: University of Texas Press, 1986, pp. 26–27, 30–31. Herbert Molloy Mason Jr., *Death from the Sea: Our Greatest Natural Disaster,* New York: Dial Press, 1972, p. 66. Eric Larson, *Isaac's Storm: A Man, a Time, and the Deadliest Hurricane in History,* New York: Vintage Books, 1999, pp. 12–13, 15, 84. Paul Lester, *The Great Galveston Disaster: Containing a Full and Thrilling Account of the Most Appalling Calamity of Modern Times,* Chicago: Co-Operative Publishing, 1900, p. v.

11. King Vidor, "Southern Storm," *Esquire,* May, 1935.

12. Patricia Bellis Bixel and Elizabeth Hayes Turner, *Galveston and the 1900 Storm,* Austin: University of Texas Press, 2000, pp. 41, 43.

13. Clarence Ousley, *Galveston in Nineteen Hundred,* Atlanta: William C. Chase, 1900, pp. 250–253.

14. Michael P. Malone and F. Ross Peterson, "Politics and Protests," in *The Oxford History of the American West,* Clyde A. Milner II et al., eds., New York: Oxford University, 1996, p. 506. Larson, *Isaac's Storm,* pp. 165–166.

15. Tang Xiren, *A General History of Earthquake Studies in China,* Beijing: Science Press, 1988, pp. 3–9, 20. Frederick Wakeman, Department of History, University of California at Berkeley, personal communication, July 5, 2003. Song Shouquan and Chen Yingfang, "Countermeasures against Earthquake Rumors and Misdissemination of Information about Earthquakes," in *Earthquake Countermeasures,* Beijing: State Seismological Bureau, 1988, pp. 46–54. Chen Yong et al., eds., *The Great Tanshan Earthquake of 1976,* Oxford, England: Pergamon Press, 1988, pp. 88–89. Bruce A. Bolt, *Earthquakes,* New York: W. H. Freeman, 1993, pp. 194–198. Fradkin, *Magnitude 8,* pp. 164–170. "The 25 Largest Earthquake Disasters in Human History," GeoHazards International, http://www.geohaz.org/member/news/signif.htm, 2003.

SCIENCE, POLITICS, AND SAN FRANCISCO

1. J. D. Whitney, "Earthquakes," *North American Review,* April 1869, p. 609.

2. Michael L. Smith, *Pacific Visions: California Scientists and the Environment 1850–1915,* New Haven, Conn.: Yale University Press, 1987, pp. 2–4, 19, 42. Carl-Henry Geschwind, *California Earthquakes: Science, Risk & the Politics of Hazard Mitigation,* Baltimore: Johns Hopkins University Press, 2001, pp. 9–12.

3. "Earthquakes," *University Echo,* April, May, June, July, 1872.

4. Stephen J. Pyne, *Grove Karl Gilbert: A Great Engine of Research,* Austin: University of Texas Press, 1980, p. 229. Robert E. Wallace, "G. K. Gilbert's Studies of Faults, Scarps, and Earthquakes," Geological Society of America, Special Paper 183, 1980, p. 37.

5. Grove Karl Gilbert, "A Theory of the Earthquakes of the Great Basin, with a Practical Application," *Salt Lake Tribune,* September 30, 1883.

6. George D. Louderback, "History of the University of California Seismographic Stations and Related Activities," *Bulletin of the Seismological Society of America,* July 1942, pp. 205–212. Bruce A. Bolt, "One Hundred Years of Contributions of the University of California Seismographic Stations," in *Observatory Seismology,* Berkeley: University of California Press, 1989, p. 472. Fradkin, *Magnitude 8,* p. 134–135. Edward S. Holden, *Catalogue of Earthquakes on the Pacific Coast 1769 to 1897,* reprinted from the Smithsonian Miscellaneous Collections No. 1087 for distribution by the Lick Observatory, 1898, pp. 12, 14, 17, 24, 30.

7. "The Earthquake," *Mining and Scientific Press,* April 28, 1906, p. 272.

8. Grove Karl Gilbert to Andrew C. Lawson, December 6, 1893, Lawson Collection, Banc. Perry Byerly and George D. Louderback, "Memorial to Andrew Cowper Lawson (1861–1952)," *Proceedings Volume of the Geological Society of America Annual Report for 1953,* May 1954, pp. 141–142. Mason L. Hill, "San Andreas Fault: History of Concepts," *Geological Society of America Bulletin,* March 1981, pp. 112–114. Fradkin, *Magnitude 8,* pp. 9, 10, 96, 216. Andrew C. Lawson, *Sketch of the Geology of the San Francisco Peninsula,* Washington, D.C.: U.S. Government Printing Office, 1895, pp. 468, 473. Frederick Leslie Ransome, "The Probable Cause of the San Francisco Earthquake," *National Geographic,* June 1906, pp. 286–287.

9. Carl W. Stover and Jerry L. Coffman, *Seismicity of the United States 1568–1989* (Revised), USGS Professional Paper 1527, 1993, p. 114. Oscar Lewis and Carroll D. Hall, *Bonanza Inn: America's First Luxury Hotel,* New York: Alfred A. Knopf, 1939, p. 320. "No Cause for Alarm in Recent Earthquakes," *Daily Californian,* December 12, 1904.

10. James P. Walsh and Timothy J. O'Keefe, *Legacy of a Native Son: James Duval Phelan & Villa Montalvo,* Forbes Mill Press, 1993, pp. ix–xii, 1–31. Robert E. Hennings, *James D. Phelan and the Wilson Progressives of California,* New York: Garland Publishing, 1985, pp. 1–10. Philip J. Ethington, *The Public City: The Political Construction of Urban Life in San Francisco, 1850–1900,* Berkeley: University of California Press, 2001, pp. 377–386. Kevin Starr, *Americans and the California Dream 1850–1915,* New York: Oxford University Press, 1973, pp. 249–253. Judd Kahn, *Imperial San Francisco: Politics and Planning in an American City 1897–1906,* Lincoln: University of Nebraska Press, 1979, pp. 59–61.

11. Franklin K. Lane to James D. Phelan, May 11 and September 29, 1906, Phelan Collection, Banc. Theodore Roosevelt to James D. Phelan, March 25 and 27, 1907, and December 28, 1908, Banc. P. I. Pilat to James D. Phelan, March 26 and 27, Banc, and Phelan to Pilat, March 26, 1906, Banc. "Memorial Services in Honor of the Late Senator James D. Phelan," Board of Supervisors of the City and County of San Francisco, August 11, 1930, Banc.

12. Major General Adolphus W. Greely to James D. Phelan, January 22 and 30, 1907, Banc. Brigadier General Frederick Funston to James D. Phelan, February 8, 1908, Banc. James D. Phelan to Captain R. B. Hobson, April 1, 1909, Banc.

13. Ruth Brooke to James D. Phelan, June 28, 1910, and other letters through July 9, 1930, Banc. James Phelan to Frank Sullivan, December 10, 1894, Banc, and the Florence Ellon–James D. Phelan correspondence from 1894 to 1930, Banc.

14. "Celebrities at Home, No. 10," *Wasp,* June 3, 1905.

15. "BROTHERS ATTENTION!" undated handbill, CSP.

16. Dawson Mayer to James D. Phelan, March 16 and 30, 1908, Banc.

17. James D. Phelan, speaking in the U.S. Senate on the Encroachments of the Japanese on the Pacific Coast—A National Peril, June 14, 1920, *Congressional Record,* pp. 9400–9401. For a view of the Progressives' racial policy in rural areas see "The Great Valley" chapter in Philip L. Fradkin, *The Seven States of California: A Natural and Human History,* Berkeley: University of California Press, 1997.

18. Gertrude Atherton, *California: An Intimate History,* New York: Harper & Brothers, 1914, pp. 311, 312. Gertrude Atherton to James D. Phelan, May 10, 1914, Banc.

19. Franklin Hichborn, *The System: As Uncovered by the San Francisco Graft Prosecution,* San Francisco: James H. Barry, 1915, pp. 12–14, 191–192. Franklin Hichborn to James D. Phelan, November 7 and 12, December 20, 1912; June 17, October 10, 1914; July 11, 1915, Phelan Collection, Banc. Walsh and O'Keefe, *Legacy of a Native Son,* p. 39.

20. George Kennan, "The Fight for Reform in San Francisco," *McClure's* magazine, September 1907. Harold S. Wilson, *McClure's Magazine and the Muckrakers,* Princeton, N.J.: Princeton University Press, 1970, pp. 159, 184–185.

21. "Abe Ruef at Bay at Last," *New York Times,* March 17, 1907.

22. Mrs. Bernard S. Gordon to Walton Bean, October 18, 1955, Banc. Mrs. Gordon was the daughter of one of Ruef's sisters.

23. Walton Bean's handwritten comment on Ruef's college transcript, "Would have been medallist, except Jew," Walton Bean Collection, Banc.

24. Alice Gerstle Levison, "Family Reminiscences," Regional Oral History Office, Bancroft Library, University of California, 1967, pp. 84–85. William M. Roberts, university archivist, Banc, personal communication.

25. James P. Walsh, "Abe Ruef Was No Boss: Machine Politics, Reform, and San Francisco," *California Historical Society Quarterly,* Spring 1972.

26. Irena Narell, *Our City: The Jews of San Francisco,* San Diego: Howell-North Books, 1981, p. 264. William Issel and Robert W. Cherny, *San Francisco, 1865–1932,* Berkeley: University of California Press, 1986, p. 41. Walton Bean, *Boss Ruef's San Francisco: The Story of the Union Labor Party, Big Business, and the Graft Prosecution,* Berkeley: University of California Press, 1952, pp. 1–27. Ethington, *The Public City,* p. 403. "Political Renaissance of Phelan," *Town Talk,* September 5, 1903.

27. Various sources culled from newspapers, magazines, and books.

28. "Banquet Given Outgoing Mayor James D. Phelan," December 28, 1901, Banc.

29. Evarts I. Blake, *San Francisco: A Brief Biographical Sketch of the Most Prominent Men Who Will Preside over Her Destiny for at Least Two Years,* San Francisco: Pacific Publishing, 1902, pp. 32–33.

30. Leigh H. Irvine, *A History of the New California: Its Resources and People,* New York: Lewis Publishing, 1903, pp. 792–794. Oscar T. Shuck, ed., *History of the Bench and Bar of California,* Los Angeles: Commercial Publishing House, 1901, pp. 1064, 1067.

31. Mel Scott, *The San Francisco Bay Area: A Metropolis in Perspective,* Berkeley: University of California Press, 1959, p. 80.

32. Will Irwin, *The City That Was: A Requiem of Old San Francisco,* New York: B. W. Huebsch, 1906, p. 47. Arnold Genthe, *As I Remember,* New York: Reynal & Hitchcock, 1936, pp. vi, 32, 34–36.

33. Ansel Adams, *Ansel Adams: An Autobiography,* Boston: Little, Brown, 1985, p. 6.

34. Christopher M. Douty, *The Economics of Localized Disasters: The 1906 San Francisco Disaster,* New York: Arno Press, 1977, pp. 53–77. Scott, *The San Francisco Bay Area,* pp. 95–98. Kahn, *Imperial San Francisco,* pp. 5–11, 26–27. Ethington, *The Public City,* p. 325. Issel and Cherny, *San Francisco,* pp. 23–39. Christopher Jenks, "Who Should Get In?" *New York Review of Books,* November 29, 2001. Judy Crichton, *American 1900: The Turning Point,* New York: Henry Holt, 1998. "San Francisco," *The Jewish Encyclopedia,* vol. 11, New York: Funk & Wagnalls, 1905, pp. 34–39.

35. "Race Suicide Not Evident Here," *San Francisco Bulletin,* May 13, 1903.

36. Kahn, *Imperial San Francisco,* p. 58.

37. Ronald Takaki, *Strangers from a Different Shore: A History of Asian Americans,* New York: Penguin, 1990, pp. 245–253. Charles J. McClain, *In Search of Equality: The Chinese Struggle against Discrimination in Nineteenth-Century America,* Berkeley: University of California Press, 1994, pp. 241, 262, 264, 276. Erica Y. Z. Pan, *The Impact of the 1906 Earthquake on San Francisco's Chinatown,* New York: Peter Lang, 1995, pp. 1, 8, 10–11, 15, 18, 23–26. Crichton, *American 1900,* pp. 164–166. Scott, *The San Francisco Bay Area,* pp. 76–79.

38. Susan Craddock, *City of Plagues: Disease, Poverty, and Deviance in San Francisco,* Minneapolis: University of Minnesota Press, 2000, pp. 126–147. Nayan Shah, *Contagious Divides: Epidemics and Race in San Francisco's Chinatown,* Berkeley: University of California Press, 2001, pp. 120–157. Marilyn Chase, *The Barbary Plague: The Black Death in Victorian San Francisco,* New York: Random House, 2003, pp. 62, 66, 70, 84–86, 114. "Ask Removal of Chinatown," *San Francisco Chronicle,* April 4, 1903.

39. Starr, *Americans and the California Dream,* pp. 290–293. Kahn, *Imperial*

San Francisco, pp. 27, 57–58, 70, 80–81, 83. Ethington, *The Public City*, pp. 381–383, 388. Scott, *The San Francisco Bay Area*, pp. 97–105.

40. Pan, *The Impact of the 1906 Earthquake*, p. 27.

41. "Make San Francisco a Great Pleasure City," *Bulletin*, January 7, 1904. "Architect to Plan City's Beauty," *Bulletin*, April 20, 1904. Scott, *The San Francisco Bay Area*, pp. 105–107.

42. "Committee of Twenty's Summary, San Francisco, October, 1905," in *Earthquake & Fire, 1906, San Francisco: Observations, Criticisms, Comparisons, and Opinions on Fire Protection*, New York: Press of J. E. Hetsch, 1907, pp. 44–45. S. Albert Reed, consulting engineer to the National Board of Fire Underwriters Committee of Twenty, "The San Francisco Conflagration of April, 1906," New York, 1906, p. 5.

43. Hermann Schussler, *The Water Supply of San Francisco, California, Before, During and After the Earthquake of April 18, 1906 and the Subsequent Conflagration*, New York: Martin B. Brown Press, July 23, 1906, pp. 7–9, 12–14, 24. Gray Brechin, *Imperial San Francisco: Urban Power, Earthly Ruin*, Berkeley: University of California Press, 2001, pp. 99–102. James J. Rawls and Walton Bean, *California: An Interpretive History*, New York: McGraw-Hill, 1997, p. 306. Reed, "The San Francisco Conflagration," pp. 2–5. San Francisco Board of Supervisors, *San Francisco Municipal Reports for the Fiscal Year 1904–1905*, 1907, p. 212. San Francisco Board of Supervisors, *San Francisco Municipal Reports for the Fiscal Years 1905–1906 and 1906–1907*, 1908, p. 722.

44. Erwin N. Thompson, *Defender of the Gate: The Presidio of San Francisco*, vol. 1, Denver: U.S. Department of the Interior, National Park Service, 1997, p. 456. San Francisco Board of Supervisors, *San Francisco Municipal Reports*, 1908, pp. 898–899.

45. San Francisco Board of Supervisors, *San Francisco Municipal Reports*, 1908, p. 719.

46. John J. Conlon Jr., "The Autobiography of John J. Conlon," n.d., unpublished manuscript, Banc; the author was the son of Battalion Chief John J. Conlon.

47. William Bronson, *The Earth Shook, the Sky Burned*, Garden City, N.Y.: Doubleday, 1959, pp. 19–20 and maps. Douty, *The Economics of Localized Disasters*, pp. 47–50. Committee of Twenty's Summary, San Francisco, October, 1905, contained in *Earthquake & Fire, 1906, San Francisco: Observations, Criticisms, Comparisons, and Opinions on Fire Protection*, New York: Press of J. E. Hetsch, 1907, pp. 44–45.

THE HOTEL AND THE OPERA HOUSE

1. Oscar Lewis and Carroll D. Hall, *Bonanza Inn: America's First Luxury Hotel*, New York: Alfred A. Knopf, 1939, pp. 4, 5, 15, 19–20, 22–24, 27–28, 55,

318, 322. Lloyd, *Lights and Shades,* pp. 52–53. USGS, *The San Francisco Earthquake and Fire,* p. 26.

2. Lewis and Hall, *Bonanza Inn,* pp. 288–297.

3. Pierre V. R. Key, *Enrico Caruso: A Biography,* New York: Vienna House, 1972. Michael Scott, *The Great Caruso,* London: Hamish Hamilton, 1988, pp. 90–91. Howard Greenfield, *Caruso,* New York, G. P. Putnam's Sons, 1983, p. 112. Alfred Hertz, "Facing the Music," unpublished manuscript, music library, University of California at Berkeley, pp. 121–123. "Grand Opera Stars Arrive," *San Francisco Chronicle,* April 16, 1906. "Opera Season Opens Tonight," *San Francisco Call,* April 16, 1906.

4. "Victims of Vesuvius May Number 2,000," *San Francisco Chronicle,* April 12, 1906.

5. "Remarkable List of Natural Calamities," *San Francisco Examiner,* April 15, 1906.

6. Greenfield, *Caruso,* pp. 82–87. Scott, *The Great Caruso,* pp. xvii–xix. Richard Barthelemy, *Memories of Caruso,* Plainsboro, N.J.: La Scala Autographa, 1979, pp. 9, 14–15. Stanley Sadie, ed., *The New Grove Dictionary of Opera,* London: Macmillan, 1992, pp. 746–747.

7. Heinrich Conried, "Prospectuses: Second Trans-Continental Tour of the Conried Metropolitan Opera Company, Spring, 1906," 1906, Banc; Conried was president and managing director of the Metropolitan Opera.

8. "Lenten Calm Marks Opening Night at the Opera," *Examiner,* April 17, 1906. "Last Night Not So Big as Expected," *San Francisco Call,* April 17, 1906. "Pomp and Crash of German Opera Opens Season with Splendor but Audience Misses Thrill of Old Favorites among the Tuneful Music-Dramas of Italy and Longs for the Golden Notes of Caruso," *Bulletin,* April 17, 1906.

9. Mary Watkins Cushing, *The Rainbow Bridge,* New York: G. P. Putnam's Sons, 1954, pp. 6, 46, 94–95. Stanley Sadie, ed., *The New Grove Dictionary of Opera,* vol. 2, London: Macmillan, 1992, pp. 299–300.

10. "New and Modern Theatre Planned for Union Square," *San Francisco Examiner,* April 15, 1906. "A Grand Opera House at Union Square," *San Francisco Chronicle,* April 15, 1906.

11. "Grand Opera," the Grand Opera House Company, 1906 season, Banc.

12. Lewis and Hall, *Bonanza Inn,* pp. 4–10. "Loungers in the Lobby Express Satisfaction with the Opening," *San Francisco Call,* April 17, 1906. "Madam Sembrich Is a Hostess," *San Francisco Call,* April 17, 1906. "Police Detail at the Grand Opera House," *San Francisco Examiner,* April 17, 1906.

13. "Fashionable Society Comes Out Radiantly on the Second Night," *San Francisco Call,* April 18, 1906. "Many Brilliant Gowns Add to Charm of Opera," *San Francisco Call,* April 18, 1906. "San Francisco Sustains Name for Gowns and Coldness," *San Francisco Bulletin,* April 17, 1906. John Castillo Kennedy, *The Great Earthquake and Fire: San Francisco, 1906,* New York: William Morrow, 1963,

p. 8. Malcolm E. Barker, *Three Fearful Days: San Francisco Memoirs of the 1906 Earthquake & Fire,* San Francisco: Londonborn Publications, 1998, pp. 63–65.

14. "Three Strikingly Beautiful Creations Are Worn at the Opera," *San Francisco Examiner,* April 18, 1906.

15. John Barrymore, *Confessions of an Actor,* Indianapolis: Bobbs-Merrill, 1925, chap. 3.

16. "Caruso Makes Don Juan the Leading Role," *San Francisco Call,* April 18, 1906. "Loungers," *San Francisco Examiner,* April 17, 1906. "Caruso Superb in Role of Don Jose," *San Francisco Chronicle,* April 18, 1906.

17. "Strollers in Foyer Discuss New 'Carmen,'" *San Francisco Call,* April 18, 1906. James D. Phelan to Marabelle Gilman, May 8, 1907, Banc.

18. Laurence M. Klauber, "Two Days in San Francisco, 1906," n.d., unpublished manuscript, Banc.

19. "Fremstad's Carmen Is Inclined to Be Dutchy While Abott's Micaela Is Pronounced Disappointment," *San Francisco Examiner,* April 18, 1906.

20. Lewis and Hall, *Bonanza Inn,* p. 325. "Caruso's Plight at the Palace," *San Francisco,* April 1967, p. 36. Pietro Gargano and Gianni Cesarini, *Caruso,* Milan: Longanesi, 1990. Elsa Maxwell, *R.S.V.P.,* Boston: Little, Brown, 1954, pp. 8, 52–53.

21. James Hopper, *Everybody's Magazine,* June 1906, p. 760a.

WEDNESDAY, APRIL 18, 1906

1. Alexander B. McAdie, *Climatology of California,* U.S. Department of Agriculture, Weather Bureau Bulletin L, 1903, p. 259. Alexander B. McAdie to Andrew C. Lawson, February 11, 1907, Banc. Alexander G. McAdie, "Earthquake Weather," *Bulletin of the California Physical Geography Club,* October 1907, pp. 8–9. Alexander G. McAdie, *Catalogue of Earthquakes on the Pacific Coast 1887 to 1906,* Washington, D.C.: Smithsonian Institution, 1907, pp. 45–46. Philip Williams Jr., "Weather and the San Francisco Fire of 1906," *Weatherwise,* June 1956, pp. 90–93.

2. Bruce A. Bolt, *Earthquakes,* New York: W. H. Freeman, 1993, p. 5. Philip L. Fradkin, *Magnitude 8: Earthquakes and Life along the San Andreas Fault,* Berkeley: University of California Press, 1999, pp. 98–100.

3. McAdie, *Catalogue of Earthquakes,* pp. 48, 51–52.

4. Fradkin, *Magnitude 8,* p. 99.

5. "The Great Fire of 1906," *Argonaut,* May 1, 1926.

6. C. F. Maravin, to Andrew C. Lawson, February 6, 1907, Banc. Francis E. Vaughan, *Andrew C. Lawson: Scientist, Teacher, Philosopher,* Glendale, Calif.: Arthur H. Clark, 1970, p. 86. "Report of the Sub-committee on State Instrument Records," n.d., Banc. David J. Wald et al., "Source Study of the 1906 San Francisco Earthquake," *Bulletin of the Seismological Society of America,* vol. 83, 1993, pp. 981–1019.

7. Bruce A. Bolt, "The Focus of the 1906 California Earthquake," *Bulletin of*

the Seismological Society of America, February 1968, pp. 457–471. David M. Boore, "Strong Motion Recordings of the California Earthquake of April 18, 1906," *Bulletin of the Seismological Society of America,* June 1977, pp. 561–576. Eric L. Geist and Mary Lou Zoback, "Analysis of the Tsunami Generated by the M 7.8 1906 San Francisco Earthquake," *Geology,* January 1999, pp. 15–18. Mary Lou Zoback et al., "Abrupt Along-Strike Change in Tectonic Style: San Andreas Fault Zone, San Francisco Peninsula," *Journal of Geophysical Research,* May 10, 1999, pp. 10719–10742.

8. Zoback et al., "Abrupt Along-Strike Change," May 10, 1999, p. 10721. Harry Fielding Reid, *The Mechanics of the Earthquake,* vol. 2 of *The California Earthquake of April 18, 1906,* by State Earthquake Investigation Commission, Washington, D.C., 1910, pp. 3–9.

9. Harry Fielding Reid, *The Mechanics of the Earthquake,* pp. 3–9.

10. *Argonaut,* May 1, 1926. Reed, "The San Francisco Conflagration," p. 5.

11. *Argonaut,* May 22, 1926.

12. *Argonaut,* May 8 and 15, 1926.

13. James D. Phelan, "Personal Notes at the Time of the San Francisco Earthquake and Fire," unpublished manuscript, n.d., Banc. Walsh and O'Keefe, *Legacy of a Native Son,* pp. 93–95.

14. Horatio Putnam Livermore to his wife, Helen Livermore, April 21, 1906, private collection.

15. *Argonaut,* October 16, 1926. *Argonaut,* October 23, 1926.

16. *Argonaut,* October 9, 1926.

17. David Howard Bain, *Sitting in Darkness: Americans in the Philippines,* Boston, Mass.: Houghton Mifflin, 1984, pp. 9–10, 14–15, 45, 88–89, 392–393.

18. "A Letter from Gen. Funston," *Argonaut,* July 7, 1906.

19. Thompson, *Defender of the Gate,* p. 462. "Meeting of the Finance Committee of the San Francisco Relief and Red Cross Funds Held at Hamilton School," June 8, 1906, transcript, Banc.

20. Frederick Funston, "How the Army Worked to Save San Francisco," *Cosmopolitan Magazine,* July 1906, pp. 239–243. U.S. War Department, "Earthquake in California, April 18, 1906," in *Annual Report,* Appendix A Washington, D.C., 1906, pp. 85–86.

21. Ballantine, "Military Dictatorship," p. 414.

22. "Earthquake and Fire: San Francisco in Ruins," *Call-Chronicle-Examiner,* April 19, 1906.

23. Governor George C. Pardee to Colonel J. C. McMullen, May 18, 1906, Banc.

24. "Over 500 Dead, $200,000,000 Lost in San Francisco Earthquake," *New York Times,* April 19, 1906. "Four-Fifths of City in Ruins," *Army News,* April 26, 1906. "Funston Relaxes the Rigor of Martial Law," *San Francisco Examiner,*

April 23, 1906. "Military Law Ends in the City by Funston's Orders, *San Francisco Examiner,* April 27, 1906.

25. Dear sister from Dell, April 27, 1906, CSL. Ronald G. Flick, *San Francisco Is No More: The Letters of Antoine Borel, Jr.,* Menlo Park, Calif.: privately printed, 1963, p. 14. Consul General C. W. Bennett to the British Foreign Office, April 25, 1906, Banc. Mrs. James T. Watkins, "The 1906 San Francisco Earthquake," *California Geology,* December 1981, pp. 260–266.

26. "Pardee Asks for the Troops: Federal forces Now Are Acting under Authority of Law," *New York Times,* April 26, 1906. Mayor Eugene Schmitz to President Theodore Roosevelt, May 22, 1906, Gleeson Library, Rare Book Room, University of San Francisco.

27. Marion O. Hooker, "Lessons of the Great Fire," unpublished manuscript, n.d., Banc.

28. Phelan, "Personal Notes." *Argonaut,* January 15, 1927.

29. "Looters Are Shot without Mercy," *San Francisco Chronicle,* April 22, 1906. "Militiamen Busy among the Ruins," *San Francisco Chronicle,* April 30, 1906. "Justice Rehnquist's Ominous History of Wartime Freedom," *New York Times,* September 22, 2002.

30. Walsh and O'Keefe, *Legacy of a Native Son,* p. 104. John Riordan, "Garret McEnerney and the Irish Pursuit of Success," May 28, 1976, Banc. Gordon Thomas and Max Morgan Witts, *The San Francisco Earthquake,* New York: Stein and Day, 1971, pp. 131–133. Bailey Millard, *History of the San Francisco Bay Region,* vol. 1, New York: American Historical Society, 1924, p. 506.

31. "The Cover" and "Earthquake, Fire & Printers in 1906," *Western Printer & Lithographer,* April 1956, pp. 12, 28.

32. "No Martial Law," *Coast Review,* October 1906.

33. Orisa to Charlotte, April 20, 1906, CSL. Annette to Elsie, April 22, 1906, CSL.

34. Reed, "The San Francisco Conflagration," pp. 1, 6.

35. *Argonaut,* September 11 and 18, 1926, and March 26, 1927.

36. Bowlen, "Fires We Have Fought."

37. Battalion Chief Fred J. Bowlen, comp., "Experiences of Captain G. F. Brown, Engine Company #3, and His Men," and various other accounts in "Reports of Fire Officers of the San Francisco Fire Department on the Fire of 1906," 1935, Banc. *Argonaut,* October 23, 30, and November 6, 1926. "Statement of F. Ernest Edwards," n.d., Banc.

38. Schussler, *The Water Supply of San Francisco,* pp. 7–8, 14, 25, 19, 29, 35, 75. "Report of Sub-committee on Water Supply and Fire Protection, to the Committee on the Reconstruction of San Francisco," May 26, 1906, Banc. *San Francisco Municipal Reports,* 1908, pp. 779–786. *Major Quakes Likely to Strike Between 2000 and 2300,* USGS Fact Sheet 152-99, Menlo Park, 1999, http://geopubs.wr

.usgs.gov/fact-sheet/fs152-99/. Fradkin, *Magnitude 8*, pp. 1995–1999. Thomas D. O'Rourke, ed., *The Loma Prieta, California, Earthquake of October 17, 1989—Marina District,* USGS Professional Paper 1551-F, 1992.

39. E. C. Jones, "The Story of the Restoration of the Gas Supply in San Francisco after the Fire," and L. E. Reynolds, "How Electricity Was Served to Consumers and Street-Car Lines by the San Francisco Gas and Electric Company after the Fire," *Proceedings of the Thirteenth and Fourteenth Annual Meetings of the Pacific Coast Gas Assn.,* 1906, pp. 350–373. Carrie Duncan to Mrs. Worthy, May 23, 1906, CHS.

40. Hanson, *The Dreadful Judgment,* p. 205. Bond, ed., *Fire and the Air War,* pp. 101–102.

41. *Argonaut,* August 13, 1927.

42. Conlon, "The Autobiography of John J. Conlon," p. 5. Battalion Chief Fred J. Bowlen, comp., "Experiences of Captain G. F. Brown, Engine Company #3, and His Men," and various other accounts in "Reports of Fire Officers of the San Francisco Fire Department on the Fire of 1906," 1935, Banc; the chief engineer was the fire chief.

43. T. A. Rickard, ed., *After Earthquake and Fire,* San Francisco: Mining and Scientific Press, 1906, pp. 37–38, 50–51, 85–86, 109.

44. Reed, "The San Francisco Conflagration," p. 9.

45. Barker, *Three Fearful Days,* p. 142.

46. *Argonaut,* August 13, 1926.

47. *Argonaut,* January 29, 1927, and February 5, 1927.

48. U.S. War Department, "Earthquake in California," pp. 217–221, 228–229.

49. "A Letter from General Funston," *Argonaut,* July 7, 1906.

50. Captain Kelly to his family, n.d., Banc.

51. James Russel Wilson, *San Francisco's Horror of Earthquake and Fire,* Memorial Publishing, 1906, p. 237.

52. "How the History of the Disaster Is Being Made," *San Francisco Examiner,* April 19, 1908.

53. *Somers & Co. v. General Relief Committee,* San Francisco Superior Court, September 22, 1908, Banc, pp. 6–8, 11, 13–14. Walsh and O'Keefe, *Legacy of a Native Son,* p. 98.

54. Bean, *Boss Ruef's San Francisco,* p. 121. *Argonaut,* January 22, 1927. Rufus P. Jennings, "Organization in the Crisis," *Out West,* June 1906, pp. 519–522. "No. 1—Minutes of Citizens' Committee," April 18, 1906, Banc. *San Francisco Municipal Reports,* 1908, pp. 755–756.

55. John P. Young, *Journalism in California,* San Francisco: Chronicle Publishing, 1915, p. 858.

56. "George Cooper Pardee, 1857–1941," *Cupola* (quarterly publication of the Pardee Home Museum, Oakland), November 2002.

57. The telegrams between Roosevelt and Pardee are in the Pardee Collection, Banc. Date Book, Pardee Home Museum, Oakland, 1906. "Governor Pardee Hard at Work for the Sufferers," *Oakland Tribune,* April 20, 1906.

58. Van W. Anderson, "The Story of the Bulletins," *Pacific Monthly,* June 1906.

59. *Argonaut,* April 9 and 16, 1927.

60. James Hopper, "Our San Francisco," *Everybody's Magazine,* June 1906.

61. *Argonaut,* April 16, 23, 30, and May 7, 1927. Young, *Journalism in California,* pp. 171–174.

62. *Argonaut,* November 6, 13, 20, 1926.

63. Scott, *The Great Caruso,* pp. 91–92. Greenfield, *Caruso,* pp. 113–115. Key, *Enrico Caruso,* pp. 227–229. "Some Earthquake Experiences," *Literary Digest,* May 5, 1906. "Facing the Music: The Memoirs of Alfred Hertz," *San Francisco Chronicle,* June 21, 1942. Bruce Charles Williams, "Caruso's Plight at the Palace," *San Francisco,* April 1967. Genthe, *As I Remember,* p. 89. "Story of the San Francisco Earthquake and Conflagration as far as It Affected the Conried Metropolitan Opera Company April 18th, 19th, and 20th," Ernest Goerlitz, n.d., unpublished manuscript, CHS. "Opera Stars Stories," *New York Daily Tribune,* April 25, 1906. Barker, *Three Fearful Days,* pp. 214–217. *Argonaut,* August 6, 1927.

64. *Argonaut,* November 27, 1926.

65. Mary Austin, *Earth Horizon,* New York: The Literary Guild, 1932, p. 302. Jordan, *The California Earthquake of 1906,* pp. 341–345. Augusta Fink, *I—Mary,* Tucson: University of Arizona Press, 1983, pp. 128–129.

66. *Argonaut,* November 27, December 4, 11, 1926. Lewis and Hall, *Bonanza Inn,* pp. 337–340.

67. U.S. Weather Bureau, Annual Summary, 1906, Washington, D.C., 1906. U.S. Weather Bureau, *Weather Bureau Journals,* Diary of Daily Activities, San Francisco Office, 1906. Testimony of Alexander G. McAdie in *California Wine Association v. Commercial Union Fire Insurance Company of New York,* February 2, 1908, Banc, p. 77. Alexander McAdie to C. F. Marvin, professor in charge of the weather bureau's Instrument Division, February 6, 1907.

68. Brechin, *Imperial San Francisco,* p. 60. Ellis L. Yochelson, "The Scientific Ideas of G. K. Gilbert," Geological Society of America, Special Paper 183, Boulder, Colo.: Geological Society of America, 1980, p. 41.

69. Frances E. Vaughan, *Andrew C. Lawson: Scientist, Teacher, Philosopher,* Glendale, Calif.: Arthur H. Clarke, 1970, pp. 86–87. Alexander G. McAdie, "The Scientific Side of It," *Sunset,* June–July 1906, pp. 170–172. "Report of the Sub-committee on State Instrumental Records," Lawson Collection, Banc.

70. State Earthquake Investigation Commission, *The California Earthquake of April 18, 1906,* pp. 377–383. Rickard, *After Earthquake and Fire,* pp. 105–108. David Starr Jordan, "The Earthquake and Professor Larkin," *Science,* August 10,

1906, pp. 178–179. Charles Davison, "Earthquake Sounds," *Bulletin of the Seismological Society of America,* July 1938, pp. 147–161. John S. Derr, "Earthquake Lights: A Review of Observations and Present Theories," *Bulletin of the Seismological Society of America,* December 1973, pp. 2177–2187.

71. Philip L. Fradkin, *Stagecoach: Wells Fargo and the American West,* New York: Simon & Schuster, 2002, pp. 163–166. F. L. Lipman, interview by Catherine Harroun, 1943–1944, Wells Fargo Archives, pp. 1–2.

72. Felice A. Bonadio, *A. P. Giannini: Banker of America,* Berkeley: University of California Press, 1994, pp. xi, 22, 27, 31, 32–36. Gerald D. Nash, *A. P. Giannini and the Bank of America,* Norman: University of Oklahoma Press, 1992, pp. 28–36. Marquis James and Bessie Rowland James, *Biography of a Bank: the Story of Bank of America, N. T. & S. A.,* New York: Harper & Brothers, 1954, pp. 21–29. Thomas and Witts, *The San Francisco Earthquake,* pp. 41–43, 117–119, 134–135, 191, 228–231. Paola A. Sensi-Isolari et al., *Struggle and Success: An Anthology of the Italian Immigrant Experience in California,* New York: Center for Migration Studies, 1993, pp. 107–110. Deanna Paoli, *The Italians of San Francisco 1850–1930,* New York: Center for Migration Studies, 1978, pp. 29, 31. Lipman, interview by Catherine Harroun, p. 3.

73. *Argonaut,* September 18, 25, 1926.

74. James B. Stetson, Statement, June 22, 1906, unpublished manuscript, Banc. James B. Stetson, *Narrative of My Experiences in the Earthquake and Fire at San Francisco,* Palo Alto, Calif.: Louis Osborne, 1969, p. 26. The manuscript and printed versions, the latter edited by Oscar Lewis, differ; Lewis's editing was inaccurate and diminished Stetson's voice.

75. *Argonaut,* October 2, 1926. Harry J. Coleman, *Give Us a Little Smile, Baby,* New York: E. P. Dutton, 1943, pp. 132–133. Barker, *Three Fearful Days,* pp. 91–95.

76. Dr. Margaret Mahoney, "The Earthquake, the Fire, the Relief," July 28, 1906, San Francisco Public Library, History Center, p. 4.

77. *Argonaut,* September 25, October 2, 1926.

78. Barker, *Three Fearful Days,* p. 95. "Fire Brings the Triumph of Auto," *San Francisco Chronicle,* April 29, 1906.

79. Wallace Everett, "Autos and the Great Fire," *Sunset,* February 1907, pp. 293–295. J. C. Cunningham, "How the Early-Day Automobile Fared in the Great Earthquake," *Motorland,* March–April 1967. *Argonaut,* March 5 and 12, 1927.

80. Laura Hillenbrand, *Seabiscuit: An American Legend,* New York: Random House, 2001, pp. 4–7.

81. *Mining and Scientific Press,* April 28, 1906.

82. Thompson, *Defender of the Gate,* pp. 320–321, 336–337, 348–356.

83. Major William Stephenson to the class of 1877, Bowdoin College, May 31, 1906, Banc. U.S. War Department, "Earthquake in California," pp. 209–230. Thompson, *Defender of the Gate,* p. 358.

84. Anna G. Blake to her mother and grandmother, various letters, April to

July 1906, Banc. "Life in San Francisco," *Andover (Mass.) Townsman,* June 6, 1906, Banc.

85. Stephenson to the class of 1877.

86. Stetson, *Narrative of My Experiences,* p. 26. Phelan, "Personal Notes," p. 6.

87. *Argonaut,* December 4, 11, 1926.

88. Jerome Barker Landfield, "Operation Kaleidoscope," unpublished manuscript, n.d., Banc.

89. John B. McGloin, "A Fearful Shock of Earthquake . . . ," *St. Ignatius Bulletin,* July 1969, pp. 2–6. Father John P. Frieden, "Some Personal Reminiscences of the Earthquake of San Francisco," n.d., Gleeson Library, Rare Book Room, University of San Francisco.

90. Pan, *The Impact of the 1906 Earthquake,* pp. 33–38.

91. *Argonaut,* June 5, 12, 19, 1926. Gladys Hansen, "The San Francisco Numbers Game," *California Geology,* December 1987, p. 271.

92. Barker, *Three Fearful Days,* pp. 119–120.

93. U.S. War Department, "Earthquake in California," pp. 214, 218, 229. *Argonaut,* February 5 and June 19, 1926.

94. Mahoney, "The Earthquake, the Fire, the Relief," p. 4.

95. *Argonaut,* January 8, 1927.

96. Paul Sinsheimer, "The San Francisco Catastrophe of 1906," *Western States Jewish Quarterly,* April 1975, p. 249.

97. Watkins, "The 1906 San Francisco Earthquake," p. 262. Sylvan Joseph Lisberger family papers, unpublished manuscript, Banc.

98. Etoile Millar Blauer to Hazel Aubry, April 20, 1906, CHS.

99. Jack London, "The Story of an Eye-witness," *Colliers,* May 5, 1906.

100. Charmian London, *The Book of Jack London,* vol. 2, New York: Century, 1921, pp. 124–130. Charmian London's diary, entries for April 18, 19, 20, 1906, HL. Earle Labor et al., eds., *The Letters of Jack London,* vol. 2 (1906–1912), Stanford, Calif.: Stanford University Press, 1988, pp. 571–575, 588–590.

101. "Report of the Committee on Earthquake and Fire History of the Second Day's Session," Grand Chapter of the Royal Arch Masons of California, 52nd Annual Convocation, April 17–18, 1906, Banc.

102. *Argonaut,* July 31, 1926.

103. Almira Hall Eddy to Mr. Trenworth, May 14, 1906, Banc.

104. McGloin, "A Fearful Shock of Earthquake," pp. 6–7.

105. Lisberger family papers.

106. Josephine Fearon Baxter to her parents, April 23, 1906, Banc.

107. *Adams: An Autobiography,* pp. 7–8. David Wyatt, *Five Fires: Race, Catastrophe, and the Shaping of California,* Reading, Mass.: Addison-Wesley Publishing, 1997, pp. 121–124.

108. Warren Olney to A. J. Ralston, May 3, 1906, Banc.

109. D. G. Doubleday to "Dear Sir," May 12, 1906, Banc.

110. Attempts to reduce the chaos of the three days of fire to a coherent narrative appear in the following documents: Board of Supervisors, "Report of Fire Department," in *Excerpts from San Francisco Municipal Reports*, San Francisco: Neal Publishing, 1908 (repr. San Francisco: George Lithography, 1971), pp. 719–723. Laurence J. Kennedy, "The Progress of the Fire in San Francisco April 18th–21st, 1906 as Shown by an Analysis of Original Documents," M.A. thesis, Department of History, University of California, 1908. S. Albert Reed, "The San Francisco Conflagration of April 1906," New York City: The National Board of Fire Underwriters, May 1906. *Argonaut*, July 23, 30, August 6, 13, 20, 1927.

111. Bronson, *The Earth Shook*, p. 46. Bowlen, "Experiences of Captain G. F. Brown." *San Francisco Municipal Reports*, 1908, p. 721.

112. Bronson, *The Earth Shook*, map. *Argonaut*, August 8, 1927. Kennedy, "The Progress of the Fire," pp. 8, 15.

THURSDAY, APRIL 19, 1906

1. Phelan, "Personal Notes." Walsh and O'Keefe, *Legacy of a Native Son*, pp. 99–103.

2. Alice Gerstle Levison, "Family Reminiscences," 1967, Banc, Regional Oral History Office.

3. *Argonaut*, July 24, 1926.

4. Document with a handwritten "Eleanor?" on its cover page, in box 2 of the Hooker family papers, n.d., Banc. Carl Gundlach to Carl, April 22, 1906, CHS.

5. Hooker, "Lessons of the Great Fire," pp. 34–35. Jerome Barker Landfield, "Operation Kaleidoscope," unpublished manuscript, n.d., Banc.

6. Marion Osgood Hooker to Ellie, April 19, 1906, Banc.

7. Ah Wing, "Earthquake of the 52nd Year of the Reign of Emperor Kwong-Hau," n.d., Stan. Kennedy, "The Progress of the Fire," pp. 18–19.

8. Aunt Bertha to her niece, Elsa Billenbeck, May 13, 1906, Banc.

9. Watkins, "The 1906 San Francisco Earthquake."

10. Reed, "The San Francisco Conflagration of April 1906," p. 10.

11. *San Francisco Municipal Reports*, 1908, p. 725.

12. Stephenson to the class of 1877.

13. U.S. War Department, "Earthquake in California," pp. 89, 219.

14. Funston, "How the Army Worked to Save San Francisco," p. 246.

15. U.S. War Department, "Earthquake in California," p. 220.

16. Cunningham, "How the Early-Day Automobile Fared in the Great Earthquake," *Presidio Weekly Clarion*, April 27, 1906; there is evidence that the newspaper, although accurate in its history, was published fifty years later as a commemorative edition.

17. Stetson, Statement, pp. 7–10, and *Narrative of My Experiences*, pp. 34–42.

18. Elizabeth Maud Nankervis, "One Woman's Experience," 1959, unpub-

lished manuscript, Banc. Rev. Edward P. Roe, *Barriers Burned Away*, New York: Dodd & Mead, 1873, pp. 402–403.

19. Various telegrams in the George C. Pardee Collection, Banc.

20. Los Angeles Chamber of Commerce Citizens' Relief Committee, *Report of the Los Angeles Chamber of Commerce Citizens' Relief Committee of Receipt and Disbursements of Funds*, Los Angeles: The Chamber, January 1908, pp. 6, 9.

21. David Nasaw, *The Chief: The Life of William Randolph Hearst*, New York: Houghton Mifflin, 2000, pp. 203–204. Ben Proctor, *William Randolph Hearst: The Early Years, 1863–1910*, New York: Oxford University Press, 1998, pp. 213–214. "Examiner Relief Workers Performed Thrilling Service," *Los Angeles Examiner*, May 1, 1906.

22. Nellie May Brown to Estrella L. Brown, April 19–May 1, 1906, Banc.

23. U.S. War Department, "Earthquake in California," pp. 176–177, 194, 196.

24. Nankervis, "One Woman's Experience," p. 10.

25. Pond, "The United States Navy and the San Francisco Fire," pp. 983–993.

26. U.S. War Department, "Earthquake in California," pp. 88–89. James D. Hudson, "The California National Guard in the San Francisco Earthquake and Fire of 1906," *California Historical Quarterly*, Spring 1976, pp. 138, 142. Funston, "How the Army Worked to Save San Francisco," p. 239.

27. Lesley Einstein, "An Eye-witness Account of the San Francisco Earthquake and Fire," n.d., CHS. Eldridge J. Best, untitled account, n.d., CHS. Captain J. T. Nance, professor of military science and tactics, to Benjamin Ide Wheeler, president of the University of California, May 2, 1906, Banc. Sayre Macneil, "Cadets in Active Service," *Blue and Gold*, 1908, Banc.

28. *Argonaut*, March 26, 1927. Barker, *Three Fearful Days*, pp. 262–266.

29. "Vigilantes Are Doing Duty," *San Francisco Examiner*, April 23, 1906. Charles Ross to A. M. von Metzke, April 26 and June 12, 1906, Banc. *Argonaut*, June 11, 1927. *Argonaut*, June 18, 1927. Rickard, *After Earthquake and Fire*, p. 45.

30. *Argonaut*, June 4 and 11, 1927. "Soldier May Be Charged with Killing," *San Francisco Examiner*, May 5, 1906; "Says Meyers Was Shot from Rear," *San Francisco Examiner*, May 10, 1906.

31. Ross to A. M. von Metzke, April 26, 1906, Banc.

32. Funston, "How the Army Worked to Save San Francisco," p. 248. U.S. War Department, "Earthquake in California," p. 92. Gladys Hansen, interview, San Francisco, July 8, 2002.

33. *Argonaut*, May 28, June 4 and 11, 1927.

34. William G. Hartley, "Saints and the San Francisco Earthquake," *Brigham Young University Studies*, vol. 23, 1983, pp. 447–448.

35. Elmer E. Enewold to Lawrence Enewold, May 3, 1906, CHS.

36. "The San Francisco Earthquake & Fire as Remembered by Charles Drummond McArron," n.d., San Francisco Public Library, History Center.

37. John R. Hubbard, Company B Hospital Corps, to Mrs. C. N. Hubbard, May 4, 1906, San Francisco Public Library, History Center.

38. Sol Lesser, "My Experiences during the Earthquake and Fire in San Francisco," April 18, 1906, CHS.

39. Harriet Lane Levy, unpublished manuscript, n.d., Banc, pp. 5–6. Harriet Levy, *920 O'Farrell Street: A Jewish Girlhood in Old San Francisco,* Berkeley, Calif.: Heyday Books, 1996, pp. x–xiii, 192–196.

40. William James, "On Some Mental Effects of the Earthquake," in *Memories and Studies,* New York: Longmans, Green, 1911, pp. 200–226. William James, "Stanford's Ideal Destiny," *Science,* May 25, 1906. Mrs. William James to relatives, April 18, 1906, Stan. Fradkin, *Magnitude 8,* pp. 19–22. Wyatt, *Five Fires,* pp. 107–110.

41. Roxanne Nilan, "A Young University Is Tested," *Sandstone and Tile,* Winter 1979, pp. 1–7. "The California Universities," *Science,* April 27, 1906, pp. 674–675. "The Earthquake at Stanford University," *Science,* May 4, 1906, pp. 716–717. "Scientific Buildings and Collections at Stanford University," *Science,* May 11, 1906, pp. 756–757. David Starr Jordan, "Stanford University and the Earthquake of April 18, 1906," *Pacific Monthly,* June 1906, pp. 634–645. David Starr Jordan, "The Earthquake at Stanford University," *Out West,* June 1906, pp. 507–513. "University Buildings Veneered," *San Francisco Examiner,* May 1, 1906. "Didn't Plan against a Temblor," *San Francisco Examiner,* May 2, 1906. Jeanette Hayward Beymer, unpublished manuscript, 1907, Stan. Earthquake Reconstruction Committee, "Report on Conditions of Buildings Constituting Leland Stanford Junior University, California, and Damages Resulting Thereto from the Effects of the Earthquake of April 18th, 1906," June 18, 1906, Stan. USGS, *The San Francisco Earthquake and Fire,* pp. 180–186. State Earthquake Investigation Commission, *The California Earthquake of April 18, 1906,* pp. 255–257. Klauber, "Two Days in San Francisco."

42. David Starr Jordan to Professor K. Otaki, April 19, 1906, Stan. David Starr Jordan to Dr. Barton W. Evermann, April 23, 1906, Stan. David Starr Jordan to Andrew C. White, April 24, 1906, Stan.

43. Olaf P. Jenkins, "Experiencing the San Francisco Earthquake at Palo Alto, California," *California Geology,* April 1980, pp. 84–87.

44. "Great Earthquake Took a Heavy Toll at Agnews," *San Jose Mercury,* April 20, 1981.

45. "State Hospital at Agnews Is in Ruins," *San Jose Mercury and Herald,* April 19, 1906.

46. "Seventy Bodies Taken Out from Agnews Ruins," *San Jose Mercury and Herald,* April 21, 1906. "Several More Bodies Taken from Agnews," *San Jose Mercury,* April 24, 1906.

47. "150 Killed at Agnews," *San Jose Mercury and Herald,* April 18, 1906. Payson J. Treat to Flora (his sister), April 23, 1906, Stan.

48. Dr. Leonard Stocking, "Report on the Disaster Which Befell Agnews State Hospital April 18, 1906," Agnews, Calif.: Agnews State Hospital, May 9, 1906. Jordan, *The California Earthquake of 1906*, pp. 186–187. USGS, *The San Francisco Earthquake and Fire*, p. 22. State Earthquake Investigation Commission, *The California Earthquake of April 18, 1906*, pp. 280–281.

49. Response of Governor Pardee to the *Seattle Times* article, n.d., Banc.

50. Dr. Leonard Stocking to Governor George C. Pardee, April 26, 1906, Banc. Leonard Stocking to Governor George C. Pardee, April 27, 1906, Banc. Leonard Stocking to Governor George C. Pardee, May 4, 1906, Banc. Leonard Stocking to Dr. Mabel E. Anthony, May 25, 1906, Banc.

51. Patricia B. Curran, "The Earthquake of April 18, 1906, in the Santa Clara Valley," Society of Pioneers of Santa Clara County, June 7, 1958. "Phelan, Block Buries Three Persons," *San Jose Daily Mercury*, April 20, 1906. "Phelan People Will Start Reconstruction Here at Once," *San Jose Daily Mercury*, April 21, 1906.

52. Jordan, *The California Earthquake of 1906*, pp. 188–191. USGS, *The San Francisco Earthquake and Fire*, pp. 21–22. State Earthquake Investigation Commission, *The California Earthquake of April 18, 1906*, pp. 284–287.

53. "Martial Law Is Placed over the City," *San Jose Mercury and Herald*, April 19, 1906. "Proclamation by Mayor Worswick" and "Why Martial Law Exits Here," *San Jose Daily Mercury*, April 21, 1906.

54. "Warning," *Argonaut*, April 21, 1906. "WARNING!" in *Early Day San Jose*, Smith & McKay Printing, 1971. "Proclamation," Mayor G. D. Worswick, April 18, 1906, San Jose Public Library.

55. "Citizens in Mass Meeting," *San Jose Daily Mercury*, April 20, 1906.

56. "Earthquake Notes," *Santa Cruz Sentinel*, April 19, 1906. "The Great Earthquake," *Mountain Echo*, April 21, 1906. "Loma Prieta Lumbermen Killed," *San Jose Mercury*, April 25, 1906. Louise Ehrmann Titus, unpublished manuscript, August 28, 1972, Banc. Jordan, *The California Earthquake of 1906*, p. 29. Dennis R. Dean, "The San Francisco Earthquake of 1906," *Annals of Science*, November 1993, p. 510. State Earthquake Investigation Commission, *The California Earthquake of April 18, 1906*, pp. 267–268. Fradkin, *Magnitude 8*, p. 222.

57. Gaye LeBaron, *Santa Rosa: A Nineteenth Century Town*, Santa Rosa, Calif.: Historia Ltd., 1985, p. 201.

58. Jordan, *The California Earthquake of 1906*, pp. 113–119. USGS, *The San Francisco Earthquake and Fire*, pp. 24–25.

59. J. Edgar Ross, "The Earthquake in Sonoma County," Healdsburg, Calif.: privately published, 1906. Fradkin, *Magnitude 8*, pp. 103–104.

60. Motley Hewes Flint, "Report of the General Masonic Relief Fund," October 1, 1906, Banc. Labor et al., *The Letters of Jack London*, pp. 572–573.

61. "A Dreadful Catastrophe Visits Santa Rosa," *Press Democrat*, April 19, 1906.

62. State Earthquake Investigation Commission, *The California Earthquake of April 18, 1906,* p. 200.

63. Jessie Loranger to Hattie and Lillian Loranger, April 19, 1906, San Francisco Public Library, History Center.

64. State Earthquake Investigation Commission, *The California Earthquake of April 18, 1906,* pp. 199–203. Monroe H. Alexander, "The Earthquake in Santa Rosa," *California Christian Advocate,* December 27, 1906. LeBaron, *Santa Rosa,* pp. 200–202. "Newsy Notes," *Democrat-Republican,* April 21, 1906.

65. "Report of Relief Committee," 1906, Sonoma County Library, Santa Rosa.

66. Martin Read to Eben Read, April 25, 1906, University of the Pacific, Special Collections.

67. William F. Nichols, *A Father's Story of the Earthquake and Fire,* San Francisco: Foster and ten Bosch, 1906, pp. 8, 14, 20–21.

68. Tekla N. White, *Missions of the San Francisco Bay Area,* Minneapolis: Lerner Publications, 1996, pp. 35, 61. "Welcome to Misión San Francisco de Asís, Properly Known as Mission Dolores," n.d., San Francisco: Mission Dolores.

69. Phelan, "Personal Notes," pp. 12–15.

70. Henry Anderson Lafler, "My Sixty Sleepless Hours: A Story of the San Francisco Earthquake," *McClure's,* July 1906.

FRIDAY, APRIL 20, 1906

1. *Argonaut,* August 13 and 20, 1927.

2. Landfield, "Operation Kaleidoscope."

3. U.S. War Department, "Earthquake in California," p. 89. Kennedy, "The Progress of the Fire," p. 25.

4. Jordan, *The California Earthquake of 1906,* p. 350.

5. Henry Anderson Lafler, Supplement to Brigadier General Frederick Funston's "How the Army Worked to Save San Francisco," *Cosmopolitan,* July 1906, printed by the Calkins Newspaper Syndicate, 1906, Banc, p. 7.

6. Bowlen, "Fires We Have Fought."

7. Conlon, "The Autobiography of John J. Conlon," p. 4.

8. Hooker, "Lessons of the Great Fire," p. 45.

9. Horatio Putnam Livermore to Helen Livermore, April 21, 22, 23, 25, 1906, private collection.

10. *Argonaut,* March 19, 1927.

11. F. H. Wheelan, "A House That Was Saved by the Flag," *St. Nicholas Illustrated Magazine,* July 1908, pp. 791–793.

12. Hooker, "Lessons of the Great Fire," pp. 36, 45.

13. Gladys Hansen and Emmet Condon, *Denial of Disaster: The Untold Story and Photographs of the San Francisco Earthquake and Fire of 1906,* San Francisco: Cameron, 1989, p. 73.

14. *Argonaut,* July 17, 24, and 31, 1926. Barker, *Three Fearful Days,* p. 188.

15. Lieutenant Frederick N. Freeman, "Navy Participation in San Francisco Disaster, 1906," April 30, 1906, Regional Archives—Pacific Region, San Bruno, Calif., pp. 2, 4. Pond, "The United States Navy and the San Francisco Fire," p. 987.

16. Charles H. Spear, president of the Board of State Harbor Commissioners, to Major General A. W. Greely, April 29, 1906, Regional Archives—Pacific Region, San Bruno, Calif. P. Christensen of A. P. Hotaling & Company to Admiral C. F. Goodrich, May 10, 1906, Regional Archives—Pacific Region, San Bruno, Calif. P. S. Rossi to Admiral C. F. Goodrich, May 1, 1906, Regional Archives—Pacific Region, San Bruno, Calif..

17. Pond, "The United States Navy and the San Francisco Fire," pp. 982, 984–985, 987, 991–993. Freeman, "Navy Participation in San Francisco Disaster," pp. 4, 7–8, 10.

18. *Argonaut,* August 20, 1927.

19. *Somers & Co. v. General Relief Committee,* deposition of James D. Phelan, September 22, 1908, pp. 6–8, 11, 14, Banc.

20. Jacob Voorsanger, "The Relief Work in San Francisco," *Out West,* June 1906, pp. 530–531.

21. Phelan, "Personal Notes," p. 15. *San Francisco Municipal Reports,* 1908, pp. 757–761.

22. Jennings, "Organization in the Crisis," pp. 519–525.

23. John P. Young, *Journalism in California: Pacific Coast and Exposition Biographies,* San Francisco: Chronicle Publishing, 1915, p. 172.

24. Phelan, "Personal Notes," p. 15. *Argonaut,* May 14, 1927.

25. U.S. War Department, "Earthquake in California," pp. 107, 114, 129. Charles J. O'Connor et al., *San Francisco Relief Survey: The Organization and Methods of Relief Used after the Earthquake and Fire of April 18, 1906,* New York: Russell Sage Foundation, 1913, p. 69.

26. Miscellaneous correspondence in the Pardee Collection, Banc. Barbara Plageman, "Stockton's Response to the Great Earthquake of 1906," n.d., University of the Pacific, Special Collections, pp. 13–14, 17–18. Sidona V. Johnson, "The Relief Work at Portland, Oregon," *Pacific Monthly,* June 1906, pp. 746–748.

27. "Los Angeles Chamber of Commerce Citizens' Relief Committee," *Report,* pp. 5, 8–9.

28. "Oakland Getting Sweet Revenge for the Old Time Gibes of San Francisco," *New York Times,* May 13, 1906.

29. "Over 20,000 Chinese Are Now in Oakland," *Oakland Tribune,* April 22, 1906. "Refugees Drenched by a Heavy Rain," *Oakland Tribune,* April 23, 1906.

30. Harris Bishop, "How Oakland Aided Her Sister City," Oakland Relief Committee, 1906, Oakland Public Library. "How the Oakland Committee Is

Handling the Food Situation and Helping the Needy," *Oakland Tribune,* April 20, 1906. "Refugees Find Ample Shelter in Oakland," *San Francisco Chronicle,* April 22, 1906. "Stop the Cinch Business," *Oakland Tribune,* April 25, 1906. "Good Work Done at Hearst City," *Oakland Tribune,* April 26, 1906. "Campers Decrease," *Oakland Tribune,* April 27, 1906.

31. Alice Hutchinson to her mother, undated, and to Helen, May 2, 1906, CHS.

32. Edward E. Ewer, "Earthquake Recollections from Health Department Standpoint," n.d., University of the Pacific, Special Collections. "Examiner Relief Workers Performed Thrilling Service," *Los Angeles Examiner,* May 1, 1906.

33. *Argonaut,* February 19, 1927.

34. *Argonaut,* June 18, 1927. Remsen Crawford, "Raising $3,000,000 for Charity," *Broadway Magazine,* June 1, 1906, pp. 115–124. Fradkin, *Stagecoach,* pp. 167–168. Nasaw, *The Chief,* pp. 203–204.

35. American National Red Cross, *Sixth Annual Report of the American National Red Cross, Covering the Period from January 1 to December 31, 1910,* Washington, D.C., 1910, pp. 35, 37. American National Red Cross, *Bulletin No. 3,* Washington, D.C., July 1906, pp. 16–17. Merchant's Association of New York, *Report of the Merchant's Association of New York Relief Committee for the San Francisco Sufferers,* New York: Merchants' Association of New York, June 1906, p. 10. Los Angeles Chamber of Commerce Citizens' Relief Committee, *Report,* p. 15. Winnifred Mears, "Spending $9,181,403.23," *Overland Monthly,* September, 1907, p. 212. Miscellaneous items, Pardee Collection, Banc. "San Francisco the Imperishable," Passenger Department of the Southern Pacific, San Francisco, 1906, Banc. U.S. War Department, "Earthquake in California," p. 128. "The Army in the San Francisco Disaster," *Journal of the United States Infantry Association,* July 1907.

36. "Report of the Sub-committee on Statistics to the Chairman and Committee on Reconstruction," April 24, 1907, pp. 1, 3–5, Banc. Reed, "The San Francisco Conflagration," pp. 1, 11–12. "Report of the Committee on Municipal Buildings," June 4, 1906, pp. 2–4, Banc. "Destruction of San Francisco and Other California Libraries," *Library Journal,* May 1906, pp. 213–215. Charles B. Faulhaber, "The Bancroft Library 1900–2000," *Chronicle of the University of California,* Fall 2000, p. 37. William F. Heintz, "California Wine and the Quake of '06," *Wines & Vines,* April 1980, p. 47.

37. Committee of Five, *Report of the Committee of Five to the Thirty-five Companies on the San Francisco Conflagration, April 18–21,* New York, December 31, 1906, p. 11, Banc. Archibald MacPhail, *Of Men and Fire: A Story of Fire Insurance in the Far West,* San Francisco: Fire Underwriters Association of the Pacific, 1948, p. 111.

38. "Metcalf Reports to the President," *San Francisco Chronicle,* April 29, 1906. Mahoney, "The Earthquake, the Fire, the Relief." Fradkin, *Magnitude 8,* p. 7. O'Connor et al., *San Francisco Relief Survey,* pp. 91–92.

39. Hansen, "The San Francisco Numbers Game," pp. 271–272. "Report of the Sub-committee on Statistics," p. 16. California Promotion Committee, *San Francisco Dauntless,* May 15, 1906, Banc. *San Francisco Municipal Reports,* 1908, p. 703.

40. Dr. William J. Walsh to Archbishop P. W. Riordan, February 3, 1911, San Francisco Public Library, History Center.

41. Gladys Hansen, *Who Perished: A List of Persons Who Died As a Result of the Great Earthquake and Fire in San Francisco on April 18, 1906,* San Francisco: San Francisco Archives, 1980. Gladys Hansen and Frank R. Quinn, "The 1906 'Numbers' Game," June 1985, San Francisco Public Library. Hansen, "The San Francisco Numbers Game," pp. 271–274. Gladys Hansen and Emmet Condon, *Denial of Disaster: The Untold Story and Photographs of the San Francisco Earthquake and Fire of 1906,* San Francisco: Cameron, 1989, p. 152. Hansen, interview. "90 Years Later Quake Victims Get Names," *San Francisco Chronicle,* April 14, 1996. Bolt, *Earthquakes,* p. 5. Dan Kurzman, *Disaster: The Great San Francisco Earthquake and Fire of 1906,* New York: William Morrow, 2001, pp. 248–249; this book is filled with factual errors. *Argonaut,* July 23, 1927. *San Francisco Municipal Reports,* 1908, p. 719.

THE RELIEF EFFORT

1. David L. Sills, ed., *International Encyclopedia of the Social Sciences,* New York: Macmillan and the Free Press, 1968, p. 202.

2. "Beneath the Surface in San Francisco," *New York Times,* July 7, 1907.

3. Carl Gundlach to Carl, April 22, 1906, CHS.

4. James H. Shore, ed., *Disaster Stress Studies: New Methods and Findings,* Washington, D.C.: American Psychiatric Press, 1986, pp. 142–149. David Alexander, *Natural Disasters,* London: UCL Press, 1993, pp. 564–566.

5. J. Eugene Haas et al., eds., *Reconstruction Following Disaster,* Cambridge, Mass.: MIT Press, 1977, pp. xxvii–xxviii, 5.

6. "The American Way of Death Becomes America's Way of Life," *New York Times,* August 18, 2002.

7. To the Finance Committee of the San Francisco Relief and Red Cross Funds (Incorporated) from its Sub-committee, memorandum, March 14, 1907, Banc.

8. Phelan, Personal Notes, pp. 16–20.

9. James D. Phelan to Sir Thomas Lipton, May 21, 1906, Banc. James D. Phelan to Secretary of War William H. Taft, May 2, 1906, Banc.

10. James D. Phelan to C. L. Duval, May 15, 1906, Banc. James D. Phelan to Edgar Carolan, May 11, 1906, Banc. James D. Phelan to Mabelle Gilman, May 8, 1906, Banc. James D. Phelan to J. Downey Harvey, July 12, 1906, Banc. James D. Phelan to George L. Duval, December 4, 1906 and May 2, 1907, Banc. James D. Phelan to Robert J. Aitkin, May 14, 1907, Banc.

11. Florence Ellon to James D. Phelan, March 30, 1905; April 14, 1905; April 10, 1906; May 19, 1906; December 9, 1906; February 24, 1907, Banc.

12. "City and Nation Celebrate Independence Day," *San Francisco Bulletin*, July 4, 1906. James D. Phelan, "The Future of San Francisco," *Out West*, June 1906, pp. 537–538. James D. Phelan, "Rise of the New San Francisco," *Cosmopolitan*, October 1906, pp. 575–582. James D. Phelan to President Theodore Roosevelt, May 4, 1906, Banc. Platt, *Disasters and Democracy*, pp. 1, 9.

13. O'Connor et al., *San Francisco Relief Survey*, pp. vii, 9.

14. Charles Hurd, *The Compact History of the American Red Cross*, New York: Hawthorn Books, 1959, pp. 103–112. Caroline Moorehead, *Dunant's Dream: War, Switzerland and the History of the Red Cross*, New York: Carrol & Graf, 1999, pp. 108–118.

15. "Roosevelt Explains," *New York Times*, May 4, 1906. "Stirred by the President's Words: President Asked to Rescind Proclamation Reflecting on San Francisco," *San Francisco Chronicle*, April 25, 1905. "Phelan Will Receive Money," *San Francisco Examiner*, April 26, 1906.

16. Phelan, "Personal Notes," pp. 22–26. "Conference Meeting of the Finance Committee," transcript, May 5, 1906, Banc, pp. 44–45.

17. O'Connor et al., *San Francisco Relief Survey*, p. 11. James D. Phelan, "Extracts from Documents Bearing on the Relations of the American National Red Cross to the San Francisco Relief and Red Cross Funds, a Corporation," April 15, 1910, Banc. American National Red Cross, *Bulletin No. 3*, Washington, D.C., July 1906, pp. 16–17. Morison, *The Letters of Theodore Roosevelt*, pp. 219–220. William W. Morrow, "The Earthquake of April 18, 1906, and the Great Fire in San Francisco on That and Succeeding Days—Personal Experiences, Inauguration of Red Cross and General Relief Work," n.d., Banc, pp. 18–26. *Somers and Co. v. General Relief Committee*, deposition of James D. Phelan, September 22, 1908. Walsh and O'Keefe, *Legacy of a Native Son*, pp. 108–109. James D. Phelan to Mayor Eugene Schmitz, June 6, 1906, Banc.

18. O'Connor et al., *San Francisco Relief Survey*, pp. 9, 39; the most complete listing of the finance committee, its various subcommittees, and its changing membership is contained in O'Connor, pp. 377–378.

19. Phelan, "Personal Notes," p. 20. Various reports and correspondence between Pardee and National Guard staff officers, April and May 1906, Banc. Meeting of the Finance Committee of the San Francisco Relief and Red Cross Funds, June 6, 1906, Banc, pp. 24–25.

20. "Friction between Militia and Mayor," *San Francisco Chronicle*, April 24, 1906. "Militia Center of Hot Conflict," *San Francisco Chronicle*, April 26, 1906. Colonel (unnamed) of the First Infantry to George Pardee, May 26, 1906, Banc. *Argonaut*, June 11, 1927. Hudson, "The California National Guard," pp. 144–147.

21. U.S. War Department, "Earthquake in California," p. 107.

22. *Argonaut*, February 26, 1927.

23. Chaplain Charles D. Miel to Lieutenant Colonel M. M. Ogden, May 2, 1906, Banc.

24. Lieutenant Colonel M. M. Ogden to Brigadier General J. B. Lauck, May 29, 1906, Banc.

25. *Argonaut,* February 19, 1927. O'Connor et al., *San Francisco Relief Survey,* pp. 12, 21, 30, 33, 40, 55, 61–62, 379–380. Conference Meeting of the Finance Committee, May 4, 1906, Banc.

26. California Promotion Committee, *San Francisco Dauntless.*

27. *San Francisco Municipal Reports,* 1908, pp. 755–767. "At Work for a Greater City," *San Francisco Chronicle,* April 24, 1906.

28. Meetings of the Finance Committee, May 4, 5, 7, 17, 1906, Banc. James D. Phelan to Secretary of War William H. Taft, May 2, 1906, Banc. O'Connor et al., *San Francisco Relief Survey,* pp. 387–388. Douty, *The Economics of Localized Disasters,* p. 101.

29. Meeting of the Finance Committee, transcript, May 14, 1906, Banc, pp. 60–61.

30. O'Connor et al., *San Francisco Relief Survey,* pp. 78–79, 87, 388.

31. "A Resume of the Work Performed by the Committee for Housing the Homeless after the Destruction of San Francisco by Fire April 18th—20th, 1906," n.d., Phelan Collection, Banc. O'Connor et al., *San Francisco Relief Survey,* pp. 70–71.

32. *Argonaut,* July 2, 9, and 15, 1927.

33. Walsh and O'Keefe, *Legacy of a Native Son,* pp. 28, 57, 67.

34. "Father Yorke to the Leader Readers," *Leader,* April 28, 1906.

35. Kahn, *Imperial San Francisco,* p. 128.

36. Meetings of the Citizens' Committee of Fifty, April 30, May 1, May 2, 1906, Banc. Jennings, "Organization in the Crisis," pp. 524–525. *San Francisco Municipal Reports,* 1908, pp. 767–770. "Spreckels Will Resign from Committee of Forty," *San Francisco Examiner,* May 16, 1906.

37. O'Connor et al., *San Francisco Relief Survey,* pp. 221–238. Marie Bolton, "Recovery for Whom? Social Conflict after the San Francisco Earthquake and Fire, 1906–1915," Ph.D. dissertation, University of California, Davis, 1997, pp. 59–64, 68, 70.

38. "Storms Not Due to Earthquakes," *San Francisco Call,* May 28, 1906.

39. O'Connor et al., *San Francisco Relief Survey,* pp. 77–78.

40. *Argonaut,* July 17, 1926.

41. F. O. Popenoe, "The San Francisco Disaster: A Personal Narrative," *Pacific Monthly,* June 1906, p. 735. Personals, *San Francisco Examiner,* April 24, 1906.

42. "The Refugees' Cookbook," pamphlet, 1906, Banc.

43. "What Society Is Doing," *San Francisco Examiner,* April 30, 1906.

44. "See San Francisco in Ruins: The Trail of the Greatest Fire in the World's History," St. Francis Hotel, n.d., Banc.

45. Anna G. Blake to Mrs. H. L. Blake, April 21, 1907, Banc.

46. "Business Firms Prepare to Adorn the City with Stately Buildings," *San Francisco Call,* April 22, 1906, Banc.

47. Mary Louise Bine Rodriguez, *The Earthquake of 1906,* San Francisco: privately printed, 1951, pp. 48–49.

48. W. D. Sohier and Jacob Furth, "Report of the Massachusetts Association for the Relief of California," September 27, 1906, pp. 6–7, Banc.

49. Mahoney, "The Earthquake, the Fire, the Relief," pp. 5–8.

50. Craddock, *City of Plagues,* pp. 147–148. *Argonaut,* July 2, 9, 16, 1927. U.S. War Department, "Earthquake in California," pp. 213–214.

51. Chairman, San Jose Relief Committee to Dr. Hirschberger, April 22, 1906, Banc.

52. Craddock, *City of Plagues,* p. 126. Chase, *The Barbary Plague,* pp. 162, 192, 211.

53. *San Francisco Municipal Reports,* 1908, pp. 481–511. Craddock, *City of Plagues,* pp. 148–160. Shah, *Contagious Divides,* pp. 153–157.

54. Dr. William W. Stiles, "The San Francisco Earthquake and Fire: Public Health Aspects," *California Medicine,* July 1956, pp. 36–38.

55. A. W. Greely, *Reminiscences of Adventure and Service: A Record of Sixty-five Years,* New York: Charles Scribner's Sons, 1927, pp. 219–224.

56. Kahn, *Imperial San Francisco,* pp. 136–153. Douty, *The Economics of Localized Disasters,* pp. 104, 128. Winnifred Mears, "Spending $9,181,403.23," *Overland Monthly,* September 1907, pp. 212, 215, 220, 218–219. C. J. O'Connor to James D. Phelan, "Grants to Charitable Institutions as Approved by Executive Committee," October 26, 1907, Banc. O'Connor et al., *San Francisco Relief Survey,* pp. 94–95.

THE UPBUILDING OF SAN FRANCISCO

1. Haas et al., *Reconstruction Following Disaster,* pp. xxv, 73–84. Douty, *The Economics of Localized Disasters,* pp. 221, 223, 363–370. Scott, *The San Francisco Bay Area,* pp. 97–107. Charles Moore, *Daniel H. Burnham: Architect Planner of Cities,* vol. 2, New York: De Capo Press, 1968, pp. 3–5. "When London Started Over," *New York Times Book Review,* September 22, 2002. Walsh and O'Keefe, *Legacy of a Native Son,* pp. 84–91.

2. James D. Phelan to Thomas M'Caleb, April 30, 1906, Banc. James D. Phelan to Daniel Burnham, May 2, 1906, Banc.

3. Daniel Burnham to C. D. Marshall (Phelan's secretary), April 17, 1906, Banc. Daniel Burnham to James Phelan, June 13, 1906, Banc. Samuel E. Moffett, "The Future of San Francisco," *Collier's,* June 30, 1906.

4. "Proceedings of Legislative Committees in Joint Session," May 17, May 21, May 22, May 23, 1906, Banc.

5. Kahn, *Imperial San Francisco,* pp. 178, 212.

6. "To Shop on the Avenue: Many Retail Stores Are Being Relocated on Van Ness," *San Francisco Call,* May 7, 1906.

7. Simon Schama, *A History of Britain: The Wars of the British 1603–1776,* vol. 2, New York: Hyperion, 2001, pp. 264–273.

8. Scott, *The San Francisco Bay Area,* pp. 112–117. Brechin, *Imperial San Francisco,* pp. 153–154. Douty, *The Economics of Localized Disasters,* pp. 161–164, 176–178. James D. Phelan to Andrew W. Crawford, July 10, 1906, Banc. James D. Phelan to Mary Dickson, January 14, 1909, Banc. "M. H. de Young Will Fight Burnham Plans for Downtown and Business Men's Association Is with Him Strongly," *San Francisco Call,* May 23, 1906. "Report of Marsden Manson to the Mayor and Committee on Reconstruction on the Improvements Now Necessary to Execute and an Estimate of the Cost of the Same," October, 1906, CSP.

9. Various letters and telegrams between J. A. Graves, vice president and manager of the Farmers & Merchants National Bank of Los Angeles, other correspondents, and Isaias W. Hellman, April 19 to May 28, 1906, CHS. Douty, *The Economics of Localized Disasters,* pp. 168–171.

10. "Big Structures Not Planned," *San Francisco Chronicle,* April 25, 1906.

11. "Stop the Cinch Business," *Oakland Tribune,* April 25, 1906.

12. J. C. Branner, "Earthquakes and Structural Engineering," *Bulletin of the Seismological Society of America,* March 1913, p. 2.

13. G. K. Gilbert, "Earthquake Forecasts," *Science,* January 22, 1909, p. 135.

14. Charles Scawthorn, "Fire Following Earthquakes," in *Earthquake Engineering Handbook,* Wai-Fah Chen and Charles Scawthorn, eds., New York: CRC Press, 2003, pp. 29-1, 29-2.

15. C. H. Bigelow to George C. Pardee, June 16, 1906, Banc.

16. John Ripley Freeman, *Earthquake Damage and Earthquake Insurance,* New York: McGraw-Hill, 1932, pp. x, 2.

17. Samuel Richard Weed, "My Early Experience and Recollections of the Great Fire and the First Fire Department in San Francisco," paper presented at the annual meeting of the Pacific Coast Underwriters Association, January 14, 1908, HL.

18. "Report of the Special Committee of the Board of Trustees of the Chamber of Commerce of San Francisco on Insurance Settlements Incident to the San Francisco Fire," November 13, 1906, p. 56, Banc. Douty, *The Economics of Localized Disasters,* pp. 203–204.

19. "Report of Special Committee on Settlements Made by Fire Insurance Companies in Connection with the San Francisco Disaster," reprinted from the monthly *Bulletin of the National Association of Credit Men,* n.d., Banc. MacPhail, *Of Men and Fire,* p. 103.

20. G. H. Marks, "Reminiscences and Lessons of the San Francisco Conflagration 18–21 April 1906," London Assurance, n.d., Banc.

21. Committee of Five, *Report of the Committee of Five,* pp. 11, 26–27, 43. *1906,* pp. 6, 9–13, 55. "Report of Special Committee on Settlements Made by Fire Insurance Companies in Connection with the San Francisco Disaster," reprinted from the monthly *Bulletin of the National Association of Credit Men,* n.d., Banc, p. 2. Douty, *The Economics of Localized Disasters,* pp. 196–197.

22. "Vast Loan Is Offered / New York Capitalists Will Advance $100,000,000 for Rebuilding," *San Francisco Call,* May 2, 1906. Douty, *The Economics of Localized Disasters,* pp. 193–195, 206–207. Haas et al., *Reconstruction Following Disaster,* p. 6.

23. Ibid., Whitney, *1906,* p. 22. Douty, *The Economics of Localized Disasters,* pp. 199–201.

24. Committee of Five, *Report of the Committee of Five,* pp. 13–14.

25. Earthquake insurance became generally available after the 1925 Santa Barbara quake. When large losses were incurred in the 1994 Northridge earthquake, the insurance industry declined to cover earthquakes any longer. The state took over that function. Governor George C. Pardee and Mayor Eugene E. Schmitz to all home offices, June 15, 1906, Phelan Collection, Banc. Bigelow to George C. Pardee. Harold Rose, Union Assurance Society, to Governor George C. Pardee, June 24, 1906, Banc. Henry Evans, Continental Insurance Company, to Governor George C. Pardee and Mayor Eugene E. Schmitz, June 16, 1906, Banc. Theo. W. Letton, Prussian National Insurance Company, to Governor George C. Pardee, June 18, 1906, Banc.

26. Various documents in the Atlas Insurance [*sic*] Company Collection, 1895–1911, Banc.

27. "Report of Special Committee on Settlements Made by Fire Insurance Companies in Connection with the San Francisco Disaster," reprinted from the monthly *Bulletin of the National Association of Credit Men,* n.d., Banc.

28. Douty, *The Economics of Localized Disasters,* pp. 196, 198–199, 202–212.

29. Freeman, *Earthquake Damage,* pp. 171, 175, 180, 182. *The Effects of the San Francisco Earthquake of April 18th, 1906, on Engineering Constructions,* American Society of Civil Engineers Transactions, Paper No. 1056, December 1907, p. 325.

30. USGS, *The San Francisco Earthquake and Fire,* p. 12.

31. James C. Wilson, "Earthquake Engineering: Designing Unseen Technology against Invisible Forces," *Journal of the International Committee for the History of Technology,* vol. 1, 1995, pp. 176–177.

32. *The Effects of the San Francisco Earthquake of April 18th, 1906, on Engineering Constructions,* pp. 211–212, 234, 237, 325. USGS, *The San Francisco Earthquake and Fire,* pp. 51, 53–54, 153. A. L. A. Himmelwright, "The San Francisco Earthquake and Fire," Roebling Construction Company, 1906, pp. 25–26.

33. *The Effects of the San Francisco Earthquake of April 18th, 1906, on Engineering Constructions,* pp. 241, 313. USGS, *The San Francisco Earthquake and Fire,* pp. 68–69.

34. The old city hall was located where the new main branch of the San Francisco Public Library now stands. "City Hall Presents Problem," *San Francisco Chronicle,* April 29, 1906. National Association of Stationary Engineeers, *Report of California No. 3 National Association of Stationary Engineers of the San Francisco Calamity,* H. S. Crocker, n.d., Banc. Hansen and Condon, *Denial of Disaster,* pp. 15, 138. Walsh and O'Keefe, *Legacy of a Native Son,* pp. 64, 88. Rickard, *After Earthquake and Fire,* p. 82.

35. USGS, *The San Francisco Earthquake and Fire,* pp. 34–35, 81–89, 144, 146, 155. Reed, "The San Francisco Conflagration," pp. 232–233. Ibid., p. 19.

36. *The Effects of the San Francisco Earthquake of April 18th, 1906, on Engineering Constructions,* pp. 277–282, 323–329.

37. F. W. Fitzpatrick, "The San Francisco Calamity," *Fireproof Magazine,* August 1906. Scawthorn, "Fire Following Earthquakes," pp. 29-19, 29-20, 29-21. James C. Williams, "Earthquake Engineering: Designing Unseen Technology against Visible Forces," *Journal of the International Committee for the History of Technology,* vol. 1, 1995, pp. 172–194. Douty, *The Economics of Localized Disasters,* pp. 207–212. Steinberg, *Acts of God,* pp. 36–38.

38. Stephen Trobriner, "The Phoenix Rising: San Francisco Confronts the Danger of Earthquake and Fire, 1906–1914," in *American Public Architecture: European Roots and Native Expressions,* Papers in Art History from Pennsylvania State University, vol. 5, University Park: Pennsylvania State University, 1995, pp. 185–193.

39. James D. Phelan to J. Downey Harvey, July 12, 1906, Banc. James D. Phelan to George L. Duvall, December 4, 1906 and May 2, 1907, Banc. James D. Phelan to Robert J. Aitkin, May 14, 1907, Banc. General Frederick Funston to James D. Phelan, February 8, 1908, Banc. James D. Phelan to Captain R. P. Hobson, April 1, 1909, Banc. General Frederick Funston to James D. Phelan, November 14, 1912, Banc. "Phelan Building," F. J. Cooper Advertising Agency, n.d., Banc. Walsh and O'Keefe, *Legacy of a Native Son,* pp. 106–108.

40. Rufus M. Steele, "Killing an Army of Horses to Rebuild San Francisco," *Harper's Weekly,* April 20, 1907, pp. 580–581.

41. Nash, *A. P. Giannini and the Bank of America,* pp. 34–35. Various issues of the *Timberman,* dating from May 1906 to December 1907. Michael Williams, *Americans and Their Forests: A Historical Geography,* New York: Cambridge University Press, 1999, pp. 290–315. Edwin T. Coman Jr. and Helen Gibbs, *Time, Tide and Timber: A Century of Pope & Talbot,* Stanford, Calif.: Stanford University Press, 1949, pp. 221–226, 441. William G. Robbins, *Hard Times in Paradise: Coos Bay, Oregon, 1850–1986,* Seattle: University of Washington Press, 1988, pp. 12–13, 28–39. James B. Meikle, "San Francisco and the Cities on Puget Sound," *Pacific Monthly,* June 1906, pp. 15–16. Tom Richardson, "The Effect of the California Disaster upon Pacific Coast Cities," *Pacific Monthly,* June 1906, pp. 13–14. Bean, *Boss Ruef's San Francisco,* pp. 70–71.

1. Morrow, "The Earthquake of April 18, 1906." Millard, *History of the San Francisco Bay Region*, pp. 404–405. Issel and Cherny, *San Francisco,* pp. 36–37.

2. Benjamin Ide Wheeler to Henry Morse Stephens, April 24, 1906, Banc. Faulhaber, "The Bancroft Library," pp. 30–39.

3. "We Want All the Facts," Committee on History, n.d., HL. "Compiling Data for Compilation of the History," *San Francisco Call,* May 5, 1906. "Will Compile Big History," *San Francisco Examiner,* May 7, 1906.

4. Various "Earthquake History [Expense] Accounts," 1907–1908, in collection of H. Morse Stephens, Banc. American National Red Cross, *Sixth Annual Report,* p. 58.

5. H. Morse Stephens, "How the History of the Disaster Is Being Made," *San Francisco Examiner,* April 19, 1908.

6. Harold L. Leupp to Farnham P. Griffiths, April 1, 1925, Banc.

7. "Henry Morse Stephens," *Nation,* April 26, 1919. "Interesting People," *American Magazine,* July 1919.

8. "Last Will and Testament of Henry Morse Stephens," January 6, 1919, Banc. Harold L. Leupp to Farnham P. Griffiths, September 1, 1924, Banc. Various correspondence between Leupp and Griffiths, and Leupp and Drum and Griffiths, 1920–1925, Banc. Leupp to Griffiths, April 1, 1925. Griffiths to Drum, January 6, 1925, Banc. Griffiths to Leupp, January 6, 1925, Banc. Leupp to Griffiths, March 19, 1925, Banc. Griffiths to Drum, March 21, 1925, Banc. Drum to Griffiths, April 8, 1925, Banc.

9. The last story in the series was number 70, but the numbering was incorrect: sixty-nine parts were actually published.

10. Documents that were sent to Wheeler were passed on to Stephens with instructions to deposit them in the Bancroft Library. Others wound up in the hands of individuals such as Phelan, who then donated them to various archives, including the Bancroft. The process, it is evident now, lacked a cohesive system. *Argonaut,* April 24, 1926, p. 12.

11. Marian Hooker to John Francis Neylan, May 18, 1950, Banc.

12. Charles S. Cushing, chairman of the History Committee of the Society of California Pioneers, and Warren Howell, transcripts of telephone conversations, October 31 and November 1, 1941, CSP. H. P. Van Sicklen, "Publication of the Society of California Pioneers," 1942, CSP, pp. 10–11. Unsigned note to Mr. Allen, CSP, June 24, 1947.

13. Charles F. Richter, *Elementary Seismology,* San Francisco: W. H. Freeman, 1958, p. 467. Byerly and Louderback, "Memorial to Andrew Cowper Lawson," pp. 141–147. Frances E. Vaughan, *Andrew C. Lawson: Scientist, Teacher, Philosopher,* Glendale, Calif.: Arthur H. Clark, 1970, pp. 73–82. Fradkin, *Magnitude 8,*

p. 137. Andrew C. Lawson to Frederick L. Ransome, March 9, 1909, Banc. Andrew C. Lawson to the president and board of trustees of the Carnegie Institution, May 1, 1907, Banc.

14. Andrew C. Lawson to Governor George C. Pardee, April 19, 1906, Banc. Governor George C. Pardee to "To Whom It May Concern," April 21, 1906, in "Preliminary Report of the State Earthquake Investigation Commission," May 31, 1906, Banc.

15. Andrew C. Lawson to Henry Fielding Reid, April 24, 1906, Banc. Andrew C. Lawson to Benjamin Ide Wheeler, May 7, 1906, Banc. Andrew C. Lawson to Grove Karl Gilbert, June 28, 1906, Banc. Andrew C. Lawson to members of the commission, May 11, 1907, Banc. Andrew C. Lawson to R. S. Woodward, president of the Carnegie Institution, November 4, 1907, Banc.

16. Pardee, "To Whom It May Concern."

17. Brechin, *Imperial San Francisco,* p. 60.

18. Andrew C. Lawson to Benjamin Ide Wheeler, December 10, 1907, Banc. Frederick L. Ransome to Andrew C. Lawson, January 12, 1910, Banc.

19. Pyne, *Grove Karl Gilbert,* pp. 228–231.

20. Grove Karl Gilbert to Andrew C. Lawson, May 24, 1906, Banc.

21. State Earthquake Investigation Commission, *The California Earthquake of April 18, 1906,* pp. 71–80.

22. Robert E. Wallace, "G. K. Gilbert's Studies of Faults, Scarps, and Earthquakes," in *The Scientific Ideas of G. K. Gilbert,* Ellis L. Yochelson, ed., Geological Society of America Special Paper 183, Boulder, Colo.: Geological Society of America, 1980, p. 41.

23. Carol S. Prentice and David P. Schwartz, "Re-evaluation of 1906 Surface Faulting, Geomorphic Expression, and Seismic Hazard along the San Andreas Fault in the Southern Santa Cruz Mountains," *Bulletin of the Seismological Society of America,* October 1991, pp. 1424–1479.

24. J. C. Branner to A. C. Lawson, April 30, 1906, Stan. J. C. Branner to G. A. Waring, June 10, 1906, Stan. Andrew C. Lawson to J. C. Branner, January 21, 1907, Banc. Andrew C. Lawson to E. P. Carey, February 5, 1907, Banc. Andrew C. Lawson to John C. Branner, February 7, 1907, Banc. Andrew C. Lawson to George D. Louderback, February 26, 1907, Banc. Andrew C. Lawson to John C. Branner, March 22, 1907, Banc. Andrew C. Lawson to John C. Branner, March 6, 1907, Banc. Andrew C. Lawson to John C. Branner, March 22, 1907, Banc. Andrew C. Lawson to John C. Branner, March 25, 1907, Banc. E. P. Carey to Andrew C. Lawson, April 7, 1907, Banc. J. C. Branner to G. A. Waring, April 9, 1907, Stan. Andrew C. Lawson to E. S. Larsen, April 22, 1907, Banc. Andrew C. Lawson to Carnegie Institution Board of Trustees, May 1, 1907, Banc. Andrew C. Lawson to G. A. Waring, May 9, 1907, Banc. Andrew C. Lawson to George D. Louderback, June 6, 1907, Banc. "Excerpts

from Genealogy and Personal Memoirs of Edgar C. Smith," Stanford Class of 1907, Stan. Dennis R. Dean, "The San Francisco Earthquake of 1906," *Annals of Science,* November 1993, pp. 517–521. Geschwind, *California Earthquakes,* pp. 32–39.

25. Andrew C. Lawson to Grove Karl Gilbert, June 14, 1907, Banc.

26. Andrew C. Lawson to David Starr Jordan, October 24, 1907, Banc. Andrew C. Lawson to William Barnum, chief clerk of the Carnegie Institution, January 21, 1908, Banc. Andrew C. Lawson to Harry Fielding Reid, January 21, 1908, Banc.

27. Harry Fielding Reid to Andrew C. Lawson, March 9, 1907, Banc. Andrew C. Lawson to A. O. Leuschner, March 12, 1907, Banc.

28. Andrew C. Lawson to Grove Karl Gilbert, May 6, 1907, Banc. Andrew C. Lawson to John D. Rockefeller, January 26, 1909, Banc. Andrew C. Lawson to W. P. Scott, January 28, 1909, Banc.

29. J. J. Litehiser, *Observatory Seismology,* Berkeley: University of California Press, 1989, p. 28. Arnold J. Meltsner, "The Communication of Scientific Information to the Wider Public: The Case of Seismology in California," *Minerva,* Autumn 1979, p. 338.

30. Andrew C. Lawson to Benjamin Ide Wheeler and David Starr Jordan, May 7, 1906, Banc. George D. Louderback to Andrew C. Lawson, June 23, 1907, Banc. George D. Louderback to Andrew C. Lawson, June 27, 1908, Banc. Geschwind, *California Earthquakes,* pp. 39–42, 44. Andrew C. Lawson, "Seismology in the United States," *Bulletin of the Seismological Society of America,* March 1911, pp. 1–4.

31. Stephen Taber, "The Earthquake Problem in Southern California," *Bulletin of the Seismological Society of America,* December 1920, pp. 287–288.

32. Gilbert, "Earthquake Forecasts," pp. 135–136. Branner, "Earthquakes and Structural Engineering," pp. 1–5. Meltsner, "The Communication of Scientific Information," p. 372. Geschwind, *California Earthquakes,* p. 44.

33. Charles W. Jenning, "New Geologic Map of California: A Summation of 140 Years of Geologic Mapping," *California Geology,* April 1978, p. 77. Meltsner, "The Communication of Scientific Information," p. 338.

34. Bruce A. Bolt, "The Development of Earthquake Seismology in the Western United States," in *Geologists and Ideas: A History of North American Geology,* Centennial Special Volume 1, Boulder, Colo.: Geological Society of America, 1985, p. 473. Carol S. Prentice, *The Great San Francisco Earthquake of 1906 and Subsequent Evolution of Ideas,* Geological Society of America, Special Paper 338, Boulder, Colo.: Geological Society of America, 1999, pp. 79–85.

35. USGS, "Is a Powerful Quake Likely to Strike in the Next 30 Years?" USGS Fact Sheet 039-03, 2003.

1. Meltsner, "The Communication of Scientific Information," p. 333.

2. William Randolph Hearst, "The San Francisco That Was and the San Francisco That Is to Be," *San Francisco Examiner,* May 13, 1906. The commentary appeared in all Hearst's papers and was made into a broadside.

3. Emerson L. Daggett, *History of San Francisco Journalism: The San Francisco Press and the Fire of 1906,* vol. 5, San Francisco: Works Progress Administration (WPA), 1940, pp. 13–45. Fradkin, *Magnitude 8,* pp. 199–206.

4. Various issues of the *San Francisco Call, San Francisco Examiner,* and *San Francisco Chronicle.* "Let Us Have Right Kind of a New City," *San Francisco Examiner,* April 23, 1906. "UNDAUNTED!" *San Francisco Examiner,* May 3, 1906.

5. "Quake Opens a Big Chasm," *San Francisco Call,* May 6, 1906. Robert Streitz and Roger Sherburne, eds., *Studies of the San Andreas Fault Zone in Northern California,* Sacramento, Calif.: California Division of Mines and Geology, 1980, p. 86. Fradkin, *Magnitude 8,* p. 102.

6. "The Divine Sara Sees City's Ruins and Weeps," *San Francisco Examiner,* May 15, 1906. Genthe, *As I Remember,* pp. 99–101.

7. Daggett, *History of San Francisco Journalism,* pp. 45–61.

8. "A Look on the Brighter Side," *San Jose Mercury* and *Herald,* April 20, 1906.

9. "All Danger Is Past," *San Jose Mercury,* April 25, 1906.

10. "Old Paper Tells of Earthquake of '68," *San Jose Mercury* and *Herald,* April 22, 1906.

11. Labor et al., *The Letters of Jack London,* p. 578.

12. Henry Anderson Lafler, "Literature in Peril of Fire," *Evening Post,* June 18, 1906.

13. Lafler, "My Sixty Sleepless Hours."

14. "San Francisco," *Literary Digest,* April 28, 1906.

15. Labor et al., *The Letters of Jack London,* pp. 575–576, 578, 580–582, 588–589, 591, 593. Charmian London, *The Book of Jack London,* pp. 127, 129, 130. Jack London, "The Story of an Eye-witness." Charmian London, *The Log of the Snark,* New York: Macmillan, 1916, pp. viii–ix, 15. Alex Kershaw, *Jack London: A Life,* New York: St. Martin's Press, 1998, pp. 172–173. Jack London to Professor Edgar L. Larkin, May 15, 1906, HL. Charmian London's diary, entries for May and June 1906, HL. State Earthquake Investigation Commission, *The California Earthquake of April 18, 1906,* pp. 173–176, 186–188, 209–210. *Mendocino Historical Review,* March 1982, pp. 4, 10, 14.

16. Maury Klein, *The Life and Legend of E. H. Harriman,* Chapel Hill: University of North Carolina Press, 2000, pp. 376–380.

17. Philip L. Fradkin, *A River No More: The Colorado River and the West,* Berkeley: University of California Press, 1996, p. 270. Fradkin, *Stagecoach,* pp. 171–173.

18. Steinberg, *Acts of God,* p. 30.

19. George Kennan, *E. H. Harriman: A Biography,* New York: Houghton Mifflin, 1922, pp. 75–76.

20. "San Francisco the Imperishable," Passenger Department of the Southern Pacific, San Francisco, 1906, Banc.

21. Charles S. Fee to Governor George Pardee, May 18, 1906, May 23, 1906, June 6, 1906, Banc.

22. James Horsburgh to the Stockton Chamber of Commerce, n.d., CHS.

23. Hansen and Condon, *Denial of Disaster,* pp. 103, 108, 109. Fradkin, *Magnitude 8,* pp. 132–133. *Sunset,* May 1906. *Sunset,* June–July, 1906.

24. "Two University Presidents Speak for the City: Vigorous Defense and Protest in Reply to Eastern Critics," *Sunset,* April 1908.

25. Wyatt, *Five Fires,* p. 108. Fradkin, *Magnitude 8,* pp. 258–259.

26. Steinberg, *Acts of God,* pp. 25–26.

27. For example: James Russel Wilson, *San Francisco's Horror of Earthquake and Fire,* Memorial Publishing, 1906; Charles Morris, ed., *The San Francisco Calamity,* Philadelphia: J. C. Winston, 1906; Samuel Fallows, *Complete Story of the San Francisco Horror,* Chicago: Hubert D. Russell, 1906; and Frank Thompson Searight, *The Doomed City: A Thrilling Tale,* Chicago: Laird & Lee, 1906. Geschwind, *California Earthquakes,* p. 14.

28. Robert V. Hudson, *The Writing Game: A Biography of Will Irwin,* Ames: Iowa State University Press, 1982, pp. 51–55. Oscar Lewis, ed., *San Francisco: 1906 & Before,* Ashland, Ore.: Lewis Osborne, 1973, pp. v, 11–29

29. Rufus Steele, *The City That Is,* San Francisco: A. M. Robertson, 1909, p. 90.

30. Schama, *A History of Britain,* pp. 267–268.

31. Lewis, *San Francisco,* pp. iv, 11.

32. Ibid., p. 33.

33. Gertrude Atherton, *Ancestors,* New York: Harper & Brothers, 1907, p. 595. Gertrude Atherton, *Adventures of a Novelist,* New York: Liveright, 1932, p. 404. Emily Wortis Leider, *California's Daughter: Gertrude Atherton and Her Times,* Stanford, Calif.: Stanford University Press, 1991, p. 207.

34. Susan Sontag, "On Photography (the short course)," *Los Angeles Times Book Review,* July 27, 2003.

35. Edgar A. Cohen, "With a Camera in San Francisco," *Camera Craft,* June 1906, p. 183.

36. Beaumont Newhall, *The History of Photography: From 1839 to the Present,* New York: Museum of Modern Art, 1982, pp. 128–132, 136, 167, 251–252. Helmut and Alison Gernsheim, *The History of Photography: From the Camera*

Obscura to the Beginning of the Modern Era, New York: McGraw-Hill, 1969, pp. 412–416, 422–424. Therese Heyman, "Encouraging the Artistic Impulse: The Second Generation: 1890–1925," in *Watkins to Westin: 101 Years of California Photography, 1849–1950,* Santa Barbara, Calif.: Santa Barbara Museum of Art, 1992, pp. 58–66. A. E. Suppiger, "The Tale of a Kodak," *Camera Craft,* March 1906, pp. 115–120.

37. Fayette J. Clute, "With Earthquake and Fire," *Camera Craft,* May 1906, pp. 149–154. Dr. H. D'Arcy Power, "Earthquake and Fire from a Photographer's View," *Camera Craft,* May 1906, pp. 155–160.

38. Cohen, "With a Camera in San Francisco," pp. 183–194. Arthur Inkersley, "An Amateur's Experience of Earthquake and Fire," *Camera Craft,* June 1906, pp. 195–200. A. Hildebrandt, *Airships Past and Present,* London: Archibald Constable, 1908, p. 332.

39. Genthe, *As I Remember,* pp. 89–97. Heyman, "Encouraging the Artistic Impulse," pp. 58–60. Wyatt, *Five Fires,* pp. 118–121.

40. Coleman, *Give Us a Little Smile, Baby,* pp. 143–145.

41. Hildebrandt, *Airships Past and Present,* pp. 168, 187, 287–291, 302, 332.

42. Gernsheim and Gernsheim, *The History of Photography,* p. 508. "Picture Takers Use Balloons," *San Francisco Call,* May 9, 1906. Simon Baker, "San Francisco in Ruins: The 1906 Aerial Photographs of George R. Lawrence," *Landscape,* vol. 30, number 2 (1989), pp. 9–14. "Will Photograph Ruins from the Sky," *San Francisco Examiner,* May 3, 1906. Coleman, *Give Us a Little Smile, Baby,* pp. 145–150.

DISASTER AND RACE

1. Pan, *The Impact of the 1906 Earthquake,* p. 105.

2. Horatio Putnam Livermore to his wife, Helen Livermore, April 25, 1906, private collection.

3. Pan, *The Impact of the 1906 Earthquake,* pp. 37–41, 50.

4. Ibid., pp. 43, 78. "Metcalf Reports to the President," *Chronicle,* April 29, 1906.

5. Lee Mong Kow to Governor George C. Pardee, April 21, 1906, Banc.

6. George C. Pardee to Denman Wagner, May 17, 1906, Banc.

7. Hooker, "Lessons of the Great Fire," pp. 54–55.

8. "Chinese Sent to the Golf Links," *San Francisco Chronicle,* April 28, 1906. Pan, *The Impact of the 1906 Earthquake,* pp. 43–44. "Metcalf Reports to the President," *Chronicle,* April 29, 1906. Bean, *Boss Ruef's San Francisco,* p. 8. "Chinese Colony at Foot of Van Ness," *San Francisco Chronicle,* April 27, 1906. "New Chinatown Near Fort Point," *San Francisco Chronicle,* April 29, 1906. Pan, *The Impact of the 1906 Earthquake,* p. 45.

9. "Looters Dig Up Valuables in Chinatown," *San Francisco Examiner,* April

28, 1906. "Blame Militia for Much Looting," *San Francisco Examiner,* April 28, 1906.

10. David Nicolai, director of the Pardee Home Museum, personal communication, March 24, 2003.

11. Judge Advocate report to Assistant Adjutant General, Pardee Collection, April 28, 1906, Banc. Second Lieutenant William H. Flood to Adjutant General L. B. Lauk, April 29, 1906, Banc. Brigadier General John A. Koster to Governor George C. Pardee, April 28, 1906, Banc. Pan, *The Impact of the 1906 Earthquake,* pp. 52–55.

12. "Will Find Work for Women Looters," *San Francisco Examiner,* May 4, 1906.

13. "For a New Chinatown," *New York Times,* August 8, 1906.

14. "Passing of Chinatown," *The Literary Digest,* May 5, 1906.

15. "Chinatown Is to Be Residence District," *San Francisco Examiner,* April 31, 1906. *Argonaut,* April 28, 1906. "Chinese Consul Pleads for Freedom," *San Francisco Examiner,* May 3, 1906.

16. Pan, *The Impact of the 1906 Earthquake,* p. 65.

17. Minutes of the Citizens' Committee, May 1, 1906, Banc. "Celestials Fight Being Ousted," *San Francisco Examiner,* May 7, 1906. "Chinese Merchants Desire to Remain on the Old Site," *San Francisco Call,* May 11, 1906. "The New Chinatown" and "Chinese Minister Is Coming," *San Francisco Call,* May 12, 1906. "To Resist Moving of Chinatown," *San Francisco Call,* May 17, 1906. Pan, *The Impact of the 1906 Earthquake,* pp. 66–76, 96–98. "San Francisco's New Chinatown," *New York Times,* February 11, 1908.

18. Takaki, *Strangers from a Different Shore,* pp. 113, 120–121, 124.

19. McClain, *In Search of Equality,* pp. 282–283.

20. Bailey, *Theodore Roosevelt and the Japanese-American Crisis,* p. 17.

21. "Experts Omori and Branner Declare California Is Now Immune from Heavy Shocks," *San Francisco Call,* May 20, 1906. Louderback, "Central California Earthquakes," p. 213.

22. "Dr. Omori Is Beaten Because of His Joke," *San Francisco Examiner,* July 7, 1906. Victory H. Metcalf, *Message from the President of the United States, Japanese in the City of San Francisco, Cal.,* Senate Document No. 147, December 18, 1906, pp. 15–16, 38–40. F. Omori to Governor George C. Pardee, June 26, 1906, Banc. Japanese Consul-General K. Uyeno to Governor George C. Pardee, July 7, 1906, Banc. Fradkin, *Magnitude 8,* p. 184.

23. Jordan, *The California Earthquake of 1906,* pp. 314–315.

24. Bailey, *Theodore Roosevelt and the Japanese-American Crisis,* pp. 17, 20–27. Metcalf, *Message from the President of the United States,* pp. 3–4, 7–15, 33–38. "President Adds Plea to Report on Japanese," *New York Times,* December 19, 1906.

25. Victor Low, *The Unimpressible Race: A Century of Educational Struggle by*

the Chinese in San Francisco, San Francisco: East/West Publishing, 1982, pp. 93–95. *San Francisco Municipal Reports,* 1908, pp. 683–685.

26. Raymond A. Esthus, *Theodore Roosevelt and Japan,* Seattle: University of Washington Press, 1966, pp. 128–145, 152–165. Morison, *The Letters of Theodore Roosevelt,* pp. 473–476, 521, 541–542, 608–615, 618–619, 656–657. James D. Phelan to the *Chicago Tribune,* telegram, n.d., Banc. "J. D. Phelan Sees Peril to Republic in Silent Invasion of Japanese," *Chicago Tribune,* December 7, 1906. Metcalf, *Message from the President of the United States,* pp. 3–7, 29. *San Francisco Municipal Reports,* 1908, p. 684. Takaki, *Strangers from a Different Shore,* pp. 202–203. Bailey, *Theodore Roosevelt and the Japanese-American Crisis,* pp. 43–67, 83, 124–125, 170–177, 184–192. Edmund Morris, *Theodore Rex,* New York: Random House, 2001, pp. 482–485.

27. "Social Order at Stake in Unhappy San Francisco," *New York Times,* May 26, 1907. Bailey, *Theodore Roosevelt and the Japanese-American Crisis,* pp. 194–217, 244–251, 262–263, 298–301. Esthus, *Theodore Roosevelt and Japan,* pp. 167–195. Morris, *Theodore Rex,* pp. 493–495. Morison, *The Letters of Theodore Roosevelt,* pp. 671–672, 717–719. Fradkin, *Magnitude 8,* pp. 167–211, 213–267, 441.

THE POLITICS OF DISASTER

1. Walton Bean to John Galvin, June 25, 1975, Banc. John Galvin to Walton Bean, August 5, 1975, Banc. Galvin, a veteran of the hurly-burly of Boston politics, wrote Bean that he understood why James Curley of Boston and Richard Daley of Chicago were called bosses: "But a well-educated man like Ruef is a different kind of political figure: more like the fellows from the big corporations who are in Washington trying to explain their 'contributions' to politicians and political parties in many different parts of the world." Galvin, who worked the Boston precincts for John F. Kennedy, added, somewhat admiringly: "He [Ruef] certainly was an 'operator.'"

2. James J. Rawls and Walton Bean, *California: An Interpretive History,* 6th ed., New York: McGraw-Hill, 1993, p. 242. Kahn, *Imperial San Francisco,* p. 3. Walton Bean to Edward I. Sugarman, January 1, 1947, Banc. Various correspondence between Franklin Hichborn and James D. Phelan, 1912–1915, Banc.

3. Rudolph Spreckels to Walton Bean, November 20, 1946, Banc. Fremont Older to Guido Marks, May 20, 1912, Banc. Fremont Older, *My Own Story,* New York: Macmillan, 1926, pp. 174–175. Fremont Older, *Growing Up,* San Francisco: San Francisco Call-Bulletin, 1931, pp. 154–155. James D. Phelan to Julia Heynemann, February 12, 1908, Banc.

4. George E. Mowry, *The California Progressives,* Berkeley: University of California Press, 1951, p. 37.

5. Older, *My Own Story,* pp. 142–144. Fremont Older to James D. Phelan,

November 1, 1907, Banc. Bean, *Boss Ruef's San Francisco,* pp. 286, 304–309, 312. Judge William P. Lawlor to James D. Phelan, November 11, 1912, Banc. Judge William P. Lawlor to James D. Phelan, March 31, 1915, Banc. Henry Ach et al., "Misconduct of Judge," Appellant's Opening Brief, District Court of Appeal, First Appellate District, *The People of the State of California v. Abraham Ruef,* July 22, 1910, pp. 34–59, 522–530, Banc.

6. Q, "Ruef—A Jew under Torture," *Overland Monthly,* November 1907, pp. 517–519.

7. Earl Pomoroy, introduction to *Upbuilders,* by Lincoln Steffens, Seattle: University of Washington Press, 1968, pp. ix, xx, xxix–xxx. Lincoln Steffens, "The Mote and the Bean: A Fact Novel," *American Magazine,* November 1907, pp. 28, 36. Lincoln Steffens, *The Autobiography of Lincoln Steffens,* New York: Harcourt, Brace, 1931, p. 556. Lincoln Steffens to Fremont Older, n.d. (1910?), Banc.

8. Harry J. Cooper, interviewed by Francis J. Farquahar, 1959, Regional Oral History Office, Bancroft Library, University of California, p. 2.

9. "Rabbi Wise Calls the Vigilante Spirit," *Liberator,* October 16, 1909. Bean, *Boss Ruef's San Francisco,* p. 289. "The Truth of the Matter," *Jewish Times,* March 20, 1908. M. Lissner to Jacob Nieto, January 14, 1908, Western Jewish History Center, Berkeley. Narell, *Our City,* pp. 295, 298. Danny Cotton, "The Curley Boss—Abraham Ruef," docent training manual, April 20, 1986, Judah Magnes Museum, Berkeley.

10. "Beneath the Surface in San Francisco," *New York Times,* July 7, 1907. Others who saw the disaster as the motivating event were the following: Bean, *Boss Ruef's San Francisco,* p. viii; and James D. Hart, *A Companion to California,* Berkeley: University of California Press, 1987, p. 459.

11. Mowry, *The California Progressives,* pp. 14–22, 91–94.

12. William Deverell and Tom Sitton, *California Progressivism Revisited,* Berkeley: University of California Press, 1994, pp. 6, 24, 26.

13. Transcript of the mass meeting at Dreamland Pavilion prepared for the League of Justice, November 14, 1908, pp. 21, 28, Banc.

14. Various communications back and forth between Phelan and the National Bank of Commerce, March and April, 1907, Banc. The New York bank—besides placing Phelan's stock orders, loaning him money, and allowing him to overdraw considerable amounts—held the large account of the San Francisco Relief and Red Cross funds. A bank official thanked Phelan for "the kindly feeling" that prompted him to deposit the relief funds in the bank. Zoeth S. Eldridge, president of the National Bank of the Pacific, to James D. Phelan, December 20, 1906, Banc. Older, *My Own Story,* pp. 16–18, 24–27.

15. "Beneath the Surface in San Francisco," *New York Times,* July 7, 1907.

16. James D. Phelan to George L. Duval, November 16, 1907 and March 19, 1908, Banc.

17. Walsh, "Abe Ruef Was No Boss," pp. 12–13.

18. Mowry, *The California Progressives,* pp. 86–104. Deverell and Sitton, *California Progressivism Revisited,* pp. 5–6. Deverell and Sitton use similar descriptions, derived mainly from Mowry, as does Kevin Starr, *Inventing the Dream: California through the Progressive Era,* New York: Oxford University Press, 1985, pp. 235–237, 268. See also Ethington, *The Public City,* pp. 287–407.

19. George Kennan, "The Fight for Reform in San Francisco," *McClure's,* September 1907, p. 555.

20. Older, *Growing Up,* pp. 146–151.

21. Older, *My Own Story,* pp. v–vii, 2–3, 14–38.

22. Cora Older to Walton Bean, April 25, 1952, Banc.

23. Older, *My Own Story,* pp. 57–69.

24. Bean, *Boss Ruef's San Francisco,* p. 69.

25. William R. Hunt, *Front Page Detective: William J. Burns and the Detective Profession, 1880–1930,* Bowling Green, Ohio: Bowling Green State University Popular Press, 1990, pp. 1–33, 37, 45, 195.

26. Bean, *Boss Ruef's San Francisco,* pp. 55–71. Cora Older, "The Story of a Reformer's Wife," *McClure's,* July 1909, p. 279.

27. Lincoln Steffens, "Rudolph Spreckels: A Business Man Fighting for His City," *American Magazine,* February 1908, pp. 390–402. Lincoln Steffens, "The Mote and the Beam: A Fact Novel," *American Magazine,* November 1907, p. 36. Bean, *Boss Ruef's San Francisco,* pp. 71–77. Cora Older, "The Story of a Reformer's Wife," p. 280.

28. "Fremont Older's Story of the Bulletin," n.d., Banc.

29. Mowry, *The California Progressives,* p. 31. Bean, *Boss Ruef's San Francisco,* pp. 161–163.

30. James D. Phelan to Francis J. Heney, December 18, 1906, Banc. Bean, *Boss Ruef's San Francisco,* pp. 140–144, 270–271.

31. Cora Older, "The Story of a Reformer's Wife," pp. 164–170, 282.

32. Theodore Bonnet, *The Regenerators: A Study of the Graft Prosecution of San Francisco,* San Francisco: Pacific Printing, 1911, p. 250.

33. George H. Boke to James D. Phelan, July 18, 1908, Banc.

34. Memo from W. H. Payson, secretary, to members, n.d., Banc.

35. San Francisco Graft Trial Collection, vol. 32, Banc, pp. 21, 26–27, 158–165, 173–174, 178, 200–201, 204, 209, 226, 231, 233–234, 237–238, 254–255, 270–289.

36. Ach et al., "Misconduct of Judge," p. 58. Lincoln Steffens, "An Apology for Graft," *American Magazine,* June 1908, p. 128. Bean, *Boss Ruef's San Francisco,* p. 180.

37. Dreamland Pavilion transcript, pp. 6, 23.

38. Fremont Older to James D. Phelan, November 1, 1907, Banc.

39. Older, *My Own Story,* pp. 168–169.

40. William P. Lawlor to James D. Phelan, November 12, 1912, and March 31, 1915, Banc.

41. Cora Older, "The Story of a Reformer's Wife," p. 292.

42. Rudolph I. Coffee, "Jewish Conditions in San Francisco," *Western States Jewish Historical Quarterly,* April 1976, pp. 252–253. Bean, *Boss Ruef's San Francisco,* pp. 179–187, 200–201.

43. Q, "Ruef—A Jew under Torture," pp. 518–519.

44. Hunt, *Front Page Detective,* pp. 42–45, 47.

45. "San Francisco's Fate in Balance," *New York Times,* July 29, 1907.

46. "Transcript on Appeal," First Appellate District Court of Appeal, *The People of the State of California v. Eugene E. Schmitz,* October 1907, pp. 643–645, Banc.

47. Q, "Ruef—A Jew under Torture," p. 519.

48. Bean, *Boss Ruef's San Francisco,* pp. 202–204.

49. Older, *My Own Story,* pp. 165–166. Almost the same account of the meeting was given by Rabbi Nieto in a deposition.

50. Older, *My Own Story,* pp. 159–160, 166–167. Bean, *Boss Ruef's San Francisco,* pp. 198–200, 204–213. "Transcript on Appeal," pp. 646–649.

51. Bean, *Boss Ruef's San Francisco,* pp. 214–218.

52. "San Francisco's Fate in Balance." "Testimony on Appeal," pp. 646–647, 654–658.

53. Bean, *Boss Ruef's San Francisco,* pp. 108–118, 131–137, 218–228, 244–245, 268–270, 315–316.

54. "Politics Play Large Part in Calhoun Case," *Boston Globe,* June 30, 1909. "Beneath the Surface in San Francisco," *New York Times,* July 7, 1907. Bonnet, *The Regenerators,* pp. 59–63.

55. Bean, *Boss Ruef's San Francisco,* pp. 256–263. Cora Older, "The Story of a Reformer's Wife," pp. 286–288. Fremont Older to James D. Phelan, May 31, 1910, Banc.

56. "Public Service Criticism Is Boomerang to Critic," *San Francisco Examiner,* September 26, 1908. James D. Phelan to George Cortelyou, secretary of the treasury, September 28, 1908, Banc.

57. Theodore Roosevelt to James D. Phelan, March 25, 1907, Banc. Benjamin Ide Wheeler to William Loeb, secretary to President Roosevelt, July 3, 1907, Banc. Franklin Lane to Fremont Older, November 20, 1907, Banc.

58. Hunt, *Front Page Detective,* p. 38. Form letter ending "Stop These Papers. Do It Today," n.d., Banc.

59. Dreamland Pavilion transcript, p. 24.

60. James D. Phelan to Dr. C. N. Lathrop, June 5, 1908, Banc. "James D. Phelan Praises Work of F. J. Heney," *Los Angeles Express,* August 21, 1908.

61. Bean, *Boss Ruef's San Francisco,* pp. 250–252. Cora Older, "The Story of a Reformer's Wife," pp. 289–290. Older, *My Own Story,* pp. 128–135. Bonnet, *The Regenerators,* pp. 171–172.

62. "James D. Phelan Praises Work of F. J. Heney," *Los Angeles Express,* August 21, 1908.

63. Older, *My Own Story,* pp. 148–149. Bonnet, *The Regenerators,* p. 166. Bean, *Boss Ruef's San Francisco,* pp. 275–277. Cora Older, "The Story of a Reformer's Wife," p. 291.

64. "The Truth of the Matter," *Jewish Times,* March 20, 1908. "Startling Revelations in the Graft Prosecutions as Disclosed by Rabbi Nieto," *Emanu-El,* January 31, 1908. Bean, *Boss Ruef's San Francisco,* pp. 272–275, 277–278.

65. Bean, *Boss Ruef's San Francisco,* pp. 282–285. Older, *My Own Story,* pp. 140–142. Dreamland Pavilion transcript, p. 2. Ach et al., "Misconduct of Judge," p. 35.

66. Bean, *Boss Ruef's San Francisco,* pp. 284–285.

67. Ach et al., "Misconduct of Judge," pp. 24–59.

68. Older, *My Own Story,* pp. 142–144.

69. Richard Coke Lower, *A Bloc of One: The Political Career of Hiram W. Johnson,* Stanford, Calif.: Stanford University Press, 1993, pp. 13–17.

70. Older to Marks, March 20, 1912.

71. Indictments against one remaining defendant were dismissed the next week. "Schmitz Indictments Dismissed," *San Francisco Bulletin,* May 25, 1912.

72. For a sampling of articles see Abraham Ruef, "The Road I Traveled: An Autobiographic Account of My Career from University to Prison, with an Intimate Recital of the Corrupt Alliance between Big Business and Politics in San Francisco," *San Francisco Bulletin,* May 20 and 21, 1912. "For the Parole of Ruef," *San Francisco Bulletin,* September 5, 1912. "The People Do Not Rule," *San Francisco Bulletin,* September 14, 1912. "Stanford Professor in Temper at the Bulletin's Attitude," *San Francisco Bulletin,* September 11, 1912.

73. Abe Ruef to Bertha Altmann, 1915, CHS.

74. Bean, *Boss Ruef's San Francisco,* pp. 306–309. A. Ruef to the Prison Directors, July 14, 1911, Banc. Frannie Heppner oral history, 1974, Western Jewish History Center.

75. Bean, *Boss Ruef's San Francisco,* pp. 309–315.

76. Rudolph Spreckels to Walton Bean, December 12, 1946, Banc.

77. Older, *My Own Story,* pp. 173–174, 179, 331.

78. Older expressed his regret in many forums, including editorials in the *Bulletin,* speeches, and his autobiography. He was castigated as a turncoat by all the Progressives, except Franklin Lane and Lincoln Steffens. Older, *Growing Up,* p. 155.

1. Numerous articles in the *San Francisco Examiner,* including those for December 2, 5, 6, 10, 1910.

2. H. Wiley Hitchcock and Stanley Sadie, eds., *The New Grove Dictionary of American Music,* vol. 4, London: Macmillan, 1986, p. 366.

3. *San Francisco Examiner,* December 13 and 21, 1910.

4. Numerous stories in the December 25, 1910, issues of the *San Francisco Examiner, San Francisco Chronicle,* and *San Francisco Call* and the December 26, 1910, issue of the *Bulletin.* Mary R. B. McAdie, ed., *Alexander McAdie: Scientist and Writer,* Charlottesville, Va.: M. R. B. McAdie, 1949, pp. 157–159.

5. Madame Tetrazzini, *My Life of Song,* London: Cassell, 1912, pp. 246–255, 294. Charles Neilson Gattey, *Luisa Tetrazzini the Florentine Nightingale,* Portland, Ore.: Amadeus Press, 1995, pp. 45–60, 130–145, 171–175.

6. "City Launches Campaign for Big Fair," *San Francisco Examiner,* December 8, 1908.

7. James D. Phelan to Rufus P. Jennings, August 14, 1908, Banc.

8. Exposition Issue, *Sunset,* December 1910. A. C. David, "The New San Francisco," *Architectural Record,* January 1912, pp. 4–26.

9. Burton Benedict, *The Anthropology of World's Fairs,* Berkeley: Lowie Museum of Anthropology, 1983, pp. vii, 13, 24, 60, 66–67, 73–74, 77, 80–81, 87–88, 98–99, 108, 114, 158, 161–163. Frank Morton Todd, *The Story of the Exposition,* vols. 1 and 5, New York: G. P. Putnam's Sons, 1921, pp. 35, 42, 44, 52, 92, 96, 247. Starr, *Americans and the California Dream,* pp. 296, 302–305.

10. Hansen and Condon, *Denial of Disaster,* pp. 137, 139, 150. Fradkin, *Magnitude 8,* pp. 194–195, 198.

AUTHOR'S NOTE

1. James C. Cooper and Karl Borden, "Making Public History Displays Understandable: The Interpretation of Wages and Prices in Public Historical Displays," *The Public Historian,* Spring 1997, pp. 9–29.

SELECTED READINGS

I have selected only those books for which there is a fair chance of finding them in larger public and higher education libraries. The selections are arranged by chapter as they were first used in the text. I have moved a few to better correspond with the principal topics they address.

Three predominantly visual records are very helpful. I recommend two photo-driven books: William Bronson's *The Earth Shook, the Sky Burned* and Gladys Hansen and Emmet Condon's *Denial of Disaster*. I also recommend one video: *The Great San Francisco Earthquake: 1906* was written and produced by Tom Weidlinger for the first PBS *American Experience* program.

Some of the books, including the two volumes of the report of the State Earthquake Investigation Commission and many of the manuscripts, are available on the Bancroft Library's 1906 San Francisco earthquake and fire online archive, which can be reached through a link at http://bancroft.berkeley.edu/collections. With the centennial of the earthquake and fire approaching, the list of books and visual materials will undoubtedly lengthen.

BEGINNINGS

Castel, Albert E. *Decision in the West: The Atlanta Campaign of 1864.* Lawrence: University Press of Kansas, 1992.

Groom, Winston. *Shrouds of Glory: From Atlanta to Nashville: The Last Great Campaign of the Civil War.* New York: Atlantic Monthly Press, 1995.

Hittell, John S. *A History of the City of San Francisco and Incidentally of the State of California.* San Francisco: A. L. Bancroft, 1878.

Key, William. *The Battle of Atlanta and the Georgia Campaign.* New York: Twayne Publishers, 1958.

Kroeber, A. L. *Yurok Myths.* Berkeley: University of California Press, 1976.

Langewiesche, William. *American Ground: Unbuilding the World Trade Center.* New York: North Point Press, 2002.

Lloyd, B. E. *Lights and Shades in San Francisco.* San Francisco: A. L. Bancroft, 1876. (Repr. Berkeley Hills Books, 1999.)

McMurry, Richard M. *Atlanta 1864: Last Chance for the Confederacy.* Lincoln: University of Nebraska Press, 2000.

Muller, Charles G. *The Darkest Day: 1814: The Washington-Baltimore Campaign.* Philadelphia: J. B. Lippincott, 1963.

Platt, Rutherford H. *Disasters and Democracy: The Politics of Extreme Natural Events.* Washington, D.C.: Island Press, 1999.

———. "Natural Hazards of the San Francisco Mega-City." In *Crucibles of Hazard: Mega-Cities and Disasters in Transition.* New York: United Nations University Press, 1999.

Steinberg, Ted. *Acts of God: The Unnatural History of Natural Disaster in America.* New York: Oxford University Press, 2000.

Whitehorne, Joseph A. *The Battle for Baltimore, 1814.* Baltimore: The Nautical & Aviation Publishing Company of America, 1997.

THE TALE OF TWO CITIES

Bond, Horatio, ed. *Fire and the Air War.* Boston: National Fire Protection Association, 1952.

Chen, Yong, et al., eds. *The Great Tanshan Earthquake of 1976.* Oxford, England: Pergamon Press, 1988.

Gess, Denise, and William Lutz. *Firestorm at Peshtigo: A Town, Its People, and the Deadliest Fire in American History.* New York: Henry Holt, 2002.

Hanson, Neil. *The Dreadful Judgment: The True Story of the Great Fire of London 1666.* New York: Doubleday, 2001.

Larson, Eric. *Isaac's Storm: A Man, a Time, and the Deadliest Hurricane in History.* New York: Vintage Books, 1999.

Mason, Herbert Molloy Jr. *Death from the Sea: Our Greatest Natural Disaster.* New York: Dial Press, 1972.

McComb, David G. *Galveston: A History.* Austin: University of Texas Press, 1986.

Miller, Ross. *The Great Chicago Fire.* Urbana: University of Illinois Press, 2000.

Pyne, Stephen J. *Fire in America: A Cultural History of Wildland and Rural Fire.* Seattle: University of Washington Press, 1997.

Pyne, Stephen J., et al. *Introduction to Wildland Fire.* New York: John Wiley & Sons, 1996.

Rosen, Christine Meisner. *The Limits of Power: Great Fires and the Process of City Growth in America.* New York: Cambridge University Press, 1986.

Sawislak, Karen. *Smoldering City: Chicagoans and the Great Fire, 1871–1874.* Chicago: University of Chicago Press, 1995.

Sebald, W. G. *On the Natural History of Destruction.* New York: Random House, 2003.

Smith, Carl. *Urban Disorder and the Shape of Belief: The Great Chicago Fire, the Haymarket Bomb, and the Model Town of Pullman.* Chicago: University of Chicago Press, 1995.

Tang, Xiren. *A General History of Earthquake Studies in China.* Beijing: Science Press, 1988.

Adams, Ansel. *Ansel Adams: An Autobiography.* Boston: Little, Brown, 1985.

Atherton, Gertrude. *California: An Intimate History.* New York: Harper & Brothers, 1914.

Bolt, Bruce A. *Earthquakes.* New York: W. H. Freeman, 1993.

Brechin, Gray. *Imperial San Francisco: Urban Power, Earthly Ruin.* Berkeley: University of California Press, 2001.

Chase, Marilyn. *The Barbary Plague: The Black Death in Victorian San Francisco.* New York: Random House, 2003.

Craddock, Susan. *City of Plagues: Disease, Poverty, and Deviance in San Francisco.* Minneapolis: University of Minnesota Press, 2000.

Crichton, Judy. *American 1900: The Turning Point.* New York: Henry Holt, 1998.

Fradkin, Philip L. *Magnitude 8: Earthquakes and Life along the San Andreas Fault.* Berkeley: University of California Press, 1999.

———. *The Seven States of California: A Natural and Human History.* Berkeley: University of California Press, 1997.

Genthe, Arnold. *As I Remember.* New York: Reynal & Hitchcock, 1936.

Geschwind, Carl-Henry. *California Earthquakes: Science, Risk & the Politics of Hazard Mitigation.* Baltimore: Johns Hopkins University Press, 2001.

Hennings, Robert E. *James D. Phelan and the Wilson Progressives of California.* New York: Garland Publishing, 1985.

Hough, Susan Elizabeth. *Earthshaking Science: What We Know (and Don't Know about Earthquakes).* Princeton, N.J.: Princeton University Press, 2002.

Issel, William, and Robert W. Cherny. *San Francisco, 1865–1932.* Berkeley: University of California Press, 1986.

Kahn, Judd. *Imperial San Francisco: Politics and Planning in an American City 1897–1906.* Lincoln: University of Nebraska Press, 1979.

Litehiser, J. J. *Observatory Seismology.* Berkeley: University of California Press, 1989.

McClain, Charles J. *In Search of Equality: The Chinese Struggle against Discrimination in Nineteenth-Century America.* Berkeley: University of California Press, 1994.

Scott, Mel. *The San Francisco Bay Area: A Metropolis in Perspective.* Berkeley: University of California Press, 1959.

Shah, Nayan. *Contagious Divides: Epidemics and Race in San Francisco's Chinatown.* Berkeley: University of California Press, 2001.

Smith, Michael L. *Pacific Visions: California Scientists and the Environment 1850–1915.* New Haven, Conn.: Yale University Press, 1987.

Starr, Kevin. *Americans and the California Dream 1850–1915.* New York: Oxford University Press, 1973.

Walsh, James P., and Timothy J. O'Keefe. *Legacy of a Native Son: James Duval Phelan & Villa Montalvo.* Los Gatos, Calif.: Forbes Mill Press, 1993.

THE HOTEL AND THE OPERA HOUSE

Barrymore, John. *Confessions of an Actor.* Indianapolis: Bobbs-Merrill, 1925.

Barthelemy, Richard. *Memories of Caruso.* Plainsboro, N.J.: La Scala Autographa, 1979.

Greenfield, Howard. *Caruso.* New York: G. P. Putnam's Sons, 1983.

Key, Pierre V. R. *Enrico Caruso: A Biography.* New York: Vienna House, 1972.

Lewis, Oscar, and Carroll D. Hall. *Bonanza Inn: America's First Luxury Hotel.* New York: Alfred A. Knopf, 1939.

Maxwell, Elsa. *R.S.V.P.* Boston: Little, Brown, 1954.

Scott, Michael. *The Great Caruso.* London: Hamish Hamilton, 1988.

WEDNESDAY, THURSDAY, AND FRIDAY, APRIL 18, 19, AND 20, 1906

(The following titles cover all three days.)

Bain, David Howard. *Sitting in Darkness: Americans in the Philippines.* Boston: Houghton Mifflin, 1984.

Barker, Malcolm E. *Three Fearful Days: San Francisco Memoirs of the 1906 Earthquake & Fire.* San Francisco: Londonborn Publications, 1998.

Bonadio, Felice A. *A. P. Giannini: Banker of America.* Berkeley: University of California Press, 1994.

Bronson, William. *The Earth Shook, the Sky Burned.* Garden City, New York: Doubleday, 1959.

Fradkin, Philip L. *Stagecoach: Wells Fargo and the American West.* New York: Simon & Schuster, 2002.

Hansen, Gladys, and Emmet Condon. *Denial of Disaster: The Untold Story and Photographs of the San Francisco Earthquake and Fire of 1906.* San Francisco: Cameron, 1989.

Hillenbrand, Laura. *Seabiscuit: An American Legend.* New York: Random House, 2001.

James, Marquis, and Bessie Rowland James. *Biography of a Bank: The Story of Bank of America, N. T. & S. A.* New York: Harper & Brothers, 1954.

James, William. *Memories and Studies.* New York: Longmans, Green, 1911.

Kennedy, John Castillo. *The Great Earthquake and Fire: San Francisco, 1906.* New York: William Morrow, 1963.

Kurzman, Dan. *Disaster: The Great San Francisco Earthquake and Fire of 1906.* New York: William Morrow, 2001.

Labor, Earle, et al., eds. *The Letters of Jack London.* Vol. 2 (1906–1912). Stanford, Calif.: Stanford University Press, 1988.

London, Charmian. *The Book of Jack London.* Vol. 2. New York: Century, 1921.

Millard, Bailey. *History of the San Francisco Bay Region.* Vol. 1. New York: American Historical Society, 1924.

Nasaw, David. *The Chief: The Life of William Randolph Hearst.* New York: Houghton Mifflin, 2000.

Nash, Gerald D. *A. P. Giannini and the Bank of America.* Norman: University of Oklahoma Press, 1992.

Proctor, Ben. *William Randolph Hearst: The Early Years, 1863–1910.* New York: Oxford University Press, 1998.

Rickard, T. A., ed. *After Earthquake and Fire.* San Francisco: Mining and Scientific Press, 1906.

Thomas, Gordon, and Max Morgan Witts. *The San Francisco Earthquake.* New York: Stein and Day, 1971.

Young, John P. *Journalism in California.* San Francisco: Chronicle Publishing, 1915.

THE RELIEF EFFORT

Alexander, David. *Natural Disasters.* London: UCL Press, 1993.

Douty, Christopher M. *The Economics of Localized Disasters: The 1906 San Francisco Disaster.* New York: Arno Press, 1977.

Hurd, Charles. *The Compact History of the American Red Cross.* New York: Hawthorn Books, 1959.

Moorehead, Caroline. *Dunant's Dream: War, Switzerland and the History of the Red Cross.* New York: Carrol & Graf, 1999.

O'Connor, Charles J., et al. *San Francisco Relief Survey: The Organization and Methods of Relief Used after the Earthquake and Fire of April 18, 1906.* New York: Russell Sage Foundation, 1913.

Shore, James H., ed. *Disaster Stress Studies: New Methods and Findings.* Washington, D.C.: American Psychiatric Press, 1986.

THE UPBUILDING OF SAN FRANCISCO

Freeman, John Ripley. *Earthquake Damage and Earthquake Insurance.* New York: McGraw-Hill, 1932.

Haas, J. Eugene, et al., eds. *Reconstruction Following Disaster.* Cambridge, Mass.: MIT Press, 1977.

Jordan, David Starr. *The California Earthquake of 1906.* San Francisco: A. M. Robertson, 1907.

Pyne, Stephen J. *Grove Karl Gilbert: A Great Engine of Research.* Austin: University of Texas Press, 1980, pp. 228–231.

State Earthquake Investigation Commission. *The California Earthquake of April 18, 1906,* Andrew C. Lawson, ed. Vol. 1. Washington, D.C., 1908. (Reprinted in 1969.)

Vaughan, Frances E. *Andrew C. Lawson: Scientist, Teacher, Philosopher.* Glendale, Calif.: Arthur H. Clark, 1970.

THE CULTURE OF DISASTER

Atherton, Gertrude. *Adventures of a Novelist.* New York: Liveright, 1932.

———. *Ancestors.* New York: Harper & Brothers, 1907.

Coleman, Harry J. *Give Us a Little Smile, Baby.* New York: E. P. Dutton, 1943.

Gernsheim, Helmut, and Alison Gernsheim. *The History of Photography: From the Camera Obscura to the Beginning of the Modern Era.* New York: McGraw-Hill, 1969.

Heyman, Therese. "Encouraging the Artistic Impulse: The Second Generation: 1890–1925." In *Watkins to Westin: 101 Years of California Photography, 1849–1950.* Santa Barbara, Calif.: Santa Barbara Museum of Art, 1992.

Hildebrandt, A. *Airships Past and Present.* London: Archibald Constable, 1908.

Hudson, Robert V. *The Writing Game: A Biography of Will Irwin.* Ames: Iowa State University Press, 1982.

Irwin, Will. *The City That Was: A Requiem of Old San Francisco.* New York: B. W. Huebsch, 1906.

Kershaw, Alex. *Jack London: A Life.* New York: St. Martin's Press, 1998.

Leider, Emily Wortis. *California's Daughter: Gertrude Atherton and Her Times.* Stanford, Calif.: Stanford University Press, 1991.

Lewis, Oscar, ed. *San Francisco: 1906 & Before.* Ashland, Ore.: Lewis Osborne, 1973.

London, Charmian. *The Log of the Snark.* New York: Macmillan, 1916.

Newhall, Beaumont. *The History of Photography: From 1839 to the Present.* New York: Museum of Modern Art, 1982.

Steele, Rufus. *The City That Is.* San Francisco: A. M. Robertson, 1909.

Wyatt, David. *Five Fires: Race, Catastrophe, and the Shaping of California.* Reading, Mass.: Addison-Wesley, 1997.

DISASTER AND RACE

Bailey, Thomas A. *Theodore Roosevelt and the Japanese-American Crisis.* Stanford, Calif.: Stanford University Press, 1934.

Esthus, Raymond A. *Theodore Roosevelt and Japan.* Seattle: University of Washington Press, 1966.

Low, Victor. *The Unimpressible Race: A Century of Educational Struggle by the Chinese in San Francisco.* San Francisco: East/West Publishing, 1982.

Morison, Elting E., ed. *The Letters of Theodore Roosevelt.* Vol. 5. Cambridge, Mass.: Harvard University Press, 1952.

Morris, Edmund. *Theodore Rex.* New York: Random House, 2001.

Pan, Erica Y. Z. *The Impact of the 1906 Earthquake on San Francisco's Chinatown.* New York: Peter Lang, 1995.

Takaki, Ronald. *Strangers from a Distant Shore: A History of Asian Americans.* New York: Penguin, 1990.

THE POLITICS OF DISASTER

Bean, Walton. *Boss Ruef's San Francisco: The Story of the Union Labor Party, Big Business, and the Graft Prosecution.* Berkeley: University of California Press, 1952.

Bonnet, Theodore. *The Regenerators: A Study of the Graft Prosecution of San Francisco.* San Francisco: Pacific Printing, 1911.

Deverell, William, and Tom Sitton. *California Progressivism Revisited.* Berkeley: University of California Press, 1994.

Ethington, Philip J. *The Public City: The Political Construction of Urban Life in San Francisco 1850–1900.* Berkeley: University of California Press, 2001.

Hichborn, Franklin. *The System: As Uncovered by the San Francisco Graft Prosecution.* San Francisco: James H. Barry, 1915.

Hunt, William R. *Front Page Detective: William J. Burns and the Detective Profession, 1880–1930.* Bowling Green, Ohio: Bowling Green State University Popular Press, 1990.

Mowry, George E. *The California Progressives.* Berkeley: University of California Press, 1951.

Older, Fremont. *Growing Up,* San Francisco: San Francisco Call-Bulletin, 1931.

———. *My Own Story.* New York: Macmillan, 1926.

Rawls, James J., and Walton Bean. *California: An Interpretive History.* New York: McGraw-Hill, 1993.

Starr, Kevin. *Inventing the Dream: California through the Progressive Era.* New York: Oxford University Press, 1985.

Steffens, Lincoln. *The Autobiography of Lincoln Steffens.* New York: Harcourt, Brace, 1931.

Wilson, Harold S. *McClure's Magazine and the Muckrakers.* Princeton, N.J.: Princeton University Press, 1970.

THE FAT LADY SINGS

Benedict, Burton. *The Anthropology of World's Fairs.* Berkeley: Lowie Museum of Anthropology, 1983.

Gattey, Charles Neilson. *Luisa Tetrazzini the Florentine Nightingale.* Portland: Amadeus Press, 1995.

Tetrazzini, Madame. *My Life of Song.* London: Cassell and Company, 1912.

Todd, Frank Morton. *The Story of the Exposition.* Vols. 1 and 5. New York: G. P. Putnam's Sons, 1921.

INDEX

Boke, George H., 318
Bolt, Bruce A., 191, 262
bombs, incendiary, 17–18
Bonanza Inn (Lewis), 94
Bonner, Geraldine, 269
Bonnet, Theodore, 318
books about the earthquake and fire, 276–80
Boulder Creek, 156
Boyce, R. W., 152–53
Bradley, Captain, 206
Branner, George, 149, 255, 256, 258–60
Branner, John Casper, 231–32
Briggs, Raymond W., 111–12
Brown, George F., 71
Brown, J. W., 159
Brown, Nellie May, 134–35
Brunswick Hotel, 106
Brunswick House, 88
Brunvand, Jan Harold, 15
bubonic plague, 35–36
building materials and design, 22, 39, 150–52, 240–42. *See also under* Gilbert
building requirements, new, 226, 243, 244, 344
buildings: crumbled like houses of sand, 54–55; damaged and destroyed, 187
Bulletin, 265, 313; alliance with Southern Pacific, 313, 314. *See also under* Older
Burkhalter, Charles, 255
Burnham, Daniel, 18, 36, 228
Burnham Plan, 226, 228
Burns, Thomas A., 55–56
Burns, William J., 246, 322–25, 334, 335; Fremont Older and, 322, 331; on Haas's death, 333; investigation of Schmitz and Ruef, 307, 315, 316, 322, 324, 325, 331; James Gallagher and, 331; jury tampering, 318; questionable investigative techniques, 307, 314, 331; William Biggy and, 322, 334; William Hunt's biography of, 322–23
Byerly, Perry, 261
Byrne, James W., 108

cadets, 137–38, 205
Calhoun, Patrick, 327–28

California Historical Society Library, 253
California National Guard, 64
California Naval Militia, 136–37
California Progressives, 312; one legacy of the, 306–7. *See also* Progressive movement
California Promotional Committee, 189
California Society of New York, 133
California Women's Hospital, 102
Call Building, 84, 88, 240–42
Call-Chronicle-Examiner, joint edition of, 64, 89
Camera Craft, 281–84
cameras, 281, 285; attached to balloons and kites, 287
Campbell, Wallace W., 255
camps, 182, 209–10, 215, 291; building, 210; closing of last, 225; drawbacks, 210–11; separate but (un)equal, 211
Camps Department, 215
Camp Sepulveda, 181
cannons, 128
Canther, D. N., 159
Carnegie, Andrew, 186
Carnegie Institution, 256
carpenters, 210
Caruso, Enrico, 198, 284–85; cross-country tour, 42–43; at Grand Opera House, 44–47; at Palace Hotel during fire, 90–92; in San Francisco, 43–44; singing, 339, 341; vowed not to return to San Francisco, 339
Cather, Willa, 44
Catholics, 28, 212
cattle, 57
Central Emergency Hospital, 99, 100
Chamberlain, George E., 132–33
Chamber of Commerce, 155, 233–35
charity workers, 220, 221
Chase, Marilyn, 223
Chicago fire of 1871, 4, 13–18, 236, 238
children, classified ads to reconnect parents and, 217
Chile Relief Committee, 199
chimneys, repairing, 206
china, stealing pieces of, 292–93
Chinatown(s), 34–35, 39, 109–11; attempts

David Street, 54, 55

dead persons brought to hospitals, 101

deaths, 56, 60–61, 70, 151–52; list of persons killed, 190; from militia/martial law, 65, 67–69, 80, 101–2, 140–43, 189

death toll(s), 4, 5, 60, 140, 150, 160, 188–91; reported by Adolphus Greely, 140; uncertainty regarding total, 345–46; underestimated, 189–91

Deenen, Jeremiah, 206

Deering, Frank, 123

Deering, Mrs., 269

democracy, 65, 82, 215

"dependent class," 199

Derleth, Charles Jr., 148–49, 152, 154, 157

Deverell, William, 310

"devil wagons," 102–4

Devine, Edward T., 201, 202, 208, 209, 291

Devlin, F. J., 236–38

Dewey, Guion H., 92–93

de Young, M. H., 176, 229, 265

diamonds, 45, 143

Dinan, Chief of Police, 64, 67

dining out in Paris, 144–45

disasters: "during" vs. "after" periods of, 195; earthquake and fire of 1906 compared with other, 3–5; natural, 6. See also postdisaster cities

disease: relief efforts and, 219, 221–24; sanitation and, 221–23. See also smallpox

dislocations, 226. See also refugees

Dixon, Maynard, 44, 274

doctors, 132, 175. See also hospitals

Dolge, William, 309

donations. See relief effort(s)

Doubleday, D. G., 117

Dougherty, John, 70, 78

Dreyfus, Alfred, 30, 307

Drum, John S., 248, 252–54

Dunne, Frank H., 319–20, 326

dynamiting. See explosives

Earth Dragon, 110

earthquake and fire of 1906: characterizations of, 3, 224 (see also books; magazines; newspapers); compared with other disasters, 3–5; economic impact, 4; experiences of, xiii–xvii, 61–62, 92–93, 145–46, 150 (see also London, Jack); experiences of ordinary people, 116–17; final statistical report on, 187–91; first seventeen hours, 118–19; first shock waves, 52–54; as "great fire" vs. "great earthquake," 231–32, 263; impact on the entire West, 4; last seventy-two hours, 187–91; lost collection of written materials on, 345; photographs of (see photography); search for historic and scientific understanding, 248–54 (see also engineers; Lawson, Andrew); second twenty-four hours, 161–63; second violent shock, 55–58; timing of earthquake, 5; as unique disaster, 4–8; written recollections of, xiii–xv, 51, 162 (see also books; magazines; newspapers). See also specific topics

earthquake catalog, 23

earthquake collection, 250–54

earthquake cottages, 210, 215, 222

earthquake damage, factors contributing to, 239–43

Earthquake History Committee. See History, Committee on

"earthquake love," 211

Earthquake of 1906, The (Jordan), 260

earthquake publications and studies, lack of support for, 261–62

earthquakes, 8, 43, 53–54, 231–32; California attitude toward, 21–22; denial of, 231, 263; early, 8–9; in 1865 and 1868, 11–12; future, 8; policy of assumed indifference to danger of, 232; portrayed positively in media, 268–69; prediction of, 262; science of, 21–25, 95–96

East Street, 174

Eddy, Almira Hall, 116

editorials. See newspapers

Edwards, F. Edward, 71

electrical lines, damaged, 73, 74

Ellon, Florence, 27, 199–200

emergency, declaration of, 136. See also martial law

emergency period, immediate, 196

encampments. See camps

Enewold, Elmer E., 141–42
Engine Company No. 2, 70, 71
Engine Company No. 3, 70
engineers, probing for answers, 239–44
epicenter of earthquake, 53
ethnic minorities, 211; (separate and) unequal treatment, 211, 224. *See also* races;
specific minority groups
ethnic prejudices, 14, 19–20, 68, 80; denial
of, 289–91, 298–99. *See also* racism
ethnic stereotypes, 277
Evelyn, John, 279
Ewer, Edward N., 183, 184
Examiner. See San Francisco Examiner
Examiner Building, 85, 86, 134
explosives, 38, 69, 121, 165, 166, 331; extensive (mis)use of, 74–79, 111–12, 123, 128;
fires caused by, 75–77, 111–12, 164; flammability of various types of, 75–77, 111;
Phelan and, 162; used on Hotaling's,
170; on Van Ness Avenue, 126–30; who
was responsible for indiscriminate use
of?, 78–79, 123
extreme solution. *See* shoot-to-kill order

Fairmont Hotel, 81
fatalities. *See* deaths
faulting theory, Grove Gilbert on, 22, 258
faults/fault lines, 6, 23, 24, 149, 187, 239.
See also San Andreas Fault
federal aid, 133, 201. *See also* relief effort(s)
Ferry Building, 134
fictional portrayals of the earthquake and
fire, 276, 280
Fillmore Street trolley line, 207
finance committee, 176, 201, 208; Adolphus
Greely and, 202, 209, 220; name change,
204. *See also under* Phelan; Roosevelt
financial assistance, 132
fireboats, 72
firebombings, 17–18
firebreaks, 74, 75. *See also* explosives
fire commissioners, board of, 38
fire department, 37–39, 55, 63, 128
Fire Dragon, 110
firefighting: by citizen volunteers, 166–67;
procedures, 39

fire hazards, 37–38, 344
fire insurance industry. *See* insurance
industry, fire
firemen, 55, 69–72; criticisms of, 165–67;
killed, 70
"fireproof" buildings and structures, 240,
242. *See also* Palace Hotel
fire(s), 55, 71–72, 85; caused by explosives,
75–77, 111–12, 164; descriptions of, 115,
120; early, 9–11; obliviousness to possibility of, 94–95; positive reactions to, 11;
total damage caused by, 187; as weapon,
17 (*see also* arson). *See also* earthquake
and fire of 1906; Van Ness Avenue;
specific topics
fire stations, 55, 70, 71
firestorms, 17; physics of, 16–17
Fisher, Lucy, 102
flag dip, 167
flammability index, 16
flat lands, 59
Fletcher, John D., 249
Flint, Frank P., 133
Flint, Motley Hewes, 158
Flood, Mary Leary, 45, 46, 167
focus of earthquake, 53
food: for children, 206, 207, 212; E. K.
Johnson on, 155; for the poor, 212; and
price gouging, 142–43; provision of, 55–
56, 132–33, 135–36, 206, 212–13; rations,
135; from shuttered grocery stores, 137.
See also relief effort(s)
food committee, 177
forests and lumber, 246–47
Fort Mason, 136
Franklin Hall, 121, 206
Freeman, Frederick N., as real hero, 171–75
Freeman, John R., 233
Freitag, J. K., 243
Fremsted, Olive, 44, 46–47
Frieden, John P., 110
Funston, Frederick, 104, 124, 137, 165; army
troops called in by, 63, 65; and assistance
for needy persons, 135, 204; background,
62; characterization of, 62; at citizens'
committee meeting, 291; Committee
of Fifty and, 82; denied shootings by

National Guard, 64, 65, 136–37, 175, 182; in Chinatown, 292, 293; departure, 205; looting by, 143, 292; Pardee and, 64, 205, 292. *See also* army troops

Native Americans, 9

natural disasters. *See* disasters, natural

natural gas leaks, 120

natural gas lines: damaged, 73–74. *See also* sewer gas

natural resources, 7; to rebuild San Francisco, depletion of, 245–47. *See also* water system

Navell, Irena, 310

navy, 136, 171–72

Nevada, 133

Nevada House, 60–61

Newhall, Beaumont, 281

news, control of, 178–79

newspaper buildings, 88. *See also specific buildings*

newspapers, 86, 250, 263, 264–69, 328. *See also specific newspapers*

New York City, 3–4, 134, 185, 186, 264–65

Nichols, William F., 161

Nieto, Jacob, 309, 324, 325

9/11, 3–4

nitroglycerine, 75–76. *See also* explosives

Nob Hill, 62–63, 68, 124

Norris, Frank, 310

North American Plate, 53

North Beach district, 97, 293

novels about the earthquake and fire, 276, 280

nurses, 132, 175. *See also* hospitals

Oakland, 64; Chinese in, 182, 290, 295; refugees find home in, 132, 177, 181–84

Oakland Relief Committee, 182–84, 224; health subcommittee, 183

Oakland Tribune, 182

"Octopus." *See* railroads

O'Farrell Street, 70

O'Keefe, Timothy J., 26

Older, Cora, 314, 317, 320, 322, 328, 330

Older, Fremont ("Q"), 324, 330; as agent of political and economic change, 310; campaign against Schmitz, 314, 316; as

editor of *Bulletin,* 265, 267, 306, 312–13, 316, 317, 334, 336; on Heney's assassination attempt, 332–33, 335; Heney's meeting with, 315; on Jewish people, 308; judges and, 320; "kidnapping" of, 306, 330; Lincoln Steffens and, 308, 309; meeting with Roosevelt, 315; Phelan and, 313, 315, 320; publications, 267, 307–8, 322; regrets about persecuting Ruef, 306, 336, 337, 393n78; resigned from Bohemian Club, 328; role in prosecution of Ruef, 306, 307, 309, 312–13, 316, 320, 337; Rudolph Spreckels and, 315, 320; on Ruef, 308; Ruef's and Older's careers compared, 313; Southern Pacific and, 313; William Burns and, 322, 331; William Lawlor and, 320–21; zealotry, 314

O'Leary, Patrick and Catherine, 13, 14

Olney, Warren, 117

Omori, Fusakichi, 297–98

Oriental Public School, 300–302

orphanages, 207

Otis, Harrison Gray, 302

Overland Monthly, 307

Pacific Plate, 53

Pacific Union Club, 107–8, 328

Palace Hotel, 41–43, 88, 108, 120; burning of, 90–94

pamphlets. *See* books

Pan, Erica Y. Z., 110, 292, 296

Panama-Pacific International Exposition of 1915, 196, 229, 340–44

Pao-hsi, Chung, 292

"paper buildings," 219

Pardee, George C., 82–84, 99, 204, 270; Andrew Lawson and, 254, 255; and assistance for needy persons, 133, 180; background, 82–83; characterization of, 82–83; and the Chinese, 290, 292; at citizens' committee meeting, 291; Committee on History and, 250; communications with Roosevelt, 65, 83, 84; functions, 82, 83; Fusakichi Omori and, 298; H. Morse Stephens and, 249; Leonard Stocking and, 153; martial law and, 64, 65; National Guard and,

San Francisco: in 1910, 339–41; in 1915, 341–44; characterizations of, 32–34; demographics, 32–34; "imperishable spirit of," 273, 275; neighborhoods, 39–40; physical setting, 32–33; recovery stages, 196; suburbs, 40; terrain and microclimates, 39–40

San Francisco Chronicle, 89, 265

San Francisco Examiner, 89, 264, 265, 316; photographs, 287–88

San Francisco (movie), 276–77

San Francisco's Horror of Earthquake and Fire, 277

sanitation and disease, 221–23

San Jose, 25, 64, 145, 153–55, 180

San Mateo County, 179–80

San Rafael, 180

Santa Cruz, 11

Santa Cruz Mountains, 145, 156–57

Santa Paula, 180

Santa Rosa, 64, 115, 145, 157–61

Sawislak, Karen, 14

scapegoating, 10, 11, 14, 316

Scawthorn, Charles, 232

Schmitt, H. C., 56

Schmitz, Eugene E., 78, 102, 111; army troops and, 65–67; arraignment, 321; citizens' committee and, 69, 204, 291; Committee of Fifty and, 82; Committee on History and, 248, 250; conviction, 326–27; in criminal (in)justice system, 317, 321–25; criticisms of, 67, 68; curfew "requested" by, 69; dethroned, 306; as director of relief efforts, 201; earthquake viewed by, 66–67; elected supervisor, 336; explosives and, 78, 123–24, 171; extortion, 317; finances, 327; fire hazards and, 58, 69; Funston and, 65, 66; H. Morse Stephens and, 249; indicted, 311, 317; indictments dismissed, 336; Jerome Landfield and, 123–24; John Young on, 82; martial law and shoot-to-kill order, 64, 67–69, 171, 205, 275; mayoral candidacy, 32; mayoral resignation, 311; not reelected mayor in 1915, 336; persecution of, 314–16; Phelan's

meetings with, 198; Phelan's opposition to, 81, 202, 228; praise for, 83, 275; recollections of April 18, 66–67; reelection in 1905, 29–30; Roosevelt and, 65, 202; Ruef as attorney for, 32; Ruef's relations with, 124, 305; as target of reformers, 310; temporary headquarters in Portsmouth Square, 78; trade unionism and, 311

schools: racial and ethnic discrimination in, 299–302; segregation, 5–6, 300–302

Schussler, Herman, 73, 120

science: of earthquakes, 21–25, 95–96; of firestorms, 16–17; men of, 94–96 (*see also* engineers; geologists)

scorched-earth policy, 128

Scotti, Antonio, 91, 92

Seaman, R. B., 140–41

Sebald, W. G., 17–18

segregation: school, 5–6, 300–302. *See also* ethnic minorities, (separate and) unequal treatment

seismic waves, first, 52–53

seismographs, 23, 94–96, 216, 297

Seismological Society of America, 261

seismology, 261, 262

Sembrich, Marcella, 92

sewage facilities, 183

sewer gas, explosion of, 79

Shafter, Payne, 266–67

shelter, 132, 135. *See also* refugees

Shinsheimer, Paul, 114

ships, military, 136

shootings, 65, 92–93, 138, 140, 205; prosecutions for, 141. *See also* deaths, from militia/martial law; looters, shot

shoot-to-kill order, 6, 15, 67–69, 81, 141–42

Sitton, Tom, 310

slaughterhouses, 116

smallpox, 181, 184, 221

Society of California Pioneers, 254

socioeconomic differences, 218; and unequal treatment, 59, 68, 211–14, 235, 264–65. *See also* poor people

soldiers, 126–27, 198. *See also* army troops

Sonoma County, 114

COMPOSITOR	BookMatters, Berkeley
INDEXER	Leonard Rosenbaum
CARTOGRAPHER	Jeffrey L. Ward
TEXT	11.25/13.5 Adobe Garamond
DISPLAY	Stymie Medium Condensed and Sackers Gothic Light
PRINTER AND BINDER	Thomson-Shore, Inc.